D0207814

Between Redemption and Perdition

Between Redemption and Perdition

Modern antisemitism and Jewish identity

Robert Wistrich

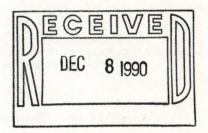

Routledge
London and New York

First published 1990
by Routledge
11 New Fetter Lane, London EC4P 4EE

Simultaneously published in the USA and Canada
by Routledge
a division of Routledge, Chapman and Hall, Inc.
29 West 35th Street, New York, NY 10001

Typeset in 10/12 Times by Times Graphics, Singapore
Printed and bound in Great Britain by
Biddles Ltd, Guildford and King's Lynn

British Library Cataloguing in Publication Data

Wistrich, Robert S. (Robert Solomon)
Between redemption and perdition: modern antisemitism and Jewish identity.
1. Jews. Racial discrimination by society
I. Title
305.8′924

Library of Congress Cataloging in Publication Data

Wistrich, Robert S.,
Between redemption and perdition: modern anti-Semitism and Jewish
identity/Robert Wistrich.
p.   cm.
Bibliography: p.
Includes index.
1. Antisemitism–History. 2.Holocaust, Jewish (1939–1945)—Causes. 3.
Jews—Cultural assimilation. 4. Jews—Identity. 5. Zionism. I. Title.
DS145.W545—1989
305.8′924—dc20—89–6288

ISBN 0 415 04233 X

Contents

v

Contents

Part 4   From Antisemitism to Anti-Zionism

Acknowledgements

The following essays are reprinted by kind permission of their original publishers; most of them have been revised or adapted in certain ways, some of them substantially. 'Antisemitism as a radical ideology' first appeared in the *Jerusalem Quarterly*, 1983, no. 28 (Summer), pp. 83–94. An earlier version of 'Karl Lueger in historical perspective' was published in *Jewish Social Studies*, 1983, vol. 45, nos 3–4, pp. 251–62 and expanded at an international colloquium in Brussels (October 1987). 'The Jewishness of Sigmund Freud' was first given as the Kaufmann Memorial Lecture at Leo Baeck College in London (6 May 1987); 'The dilemmas of assimilation in central Europe' began life in a slightly different form as a plenary lecture to the International Council of Christians and Jews at Buckow, East Germany, on 15 September 1987. A first draft of 'The Fassbinder controversy', later substantially revised, was presented at the international conference 'Remembering for the Future' at Wadham College, Oxford (11 July 1988). 'The strange case of Bruno Kreisky' appeared in an earlier, abbreviated version in *Encounter*, May 1979, pp. 78–86. 'French socialism and the Dreyfus affair' was originally published in the *Wiener Library Bulletin*, 1975, vol. 28, nos 35–6, pp. 9–19, and the article on Jabotinsky was first delivered as a lecture at University College, London in December 1979. 'Soundings in the Gulf' was published in *The Times Literary Supplement*, 23 May 1980, 'The new war against the Jews' in *Commentary*, May 1985, pp. 35–40, and an earlier version of 'The fundamentalist challenge' in *Encounter*, March 1989. 'Global anti-Zionism in the 1980s' began as a lecture in Hebrew to the Study Circle on World Jewry in the home of the President of Israel at the end of December 1984. 'The myth of the Jew in contemporary France' was written in April 1987 as a preface to the book by Henry Weinberg and has been considerably revised. 'Under the sign of *glasnost*' appeared in a slightly different form in *Present Tense*, January/February 1989. My special thanks to Andrew Wheatcroft for having read through these essays and for his pertinent comments.

Introduction

The essays in this volume were written or delivered as public lectures on different occasions over the past fifteen years. They cover a wide range of subjects from the first essay on the young Marx and the Enlightenment to the concluding article on the rise of fundamentalism in the contemporary Middle East. Some of the essays are passionate, polemical, and committed; others are more dispassionate, detached, and reflective in their approach. But, underlying them all, there are a number of convergent themes which have consistently informed my thinking and research into the modern Jewish experience.

In the first place there is the emergence of the so-called *Judenfrage* in nineteenth-century Europe – a corollary of the struggle for and against Jewish emancipation and the rise of modern antisemitism which accompanied it. By the turn of the century the 'Jewish question' had already become a significant political issue, one whose importance would constantly grow in the period between the two world wars especially in central and eastern Europe – culminating in the savagery of the Nazi Holocaust. Yet, for a variety of reasons that are examined in some of these essays, antisemitism did not disappear in the post-war world. In countries like France, Germany, Austria, and in the lands of eastern Europe which fell under communist domination, as well as in the Soviet Union and, above all, in the Muslim Arab world, antisemitism has continued to flourish, though at times it has assumed a novel intellectual framework, vocabulary, and mode of discourse. One of the central objectives in these essays is to try and decode this constantly changing language of antisemitism, to explore its multiple and variegated social dimensions, its shifting historical and geo-political context, and its continuing impact on relations between Jews and non-Jews in the contemporary world.

Central Europe epitomized, of course, the most complex, creatively anguished, and ultimately tragic of such Jewish–Gentile encounters in the past 150 years, so that it naturally provides one of the central axes of the book. Nowhere else in Europe did the late-eighteenth-century ideal of *Bildung*, and its incarnation for a time in German language and culture, exercise such a mesmeric influence on Jews. At the same time the Jewish–German encounter (sometimes misleadingly subsumed under the heading of 'symbiosis'), for all its dazzling cultural achievements, produced acute identity conflicts and tensions, especially for the largely dejudaized, secular Jewish intelligentsia. Examples such as Marx, Freud, the Polish-born Rosa Luxemburg, Walter Benjamin, and more recently Bruno Kreisky, are analysed in some detail in order to bring out the high degree of ambivalence about Jewish identity that resulted from living in a nationalistic and antisemitic environment.

Marxism, psychoanalysis, and the faith in liberal high Culture based on the cult of Reason, enlightenment, and cosmopolitanism can be seen, up to a point, as 'Jewish' strategies to cope with this problem of a hostile majority culture, of religious and racial stigmatization, and the anguish of a divided self. Tragically, however, for the fate of the Jews, this very identification with the forces of modernity and the important, pioneering role of many Jews in entrepreneurial capitalism, in the press, in radical and socialist movements, in cultural innovation, etc. simply lent added plausibility to the pre-existing anti-Jewish stereotypes embedded in most European societies since the Christian Middle Ages.

Much of this antisemitic backlash which had already begun in the mid-nineteenth century was, as I seek to show in a number of essays, a populist, plebeian revolt of the lower middle classes, the semi-intellectuals, the misfits, the disoriented and *déclassé* elements traumatized by the rapid social changes which accompanied the advent of industrial capitalism. In this respect, Austria, arguably the classic land of European political antisemitism since the late nineteenth century, offers an excellent laboratory for grasping the interplay between tradition and modernity, ideology and the masses, religion and politics, in the making of Hitler and the Nazi movement. National socialism, it might be argued, was ultimately a kind of perverse synthesis between Prusso-German authoritarianism, militarism and will-to-power, and the *völkisch*, antisemitic obsessions of the threatened Austro-German minority on the Slavic frontiers of the Habsburg monarchy.

Several essays deal also with France, whose antisemitic traditions are no less significant than those of Germany, Austria, Russia, or of a number of east-central European successor states to the Austro-Hungarian empire. Nevertheless the French case is different in so far as the revolutionary legacy of 1789 struck deeper roots here than it did elsewhere in Europe, at least until the late 1930s and the advent of Vichy. The legacy of Vichy, the impact of the mass Sephardi immigration from North Africa to France in the 1950s and 1960s, as well as of the Six Day War in the Middle East, have however profoundly modified the self-definition of French Jews. Moreover, outside of the Soviet Union, this is now the largest Jewish community in Europe (nearly twice the size of

Anglo-Jewry) and one which has come to play once more an active role in French cultural, economic, and political life. Clearly, it feels no need to adopt the low profile of the small German Jewish community (whose position is briefly analysed in my essay on the Fassbinder controversy) or of its 'assimilationist' ancestors in nineteenth-century France, who regarded themselves as 'israélites' rather than 'juifs'.

The bolder, more self-assertive attitudes of contemporary French Jewry have obviously been influenced by the existence of Israel and the new patterns of behaviour among Jews which it has engendered in the post-war era. The genesis, development, and impact of Zionism on Jews and Gentiles alike is indeed the second major axis around which this book revolves. For Zionism, from the very outset, aimed at creating a new kind of Jew, one who would no longer merely be the object of history, its passive victim and nomadic refugee. It passionately believed that only in land, territory, and national sovereignty could the Jews find *ge'ulah* (redemption) from the rootless alienation and misery of *galut* (exile). Several essays explore the secular socialist and nationalist rationale behind early Zionist ideology and its roots in the condition of Russian Jewry in the Tsarist empire.

Although the labour Zionists and the right-wing 'Revisionist' trend within the movement shared a common antagonism to the *galut* (Diaspora/exile), their diagnosis and vision of the future nevertheless remained significantly different. As the essay on Jabotinsky (the intellectual godfather of the present-day Likud party in Israel) seeks to illustrate, the 'Revisionists' emphasized the statist, political elements in Zionism far more than their socialist adversaries, for whom auto-emancipation meant above all the transformation and 'normalization' of the Jewish social structure. Labour Zionism was also more flexible in its approach to the Arab question, though it persisted in the self-serving illusion that the Palestinian Arab population had no authentic national demands which needed to be faced. The reality of the gulf between Jewish and Arab nationalism in Palestine was a painful fact for many Zionists to concede. It has also been consistently underestimated by most decision-makers in London, Washington, and Moscow during the past forty to fifty years.

In contrast to the west, Soviet attitudes to the Arab–Israeli conflict have, however, been influenced in important ways by the existence of an unresolved internal 'Jewish question'. This is the subject of two essays in the book which examine some of the causes and consequences of antisemitism in the Soviet Union both before and during the Gorbachev era. In particular, I have analysed the domestic and also the wider international impact of the intensive Soviet propaganda effort to blacken and delegitimize Zionism as a racist, fascist, and even as a 'Nazi' type of movement – a campaign that particularly flourished under the Brezhnev regime. This extremist mode of 'anti-Zionism' (which previously had a semi-official character) has in more recent years combined with the older traditions of Slavophile and Great Russian chauvinism that are currently being revived by the Pamyat organization in the USSR. The myth of the 'world Jewish conspiracy' – popularized by that notorious turn-of-the century Tsarist Russian forgery known as the *Protocols of the Elders of Zion* – is once again being openly advocated in its country of origin.

Not only in Russia or eastern Europe, one must add. Even in western countries one finds more or less sophisticated variations on the belief in an international Jewish network of power. Both right- and left-wing extremists are especially prone to such fantasies, which today are invariably linked to the long arm of Israel and its military, political, and propagandistic needs. This has also led to a rewriting of history in some quarters, in which imagined 'Zionist' power and influence is even used to explain away and 'demystify' the Holocaust as a perfidious Nazi–Zionist conspiracy to massacre the Jews of Europe. In this respect the thesis behind Jim Allen's anti-Zionist play *Perdition* echoes familiar themes from Soviet propaganda and disinformation whose origins go back to the last years of Stalin's rule.

The malevolent misrepresentation of Israel and Zionism acquired a new resonance in the west mainly during and after the Lebanon war of 1982, though its roots go back almost fifteen years earlier to the rise of a new left counter-culture at the end of the 1960s. The changes in Israel's own policies, behaviour, self-image, and self-projection (which are looked at in a number of essays) helped to reinforce these trends in various ways. Repression of Arabs in the territories, the emergence of a hard-line messianic Zionism preaching a mystical bond with the whole of the biblical land of Israel, and the increasing dominance of the right in Israeli politics since 1977 have not improved Israel's image abroad. On the other hand, they can also partly be seen as an understandable Israeli response to the chronic political instability of the Middle East, the constant pressures of terrorism, and the uncompromising position for so long adopted by the PLO and the Arab States on the Palestine question.

It must be remembered that before Sadat, more Arab states regarded the existence of Israel as illegal, illegitimate, and immoral. It took a full decade after Egypt's peace treaty with Israel for it to be accepted back into the Arab fold. Moreover, even today – when 'moderate' Arab leaders are more flexible and realistic in their attitudes to the Arab–Israeli conflict – the attitude to 'Zionism' remains intransigently negative.

In the Arab world, as several essays in the book underline, Zionism has long been perceived as part of a shadowy, occult Jewish and 'imperialist' conspiracy. Successive Arab defeats at the hands of Israel encouraged the view that vast forces of a demonic and superhuman kind were at work to subvert, undermine, and fragment Arab efforts to achieve unity and national liberation. This essentially 'antisemitic' perception of Zionism has in some cases been superimposed upon (and in others co-exists alongside) the more rationally conceived territorial–political conflict that opposes the neighbouring Arab states to Israel; and it is also being grafted on to the hitherto mainly nationalist confrontation between Israelis and Palestinian Arabs. The most recent Palestinian uprising in the territories occupied by Israel after the 1967 war has reinforced this trend by aggravating the mutual hatred and recriminations between Israelis and Palestinians, though it has also underlined the necessity for greater political realism on both sides.

The rise of Islamic fundamentalism at precisely this juncture in the history of the Arab–Israeli conflict is therefore especially unfortunate for all the parties concerned. It threatens to transform what is already a seemingly intractable national–territorial conflict into a major religious confrontation; to give a metaphysical, cosmic dimension to atavistic, tribal enmities; to reinforce Arab antisemitism by infusing it with an indigenous and traditionalist Islamic fervour; to exacerbate hatred of the west and the great 'Satan', the United States; and to threaten the stability of the 'secular' Arab regimes who are perceived by the fundamentalists as 'heretics' and traitors to Islam. The Soviet Union, too, having suffered a humiliating defeat in Afghanistan at the hands of Muslim fundamentalist guerrillas and faced with the potential disaffection of its very large Muslim minorities in central Asia, has every reason for concern.

As the concluding essay intimates, for a majority of Israelis and for most Jews in general, fundamentalism is profoundly disturbing – partly for some of the above reasons. Moreover, it has the danger of further widening and globalizing the conflict with the Arabs and injecting into it a new dimension of violence, terror, and religious fanaticism which may escalate on both sides and be impossible to contain. Such an inevitably bloodstained path to 'redemption' can only lead to mutual destruction. But given the current realities it will require political wisdom of a high order to avoid the downward spiral that has characterized so much of the recent history of the Middle East.

Robert Solomon Wistrich
Jerusalem/London, August 1989

Part 1

Nemesis in Central Europe

1

Karl Marx and the Enlightenment

The western Enlightenment intended to regenerate the Jews by liberating them from superstition and despotism. Its proclaimed goal was spiritual and political emancipation which, in the case of the Jews, presupposed severing the religious and national elements in Judaism. The Jew was henceforth to become a citizen, abandoning the separatism of his ghetto existence, and adopting the habits, customs, clothing, and speech of his Gentile neighbours. Israel was to leave its tents and intermingle with the nations on the basis of the new gospel of civic equality.

Until the Enlightenment the Jews had been a people, at least in the ethnic sense. Now they were assumed to be no more than a religion. But the enlighteners had no doubt that all religion, and especially Judaism, was essentially obscurantist, fanatical, and tyrannical. The appeal of the Enlightenment was aggressively secular and hence Jews who clung to their religious tradition were viewed with undisguised hostility. The war-cry of Voltaire and the 'philosophers' – '*Écrasez l'infâme*' – did not spare Jewish customs, manners, and sensibilities. The Enlightenment had many virtues, not least that it offered the Jews a way out of the ghetto and into the mainstream of European history. But the process of adaptation created a new problem for the self-image and self-esteem of the Jews. It demanded a progressive sloughing off of time-honoured traditions, a reform of Jewish life, and a gradual elimination of those 'Jewish' characteristics which were deemed unattractive by the Gentile world. Paradoxically, the secular humanism of the Enlightenment was also at the root of modern Jewish self-hatred.

Examples of Jewish antisemitism can certainly be found which predate the nineteenth century, notably among baptized Jews who turned against their former co-religionists with all the passion of the neophyte. Indeed, 'Jewish antisemitism' was scarcely surprising in a Christian environment which for nearly 2,000 years had encouraged open or latent Judeophobia. This historical factor, which should never be underestimated, was also pertinent to the case of Karl Marx. The psychological interpretation of Marx as a neophyte must, however, explain how radical and consistent secularism could also generate Jewish self-hatred. Even more than his radical young Hegelian contemporaries, Bruno Bauer, Feuerbach, Arnold Ruge, and Moses Hess, Marx insisted, in *Zur Judenfrage* (1844), that 'we convert theological questions into secular questions'. If Marx's analysis of the Jewish question was based, as he himself asserted, on a thoroughgoing *secular*, 'scientific' approach which rejected theological prejudices, can the charge of antisemitism be sustained?

The answer must lie in Marx's own definition of the way secularization affected the Jewish problem, and in his efforts to differentiate his approach from that of Bruno Bauer. Marx's essay on the Jews was clearly framed as a polemic against Bruno Bauer, his left-wing Hegelian mentor – a Protestant theologian turned atheist and free-thinker. But what are all too frequently overlooked in Marx's critique of Bauer are the similarities and points of agreement between the two young Hegelian thinkers. The assumption has been that, because Marx rejected Bauer's position on Jewish emancipation and formulated a different theory of society and the state, his attitude to Judaism was less hostile. What is forgotten is that Marx praised Bauer's antisemitic propositions on the religious antithesis between Judaism and Christianity in no uncertain terms. Thus at the outset of his essay he emphasized the 'boldness, sharpness, wit and thoroughness' with which Bauer had dissected the essence of both the Jewish and Christian religions. He also relied on Bruno Bauer's characterization of Judaism as a religion which 'could not be further developed theoretically, because the ideology of practical need is by its nature limited, and exhausted in a few strokes'.

Similarly, Marx quoted with approval his mentor's verdict on 'Jewish Jesuitry, the same practical Jesuitry that Bauer points out in the Talmud', which merely reflected the logic of egoism in the everyday world. Marx passed over in silence the antisemitic features in Bauer's portrayal of Judaism, because for him they were self-evidently true and therefore not worth discussing. Bruno Bauer, like his teacher Voltaire, blamed Judaism for the rise of Christianity, for tyranny and superstition. He considered that the essence of Judaism lay in the fanatical intolerance and narrow-mindedness of the Jewish national spirit. In common with the French Enlightenment, Bauer regarded Jewish particularism as incompatible with the spirit of emancipation. If the Jews wanted human rights, then Bauer insisted that they strip off their 'Jewish essence' and abandon their 'privileges' as a medieval corporation. German Jewry must recognize that a Christian state could never emancipate them, only an *atheist* state, which had no room for Christians or Jews. Radical, abstract secularism as exhibited in Bruno Bauer's essays on the Jewish question demanded that German Jews renounce unconditionally their 'chimerical nationality' and their religious affiliation.

This was the weak point in Bauer's case which Marx attacked with remorseless logic, offering in its place a different and more convincing interpretation of the meaning of secularization and of *human rights* as proclaimed by the American and French revolutions. But it is essential to notice that, in so doing, Marx did not in the least quarrel with Bauer's *antisemitic* falsifications of Jewish history and of the Jewish religion. On the contrary, he radicalized Bauer's critique of Judaism, transferring it from the realm of theological abstraction to that of *social* analysis.

Moreover in putting forward his own version of the Jewish 'practical essence', Marx built on the young Hegelian assumptions of Bruno Bauer, Feuerbach, and Moses Hess. The consensus among the Left Hegelians on this subject was remarkable: they all emphasized that the 'Jewish' character of Christianity made it inhuman, and that in this sense emancipation from Judaism was desirable. For Feuerbach, 'Judaism is worldly Christianity', for Bruno Bauer 'Judaism is unachieved Christianity', for Moses Hess the blood-mystique of Judeo–Christianity is realized 'in the modern Jewish–Christian peddler world'.

The young Marx did not disagree with any of these opinions, although his own formulation was more dialectical. 'Christianity overcame real living Judaism in appearance only. It was too respectable, too spiritual, to remove the crudeness of practical need, other than by raising itself into heaven.' When the young Marx sought in 1844 the key to the negativity of his own age, it was decidedly within the framework of Left Hegelianism. 'Christianity arose out of Judaism. It has now dissolved itself back into Judaism.' The implications of this standpoint for Jewish emancipation in Germany were clear. The post-revolutionary western society which had emerged after 1789 in the Christian world was already the apogee of 'Judaism'. Or as Marx put it in more provocative terms – 'The Jews have emancipated themselves, in so far as the Christians have become Jews'.

What, then, was the purpose of Marx's polemic against Bruno Bauer on the issue of Jewish emancipation? Why did he declare in a letter to Arnold Ruge on 13 March 1843 that 'Although the Israelite faith is repugnant to me, yet Bauer's opinion seems to me too abstract.' Why did he welcome the bitterness which 'grows with every petition rejected amid protests' and insist that 'We must riddle the Christian state with as many holes as possible and smuggle in the rational as far as we can'? Certainly it was not out of any love for the Jews, but rather out of hatred for the Christian-Germanic state, where 'the domination of religion is the religion of domination'. Jewish emancipation in Germany was, from the standpoint of radical politics, a useful weapon against Prussian absolutism. If German Jews were demanding their *civil* (that is, human) rights, then this for Marx was a blow struck in the name of secularization. It exposed the hypocrisy and backwardness of the Prussian state by comparison with the more progressive 'constitutional' bourgeois societies of France and America. With reference to Prussian conditions, Marx wrote:

'As the State *evangelizes*, when although a State, it adopts the attitude of a Christian toward the Jews, so the Jew *acts politically* when, although a Jew, he demands the rights of the citizen.'

This was the nub of Marx's quarrel with Bruno Bauer over Jewish emancipation, which comes out with greater clarity and force in *The Holy Family* of 1845. There, he approvingly quoted Gabriel Riesser, the leading spokesman for German Jewish emancipation, who (in Marx's view) 'correctly expresses the meaning of the demand of the Jews who claim the recognition of free humanity, when he calls among other things, for the freedom of movement, to sojourn, travel and trade'. Against the clerical-authoritarian state which denied the Jews rights guaranteed by the American and French constitutions, Marx was ready to support the Jewish critics of Bruno Bauer. As a consistent secularist and enemy of the Christian-Germanic ideology which sought to confine the Jews to the ghetto, any other position would have struck Marx as regressive. But Bruno Bauer, from whom Marx had imbibed his secularism and his hostility to the Christian state and Jewish religion, did not share this view. Hence, Marx felt obliged to justify his tactical position in theoretical terms, by showing that Bauer's concept of secularization was inadequate. The object of this demonstration was, however, in no sense intended to justify or defend Judaism. On the contrary, the arguments developed by Marx were all designed to show that political emancipation was insufficient to achieve the necessary and desirable abolition of Judaism.

For the purposes of this demonstration Marx appealed, in particular, to the example of North America, which evidently in 1844 represented for him the model of a secular society. In the blossoming of religious sects in American society Marx saw decisive evidence for his argument that political emancipation did not necessitate the abolition of religion. Quoting such European observers of American life as Hamilton, Beaumont, and De Tocqueville, Marx argued that religion and commerce were inextricably related features of a secularized civil society. He cited Hamilton's comments on the religion of Mammon in New England – where 'the earth in their eyes is nothing else but a stock-exchange, where they have no other calling than to become richer than their neighbors'. But if Mammon was the *worldly* God of the New Englanders, this only proved to Marx how 'judaized' the Christian world had become: 'Indeed, the practical dominance of Judaism over the Christian world has reached its unambiguous normal expression in North America.'

In secular America, Marx found the evidence he had been looking for to confound Bauer's thesis that Jewish emancipation implied the victory of atheism. However, it is highly significant that none of the writers on America whom Marx quoted had discussed Judaism, let alone the incarnation of vulgar commercial practice in the Jewish spirit. This was gratuitously introduced by Marx himself, in terms which even the most uninhibited antisemite would have been hard put to surpass. 'With the Jew and without him, money has become the practical spirit of the Christian peoples.' In 1869 Gougenot des Mousseaux was to write one of the classic antisemitic works of the nineteenth century, *Le Juif, le Judaisme et la Judaïsation des peuples chrétiens*, which elaborated similar propositions.

Marx's references to America intended to show that Judaism would survive and even flourish under conditions of political emancipation and the separation of church and state. The elimination of Judaism required a far more radical transformation which would abolish the contradiction between civil society and the state, between the private and public sphere, between the 'bourgeois' and the 'citoyen'. This solution, which would finally restore to man his collective species-essence and overcome his alienation from nature, society, and his fellow man, Marx called human emancipation. This was the radical, *revolutionary* form of secularization which Marx proposed in answer to Bruno Bauer and it was indeed the embryonic germ of his scientific socialism. But human emancipation was impossible as long as egoistic man, the atomized privatized bourgeois, was governed by money, which Marx in common with Moses Hess saw as the omnipotent and radically self-alienating power in modern bourgeois society. In Judaism and to a lesser extent in Christianity (which, like Hess, he saw as merely the 'theoretical' expression of practical need) Marx felt he had discovered the source of his alienation. 'Thus we recognize in Judaism a general, *contemporary*, *anti-social* element which has been brought to its present height by a historical development which the Jews zealously abetted and which must necessarily dissolve itself.' The Jews had not only aided and abetted the process by which money had become a dominant factor in the modern secular world, they had actively corrupted the Christian bourgeoisie.

It is not difficult to see in this method of argument the classic procedure of the antisemite. First Marx defines the Jewish 'essence' in abstract, *mythical* terms as a homogeneous, unchanging entity rooted in the Jewish religion. Then, having equated this negative essence with the Jewish group as a whole, he calls for its elimination and thereby the elimination of the related social evils of egoism, money, and avarice. Far from transcending Bruno Bauer's 'theoretical' antisemitism, Marx simply generalized and radicalized it. Whereas Bauer had projected on to the Jews his hatred of Christian intolerance and fanaticism in the classic style of the Voltairean Enlightenment, Marx blamed Judaism for the alienation of the secular world created by the Christian bourgeoisie. The mythologizing of the Jewish 'essence' simply took different forms in the two cases. For Bauer, the Jew was unchanging, static, Oriental in his passivity and indifference to modernity. For Marx, the Jew was unchanging in his practical activity, narrow-minded, money-grabbing, and parasitical. Bauer's antisemitism combined traditional Christian and secular humanist motifs. Marx's antisemitism was thoroughly modern, *materialist*, and pseudo-revolutionary.

In both cases the options left open to the Jews involved their disappearance as a social group and as a religious entity. Bruno Bauer envisaged the possibility that once the Jews were liberated from Judaism they could enjoy human rights in an atheist society. Marx held out the equally uninviting prospect that 'if the Jew recognizes the futility of his practical existence and strives to put an end to it, he will work . . . toward *human emancipation* in general and turn against the *highest practical* expression of human self-alienation'.

What motivated Marx, at a time when he was formulating the foundations of his socialist humanism, to give such a grossly distorted account of his people? How was it possible for radical secularism to coexist with such manifest antisemitism? What were the roots of his Jewish self-hatred? Many explanations have been offered and all of them have a grain of truth without being wholly convincing. It has been suggested by Isaiah Berlin that Marx's self-hatred was a response to the nationalist antisemitism of post-Napoleonic Germany – that is, he merely reflected the norms of his society. The socialist historian Werner Blumenberg also regarded self-hatred in Marx as 'the reaction of sensitive natures who were inwardly remote from Judaism, to a hostile milieu, a reaction which was itself the product of anti–Semitism'. Some commentators like Otto Rühle felt that Marx was trying to ostentatiously dissociate himself from a despised race and proclaim himself a non-Jew. Arnold Künzli has suggested that by identifying the Jews with capitalism, Marx found a means of escaping his Jewish origin and defining for himself a new revolutionary self-image. 'Judaism' represented, in this interpretation, the *primal vision of alienation*, namely those destructive forces which threatened the free personality. Subsequently, the working class became for Marx his unconscious, repressed 'ideal projection' of the Jew, whose suffering and oppression will ultimately redeem the world. For Albert Massiczek, Marx's Jewish antisemitism was the result of a tragic misunderstanding of the Hebrew roots of his humanism, produced by the distorting glass of the Christian world's endemic Judeophobia. For Helmut Hirsch, Jewish self-hate in Marx was a projection of his obsession with money, his frustration at finding himself without an inheritance, and his desire to wreak vengeance on the ethnic group from which he descended.

Others have seen in Marx's attitude the natural reaction of a baptized Jew, one who had grown up as a Protestant in the Catholic city of Trier, and had little or no knowledge of Judaism. Finally, there are those who would see in Marx's difficult relationship with his mother the initial source of his contempt for an older ghetto tradition and for narrow-minded egoism in money matters. An even more remarkable variation on the Oedipal hypothesis is the suggestion by Robert Misrahi that Marx wished unconsciously to expiate his father's guilt and complicity with the Prusso-Christian monarchy for having baptized his family to pursue his legal career. By proving to himself and others that Judaism was essentially worthless, Marx could rationalize his father's decision and maintain his own self-esteem.

All such explanations, however interesting and whatever their merits, remain fundamentally speculative and impossible to prove or disprove. We cannot psychoanalyse the dead with any degree of certainty, nor can we ever be sure about the inner motivations of such a complex personality as Marx on the basis of the incomplete evidence which exists. But self-hatred was not an uncommon phenomenon among Jewish intellectuals, especially in societies where the antisemitic pressures of the environment were strong. Both the Left Hegelian milieu of Germany and the socialist circles in Paris in which Marx moved in 1843–4 were indubitably hostile to the Jews. Even Moses Hess, who came from an orthodox Jewish background and never altogether lost his Jewish national sentiments, exhibited a similar attitude to Marx in the early 1840s. Heinrich Heine, another Rhinelander and baptized Jew (although one who, like Hess, eventually returned to the fold) also could write in 1840 that 'Money is the God of our time, and Rothschild is its prophet.' Such statements were commonplace. In radical, progressive, and socialist circles they were almost *de rigeur*. Did not Fourier, Proudhon, and Toussenel, the French socialists, blame the social evils of capitalism and *laissez-faire* in France on Jewish bankers? Was it not a fact that the Rothschilds wielded extraordinary influence in politics as well as finance over the destinies of counter-revolutionary Europe in the age of Metternich? This should be borne in mind when one discovers even in a thinker of Marx's penetration and iconoclasm the repetition of vulgar and tendentious anti-Jewish prejudices.

Certainly there must have been specific psychological causes for Marx's peculiarly visceral self-hatred, but they will inevitably remain inaccessible to our understanding, since we cannot interrogate the chief witness. What can be more confidently asserted is that since the Enlightenment such reactions have become increasingly frequent. For the appeal of secularism initially pushed the Jews onto the defensive, undermining their self-image, and exposed them to the full blast of previously alien values. It ended the centrality of the Jew for himself, thereby opening up unsuspected possibilities and new abysses. It denounced religion but did not end antisemitism. Jewish characteristics were as offensive to the Gentiles as before, but the burden of responsibility was placed on the Jews to change themselves. If they stayed as they were, then they deserved the criticism and even hatred of the world. Many Jews displayed amazing adaptability, energy, and ingenuity in adapting to the challenge of modernity while preserving their Jewish identity. Others found no way of reconciling their devotion to humanity with an equal concern for their own people. Probably no Jew has influenced modernity as much as Karl Marx but few have cast their harsh glare with so little empathy upon the Jewish people.

2

The internationalism of Rosa Luxemburg

Rosa Luxemburg was without question the greatest woman figure in the history of revolutionary socialism. Her impact on the Polish, Russian, and German labour movements was deep and enduring. In more recent times her theoretical writings have also been a source of inspiration to the radical New Left. Among critical Marxists in the 1960s and 1970s her works once more came into vogue, and the richness of her intellectual and political legacy was rediscovered by a new generation of historians, political scientists, and committed socialists.[1] There are several possible explanations for this revival of interest. In the first place Marxism itself underwent something of a renaissance in the western world in the post-Stalin era. The polycentric character of the world communist movement and the emergence of a more 'liberal' form of communism in western Europe and of an anti-authoritarian student movement in the 1960s helped to give a greater actuality to certain features of the Luxemburgist legacy. Attempts to reconnect with pre-Leninist traditions of revolutionary Marxism and disillusionment with the authoritarian, despotic brand of communism in Russia and eastern Europe have focused attention once more on the relevance of Rosa Luxemburg's contribution to socialist thought.

As a former German student leader, the late Rudi Dutschke, once pointed out, Rosa Luxemburg's ideas have potentially explosive implications for the autocratic communist societies of Asia and eastern Europe which are totally removed from her ideal of socialist democracy.[2] Precisely for this reason, ruling communist parties in Russia, China, and eastern Europe have consistently disregarded Lenin's famous injunction in 1922 to bring out 'the complete edition of her works'. The bureaucratic elite of the communist world has successfully absorbed her into the pantheon of great revolutionary fighters but at the same time anaesthetized her message. The personality of Rosa Luxemburg is still honoured in Poland, East Germany, and even Russia as a shining example of revolutionary struggle but 'Luxemburgism' remains a false doctrine, a deviation from Leninist orthodoxy.[3] Having died a martyr to the communist cause during the Spartacist revolt of 1919, she could not of course be dismissed or execrated as a heretic like Trotsky or Bukharin. But her independent spirit, her sharp critique of bureaucratic socialism, and her burning faith in the creative spontaneity of the masses were too subversive to be allowed to survive in uncensored form. The humane spirit of her Marxism had first to be extinguished by selective editing of her works before her memory could be honoured by the ruling Panzer-communists of the post-war world.

Such political considerations do not apply to the same degree in America and western Europe, though here, too, Rosa Luxemburg's legacy has been manipulated as a weapon in a variety of causes. There is for example the anti-Leninist Rosa Luxemburg of 'social-democratic' pedigree, chiefly remembered for her penetrating criticism of the Bolshevik Revolution. There are liberal and anarchist variations on this same theme which emphasize her belief in democratic institutions or in direct action from below. There is the 'New Left' Rosa Luxemburg, a pure exponent of socialist internationalism and permanent revolution. All these versions of the Luxemburg legend have their grain of truth. Significantly, they all place her in opposition to Leninist concepts. Certainly, her critique of Lenin's bureaucratic ultra-centralism, first articulated in 1904, has its relevance.[4] Few contemporaries foresaw so quickly the implications of the militaristic organizational concept that underlay Leninism, its tendency to throttle any independent initiative of the working class and bind it within the straitjacket of bureaucratic control.[5] Rosa Luxemburg regarded Lenin's tightly knit nucleus of professional revolutionaries as a mirror image of Tsarist absolutism which would reinforce the psychological servitude of the masses engendered by capitalism. As a result, the party would take the place of the proletariat and impose its own concept of socialism on the masses.

Her critique of the Bolshevik Revolution in 1918 similarly emphasized the dangers of domination by a narrow, dictatorial clique in which the bureaucracy would become the only active element, once all political life had been repressed in Russia as a whole. 'Public life gradually falls asleep. The few dozen party leaders of inexhaustible energy and boundless experience direct and rule .... A dictatorship to be sure; not the dictatorship of the proletariat, however, but only a dictatorship of a handful of politicians in the bourgeois sense'.[6] In contrast to Lenin and Trotsky, with their dismissal of 'formal democracy' as a bourgeois fetishism, she pointed out that 'the dictatorship of the proletariat consists of the way one applies democracy and not in its abolition'. Her critique of the Bolsheviks was made from the standpoint of classical revolutionary Marxism, imbued, however, with a highly personal regard for the preservation of fundamental liberties. Freedom, she argued, without free elections, without the most complete liberty of the press, of association and assembly, would become meaningless. If reserved only for supporters of the government or members of the party, it would stifle the very *raison d'être* of socialism – the auto-emancipation of the proletariat through political education, free debate, and criticism.[7] 'Freedom', she pointed out, 'is always and exclusively freedom for the one who thinks differently' – an insight as relevant today as it was sixty years ago – above all in Russia and eastern Europe. No less relevant were her warnings against Bolshevik reliance on terror.

> Lenin is completely mistaken in the means he employs. Decree, dictatorial force of the factory overseer, draconic penalties, rule by terror, all these things are but palliatives. The only way to rebirth is the school of public life itself, the most unlimited, the broadest democracy and public opinion. It is rule by terror which demoralizes.[8]

More than any other revolutionary Marxist of the twentieth century, Rosa Luxemburg, therefore, represents a genuine alternative to the coercion implicit in the Asiatic (especially the Russian) model of socialism. With her humanism, her broad political culture, her respect for individual freedom and awareness of the indivisibility of socialism and democracy, Rosa Luxemburg can fairly be said to represent the most positive values in the European tradition of communism.

At the same time it must be recognized that some more utopian features of her legacy have not survived the harsh realities of historical experience in the twentieth century. Nowhere is this more apparent than in her assessment of the national problem. Rosa Luxemburg lived in a period when it was still possible to believe that the nation-state was an anachronism, a temporary arrangement of bourgeois society which would fade together with capitalism. In contrast to Lenin, who recognized that national differences would survive long after world socialism had been achieved, she transformed socialism and national self-determination into mutually exclusive concepts. In her view any concessions to nationalism would subordinate socialism to bourgeois ideology and therefore betray the interests of the working class. The national question, like the issue of ethnic minorities, the Jewish question, the 'woman question', and the agrarian problem, would be solved as a by-product of the class struggle. As she put it, in her long polemic on 'The national question and autonomy' in 1908: 'In a society based on classes, the nation as a uniform social-political whole simply does not exist.'[9]

Her rejection of the principle of national self-determination grew largely out of the political situation in her native Poland, still partitioned at the end of the nineteenth century between Prusso-German, Austro-Hungarian, and Tsarist empires. Rosa Luxemburg opposed the Polish socialist party (PPS), which aimed at the restoration of Polish independence, for neglecting the primacy of the class struggle and the goal of proletarian revolution. Her thesis that Polish national independence was a 'petty-bourgeois utopia' brought her into conflict with Karl Kautsky, Wilheim Liebknecht, Victor Adler, and other veteran leaders of the Second International. It was also an unending source of her disagreement with Lenin, who championed the right to self-determination of oppressed nationalities in the Russian empire as a tactical lever with which to overthrow Tsarism.[10] While Lenin respected Rosa Luxemburg's internationalist convictions and her distaste for rampant Polish nationalism, he considered that her policy was simply playing into the hands of Great Russian chauvinism.

Rosa Luxemburg's intransigence on the national problem may seem at first sight puzzling, particularly as, being Polish-born and a Jewess, she was a member of two oppressed nationalities in the Tsarist empire. Why then was this great woman revolutionary so bent on the assimilation of Poles and Jews? The examination of this question inevitably brings into focus the cosmopolitan nature of her socialism and the insufficiently studied problem of the legacy of Jewish intellectuals to the revolutionary movement.[11] Was her internationalism in the last analysis not an escape from her Jewishness?

In a letter written from Wronke prison in February 1917 to her Jewish friend and correspondent, Mathilde Wurm, Rosa Luxemburg significantly reproached her for raising the issue of antisemitism, adding:

> What do you want with your special Jewish sorrows? For me the poor victims of the rubber plantations in Putamayo, the Negroes in Africa, with whose bodies the Europeans play ball are just as close . . . . Oh, this 'majestic stillness of infinity' in which so many cries have echoed away unheard. It rings so loudly in me that I have no special corner in my heart for the ghetto; I feel at home in the entire world, wherever there are clouds and birds and human tears.[12]

Rosa Luxemburg's biographer, Peter Nettl, considered this statement proof of her profound internationalism which also happened to coincide with a distaste for any self-conscious expression of Jewishness. Elsewhere, explaining her attitude to female emancipation, he suggests: 'Like anti-Semitism, the inferior status of women was a social feature which would be eliminated only by the advent of socialism; in the meantime there was no point in making any special issue of it'.[13] There is some truth in this explanantion, but it does not get to the root of her indifference toward the ghetto and what she somewhat contemptuously dismissed as 'Jewish sorrows'. For however much Rosa Luxemburg demonstrated her public disinterest in such 'secondary' issues as antisemitism (and her indifference was not as total as is generally assumed) her ethnic origins willy-nilly played a role in her career.

It is my contention that Rosa Luxemburg ignored the importance of ethnicity and underestimated the power of nationalism because she failed to recognize the distinctiveness and specific character of her own heritage. Her denial of the rights of Jews as an ethnic group, and of national independence to the Poles and smaller nationalities in eastern Europe, was not simply a theoretical application of Marx's teachings on the national problem. Her internationalism was also a product of an imposed situation of national dispossession (Polish and Jewish) which ultimately drove her to a transcendent, quasi-mystical embracing of the concept of a proletarian 'fatherland'.

Estranged like Karl Marx from her Jewish background, she found in international socialism not just a religion but a new political home. The charismatic idea of socialism, its dream of a classless internationalism and a universalist, harmonious society in which all religious, racial, and class barriers would disappear, resolved the ambiguity of her Jewishness and of her condition as a *sans-patrie*. It enabled her to turn her social marginality and lack of roots into an asset and to play a unique mediating role in the German, Polish, and Russian labour movements. She could communicate her Russo-Polish revolutionary *élan* to the reformist labour parties of western Europe and the democratic, self-reliant spirit of the west to the more violent, conspiratorial atmosphere of socialism in eastern Europe. With her Russian political formation, her Polish and German cultural background, and Swiss university education, she was superbly equipped to become the leading apostle of international socialism in the period before the First World War.

However much she disregarded the part which her Jewish origins played in favouring this role, it would be absurd to dismiss its possible influence on her temperamental personality. Her first biographer, the German communist Paul Fröhlich (who knew her personally), observed that the comfortable and secure existence in the Luxemburg household was 'marked by that intense intimacy characteristic of Jewish families'.[14] He described her father, Eliasz Luxemburg, a businessman with marked sympathies for Polish culture and its national traditions, as belonging 'to that social stratum from which emerged the Jewish intellectual type, best represented by the great Jewish artists, men of science and fighters for a better world'.[15] Rosa's mother (*née* Line Löwenstein) was also a remarkably cultivated woman whose 'education and interests were far above those of the average Jewish woman'.[16] Line Luxemburg had a passion for classic Polish and German literature which she transmitted to her daughter with, also, a traditional Jewish reverence for the Bible. In one of her prison letters, Rosa Luxemburg recalled this love of the Bible with a touching self-irony:

> My mother, who considered that Schiller and the Bible were the supreme sources of wisdom, was firmly convinced that King Solomon understood the language of birds. In the pride of my fourteen years and my training in natural science, I used to smile at my mother's simplicity. But now I have myself grown to be like King Solomon; I too can understand the language of birds and beasts.[17]

In the case of Rosa Luxemburg as of Karl Marx one cannot altogether dismiss the subconscious and hereditary influences of a Jewish background which included centuries of rabbinical scholarship and learning.[18] The profound ethical convictions which animated Rosa Luxemburg's socialism, the passionate belief in the final triumph of social justice and the dream of a new humanity united in the bond of universal brotherhood, were as much part of prophetic Judaism as they were of the Marxist vision of history.[19] Admittedly Marxism expressed in the scientific language of political economy a view of the past, present, and future of humanity congenial to many Jewish intellectuals in eastern Europe, precisely because they were already estranged from the Jewish heritage. It offered a total *Weltanschauung* for transforming an environment from which they were alienated as Jews and at the same time a way of synthesizing a newly acquired westernized identity with the Russo-Polish background into which they were born. Marxism replaced Judaism with a militant activism, a programme for changing the world from which they were excluded. But the skill in logical exposition and the genius for abstract interpretation which Jewish intellectuals like Rosa Luxemburg exhibited, as well as her profound ethical humanism, were in many ways reminiscent of remote rabbinical and Talmudic ancestors.

Though Rosa Luxemburg knew no Hebrew and probably spoke no Yiddish (despite the Yiddishisms sprinkled through her letters), though she came from an emancipated middle-class family assimilated both to Polish and German culture, the milieu in which she grew up nevertheless encouraged the transmission of certain traditional Jewish virtues. According to Hannah Arendt, these included respect for learning, freedom from conventional prejudices, a simple trust in humanity, and an 'almost naive contempt for social and ethnic distinctions' which was simply axiomatic.[20] It was perhaps not without significance that Rosa Luxemburg remained close to her family. Neither her parents nor brothers and sisters shared her revolutionary views yet they unquestioningly helped her when she was in prison and later to hide from the Tsarist police. Rosa Luxemburg's revolutionism may have been in part a revolt against a parochially confining milieu but it did not entail a rupture with her own family. This may be one reason why her personality appears to have been more integrated than that of many other revolutionaries who also felt the need to repudiate their Jewish background yet lacked her moral integrity and inward self-assurance.[21] Though Rosa Luxemburg, like Marx, avoided all reference to her Jewish origin, she does not appear to have suffered from the more obvious symptoms of self-hatred which many revolutionaries from a similar background exhibited. There are in her correspondence, for example, very few of the sarcastic remarks about Jews that one can readily find in Marx, Lassalle, or Victor Adler. She was indeed emotionally nauseated by the antisemitism endemic in her native Poland and reacted to it with polemical sharpness and incisive irony.

This was particularly true of her reply to Andrej Niemojewski, editor of *Mysl Niepodłegla* ('Independent Thought'), a free-thinking, anti-clerical journal in Warsaw which had accused her left-wing social democratic party (the SDKPiL) of nourishing 'a passionate hatred for Poland'.[22] Niemojewski identified 'Mosaism' with servility, corruption, and pharisaism, blaming all Polish problems on the 'judaization' of social democracy. His polemics against Rosa Luxemburg even descended to the ludicrous level of equating her brochures and articles with the adulterated schnapps that her forefathers had allegedly sold to Polish peasants.[23] Rosa Luxemburg answered the 'half-wit' and 'mongrel' Niemojewski in kind, ridiculing the 'bestial idiotism' and depravity behind antisemitic pretentions to defend the purity of Polish culture against Jewish influence. Polish 'progressives', she angrily pointed out, had dragged the noble heritage of cosmopolitanism into the mud, reducing it to 'the level of an anti-Semitic *Hetzblatt*'. The Polish middle-class intelligentsia in Warsaw, she alleged, had become contaminated by the virus of racial chauvinism in the aftermath of the Russian Revolution of 1905. Writing in the German socialist newspaper, *Vorwärts*, in 1910, she sarcastically observed that 'even liberal writers were also dragged into the mud, simply because they were Jews. In comparison with the tone of these attacks, our own Stoecker and Ahlwardt [German antisemites] must be considered as highly civilized'.[24]

Less convincingly, in a further series of articles in *Młot* ('the hammer'), the organ of the SDKPiL in Warsaw, she placed the 'literary pogrom' of the Polish intelligentsia in Warsaw on a par with the hooliganism of the Russian Black-Hundred gangs under Vladimir Purishkevitch.[25] Both the Polish and Russian antisemites, she remarked, claimed to be against 'Jewish revolutionaries' and ready to leave Jewish bankers and millionaires in peace, but in practice it had proved impossible to keep order among 'the pogromist bands'. Antisemitism was in fact only a mask for the counter-revolutionary struggle of monarchist and bourgeois reaction against the growing militancy of the workers' movement. It was the revenge of the Polish middle classes for the wave of strikes and agitation against capitalist exploitation. In Tsarist Poland, Rosa Luxemburg added, its function was to unite under a single banner anti-clerical 'progressives' as well as clerical and nationalist reactionaries, all of whom regarded the Jews as the enemy of the Polish nation.[26] In answer to Niemojewski's not wholly implausible assertion that socialism itself, from Marx and Lassalle to Bebel, Singer, and Mehring, had been antisemitic in tendency, Rosa Luxemburg retorted that German social democracy had always been attacked by the antisemites as being 'anti-national' and 'judaized' precisely because its founders were 'the Jewish cosmopolitans Marx and Lassalle'.

Marx himself, she asserted, had analysed the Jewish question in his famous essay of 1844 as a *social*, not a racial or a religious problem. For him (as for his disciples), Jewish emancipation meant the liberation of society from all forms of exploitation. What Marx had called *Judentum* was therefore 'nothing but the huckstering and swindling spirit, which exists in every society', including modern Christian nations.[27] Marxism had nothing in common with racism, and its methodology rejected the very concept of 'races' or 'nations' seen as undifferentiated anthropological groups or homogeneous supra-class entities. For international social-democracy there were 'only two nations, the exploiters and the exploited – and only two religions – the religion of capital and the gospel of the emancipation of labour'.[28]

The Jewish question did not exist for Marxists, any more than the 'Negro question' or the Chinese 'Yellow Peril'.[29] Such symptoms of class antagonism would be resolved along with a thousand other tasks in the future socialist society. Those who raised the 'Jewish question' as a separate issue were engaging, declared Rosa Luxemburg, in the classic manoeuvre of the counter-revolution – to divert the workers from their goals by artificially fomenting racial and religious hatred.

Rosa Luxemburg's analysis of antisemitism in Poland and Russia followed the conventional Marxist pattern. Curiously, she did not apply it to German antisemitism, though as a prominent left-wing socialist she had been exposed to similar attacks in the society for which she eventually laid down her life. This omission is all the more puzzling since she was certainly aware of her hostile reception in certain circles of the German Social Democratic Party in which she began to be active after 1898. The resentment against her which had a definite antisemitic tinge as well as Russophobic and anti-feminist undertones was ostensibly a result of her role in the 'revisionist' controversy at the turn of the century. The trade union bureaucracy in the German party, and the Bavarian socialists under Georg von Vollmar who supported Edward Bernstein's 'revisionism', were embittered by her sharp polemics, her lecturing tone, and her obvious intellectual superiority. Their anger was increased by the fact that it was another political *émigré* from the east, Alexander Israel Helphand (Parvus), at that time closely associated with Rosa Luxemburg, who spearheaded the assault on Bernstein's 'revisionism' in the German party press. Helphand-Parvus was a Russian Jew of great political talent, imaginative and unscrupulous, who like Rosa Luxemburg was able to straddle the German and Russian worlds with astonishing ease. The tactlessness of Parvus and Luxemburg, who were described by Richard Fischer (business manager of *Vorwärts*) as a 'pair of literary ruffians', was to provoke a bitter backlash at the Lübeck Congress of the German social democratic party in 1901.

Wolfgang Heine, a leading revisionist, described their behaviour as that of 'someone who comes as a guest to us and spits in our parlour'.[30] Luxemburg and Parvus, he claimed, had abused 'German hospitality' and made the struggle against antisemitism more difficult! Other delegates also deplored the manners of the new 'immigrant arrivals from the East'. As the German socialist leader August Bebel predicted in a letter to Kautsky, shortly before the congress, the animosity against Parvus and 'La Rosa' among the rank and file could not be ignored. The party leaders, including the chairman of the congress, Paul Singer (himself a Jew), maintained a discreet silence. Only Clara Zetkin, the great feminist leader and friend of Rosa Luxemburg, rose to defend the absent easterners against these aspersions on their national origins. 'They are with us not as Russians and Jews', she declared, 'but as party comrades (loud applause) who stand for the same program as us and share our struggles'.[31]

The anti-eastern prejudice in the German party surfaced again in 1905 when Rosa Luxemburg began to write a series of articles and pamphets recommending the lessons of the revolutionary mass strikes in Russia to German workers. The German Right and middle-class opinion in general saw in this attitude further confirmation of their suspicion of 'Jewish' radicalism. 'Russian', 'radical', and 'eastern Jew' had become virtually synonymous in the eyes not only of Emperor Wilhelm II, government circles, nationalists, and antisemites, but also on the right wing of the social democratic party. In these circles, Rosa Luxemburg was also considered a 'Russian patriot' and her anti-nationalism as well as her ultra-radicalism was viewed with profound suspicion.[32] Gustav Noske, the SPD spokesman on military and naval affairs (subsequently responsible in 1919 for Rosa Luxemburg's assassination, as Minister of the Interior), epitomized this native distrust of Russian and Polish-born revolutionaries in the German party. Rosa Luxemburg and Parvus symbolized in his eyes a clique of 'unworldly idealists' (*weltfremden Idealisten*) who had 'stepped forward as schoolmasters for the German proletariat'.[33] In his posthumously published memoirs he disclaimed any feelings of antisemitism, but baldly stated that east European Marxists of Jewish descent had a special gift for transforming platitudes into 'articles of dogma' incomprehensible to the German workers.[34] Similar feelings were earlier expressed by other revisionist socialists like Carl Grillenberger, August Winnig, and Eduard David.[35] Rosa Luxemburg was well aware of her peculiar reception in the SPD and of being as she once ironically put it '*nicht de la maison*'. In a bitter comment to her lover and associate, Leo Jogiches, written at the height of the revisionist controversy (27 April 1899), she quoted a well known Polish saying: '*Jak bieda to do żyda po biedzie precz Żydie*' ('When embarrassed – to the Jews for help – and when it is over – away with you, Jews').[36]

Nevertheless she did not publicly answer the personal attacks on her in the German party, at least not in the violent polemical form which she reserved for her Polish opponents. Perhaps she felt it would weaken her political position to confront such slurs. Perhaps, like Marx, she ignored the anti-Jewish flavour of these attacks to avoid drawing further attention to her origins. She was certainly opposed to any self-conscious identification as a Jewess and channelled any suppressed resentment that she felt into her defence of revolutionary Marxism against its enemies.

Nevertheless it is probably significant that she continued to feel an outsider in the SPD, and her temperamental dislike of German discipline and organization tended to grow with the years. It contrasted strikingly with the pre-1914 attitudes of other east European Jews towards Germany, including revolutionary *émigrés* like Parvus, Karl Radek, or Eugen Leviné.

For Rosa Luxemburg, however, the German party was essentially the springboard towards her dream of world revolution. Her almost mystical commitment to the abstract ideal of the proletarian 'fatherland' from the outset precluded any form of territorial patriotism or national identification.

This also determined her attitude towards the national liberation movement among the Jewish masses in Russia and eastern Europe. Along with other revolutionary Marxists she was convinced that assimilation was the only long-term solution to the Jewish national problem.[37] But her position was complicated by the peculiar triangular relationship that existed between her own social democratic party in Poland, the PPS, and the emerging Jewish labour movement (the Bund) which had also embraced a Marxist class ideology.

Rosa Luxemburg was familiar with the existence of a Jewish Workers' movement in Tsarist Russia as early as 1892. Her closest collaborator, Leo Jogiches, the son of wealthy 'Russified' Jewish parents in Vilna, had become involved in its beginnings in the late 1880s.[38] From their exile in Switzerland, both Jogiches and Rosa Luxemburg maintained close contact with Jewish labour leaders in Vilna, smuggling propagandist literature into Russia through this channel. In 1893 Leo Jogiches had published the *Four Speeches of Jewish Workers* in Russian (the original speeches had been in Yiddish) with an introduction by Boris Krichevskii, a Russian social democrat of Jewish origin who later became a leader of the 'Economist' faction of the RSDRP. Rosa Luxemburg almost certainly had a hand in this publication and may even have helped edit the introduction.[39] In January 1894 Jogiches contributed an enthusiastic review of the Vilna speeches to the SDKP organ, *Sprawa Robotnicza*, which was edited by Rosa Luxemburg.[40] In his review, Leo Jogiches welcomed the Russian Jewish workers as 'new comrades' in the common struggle of the Russian and Polish proletariat against Tsarist absolutism and capitalist exploitation. He emphasized the fact that the Vilna speakers repudiated the 'Palestinian' (that is, Zionist) solution to the Jewish problem even though their miserable situation in the Pale of Settlement made it difficult for Jewish workers to become conscious of their class interests. Jogiches pointed out that nationalism would alienate the Jewish workers from their Polish and Russian 'brothers'. But the Vilna speeches, according to Jogiches, showed that Russian Jewish workers had not been seduced by the dream of rebuilding a Jewish state in Palestine. They recognized that they would encounter the same system of exploitation there as in the Pale of Settlement. 'And so our comrades understand', wrote Jogiches, 'that the rebuilding of their own State will not destroy capitalism ... as for political freedom which is indispensable for the improvement of the workers' welfare and for the struggle against capitalism, the Jewish comrades also understand clearly that this and not the rebuilding of a utopian Jewish State, is their goal'.[41] Political liberty in the Tsarist empire could only be achieved by a common struggle of all nationalities. Jogiches praised the Vilna workers for adhering to this class standpoint 'notwithstanding all national persecution and patriotic agitation'. In his view, the Palestinophile movement (the reference was to the *Hovevei Zion* circles in Vilna) was recruited chiefly among the Jewish petty bourgeoisie and a certain section of the intelligentsia. It was a 'social-patriotic' deviation which could only distract the Jewish workers from the common class struggle against capitalism and Tsarism.

There is little doubt that this position was completely shared by Rosa Luxemburg. She was adamantly opposed to any attempt to reconcile nationalism with socialism and dismissed Zionism as a typical expression of the 'social patriotism' rampant among smaller, backward nationalities in eastern Europe. As a counterweight to it, she welcomed the emergence of a social democratic movement among the Jewish working class in Russia and Poland. In the 1890s she even saw it as a useful ally in the struggle to overthrow Tsarism. Subsequently, with the emergence of the Bund as an autonomous organization of the Jewish proletariat in Poland, Lithuania, and Russia (1897), the relationship of her SKDPiL to the new movement became more complex.

On the one hand she was personally acquainted with some leaders of the Bund, notably John Mill, who frequently visited her in Switzerland. She also shared with the Bund an *all-Russian* perspective in relation to solving the national problem in the Russian empire. The leaders of the Bund believed like Rosa Luxemburg that the proletarian revolution in Russia would automatically bring about the solution of the Jewish question. Both the SDKPiL and the Bund opposed, moreover, the secession of Poland from the Russian empire and the restoration of an independent Polish nation-state. The Bund was, however, far more tactful on this issue than Rosa Luxemburg and reluctant to take a definite stand. Its hand was forced by fears that the PPS, with its claim to exclusive hegemony on Polish 'soil', would not tolerate the existence of a separate Jewish labour movement in an independent Polish state. The Bund had emerged as an autonomous organization largely through having to defend itself against the efforts of the PPS to absorb it;[42] hence it had every reason to be suspicious of a renascent Polish nationalism.

The SDKPiL and the Bund were drawn together more closely by the frequent attacks of the PPS on both movements as instruments of 'Russification' in Poland. These polemics sometimes contained an antisemitic nuance, with the Bund and the Luxemburgist social democrats being accused of serving 'Jewish' rather than Polish interests. Rosa Luxemburg from the outset of her political career had been subject to this type of insinuation by her Polish socialist opponents. At the International Socialist Congress in London (1896) the leader of the Galician PPS, Ignacy Daszynski, openly called for the liberation of Polish socialism from her 'band of publicist brigands who are out to destroy our struggle for freedom'.[43] *Naprzód* (the PPS organ in Cracow) accused her and her 'Berdichev Russians' in May 1896 of suffering uncontrollable spasms 'on account of our Polish patriotism'.[44] Openly antisemitic socialists like Sedecki (Julian Unszlicht) identified her with attempts by so-called 'Social-Litvaks' (Lithuanian Jews) to 'russify' Poland.[45] Hence it is not altogether surprising that Rosa Luxemburg sympathized with the Bund when it was subjected to a similar onslaught by the PPS. Reviewing a pamphlet of the Bund against the PPS in 1903, she did not deny that the latter had inflamed antisemitism among Polish workers.[46]

But while she and her closest colleagues in the SDKPiL admired the 'superior organization of the Bund' and its 'revolutionary enthusiasm', they were increasingly disturbed by its self-assertive 'Jewish' character. Its emphasis on *Yiddishkeit* and insistence on maintaining a separate Jewish identity was contrary to the internationalism of the SDKPiL. Adolf Warski, the close associate of Rosa Luxemburg and editor of

Przegląd Socjaldemokratyczny (Social Democratic Review), wrote to Karl Kautsky in June 1903:

> Quite apart from the question as to whether the Jews are really a nation and have a national future in Russia – as the Bund asserts – the problem of party organizations and the relation of the Jewish workers to the working-class as a whole – must be solved according to common interests – and not according to burning national interests.[47]

Karl Kautsky responded to Warski's letter and Rosa Luxemburg's request for an article on the Kishinev pogrom (1903) by expounding one of the most authoritative versions of the Marxist theory of assimilation.[48] Rosa Luxemburg's position was equally assimilationist. But she did not go as far as the PPS or the Bolsheviks in demanding the total sub-ordination of the Bund to the general interests of the Polish and Russian working class. She accepted the need for local agitation in Yiddish among the Jewish masses, and even acknowledged that the Bund had achieved 'excellent results' in this field. But the cultural and linguistic peculiarities of the Jewish proletariat did not necessitate a separate Jewish organiza-tion along national lines, which in her view could only be divisive.[49] For Rosa Luxemburg the struggle to abolish anti-Jewish discrimination in the Tsarist empire and to achieve full civic equality was an inseparable part of the struggle for proletarian democracy in Russia and Poland.

In the long term she was convinced that a separate Jewish labour movement could not survive and that the Jewish proletariat in Poland would have to adopt the Polish language, national customs, and culture. But this was not a matter of coercion nor could there be any question of adopting a policy of *forced* assimilation. The process of economic development itself, which was leading to socialism, would peacefully eliminate the prospects for an independent Jewish culture. The survival of the Jewish 'nationality' in eastern Europe had been due solely to the predominance of social conditions which favoured small-scale produc-tion, commerce, and small-town life. These conditions had not permitted the emergence of a 'bourgeois national culture' among the Jewish people.[50] The efforts of a 'handful of publicists and Yiddish translators' could therefore be no substitute for this lack of national culture. The modern socialist culture which the Bund was introducing to the Jewish masses in Russia and Poland was, on the other hand, internationalist in its essence.[51] This proletarian culture would lead inevitably to the assimilation of the Jews.

In her analysis of this problem, Rosa Luxemburg came to similar conclusions as Karl Kautsky, Otto Bauer, Lenin, and other leading Marxists who believed that there was no independent future for the Jewish nation. In this respect, as in her attitude to the national problem in general, Rosa Luxemburg's prognosis has undoubtedly been falsified by history. In spite of her profound originality in various fields of theory she failed, like Marx, to understand the driving power of modern nationalism. Her vision of the proletarian 'fatherland' was buried in the carnage of the First World War. But even a decade earlier it was becoming apparent that Marx's slogan that the workers have no country no longer corresponded to political reality. National competition among workers, linguistic barriers, economic and colonial rivalries, and the growing integration of the proletariat in the structure of the nation-state belied the utopian prophecy of the *Communist Manifesto.* It is no accident that subsequent communist movements have come to power only where they have been able to mobilize nationalist sentiments in their service. The development of socialism and communism in the twentieth century, for good or for bad, has manifestly disproved the Luxemburgist negation of national self-determination.

I have suggested elsewhere that one of the psychological roots of this weakness in Rosa Luxemburg's political thought lay in her failure to come to terms with her own origins.[52] As with Marx and many other revolutionary Jews, her idealization of the 'international' proletariat appears at a subconscious level to have been a substitute for her own vulnerability as a *sans-patrie.* Perhaps this is one reason why she has proved to be a poor prophet in a world of resurgent nationalisms and ethnic self-assertion. Nevertheless her ideals remain rooted in the best traditions of socialist humanism and her vibrant personality will continue to exert its fascination on generations to come.

3

Antisemitism as a radical ideology

It is generally recognized that antisemitism as a modern ideology and as an organized political movement first emerged in Europe in the latter half of the nineteenth century. There is, however, far less agreement as to the nature and cause of this phenomenon, the significance of the term 'antisemitism' itself, and to what extent it can be seen as expressing a coherent world view, let alone a consistent policy or platform – at least in the conventional framework of nineteenth-century political parties. If by 'ideology' we imply the search for a *total* explanation of history and society, a system of belief which, without necessarily being 'rational', seeks to account for fundamental changes in the world and, more specifically, to articulate the sense of an existing or impending social crisis, then antisemitism can indeed be included under this heading. By the end of the nineteenth century, without always assuming the form of a systematic philosophy, antisemitism had none the less become a recognizable *Weltanschauung* – an interconnected way of thinking, feeling, and acting in the world, a distinctive cultural code and at the same time a vehicle for the expression of all kinds of economic and political grievances.

I shall be concerned here both with the process of crystallization of this 'ideology' and with its origins and content, as well as with some of its party political manifestations as they emerged in the 1880s and 1890s. In particular, I want to examine how far modern antisemitism, in its early phases (before 1900), was a movement of the Left or Right, radical or conservative – or whether it belongs to some more heterogeneous, hybrid category. In attempting to answer this question my angle of approach will be to examine its credentials as a species of radicalism and to consider in what ways it derives from, resembles, and differs from other 'leftist' ideologies in nineteenth-century Europe.

For this purpose it is also necessary to consider briefly the earlier part of the nineteenth century – before the term antisemitism with all its ambiguities and subsequent associations had become a fixed part of the European political vocabulary – and before the movement that fostered this ideology had itself been definitively absorbed into the whole cultural matrix of *fin-de-siècle* nationalism, *völkisch* racism, conservatism, and aggressive imperialism, especially in Germany and Austria-Hungary. In considering antisemitism as a form of political radicalism, and in re-examining its social dimension and its claims to have been a vehicle for *anti-establishment* protest, I do not, of course, wish to deny the strong elements of traditional-conservative Christian and medieval influences that were inherent both in the genesis of the ideology and in the mass organizations that it subsequently produced. Thus, in predominantly Catholic countries such as France and Austria there is no doubt that believing Catholics provided the bulk of the leadership and the main support for the nineteenth-century antisemitic parties as well as contributing to the elaboration of their ideology (although the Berlin movement in Germany – the first example of organized political antisemitism – was founded and led by the Protestant court-preacher, Adolf Stoecker). But even here, theological concerns played only a secondary role. Moreover, in the Christian-Social movement of the 1880s and 1890s in Germany, Austria, and France, it is significant that it was predominantly the urban lower middle classes, the peasantry, and the lower clergy rather than the ecclesiastical hierarchy which provided wholehearted support for antisemitism – while the leadership from Adolf Stoecker in Germany to Karl Lueger in Austria or the Abbé Garnier in France exploited all the resources of radical populist, anticapitalistic demagogy to revive the fortunes of the church in an era of rapid *dechristianization*, secularism, and rampant anti-clericalism.

While it is true that Catholic and Protestant antisemites in the late nineteenth century maintained all the traditional religious accusations against the Jews (such as diatribes against the Talmud, deicide, and blood-libel charges, especially potent in eastern Europe and the Habsburg empire), even these medieval superstitions owed their power to essentially modern techniques of mass agitation and to the crisis of insecurity afflicting lower-middle-class rural and urban strata whose imminent proletarization made them more receptive to such demogogy. What was novel and significant about Lueger's Christian-Social Party in Austria was precisely the way it blended such indigenous clerical traditions of Judeophobia as had existed for centuries with concrete social protest, with the revolt of the Viennese *Spiessbürger* in the 1880s against liberalism, high finance, and the so-called *Judenherrschaft*. The subsequent Habsburg, loyalist and Catholic 'traditionalist' image of Karl Lueger – once he had conquered Vienna in 1897 – should not disguise the social radicalism which made it possible in the first place for him successfully to mobilize the mass of small-scale producers, craftsmen, tradesmen, and shopkeepers in the Austro-Hungarian capital. Lueger's cynical exploitation of what his liberal rival Ferdinand Kronawetter called 'the socialism of fools' in order to win political power was so successful not only because of favourable local conditions and his own charismatic leadership (although these were important factors), but also because Christian-Social antisemitism so perfectly expressed the vacillating radicalism of the Viennese *Kleinbürger*. It was both anticapitalist (against the modern manufacturing methods pioneered in Austria by Jewish entrepreneurs, which were indeed swamping skilled craftsmen and small businesses), anti-liberal (the Jews were invariably seen as the backbone of the liberal establishment in Austria), and anti-immigrant – that is, directed against the unwelcome competition of poor immigrant Jewish pedlars from Galicia, Hungary, and Russia.

In addition, Christian-Socialism in Vienna held out the promise of a more democratic socio-political order which would protect the interests of the 'little man' against a narrow and unrepresentative liberal-capitalist oligarchy. The ideology on which Lueger's Christian-Socialism was based, as formulated by Karl Freiherr von Vogelsang two decades earlier, did admittedly contain strong conservative, neo-feudal elements with its dream of a corporatist society, a restoration of the guilds, and its emphasis on the Catholic prohibition of 'usury' as well as in its attack on the materialist, anti-clerical, and subversive ethos of modern bourgeois civilization. Yet even here, in the aristocratic critique of social atomism, *laissez-faire* capitalism, and the so-called 'Jewish spirit', there are parallels with the young Marx that not only von Vogelsang but even some of the Austro-Marxist theoreticians, such as Karl Renner and Otto Bauer, pointed out.

While it is undeniable that many Catholic antisemites frequently expressed a romantic anti-modernist outlook similar to von Vogelsang in Austria or La Tour de Pin in France as a reaction to the growth of industrial civilization – dreaming of a pre-capitalist way of life or expressing nostalgia for the traditional Christian order – this was not necessarily incompatible with social radicalism. Many social democrats, especially in Germany – where after 1880 the working classes were more effectively mobilized against the antisemitic groups – tended to dismiss the 'radicalism' of the antisemites as a backward-looking utopian folly, directed to the past not the future. They were sometimes compared to the machine-breaking Luddites in England or to anarchists, depicted as primitive rebels or as homeless, uprooted, dispossessed strata, who had failed to grasp the dialectics of social change or the significance of technological development.

Marxian socialism, especially as it developed in Germany after 1880, proudly regarded itself (and its evaluation has been accepted by many historians) as standing at the opposite pole of the political world to the antisemites – as an optimistic *emancipatory* creed which shared the liberal belief in education, progress, and inter-racial tolerance, and at the same time as an internationalist revolutionary movement based on class identification and opposed to all forms of national and religious discrimination. Antisemitism, as Peter Pulzer has written, was 'concerned not with more emancipation but with less, with the interests of traditional, not of new classes, with the primacy of the national and the integral over the universal'. There is some truth in this basic distinction, especially with regard to Bismarckian and Wilhelminian Germany, but it is certainly not universally valid and it unjustifiably assumes an *a priori*, inborn immunity to antisemitism within the socialist movement. Moreover, it underestimates the social and political radicalism of the antisemites. In both Austria-Hungary and France, where they organized a more formidable political movement than in the Second Reich, the antisemites could nourish themselves on a radical leftist tradition, and even in Germany before 1880 one can observe a similar phenomenon.

Nor is it an adequate explanation to present modern antisemitism simply as a *reaction* to the economic depression after 1873 or to the political crisis of post-1879 liberalism in Germany. The corollary propounded by Reinhard Rürup, that modern antisemitism is essentially 'a post-emancipation phenomenon' directed by its proponents 'against an influential powerful Jewry at the very centre of that society', is also somewhat misleading, taking too literally the claims of the antisemites themselves. While plausibly seeing the decline of bourgeois liberalism in central Europe in the 1870s as a crucial turning point in the emergence of modern political antisemitism, this approach does not adequately explain why the Jews were selected as scapegoats to explain the stockmarket crash of 1873, the socio-economic crisis of capitalism, and the backlash against liberal political culture. The implication in Rürup's argument appears to be that, in Berlin at least, the Jews really were the representatives of capitalist economy and culture and that therefore German antisemites were perhaps justified in regarding themselves as the organizers of a 'defensive movement' opposed to 'Jewish rule'. Certainly many contemporaries did see the new antisemitism of the 1870s as just such a movement against Jewish 'domination' in cultural and economic life, as did their imitators in Austria and France a few years later. On this point conservative, Catholic, radical, and even socialist critics of *laissez-faire* liberalism could unite. However, what is interesting here is that although it was the radical antisemites who made the running in the 1880s, the clerical-conservative elements reaped the fruits in the following decade, absorbing and 'recuperating' the benefits of antisemitism in the service of their own class interests.

Otto Glagau, the *petit-bourgeois* German pamphleteer who initiated the new assault on 'Jewry' in the 1870s as 'applied Manchesterism carried to extremes' and called for emancipation from the Jews, was a classic representative of the earlier radical tradition along with his fellow journalist Wilhelm Marr – the German originator in 1879 of the novel political concept 'antisemitism'. Along with other initially obscure publicists of the nineteenth century who created a *succès de scandale* with their revelations, like Drumont in France and August Rohling in Austria, they gave a sensational journalistic expression to anti-Jewish feelings that were already apparent in public as a reaction to the stockmarket crash and the general climate of social aggression and overheated nationalism. Glagau's originality was to identify the Jewish question explicitly with the social question and to rouse the embittered German *Mittelstand* with his revelations concerning the stock-exchange swindles of the *Gründerzeit*. There are more than a few echoes of Karl Marx in Glagau's denunciation of the cash nexus, the bourse-wolves, the plight of the ruined artisan class, and the iniquities of 'Manchester liberalism'. In identifying the Jewish merchant and banker with *homo capitalisticus*, Glagau and other radical antisemites of the 1870s were in fact continuing the tradition of Marx's *Zur Judenfrage*, admittedly without the intellectual sophistication of Hegelian dialectics – just as Eduard Drumont in France could draw on the anti-Jewish writings of early nineteenth-century utopian socialists such as Fourier, Toussenel, and Proudhon.

Admittedly there were some important differences – Marx defended the principle of Jewish civil rights within bourgeois society even while calling for the emancipation of humanity from 'Judaism' – whereas Otto Glagau and his disciples were primarily interested in the social and *national* liberation of 'Christian' Germans. Moreover, Marx's anti-Judaism did not utilize the naturalistic imagery derived from the biological sciences already in vogue by the 1870s but not widely current thirty years earlier. Furthermore, Marx's concept of Jewish parasitism, like that of Fourier and Toussenel in France, remained social rather than racial. The Jews were never viewed by Marx and his disciples as an alien *Volkskörper* (racial body) corroding the national organism in the sense that Glagau, Marr, and Dühring – the leaders of radical German antisemitism – and the neo-Lassallean agitator, Wilhelm Hasselmann, maintained. For Marx, they were still 'Jews' rather than 'Semites', bearers of the commercial ethos that had infiltrated the Christian world rather than a nomadic, malevolent *Volk* which aimed at imposing its racial domination over the Germans whether through the banks, the stock exchange, the state, or the political parties. But these differences should not obscure the fact that there is a line of continuity between the anti-Judaism of the young Hegelians in the early 1840s and the emergence of the new antisemitism in Germany three decades later – just as there is a connection between the early socialist *anti-juif* movement in France and the antisemitic politics of Drumont, Barrès, and Guérin in the 1890s.

One important link in this chain was the radical tradition of anti-clericalism, which goes back to the French *philosophes* of the eighteenth century. It was from this background that Wilhelm Marr himself emerged and it is not surprising that he denied so vehemently that his anti-semitism was motivated by *confessioneller Hass*. As a veteran revolutionary of 1848, an ex-radical democrat convinced by his reading of Voltaire, Feuerbach, and Daumer that monotheism was 'a malady of human consciousness' and the root of all tyranny and evil, Wilhelm Marr's antisemitism was also virulently anti-Catholic. Together with Eugen Dühring, himself a former socialist and the most influential ideologist of radical antisemitism in central Europe in the 1880s, Wilhelm Marr believed that no Christian could be a genuine antisemite because Christianity was itself based on and corrupted by Jewish racial tradition. This was a logical enough development of Marr's earlier radical negation of monotheistic religion – an evolution paralleled in France by the Blanquist socialists and continued in Germany by Eugen Dühring and Theodor Fritsch. In his socialist phase, Dühring had already presented Christianity as a doctrine which negated the life force and had sundered man from nature, sapping his vitality and spontaneous attachment to his native land. Within a few years, Dühring, by this time a determined opponent of the Marxist labour movement, was calling for the complete emancipation of the modern 'Aryan' peoples from the Judeo-Christian yoke – basing his argument for the renewal of German culture on the radical repudiation of both the Old and the New Testaments.

The *völkisch* anti-Christian antisemitic tradition in nineteenth-century Germany and Austria embodied by Theodor Fritsch, Otto Boeckel, and Georg von Schoenerer followed in Dühring's wake and found expression in a plebeian populist agitation that claimed to be *above* party and religious denominations. The social radicalism of Otto Boeckel's Hessian peasant movement in the late 1880s, which was typical of this trend, went hand in hand with a racist, neo-pagan *Blut und Boden* romanticism and denunciations of Jews, Junkers, and clerics, as well as with serious efforts to establish producer and consumer self-help organizations in the Hessian countryside to eliminate the Jewish middleman and trader. Boeckel's *Antisemitische Volkspartei*, which won a number of parliamentary seats in the 1890s, expressed a radical plebeian revolt against the existing parliamentary system in the Second Reich, against metropolitan Berlin culture, big business, the world of industry, the Jews, and the Prussian aristocracy. Boeckel's anti-modernist nostalgia admittedly embodied the conservative side of modern German antisemitism – its romantic *völkisch* aspirations for a pre-industrial culture; but as a follower of Glagau and Dühring who totally rejected the Judeo-Christian outlook and defended *Mittelstand* interests against the Junkers, capitalists, and Jews, Boeckel was undoubtedly a populist radical. Even the title of one of his best-known pamphlets, *Die Juden – Die Könige unsere Zeit* (1887), which *inter alia* attacked the Rothschilds, consciously recalled the famous work by the French socialist Toussenel written in 1845 – *Les Juifs – Rois de l'Époque*.

Georg von Schoenerer in Austria stood even more clearly in the radical camp as the undisputed leader of the leftist opposition in the Habsburg monarchy during the early 1880s. His populist attacks on the Austrian Rothschilds in 1884 accusing them of transport usury (a campaign denounced by the liberal *Neue Freie Presse* as 'communistic') was the high point of his career as the anticapitalist Führer of the masses. Von Schoenerer at this time still enjoyed the support of the future leaders of Austrian Social Democracy, Victor Adler and Engelbert Pernerstorfer, and of the Christian-Socials Karl Lueger and Ernst Schneider, not to mention the Pan-German nationalists. Anti-liberalism, anticapitalism, and anti-clericalism were the unifying threads in von Schoenerer's national-socialist ideology expressed in the Linz programme of 1882, formulated with the help of two assimilated Jews – Heinrich Friedjung and Victor Adler. Von Schoenerer's anticapitalist rhetoric in favour of productive classes, the call for universal suffrage, a progressive income tax, a tax on stock-exchange transactions, the nationalizing of railways and insurance companies, the limitation of working hours, and the subsequent addition in 1885 of the notorious *Judenpunkt* calling for the removal of Jewish influence from all areas of public life regarded as 'indispensable for realizing these reforms', were typical enough of quasi-socialist, antisemitic populism in this period. Calls for social reform and democratization of the political system went hand in hand with nationalism and a growing emphasis on the racial gulf between 'Aryan' and Jew, fused together in a militant anti-liberal platform. Significantly, von Schoenerer, like Marr in Germany, saw himself as the descendant of the radical generation of 1848 with its republican, anti-clerical, romantic nationalist ideals. He called for the destruction of the Catholic Church and Jesuit influence as well as for an end to the 'Semitic' domination of banking, credit institutions, and the press in accordance with the Pan-German slogan, *'Ohne Juda Ohne Rom wird gebaut Germaniens Dom'*. The radical, racist dynamic behind Austrian Pan-Germanism, evident in von Schoenerer's insistence on the eternal, biological necessity of combating the Jew, clearly influenced German national socialism, as Adolf Hitler openly stated in *Mein Kampf* – just as (in a different way) Lueger's ability to organize the Catholic *petit-bourgeois* masses in Vienna, his grasp of the social question, and his tactical flair shaped the young Hitler's views on propaganda. It was from these prewar Austrian models that Hitler learned the political significance of antisemitism as a weapon for mobilizing the masses against one enemy which could simultaneously symbolize both liberalism, capitalism, socialism, and the supra-national state.

This type of radical antisemitism involved not simply a traditional religious rejection of Jews and Judaism but also a negation of Christianity itself, of capitalism, of parliamentarism, and frequently of 'modernism' as a whole. Its ideological development appears to have coincided with a general socio-economic, religious, and political crisis in European society. The antisemites claimed, of course, to be reacting purely to the 'Jewish peril' and advocated all kinds of measures for banning Jewish immigrants, reducing or abolishing Jewish employment in certain professions (especially public office), withdrawing citizenship and restoring the ghetto, encouraging the expropriation of Jewish fortunes, favouring repatriation, and even physical elimination of the Jews. But much of this agitation in western and central Europe as opposed to the pogromist barbarism of Tsarist Russia remained at a purely verbal level – however violent the rhetoric.

The 'fantasy' element was strong in this nineteenth-century genre of plebeian antisemitism and its mythical quality (transcending theological hatred of Jews which sounded medieval and reactionary) was strengthened by the new emphasis on 'race' – a concept which conveniently lent itself to all kinds of mystification in spite of its modern 'scientific' ring. The very abstractness of the antisemitic 'ideology' – itself largely a creation of semi-radicalized, frustrated intellectual misfits and some sensation-mongering journalists – succeeded in activating the sense of an ideal world beyond the social atomization, the class antagonisms, and the decadence of contemporary bourgeois society. The diffuse radicalism expressed by this antisemitic mythology offered a kind of anchor for the psychologically unhinged, the economically insecure, the social misfits, the unemployed intellectuals, and the bankrupt aristocrats, as well as serving the material interests of the 'respectable' professional middle classes suddenly confronted by unwelcome Jewish competition.

As the French Catholic writer Anatole Leroy-Beaulieu put it, antisemitism was as much the socialism of 'snobs' and 'clubmen' as of the 'fools' (to use the Marxist formula) in France, as in Austria and Germany; already in *fin-de-siècle* Europe it proved its efficacy in bringing together the aristocracy and the mob, the men of capital and the honest labouring artisans, the peasants and the disaffected, culturally disoriented *Mittelstand* in a national front against the alleged domination of an 'alien' race. It was this social functionality of antisemitism along with its protean quality and ability to fuse with a whole series of other views which, among other things, distinguished it from traditional Jew-hatred and gave it a distinctively modern quality. By the 1890s it had clearly emerged as an identifiable world view, as an ideology and a political movement able to compete with conservatism, liberalism, or socialism – one, moreover, with its own *quasi-apocalyptic* view of social reality and its own peculiar methods of operation. On the one hand it exuded a brutal simplicity and aggressive demagogy which was part of its strength while at the same time the social radicalism which had made it potentially dangerous and unacceptable to bourgeois society was masked and effectively neutralized by the willingness of respectable establishment figures and political organizations to sponsor its aims. It was not the noisy, unstable radicals like Marr, Glagau, Boeckel, Ahlwardt, Fritsch, or von Schoenerer who made antisemitism *salonfähig* in Germany and Austria, but conservative nationalists like Heinrich von Treitschke, Protestant clerics like Adolf Stoecker, or Catholic aristocrats like Freiherr von Vogelsang and Prince von Liechtenstein. Needless to say, the task of integrating antisemitism into the mainstream of central European culture was greatly facilitated by the long list of illustrious German thinkers and artists from Luther, Kant, Goethe, and Fichte to Hegel, Feuerbach, Schopenhauer, and Richard Wagner, whose derogatory views of Jews and Judaism could be called upon and were in fact utilized to justify antisemitic opinions in the second half of the nineteenth century.

In France the tradition of literary antisemitism was no less distinguished than in Germany and also contributed its share towards making the new ideology socially respectable by the end of the century. Indeed in France antisemitism had been indigenous to the rationalist, anti-clerical, and socialist traditions from the beginning of the nineteenth century, giving it an intellectual prestige that it did not initially enjoy in other countries. The Voltairean contempt for the Jews (with its dual attack on the inherently debased character of the race and on the iniquities of Judeo-Christian monotheism) and the Fourierist onslaught against commercialism, mercantile parasitism, and Jewish 'usury' gave a modern, secular edge to French antisemitism well before 1848. Proudhon's visceral diatribes 'against this race which poisons everything, by meddling everywhere without ever joining itself to another people' or his call for the abolition of the 'cult' of Judaism – 'One must send this race back to Asia or exterminate it' – make even Marx's more extreme remarks on the subject seem like models of cool objectivity. For all his anti-clericalism, Proudhon felt obliged to point out that it was not for nothing that the Christians called them (the Jews) 'deicides', and his teaching that 'la haine du juif, comme de l'anglais, doit être un article de notre foi politique' was readily absorbed by many French socialists in the nineteenth century.

The socialist tradition of Fourier, Proudhon, and Blanqui appears to have digested the medieval popular feeling against the Jews as usurers into its mainstream, helped, no doubt, by the prominence of the Rothschilds and a number of other Jews (and Protestants) in the French banking oligarchy.

Indeed, modern antisemitism in France first developed primarily as an offshoot of the early radical attack on the *féodalité financière* – the new financial plutocracy, which had established its hegemony under the bourgeois Orleanist monarchy (1830–48). The French socialist stereo-type of the Jew as the incarnation of Mammon and the mercantile spirit retained a noticeably Christian tinge in the writings of Fourier, Proud-hon, Pierre Leroux, and Alphonse Toussenel. The latter's book, *Les Juifs, Rois de l'Époque*, directly related the iniquities of the Protestant capitalist ethos to 'biblical' morality and 'Jewish' racial traits – particu-larly those exemplified by cosmopolitan Jewish financiers – in such a way that Edouard Drumont had a ready model before him when he came to compose *La France Juive* forty years later. Not for nothing did Drumont refer to the 'wonderful book' of the Fourierist disciple, Alphonse Toussenel, 'the work of a poet, of a thinker, of a prophet', and declare his sole ambition to be that his own work would stand alongside it 'in the libraries of those who would understand the causes which have brought ruin and shame to our country'. In Toussenel's work one can in-deed see one of the primary sources of modern French antisemitism which was admiringly quoted not only by Drumont but also by the integral socialists who contributed to Benoît Malon's *La Revue Socialiste* in the 1880s and by the integral nationalists around *Action Française* in the 1900s. They all shared Toussenel's hatred of *la haute banque*, of the unproductive middleman and merchant, of 'Judaism', Protestantism, *laissez-faire*, and Anglo-Saxon capitalism.

No less significant is the fact that a section of the French socialist movement should have been so receptive to the 'Aryan' myth which had been first developed in France during the 1850s primarily by aristocratic and liberal-bourgeois scholars like the Comte de Gobineau and Ernst Renan. One can already find examples of this racist antisemitism in Proudhon, where he writes that the Jew 'is the evil element, Satan, Ahriman, incarnated in the race of Shem'. Proudhon had, for example, argued in *De la justice dans la révolution et dans l'église* (1858) that 'monotheism is a creation of the Indo-Germanic spirit, and could not have arisen from any other source'. Elsewhere he blamed the Jews, this 'race insociable, obstinée, infernale' for that 'superstition malfaisante' called Catholicism – it was the influence of the 'Jewish' element which (following Voltaire) Proudhon held responsible for Christian intolerance and fanaticism. It is difficult to resist the conclusion that the racist diatribes in Proudhon were grafted on almost as an appendix to justify his visceral hatred of Judaism. Significantly enough, this racist streak was shared by the Russian revolutionary anarchist Mikhail Bakunin who expressed an even more paranoic view of the Jews than Proudhon, calling them 'an exploiting sect, a bloodsucking people, a unique devouring parasite, tightly and intimately organized'. Bakunin shared Proudhon's primitivist view that only peasants and workmen were real producers, as well as his bitter hatred of Marx and Marxism – pointing out that 'the communism of Marx wants a mighty centralization by the state, and where this exists there must nowadays be a central State Bank and where such a bank exists, the parasitical Jewish nation, which speculates on the labour of the peoples, will always find a means to sustain itself.'

On the issue of Jewish 'parasitism', it would paradoxically appear that Bakunin's Russian revolutionary populism, Proudhon's French anarchism, and early German Marxism could find some common ground. What however made the French socialists particularly susceptible to this type of anticapitalistic antisemitism was the dramatic predominance of the *haute banque* in French economic and political life in the first half of the nineteenth century. The combination of this fact with the extensiveness of *petit-bourgeois* enterprise in France, its predominantly agrarian peasant Catholic culture, and the lack of a sophisticated economic theory to compare with mature Marxism, made it easier to equate the Jew with the capitalist and with the updated traditional, Christian image of the usurer. For most French radicals as for the mass of shopkeepers, artisans, and workers, the Rothschilds remained the embodiment of big capital and the entire propaganda against banking capital in France was thus easily diverted into antisemitic channels. Among some of the Blanquists this hostility towards the Jew as the incarnation of swindling, usury, and rapacity was still further intensified by their acceptance of the 'Aryan' myth and of 'Semitic' inferiority. The violently anti-clerical trend within French socialism took on, moreover, pathological proportions in the work of the French Blanquist Gustave Tridon (notably in his *Du Molochisme Juif*) – he even accused the biblical Jews of cannibalism and originating human sacrifice. This was a malevolent charge already to be found in Voltaire and also in the writings of some of the left-Hegelian radicals in Germany such as Friedrich Daumer and Ghillany. But it was left to the Blanquist socialists to demonstrate that the prime task of modernity and of revolutionary radicalism was to sweep away the last particles of 'l'esprit Sémitique' from the face of the earth.

What had distinguished France from both Germany and Austria was that antisemitism, at least until 1885, came mainly from the socialist camp and that even after Edouard Drumont's emergence it still retained its leftist character and its anticapitalist pretensions for considerably longer. As recently pointed out by Professor Zeev Sternhell, the synthesis accomplished in the 1890s by ideologists of the calibre of Drumont and Barrès, by radical polemicists like Henri Rochefort and agitators like de Morès and Jules Guérin, was to fuse the socialist with the populist-Catholic and, above all, with the nationalist current in French antisemitism and to make it the most sophisticated politico-cultural conceptualization of Judeophobia achieved anywhere in Europe in the nineteenth century. It was to take another thirty years before the full destructive potential of this 'radical' nineteenth-century ideology was to become apparent, not in Paris, its original laboratory and intellectual seed-bed, but in Munich, Berlin, and Vienna, as a central plank in the national socialist onslaught against liberal-bourgeois democracy and the Marxist labour movement. The dynamic role played by antisemitism in the ideological political synthesis represented by German Nazism would however have been inconceivable without the radical intellectual framework which first developed in the womb of the declining bourgeois society of *fin-de-siècle* Europe.

4

Karl Lueger in historical perspective

In a prescient article published in 1900, the editor-in-chief of the Viennese socialist *Arbeiter-Zeitung*, Friedrich Austerlitz, tried to explain in Marxist terms the extraordinary popularity of the lord mayor of Vienna, Karl Lueger, leader of the Christian-Social Party. With characteristic irony, he pointed out that

> the career of this former lawyer is truly one of the most interesting phenomena of our times: the key to following and understanding it is provided by a knowledge of the psychology of the petite bourgeoisie. Lueger enriched political science by a great discovery: he transformed democracy, a political orientation that was dying of boredom, into modern demagogy, into the art of fobbing people off with the appearance instead of the reality of the situation.[1]

Eleven years later, following the death of the man who was widely known and loved by his followers as the 'King of Vienna', the social democrat Austerlitz acknowledged that Lueger was indeed 'the first bourgeois politician who recognized the importance of the masses in politics'.[2] The social democrats, by 1911 already the chief rivals of Christian-socialism, could afford to be generous, for with Lueger's exit from the scene his party lost 35,000 votes in Vienna and held on to only four of the imperial capital's thirty-three seats in the general elections of that year. Although the setback proved to be only temporary and it would be an exaggeration to present the Christian-Social Party as the work of one man, however commanding his presence, it is certainly true that Dr Karl Lueger was the representative political phenomenon of his time and place.

It is, however, less easy to define precisely what constituted this representative character of his political personality and to asssess his historic significance from the perspective of the late twentieth century. Can he be viewed properly as a mentor of Adolf Hitler, as a proto-fascist leader, or as a pioneer of 'post-rational politics', as one influential cultural historian has claimed?[3] Or should he rather be seen as an ex-radical, traditionalist conservative, a Habsburg loyalist who restored the decaying fortunes of political Catholicism in Austria and ultimately substituted clerical for liberal rule? If so, what is one to make of his impressive record as the civic-minded architect of Viennese 'municipal socialism'; as a social reformer who expanded the water supply, built schools, hospitals, publicly owned abattoirs, while transforming the topography of Vienna by providing it with new city gas, electricity, tramlines, and railways, as well as a green belt, and a coherent architectural concept? In short, is it fair to see in Karl Lueger a harbinger of the twentieth-century politics of the 'radical Right', the paradigm for later *déclassé* desperadoes and ambitious demagogues such as Mussolini and Hitler, determined to rouse the atomized masses to a frenzy; or was he rather a Catholic reformist version of the archetypal Habsburg political leader – patrimonial, even patriarchal in manner, more baroque than fascist in his *modus operandi*?

To put forward the alternatives in these stark terms itself reveals the degree to which contemporary historical judgements have been unavoidably influenced by the ideological polarizations of the twentieth century. Thus a recent historian of modern conservatism, John Weiss, describing the rise of the radical Right in Europe between 1890 and 1914, places Lueger unequivocally in the reactionary tradition.[4] Starting with the premise that Austria was the cradle of the 'most strident and popular radical right-wing social movements that Europe was to see before the days of Mussolini and Hitler', and that 'the voters of the Empire were more polarized into radical right and radical left than the citizens of any other European nation', he labels Lueger's Christian-Social Party as a vehicle of ultra-conservative Catholic rightism.[5] The 1907 parliamentary elections in Austria, he claims, 'marked the emergence of the first political genius of the radical right in Europe'.[6] It is no surprise, therefore, that the young Hitler, whose arrival in Vienna from rural upper Austria coincided with the electoral triumph of 1907 (when the Christian-Socials emerged with the largest *Klub* in the first democratically elected *Reichsrat*), should have been vividly impressed by the Viennese lord mayor. Though Hitler's views on political matters were 'an amalgam of the popular commonplaces of Austro-Pan-Germans' (derived from the anti-Catholic racialist ideology of Georg von Schoenerer), his oratorical and propaganda techniques were, by his own testimony, learned from Karl Lueger.

In Lueger, the 18-year-old Hitler did indeed see the ideal modern mass leader even if he remained critical of his mentor's pro-Austrianism and half-hearted antisemitism, 'an apparent anti-Semitism [*Scheinantisemitismus*] that was almost worse than none'.[7] In matters of principle, Hitler certainly had no doubt that von Schoenerer (rather than Lueger) was 'the better and more profound thinker', that is, he had grasped the centrality of the issues of race and of the 'Jewish question'. Hitler could identify moreover with the Pan-German hatred of the Habsburgs and their call for *Anschluss* with Germany far more than with the Austro-Catholic loyalism of Lueger's party. Nevertheless, in *Mein Kampf* Hitler praised the Christian-Social Party for 'its shrewd judgement concerning the worth of the popular masses', and for its 'practical wisdom, and particularly their attitude towards socialism': he admitted that he had learned from Lueger 'the importance of the social question' and that of understanding the lower strata of the population.

> He [Lueger] saw only too clearly that, in our epoch, the political power of the upper classes is quite insignificant . . . . Thus he devoted the greatest part of his political activity to the task of winning over these sections of the population whose existence was in danger and fostering the militant spirit in them rather than attempting to paralyse it. He was also quick to adopt all available means for winning the support of long-established institutions, so as to be able to derive the greatest possible advantage for his movement from those old sources of power.[8]

Hitler, the aspiring mass politician, stressed the shrewdness, practicality, and flair for propaganda of Lueger and his lieutenants – 'they were veritable virtuosos in working up the spiritual instincts of the broad masses of their adherents' – the tactical sense for possibilities, and 'the true genius of a great reformer'. The concrete lessons that he learned from his Austrian Catholic predecessor were not in the realm of ideology but of political praxis and technique – the needs to address oneself to the masses and not just to the middle classes, to appeal to those social groups 'threatened with extinction' who provided the base for mob demagogy, and at the same time not to forgo the support of the old establishment, especially the Catholic church against whom von Schoenerer's Pan-Germans had engaged in such a foolish and disastrous struggle.

The lessons that Hitler absorbed from his stay in Vienna (1908–13) are important to one's understanding of his biography and the genesis of national socialism; yet how far should they be allowed to affect one's judgement of Karl Lueger and of the Christian-Social Party? The ideological affiliation (aside from anti-socialism and antisemitism) appears rather weak between Lueger's party and the German Nazis, not to mention the problematic continuity with the Austrian fascist movements during the First Republic.[9] Even the antisemitism of the Christian-Socials, with its strongly Catholic traditionalist and economic colouring, seems qualitatively different from that of the Nazis as Hitler himself clearly recognized. In Lueger's case, it was never truly *racial*, though the public rhetoric of his more vicious Jew-baiting lieutenants (such as Schneider, Vergani, Gregorig, Father Deckert, and so forth) was frequently indistinguishable from that of the most raucous, beer-drinking Pan-Germans. Thus the Christian-Social deputy, Ernst Schneider, a close associate of Lueger (who highly valued his indispensable knowledge of conditions in the Viennese artisanal trades), declared in the *Reichsrat* in 1901:

> The Jewish Question is a racial question, a question of blood, a culture question which can only be solved by blood and iron as hundreds of thousands of years of ancient history taught not only our people, but all peoples, and you will not escape this truth.[10]

The racist gutter journalism of the *Deutsche Volksblatt*, edited by another leading Christian-Social politician, Ernst Vergani, was no less extremist than Schneider's primitive street-corner Jew-baiting. Lueger saw no need to discipline such extremists in his own party even if his particular antisemitism, by all accounts, was little more than cynical opportunism and political calculation. This sin of omission, taken in the context of the brutal anti-intellectual and antisemitic demagogy of the time, must give more credence to those historians sceptical of the cosy picture manufactured by earlier Austrian (and some Jewish) writers of the 'Golden Age of old Vienna' under *der schöne Karl*'s benevolent rule. It is true that Lueger, himself a reasonably cultured, amiable man of immense charm, a shrewd operator with a fine sense of public relations, and (in character) the very opposite of a fanatic, generated precisely that aura of *Gemütlichkeit* around which the myth of *fin-de-siècle* Vienna has been revolving ever since.[11] In this traditionally easygoing society at a time during the 1890s when the suburban *petite bourgeoisie* and little tradesmen came into their own, politically, for the first time, even Jew-baiting might indeed appear to be no more than 'an excellent means of propaganda and of getting ahead in politics . . . the sport of the rabble', as Lueger once confided in private. Similarly there is a peculiarly Viennese geniality in the mayor's personally benign attitude towards Jews epitomized by his reported statement to Sigmund Mayer, a leading figure in the Vienna *Kultusgemeinde*:

> I like the Hungarian Jews even less than the Hungarians but I am not an enemy of our Viennese Jews; they are not so bad and we cannot do without them . . . . The Jews are the only ones who always feel like being active.[12]

Most historians agree that Lueger was probably never a convinced antisemite any more than he was a genuinely pious Catholic, though he exploited both ideologies to excellent effect during his own lifetime in order to propagate his career. If, however, one accepts this picture (which does indeed appear to be corroborated from many sources) then what remains of Lueger beyond the endearing manner, the jovial *persona*, the political skills, and a considerable administrative talent, is a hollow core without any real convictions or genuine substance. Interestingly enough, this was very much the view of the social democratic press in Austria-Hungary at the time of his triumphs. A number of left-wing and liberal writers linked the opportunistic character of Lueger's antisemitism with the peculiar temperament of the Viennese *petite bourgeoisie* and its confused backlash against an underdeveloped Austrian capitalism. Thus Wilhelm Ellenbogen, a leading left-wing Austrian socialist (and a Jewish physician), argued in 1899 that Lueger's Jew-baiting was pure fraud and had nothing to do with the 'deep-rooted Jew-hatred' inspired by the Catholic church which had long existed in Austria.[13] The new political antisemitism, he argued, flourished against the background of provincial backwardness, superficiality, and the Austrian tendency to trivialize everything,[14] 'that Viennese *Gemütlichkeit* which is almost synonymous with good-natured weak-mindedness, but which, as is well-known, may just as easily turn malevolent; phenomena which have for centuries been cultivated by the priests and princes of Austria'.[15]

Ellenbogen, like other Austrian socialists, regarded economic antisemitism in Vienna primarily as the 'socialism of fools', an attempt to manipulate and direct the frustrated and disoriented *Kleinbürger* into a mythical struggle against 'Jewish capital'. Lueger, the *condottiere* of this *petit-bourgeois* crusade against big capital, who claimed to speak in the name of the oppressed Christian *Volk* (the tailors, grocers, shoemakers, depressed artisans, peasants, and small businessmen) – this would-be dragon-slayer of 'Jewish capitalism' – was in reality delivering the city of Vienna to the big bankers and to clerical rule. The social democrat Ellenbogen described him as the 'archetypal, ambitious demagogue . . . equally well equipped with wit and pathos, an almost amoral frivolity with regard to political principles, ruthless or pliable as the occasion demands'.[16] His 'apparent anti-semitism', as the rest of his politics, was built (as Ellenbogen noted) on an unstable coalition of socioeconomic interests. His was a movement that 'lives from negation and the sins of its opponents'.[17] A similar verdict was delivered by Friedrich Austerlitz in 1900. He regarded Lueger as the one mass leader of virtuoso skill that the Austro-German bourgeoisie had produced in modern times; he was a man who had not invented antisemitism but merely had given it political expression, in order to ventilate and exploit mass grievances against liberal hegemony, which in Vienna had acquired an unmistakably Jewish flavour in the late nineteenth century.[18]

The *Scheinantisemitismus* of Lueger was undoubtedly part of the theatricality, the attitudinizing, and the oratorical flair for mass politics which he had brought to his role. As the perfect embodiment of the

Viennese common man in the age of democracy, Lueger reflected all the contradictions and dissonances of the heterogeneous groups which made up the Christian-Social Party at the turn of the century. The anti-Jewish demagogy was ultimately as empty as the claim to be simultaneously a radical and a Habsburg loyalist, a Germanophile and a Czechophile, a centralist and an autonomist. 'He only attacks the Jews, that is, the attack has no specific goal, it is an end in itself, and degenerates into demagogy.'[19] This socialist criticism was intended, of course, to expose the fraudulent, hypocritical, playful character of Lueger's posture towards the Jews though it appears decidedly inappropriate today, in the light of Hitler, Nazism, and subsequent history.[20]

Lueger's famous remark 'Wer ein Jud ist, das bestimme ich' with which he answered attacks on his associations with wealthy Jews – epitomizing his pliable, unprincipled, cynical, though essentially genial, character – belongs to an age when it was still possible to be an antisemite in public and a *Judenfreund* in private. As one Austrian biographer, Kurt Skalnik, has noted, however, 'after Auschwitz and Maidanek one may speak of this subject . . . only with seriousness'. This same historian unfortunately cannot avoid a rather doubtful if well-intentioned whitewash of the subject. 'Dr. Karl Lueger can maintain himself before the verdict of history', he writes. 'In 1880, 1890, 1900, life ran inside such a well-defined order, that one could afford, among other political escapades, to play with anti-semitism, without at the same time breaking the principles of civilised humanity and falling into a daemonic abyss'.[21]

Jewish reactions to confirmation of Lueger's election as mayor of Vienna in 1897 have yet to be studied in depth but the available evidence does not support the thesis that they would have regarded Christian-Social antisemitism as no more than a 'political escapade'. The prospect that, as the *Neue Freie Presse* put it on 30 May 1895, 'Vienna should be the only great city in the world whose administrator is an anti-Semitic agitator' was inevitably alarming to the Jewish community, as it was for different reasons to the imperial government, the church hierarchy, the Magyars, and sections of the aristocracy. The Austrian establishment of the time had good reason to distrust the social radicalism of the Lueger movement, of which antisemitism with its appeal to the coarser instincts of the mob was only one (though clearly a major) component. For the Jewish community, however, the threat was much more direct, for the initial programme of the *Vereinigte Christen* (as the Christian-Socials were originally called) clearly demanded the elimination of Jews from the civil service, medical and legal professions, and small businesses, as well as the abolition of peddling. The fact that a plebeian movement had triumphed in Vienna in large part owing to an antisemitic programme, that it was immensely popular, and seemed to represent the very antithesis of political liberalism (moreover that it was a party led by men whose *raison d'être* was to engage in violent verbal abuse of Jews) could not but be a cause for concern. No one familiar with the press of that period, with the parliamentary debate in the *Reichsrat*, or those in the city council or the lower Austrian *Landtag* can fail to be struck by the aggressive intensity of Viennese antisemitic rhetoric.[22]

Admittedly, the immediate effects were surprisingly limited. There was no serious attempt to strip Austrian Jews of their civil rights; there was no expropriation of Jewish wealth (indeed Lueger constantly consulted with Jewish businessmen in order to carry out his ambitious municipal programmes); and there was very little violence against individuals in Vienna, certainly nothing to compare with the pogroms in Galicia in the summer of 1898 or the unrest in Bohemia the following year during the Hilsner ritual-murder trial. Antisemitic efforts to boycott Jewish businesses were a singular failure in Vienna (though more successful in Polish Galicia), and in both the economic and cultural spheres Lueger's Christian-Social rule can scarcely be said to have undermined the very substantial and even preponderant Jewish presence. Apart from legislation against pedlars and the sacking of some Jewish stenographers from municipal service – cheap gestures to satisfy Lueger's more rabid followers – the new mayor's practical moves clearly indicated his desire for reconciliation rather than confrontation with the Jewish community. Even on the level of propaganda there was a slight mellowing of tone as the social democrats and Pan-Germans came in for a barrage of insults no less hostile than that which had once been directed at the increasingly impotent 'Judeo-Liberals'.

Nevertheless this does not mean that Jews could feel secure or comfortable with the demonic image of their activities fostered by various Pan-German and antisemitic Christian-Social groups or that they did not suffer from the pain of social ostracism. Even if Lueger had partially succeeded in taming and domesticating Viennese antisemitism with a heavy dose of Austrian *Gemütlichkeit*, and the threat was no longer perceived as immediate by most assimilated Jews, nevertheless in the universities and among the younger generation and the immigrant *Ostjuden* the pressures were real enough, and it is surely no accident that Jewish nationalism grew steadily in precisely these social strata after the turn of the century. Even among the prosperous Jewish middle class and the assimilated big bourgeoisie in Vienna, which was arguably as alarmed by Herzl's Zionism as it was by Lueger's antisemitism, one has the impression of a sense of malaise, a feeling that things were no longer so secure, of social tension, flight from reality and – among the Jewish intelligentsia – symptoms of acute anxiety and even demoralization.[23] It is difficult to determine how far this general mood of the European *fin-de-siècle*, so well reflected in the literature of *Jung Wien* (largely written by Jews), can be traced to the effects of Lueger's anti-liberal victory, just

as it is not easy to ascertain how deeply the antisemitism of the age penetrated into the daily lives of people, whether Jews or non-Jews.

It is of course undeniable that the deeds of the Lueger years were very
tame compared to what was to follow, though the verbal assault on Jews,
for all the official bonhomie of the mayor of Vienna, was by no means
benign. The most serious consequence was the long-term cultural and
political legitimization of antisemitism in Austrian public life, through
which anti-Jewish activities, organizations, and the most rabid demagogy
came to seem thoroughly normal and respectable. Moreover, precisely
because Lueger was the most popular mayor that Vienna had ever
known, his behaviour and mannerisms were liable to be imitated, and
even his antisemitic rhetoric could then become a necessary ingredient
for aspiring followers who looked to him as a role model.[24] Equally, the
nature of Lueger's constituency and his hold over it was such that he
could not simply abandon the anti-Jewish rhetoric which had helped him
to climb to power. Christian-Socialism, it must be remembered, com-
prised a large, diverse, and heterogeneous group of frustrated *Mittelstand*
groups for whom the Jews provided most unwelcome economic competition. They included shopkeepers, merchants, artisans, school teachers,
and clerics, but also *Hausherren* and middle-ranking government
officials. The central core of this party was the urban *Bürgertum*, the
middle section of Viennese society, which for all its subtle, internal class
distinctions had remained remarkably faithful to pre-industrial values
and the *Bürger* political culture which they had inherited from Austro-liberalism.[25] Lueger himself was a typical product of this lower *Bürgertum*,
which eventually came to reject the liberal order and liberal outlook, not
so much in favour of a 'post-rational politics', but out of a desire to
restore its fragmented unity and traditional ideals, threatened by
modernization.

Both social Catholicism and antisemitism had emerged in the 1880s as
the ideological articulation and political vehicles for these endangered
strata in the Austro-German *Bürgertum* to express their protest against liberal political parties which had sacrificed them to the 'Moloch of
capitalism'. Moreover, precisely the two most antisemitic groups in the
delicate coalition of interests that eventually made up the Christian-
Social Party – the depressed artisans and the Catholic clerics – were truly
indispensable to it for the mobilization of cadres and the winning both of
mass support and official respectability. Given the character in the 1890s
of Christian-Socialism as a bourgeois social protest movement determined to enhance the material security and social status of the lower
Bürgertum by gaining a greater share of the spoils of power – and being
dependent on groups for whom the 'Jewish question' was far from being
an academic issue – it could not be easily expected to forgo the use of
antisemitism, which had been so successful in bringing down Austro-
liberalism.

Christian-Socialism was, of course, more than simply a Jew-baiting party, just as it was more than a purely Catholic movement in spite of the major clerical input in its theory and practice. It was above all an instrument of traditional *Mittelstand* aspirations long neglected by the Austrian Liberal Party – an anticapitalist movement of radical artisans, frustrated democrats, lower clergy, and small businessmen in its origins – which later expanded to embrace more conservative elements such as the big property owners, middle-ranking officials, and peasants in the countryside. Its success was predicated on the skilful adaptation of an older, pre-1848 political language to a new class situation, the blending of cultural traditionalism with the desire for radical change, *Vormärz* conservatism with modern techniques of political mobilization, notable with mass politics. For all its populist radicalism in the early 1890s, its historical function was clearly to stabilize and reunite bourgeois society around interest politics and the defence of its privileges. This became ever more apparent after 1897 with the growing interest of the Viennese Christian-Social *Bürgertum* in maintaining its newly-won political privileges against the rising social democratic threat. It was the impressive cultural and political strength of the working classes organized in the internationalist Pan-Austrian social democracy which in fact obliged the Christian-Socials to underline the internal social homogeneity of the Austrian *Bürgertum* and to paper over existing class and cultural differences between *Hausherren* and artisans, prosperous merchants and small shopkeepers, free-thinkers and Catholic clerics. Under Lueger's charismatic leadership – patriarchal, authoritarian, but also conciliatory – the Viennese German *Bürgertum* consciously began to identify itself with the Christian *Volk* of Austria. Aided by the absence of a strong radical or secular bourgeois-democratic tradition, a powerful new force had emerged in Austrian politics; it was culturally no less *bürgerlich* than classical liberalism, but ideologically anti-liberal, anti-Marxist, social Catholic, and antisemitic.

It is not difficult to see how an antisemitism based on the real issue of artisan distress in Vienna, whose hostility to free competition in the economic sphere was given a traditionalist anchor by Baron Karl von Vogelsang in medieval church teachings on usury, could in the unstable circumstances of the 1890s emerge as the integrating ideology of the lower middle classes, making possible the unification of previously fragmented strata in the Austrian *Bürgertum*. This is indeed the thesis of the American social historian, John Boyer, who in a stimulating and important book has recently examined political radicalism in late imperial Vienna.[26] He correctly points out how well Lueger's type of antisemitism fitted into the political traditionalism and cultural patterns of deference of a conservative Viennese *Bürgertum* which, ever since 1848, had intended to define its own class consciousness by marking itself off from the proletariat. Christian-Social antisemitism in Vienna from this sociological standpoint can indeed be viewed as the functional equivalent in class terms of the liberal anti-clericalism that preceded it in the 1860s and 1870s, and of the strident Pan-German nationalism dominant among provincial Austro-Germans (bourgeois, intelligentsia, and workers) living in the Slavic border areas of the Habsburg monarchy. For ambitious politicians such as Lueger, it had all the populist attractions of appearing to be anti-plutocratic, anti-corruptionist, and even 'democratic' to his heterogeneous Viennese and lower Austrian constituency without threatening the foundations of the bourgeois order or the semi-constitutional Habsburg *Rechtsstaat*. Opposing the international and 'Jewish' character of capitalism did not mean that one was against private property or even the stock exchange *per se* in Austria or anywhere else in Europe.

The economic class basis of the Christian-Social Party is important for an understanding of why Lueger could not afford to ignore the emotions and prejudices of his constituency, particularly since he risked being outflanked by the uncompromising racial antisemitism of the Pan-Germans should he ignore the Jewish issue altogether. On the other hand, the role of the Catholic church in providing an institutional cover of respectability and traditionalism which eventually allowed the Christian-Socials to be accepted as the conservative party in Austria, helps explain the limits on their antisemitism. The latter was indispensable, primarily as a catch-all slogan which could unite white- and blue-collar types, bourgeois and artisans, landowners and peasants, lower- and middle-ranking officials as well as teachers and clerks in one fighting anti-liberal movement. On its own, however, it could never be a very effective ideology for an Austro-German party already in office, which was intent on working within the imperial Habsburg structure. Moreover, as Lueger shrewdly realized, it was precisely the skilful mix between Catholic tradition and modernity in his populist antisemitism which was such an important component in its acceptability to broad strata of the Viennese middle-class population. Only a *Volksmann*, born and bred in Vienna, who championed 'democracy' (in its anti-liberal form) while recognizing the potency of the feudal Catholic traditions of imperial Austria, could have achieved such a political *tour de force*.

Carl Schorske has problematically described this feat as 'politics in a new key', a post-rational form of demagogic artistry built on the composition of ideological collages: 'collages made of fragments of modernity, glimpses of futurity, and resurrected remnants of a half-forgotten past'.[27] Lueger, who began his career as a left liberal and radical democrat before embarking on the destruction of the liberal political tradition, appears to Schorske as the most successful political practitioner of this art of ideological collage, an agitator and popular tribune who conquered Vienna and 'then organised a great party with its stable base in the countryside',[28] The *Herrgott von Wien* was not (as Schorske realizes, of course) an ideologue and certainly – unlike Hitler – no fanatic, least of all on the Jewish issue. He was however a quintessentially Viennese politician who understood the potential uses of bourgeois social disaffection and adopted the new corporatist theories of Baron Karl von Vogelsang as a catalyst and means of welding together a broad anti-liberal coalition, just as he saw the political value of antisemitism as a lower-middle-class battering ram against *laissez-faire* capitalism. Precisely because Lueger was 'less alienated and more traditional' than his arch-rival, the Pan-German leader, Georg von Schoenerer, he was better able to organize his troops for electoral victory, by tapping the culturally conservative instincts of his urban lower-middle-class constituency and of his clerical-aristocratic sponsors. Similarly, his underlying traditionalism rather than his addiction to novelty and 'postrationalism' (Schorske) would help to explain how he was able to blunt the subversive potential of Viennese antisemitism after 1897 in the interests of the monarchy, the church, and even of the Jewish capitalist groups he had previously attacked.

Moreover, it is incorrect to suggest (as Schorske does) that Lueger confined 'the uses of racist poison to attacking the liberal foe', as if he were some kind of political chemist capable of carefully measuring the dosage of the toxic effects of the pathology on which his career had in part been built.[29] With the rise of social democracy as a dangerous rival, what had once been considered as an anticapitalist movement or as 'the socialism of the fools of Vienna' – a term coined by the radical Austrian democrat, Ferdinand Kronawetter – turned irrevocably into the anti-socialism of fools. Christian-Socialism now consciously became the political party of the Austro-German bourgeoisie mobilized against the 'Red Menace', and its antisemitism was accordingly adapted after 1900 to this priority. This crucial transformation of the central thrust of Viennese antisemitism from anticapitalism to anti-Marxism, which happened at the turn of the century, was a major legacy of Lueger to the Christian-Social Party. Here one can see an element of continuity with the situation in the First Austrian Republic. The rivalry between the clerical statesman, Ignaz Seipel, and the 'Jewish' Austro-Marxist intellectual, Otto Bauer, had its precedent in the conflict between Lueger and the Jewish-born leader of the Austrian social democrats, Victor Adler.[30] The 'Red Fear' had indeed already begun to absorb the 'Jewish question' in Lueger's time as the focal point of Christian-Social bourgeois anxieties. It began to take on hysterical proportions only in the 1920s, with the collapse of the imperial Habsburg framework, when a socialist-dominated Vienna with a large Jewish population – in a truncated Austria – confronted the conservative provinces under the sway of clerical ideology and anti-Marxist propaganda.

Nevertheless, it was the pre-1914 Christian-Social agitation which first synthesized hatred of socialists and Jews in Austria. Motives of economic competition, professional jealousy, anti-intellectualism, fear of proletarization, the struggle for scarce resources, and a fierce conflict over secularism and religious education all played their part in animating this conflict. By 1914 it had become part of the staple diet of Austrian public life.

One might see, therefore, Hitler's hysterical anti-intellectualism, as well as his identification of Marxism and Bolshevism with European Jewry, as a later reformulation of post-1900 Christian-Social rhetoric, which he had certainly encountered in Vienna. Nevertheless, whatever importance such influences may have had on the ideological origins of national socialism, it is no less essential to distinguish between different epochs, particularly with respect to the 'Jewish question'. In this context it is salutary to recall that Luegerite antisemitism operated within the framework of a conciliatory, supranational Habsburg dynasty which was not hostile to Jews; mass violence within this political system was rare; and economic life was not yet caught up in the disastrous cycles of depression, inflation, and mass unemployment of the post-1918 era. Most importantly, the inviolate character of the *Rechtsstaat* and of a political culture based on law still existed. All these structural factors were serious barriers to the translation of antisemitic rhetoric in Vienna from words into deeds during the Habsburg era. Thus, while Lueger and his followers should not be absolved from all responsibility for what happened after 1918, it cannot be denied that the conditions in the First Austrian Republic, as in Weimar Germany, were vastly different from anything that they could have imagined.

5

Hitler and national socialism: the Austrian connection

Karl Kraus once described *fin-de-siècle* Austria as an 'experimental station for the end of the world' (*Versuchs-Station für Weltuntergange*). It was above all Vienna, the capital of this multinational state of old Austria, which can be seen in retrospect as the seed-bed of the catastrophes which were to overtake central Europe in the twentieth century, as it was the cradle of much that was most exciting in modernist culture. This Janus-face of early-twentieth-century Vienna, the cosmopolitan *Kaiserstadt* of an ultra-conservative dynasty and the source of so many cultural and political revolutions silently incubating in its womb, is of the first importance for the understanding of Adolf Hitler and the genesis of Nazism.

The young man from Linz, who spent the formative years of his life between 1907 and 1913 in the Austrian capital, recalled in *Mein Kampf* in 1924 that Vienna represented 'die Erinnerung an die traurigste Zeit meines Lebens'. For Hitler, Vienna was and remained 'die schwerste, wenn auch gründlichste Schule meines Lebens'.[1] It was here that he confronted for the first time the problems of personal survival, sexuality, society, and politics, developing the bases of what was to become in postwar Munich his iron-clad *Weltanschauung* of national socialism. The long discourse in *Mein Kampf* on his Vienna years is a testament to the importance which Hitler himself attached to this period of his life, and the internal contradictions in his narrative in no way diminish the centrality of this experience.[2]

The imperial capital which both fascinated and repelled the 18-year-old Hitler in 1907 was the centre of a declining European Great Power, increasingly paralysed by the endless conflict between its warring nationalities. Hitler had nothing but contempt for this political structure, this 'impossible state', which in his eyes was a 'living corpse' (*Leichnam*) and *Völkerbabylon*. Its hybrid character as a *Rassenkonglomerat* doomed it to destruction. Vienna, with its 'Babel of races', was the living proof to

Hitler of the nefarious effects of race-mixing, which was the incarnation of *Blutschande* and the antithesis of his own ideal of ethnic homogeneity.[3] In this respect the young Hitler was largely echoing the *Angst*-ridden racist philosophies of his time, especially the views of Houston S. Chamberlain, who had composed his epoch-making *Grundlagen des Neunzehnten Jahrhunderts* in Vienna at the end of the 1890s.

Moreover the young Hitler, as a teenager in Linz, had already absorbed the ideological influence of Georg Ritter von Schoenerer's Pan-German movement which denounced the Habsburg dynasty for betraying the Austro-Germans, monotonously fulminated against race-mixing, and constantly underlined the Slav and Jewish perils.[5] A Pan-German adolescent from Linz, already impregnated with such prejudices, could only regard the Viennese melting pot with indignation and horror. In 1907 the Austrian capital already had more Czech inhabitants than Prague, and by 1910 it contained 175,294 Jews, no less than 8.6 per cent of the total population, who played a decisive role in the economic and cultural life of the city.[6] Hitler's hatred for this 'Babylon' of nationalities was therefore a natural enough outcome of his earlier upbringing, education, and provincial Austrian background. There is some reason to believe that it was indeed partly an inherited hatred, if Hitler's remarks to a German newspaper editor in 1931 are to be believed:

I have much to thank my father for. He was a customs official. He knew Austrians and Bavarians, Germans and Slavs, Italians and French. For him Austria was always just a part of the great German Fatherland. Even as a child I heard my father say that Vienna was ruled by a clique, a mongrel crew which had collected in the capital. Later I was able to check this for myself. This hotch-potch of so-called liberals could not be expected to have any leaning towards a pan-German policy. Their cultural policy was Austrian in name only . . . . There can be no true racial policy which does not safeguard our biological Aryan roots. We intend one day to give this ideological principle the force of law. Even today our youth is crying with good reason: Germany awake, down with Jewry! In Vienna I learnt to hate the Jews. Any license given the Vienna Jews was tantamount to an increase in the number of destructive parasites. In Munich or Berlin, Hamburg or Vienna I shall judge the depth of people's love for their country by the degree of hatred which they show to this rabble . . . . Vienna has turned itself into the metropolis of decay and filth. People there sponsor books opposing the reawakening of Germany. Obviously we shall burn this rubbish and have a clean-up in Vienna as in Berlin.[7]

I have quoted this interview of 1931 at some length not only because it is *echt*-Hitler in its vengeful, ideological obsessions and Pan-Germanism, but also for its revelation of a deep and permanent loathing of Vienna. In the same interview, Hitler even blames the Vienna Jews for frustrating his career as an architect (presumably he held them responsible for his failure to enter the Vienna Academy of Fine Arts in 1908), as a result of which 'now they have a politician on their hands'.[8] The desire to avenge himself 'for early years of poverty, for disappointed hopes, for a life of deprivation and humiliation' was also apparent to Hermann Rauschning in his conversations with the *Führer* in 1933–4;[9] Hitler confided to his fellow Nazi that 'Slav mestizos' had overrun Vienna, which was 'no longer a German city'. The priests and Jews who ruled the country would have to be expelled. The easy-going, lazy, *gemütlich* Austrians could then be trained in Prusso-German ways in order to be fit for incorporation into the greater German Reich.

It is remarkable that more than twenty years after leaving Vienna, Hitler retained his old repulsion for the inhabitants of the former Habsburg capital and his conviction that Austria, his own homeland, had no right to independent existence. As a youth from the provinces he had been sickened 'by the whole mixture of Czechs, Poles, Hungarians, Ruthenians, Serbs and Croats, and everywhere, the eternal mushroom (*Spaltpilz*) of humanity – Jews and more Jews'.[10] Turn-of-the-century Vienna, 'this ancient site of German culture', had been corroded by this 'foreign mixture of peoples', by the 'poison of foreign nations gnawing away at the body of our nationality'.[11]

As the *Führer* of greater Germany, Hitler was to remain faithful to this nightmarish vision of his youth, degrading Vienna after 1938 from its traditional Habsburg status as a *Weltstadt* to that of a second-rate provincial city within the Reich. This was his punishment for Vienna's original sin of having betrayed the cause of *Deutschtum* and at the same time his draconian revenge for the personal failures and humiliations he had experienced there in the years before the First World War. Even Vienna's primacy within the Austrian homeland would have to be broken, and Hitler busied himself as early as 1942 with plans to turn Linz at the end of the war into the 'neuen Weltstadt an der Donau'.[12] Linz, the fondly recalled city of Hitler's boyhood and a prewar stronghold of von Schoenerer's *Alldeutschen*, was destined to supersede the memory of a cosmopolitan Vienna which was irredeemably *verjudet* and Slavicized, on the point of being lost to *Deutschtum* forever. As for Austria, it was to be dissected into *Gaue*, sacrificed on the altar of the greater German *Reichsgedanke*.[13]

As Hitler phrased it in a speech in Linz on 7 April 1938, it was his personal mission to bring his homeland *heim ins Reich* as part of the national socialist dream of reunifying all the Germanic tribes: 'probably it was only a South German [sic] who could effect the second unification', he told his audience in Linz (referring to Bismarck's incomplete *kleindeutsch* unification of 1871), 'for he must want to lead back into the great Reich that part which in the course of our history had lost its connection with the Reich'.[14] Hitler's *deutschnationalismus*, like that of von Schoenerer, was very explicitly anti-Austrian, and designed to obliterate the memory of an independent Austrian history in the name of a tribal, imperialist Pan-Germanism.

Hitler's version of the Germanic past and future was thus completely *antithetical* to that still prevailing in the Habsburg Vienna of his youth. He had seen his decaying world from its lower depths, had been exposed to its sexual and political underground, to its grinding poverty and housing shortages by his bitter struggle for existence between 1907 and 1913.[15] It was here that he discovered for the first time the problems of subsistence, of prostitution, the mass organizations of the proletariat and the potency of antisemitism as a political weapon. This was the reverse side of the impressive imperial façades of the Ringstrasse and the glittering world of the Viennese opera which had initially so entranced the provincial Hitler.

The trauma of the deracinated provincial unhinged by his *déclassé* status, disoriented by metropolitan life, threatened by the class struggle, and by democracy, feminism, and the omnipresent Jews, was to leave its mark on the young Hitler as it did on another contemporary, Charles Maurras, who in the Paris of 1900 was to found the Action Française.[16] Not only this early French proto-fascism but above all German national socialism can in part be seen as a revolt of the provincial backwoods against the threatening predominance of the megalopolis and the irreversible thrust of modernity – a revolt that fell back on the primitive appeal to the certainties of blood and race. In the specific case of Hitler, the malignant fear of Jews and social democrats which he developed in Vienna clearly had something to do, not only with nationalist ideology, but also with his subjective experience of descending from a life of relatively comfortable, lower-middle-class respectability to the non-status of a failed bohemian dropout. In a curriculum vitae to an unknown recipient, composed in 1921, three years before the writing of *Mein Kampf*, Hitler himself remarked that 'though I came from a fairly cosmopolitan family, the school of harsh reality turned me into an antisemite within a year'.[17] (The 'cosmopolitanism' of Hitler's family can be taken with a grain of salt but the dating of his antisemitic conversion to the period around 1908 seems to me reasonable enough.)

Hitler's antisemitism was probably the most important single outcome of his Vienna years and certainly its most lasting consequence. At the simplest level it can be seen as a rationalization of his own rejection by Vienna and his gnawing sense of personal failure. The Academy of Fine Arts put paid to his dreams of becoming a famous painter or architect; he had lost his mother under tragic circumstances in December 1907 and was unwilling or unable to secure a regular job in Vienna.[18] In such a situation self-accusation could all too easily turn into vehement denunciations against the whole world and above all against upwardly mobile Jews, especially in a personality as violent and intractable as Hitler's. His hatred of intellectuals and pedants, of everything 'un-German', his obsession with the music of Richard Wagner and the world of Germanic legends and myths, could moreover be said to have almost predisposed him to absorbing antisemitic prejudices.[19] Significantly, in *Mein Kampf*, his vulgarly dramatized encounter with an exotic-looking, Galician *Ostjude*, the antithesis in outward appearance of a German Gentile, is used to stress the foreignness of the Jews and explain his own conversation to antisemitism:

> Once as I was strolling through the Inner City, I suddenly encountered an apparition in a black caftan and black hair locks. Is this a Jew? was my first thought.
>
> For, to be sure, they had not looked like that in Linz. I observed the man furtively and cautiously, but the longer I stared at this foreign face, scrutinizing feature for feature, the more my first question assumed a new form:
>
> Is this a German? ... Wherever I went, I began to see Jews, and the more I saw, the more sharply they became distinguished in my eyes from the rest of humanity. Particularly the Inner-City and the districts north of the Danube Canal swarmed with a people which even outwardly had lost all resemblance to Germans .... [20]

Hitler had discovered the *Urjude*, the pristine east European ghetto Jew, whose appearance and smell ('you could tell that these were no lovers of water') sharply marked him off from the Germans.[21] No doubt the encounter with these caftaned Jews from Galicia who had settled in Vienna's Leopoldstadt ghetto (the II District) did shock the adolescent Hitler. No less significant, however, was the *visual* stereotyping, crudely building on Austrian Gentile prejudice against eastern Jews to justify exclusionary racial antisemitism. About the assimilated, Germanized Jews of Vienna, on the other hand, Hitler had virtually nothing of substance to say. Their extraordinary creative achievements seem to have passed him by, much as he missed all the exciting developments in modern art at the turn of the century. The reader of *Mein Kampf* will find no reference to Schnitzler, Hoffmanstahl, Zweig, Altenberg, Beer-Hoffman, Kraus, Mahler, Freud, or Schoenberg any more than he will find mention of the non-Jewish pioneers of modernism in the visual arts like Otto Wagner, Gustav Klimt, Egon Schiele, Oscar Kokoschka, or Koloman Moser. As Albert Speer observed, 'in the realm of architecture, as in painting and sculpture, Hitler really remained arrested in the world of his youth; the world of 1880 to 1910, which stamped its imprint on his artistic taste as on his political and ideological conceptions'.[22] A reactionary bourgeois conservative in his tastes, an inveterate addict of the pseudo-grandeur of Ringstrasse architecture, Hitler was no less a child of *fin-de-siècle* Vienna in his antisemitic politics.

The *sexual* component in Hitler's Judeophobia was perhaps its most obviously Viennese characteristic. The combination of Victorian prudery and furtive obsessions with prostitution and white slavery – associated by many Gentile Austrians with Galician Jews – had left their mark on Viennese antisemitism since the early 1890s.[23] Hitler's own suppressed sexuality encouraged the development of lurid fantasies concerning a 'Jewish conspiracy' to bastardize the white race through the medium of prostitution and the deliberate spreading of syphilis.[24] A genuine social problem, particularly acute in *fin-de-siècle* Vienna, was diverted by Viennese antisemites (with Hitler in their wake) into the murky channels of race and blood. Obsessed with the dangers of venereal infection and, according to his boyhood friend August Kubizek, personally adhering to a monklike asceticism, Hitler projected on the Jews his own repressed erotic drives, declaring in *Mein Kampf* that in the streets of Leopoldstadt (a predominantly Jewish district) 'one could witness hideous sexual proceedings that most German people could not even imagine'.[25] The Jew, he rapidly concluded from his own outings to Vienna's red-light districts, was the 'cold-hearted, shameless and calculating director of this revolting vice traffic in the scum of the city'.[26] The mastermind behind this sexual underground was however also the hidden hand behind the revolutionary subversion of social democracy, which so aroused Hitler's anxiety and rage during his Vienna years.

The hatred of the *Judensozi* (so-called 'Jewish' social-democracy was perhaps natural to someone from Hitler's *petit-bourgeois* Austrian background. But it was undoubtedly exacerbated by the impact of Christian-Socialist agitation in Vienna at the turn of the century. Ever since 1900 the ruling *Christlich-soziale Partei* in Vienna had directed the burden of its electoral propaganda against the rising social democratic movement, which had emerged as its most dangerous rival for political power in the imperial capital.[27] Christian-socialism consciously sought at the turn of the century to become the party of the Viennese German bourgeoisie and the defender of *Mittelstand* interests against the 'Red Menace'. The able leader of this Catholic populist party and the highly successful Lord Mayor of Vienna, Dr Karl Lueger, destined to be Hitler's first role model in politics, adapted the endemic antisemitism of his urban lower-middle-class constituency to this new situation.

The 'Red Fear' and the 'Jewish question' merged in the propaganda of the *Christlich Soziale*. Anti-intellectualism, fear of proletarization, anxiety over liberal and socialist anti-clericalism and economic jealousies were cleverly exploited by Lueger and his followers to frighten their bourgeois clientele.[28] Hitler, who thoroughly approved of the anti-

Marxism of the Lueger movement and learned much from it, later emphasized the tactical 'wisdom' of the Christian-Socials in their fight against social democracy. Here was a mass movement which had demonstrated 'its shrewd judgement concerning the worth of the popular masses', its grasp of the social question and of the necessity to foster a 'militant spirit' in the lower *Bürgertum* which was struggling for its economic existence.[29]

In all these respects Hitler came to rate Lueger much higher than his boyhood political idol, Georg von Schoenerer, who by 1907 was a fading, insignificant force in Austrian politics. On the other hand, on questions of ideology and especially those involving racial issues, Hitler retained his undeviating loyalty to the Pan-German programme. There was to his mind no comparison between Lueger's clerical *Scheinantisemitismus* (which Hitler despised as dishonest and ultimately ineffective) and the uncompromising racial stand against the Jews adopted by von Schoenerer and the *Alldeutschen*.[30] In this respect, as on the question of anti-Austrianism and ruthless opposition to the Habsburg dynasty, Hitler remained a Pan-German, fundamentally in conflict with Christian-socialism. Hitler's remoteness from Vienna, from its *Lokalpatriotismus*, its instinctive Habsburg loyalism, Catholicism, and popular spirit (which Lueger knew so well how to manipulate) was strikingly revealed in these political preferences.

All his life Hitler despised the Viennese, their subservience, indifference, muddling-through, and superficiality, their partiality to wine and lightheartedness.[31] He was soon repelled by the sycophantic style of the Viennese liberal press, by its lack of sufficient Pan-Germanic fervour and its exaggerated respect for the Habsburg court. Moreover, compared with the *martial* virtues of the Prussians and the relative ethnic homogeneity of the new German Reich, the Austrians (and especially the Viennese) could only appear as a feckless, decadent hodge-podge of races loosely strung together in a ramshackle empire. Further-more, what did Austria have to show compared to such radiant Germanic figures as Otto von Bismarck or Hitler's artistic idol, Richard Wagner? Its 'judaized' culture was to Hitler, as it had been to Wagner before him, a symbol of decadence and degeneration. What then did Hitler ultimately learn in Vienna, which was later, as he put it in *Mein Kampf*, to provide 'the granite foundation' of his world view?

The lessons were not only political but more importantly they were occult – that is to say, it was in Vienna that Hitler picked up the essentials of his apocalyptic, sectarian, and fanatic ideology of biological racialism.[32] The sources of this Manichean world view derived more from Lanz von Liebenfels and other antisemitic pamphleteers of the time than from the politics of Lueger and von Schoenerer, important as these two demagogues were to Hitler's subsequent development. Sectarians like Lanz with his Ostara pamphlets provided a dualistic *Weltans-chauung* whose morbid racism and dreams of genetic selection, sterilization, or deportation of lower races, and cult of a Promethean Aryan race of blood, blue-eyed heroes, fired Hitler's imagination.[33] This literature on the borders of politics and pornography (and obsessed with the theme of racial purity) was peculiarly suited both to Hitler's perverse tastes and to his degraded social situation in Vienna. From this underground literature he almost certainly derived the sensational, extremist character of his racist antisemitism and his conviction that he was fighting an apocalyptic war for the future of 'Aryan' humanity against the destroyers of culture. From occult Austrian racist thinkers like Lanz and Guido von List, Hitler probably acquired the fanatical, almost magical drive that animated his Pan-German nationalism and sense of personal mission.[34]

The world of the Mannerheim asylum for the homeless, where he spent his last three years in Vienna, was ideally suited for a down-and-out loner like Hitler to crystallize his wild theories before a captive audience. Here, among the downtrodden, *lumpenproletarian*, and *déclassé* elements of Vienna, he could indulge in his rage against the world and his dreams of German racial supremacy. This was still some way removed from the systematic world view first elaborated in Landsberg prison in 1924. But there is no strong reason to believe that when he attributed such importance to his prewar Austrian experiences Hitler was really project-ing backward those lessons he had only learned in post-1918 Germany. Even the theory of the Jewish–Marxist conspiracy which is generally explained by historians as a reaction to the Bavarian Soviet Republic of 1918 had its clear antecedents in Hitler's Vienna years.

There is no doubt that Hitler was struck with awe and fear by the mass demonstrations of the Viennese workers and frankly alarmed by the predominantly Jewish leadership of the pre-1914 Austrian social democracy.[35] His hatred of Marxism and its doctrines of class struggle, economic equality, and human brotherhood was undoubtedly intensified by the 'discovery' of the decisive role which Jewish intellectuals had played in formulating its theory and praxis. Furthermore, the fact that the Austro-Marxists were a *staatserhaltend* factor (like the *Christlich-Soziale*) in the empire did not recommend them in Hitler's eyes, since his commitment to the destruction of dynasty was absolute. The 'Jewish' Marxists, according to Hitler's unshakeable dogma, had always operated against the interests of the German *Volk*, and their compromise with the empire and alleged favoring of Slavs was the ostensible proof of this assertion. The fact that for the majority of Slav socialists (especially the Czechs) the Austrian social democrats were perceived as *too German* was a fact that altogether escaped Hitler's understanding.[36]

Hitler left Vienna in 1913 at the age of 24, a convinced Pan-German, anti-Marxist, and antisemite. He was determined not to do military service in the Austrian empire to whose downfall he was committed. He was headed for the German Reich, which since his early youth he had looked to as the promised land, as 'the land of my dreams and of my longing'.[37] Presumably he had no regrets concerning Vienna, though eleven years later in *Mein Kampf* he stressed the importance of his years there, as a school of experience:

> I had set foot in this town while still half a boy and I left it a man, grown quiet and grave. In it I obtained the foundations for a philosophy in general and a political view in particular which later I needed to supplement only in detail, but which never left me. I do not know what my attitude toward the Jews, social democracy, or rather Marxism as a whole, the social question, etc. would be today if at such an early time the pressure of destiny – and my own study – had not built up a basic stock of personal opinions within me.[38]

The ideas of Pan-Germanism and racial antisemitism which so influenced the young Hitler were to leave a lasting legacy in Austria. Many of the future leaders of National Socialism in that country had been active members of Pan-German *Burschenschaften* in their younger days and it was no accident that in the student milieu during the 1920s and 1930s the rhetoric of violent racist antisemitism found an especially powerful echo. Gentile students since the late nineteenth century had seen the influx of Jews into Austrian universities as a direct threat to their own well-being and economic prospects. At the University of Vienna *grossdeutsch* sentiment was particularly strong after 1918 and agitation for a *numerus clausus* against Jews (as well as hostility to pacifist, socialist, and Slav students) an everyday reality. The bleak economic prospects for many students in the post-war era heightened the receptiveness to Nazi ideology and commitment to a *völkisch* community that would rigorously exclude Jews.[39]

Antisemitism was of course only one component of the *völkisch* ideology but it was to be an increasingly central one in the German Austrian Republic that emerged following the collapse of the Habsburg monarchy. In the early years of the Republic it had been exacerbated by the large immigration of eastern Jews from Galicia and Bukovina which had begun during the First World War. Slogans against eastern Jews (later extended to attack all Jews without distinction) were an integral part of the propaganda of the Austrian national socialists from 1918 until the *Anschluss* of 1938. Like their counterparts in Weimar Germany, the Austrian Nazis called for a united struggle against Jewry which would embrace the entire German people.[40] The *Grossdeutsche Volkspartei*, the strongest of the *völkisch* parties in Austria in the 1920s, also affirmed in its official programme the need to struggle against 'the pernicious influence of the Jewish spirit and the necessity of racial antisemitism caused by it', declaring that it would 'oppose the Jewish influence in all spheres of public and private life; the immigration of foreign Jews is to be curtailed; the eastern Jews are to be expelled'.[41]

In the mid-1920s in Austria, national socialists, Pan-Germans, antisemitic leagues, and organizations like the *Deutscher Turnerbund* frequently co-operated and combined around a programme of violent antisemitism, knowing that this was a popular cause – especially in Vienna with its large Jewish population, but also in the provinces where Heimwehr fascism was steadily taking root. The Christian-Social Party, too, continued the antisemitic legacy of the prewar *Luegerzeit*, and in its first 1918 electoral campaign called for a determined fight against the 'Jewish danger', depicting even assimilated Jews as *volksfremd*. Subsequent programmes of the party in 1926 and 1932 rallied against the 'destructive' influence of the Jews on Austrian cultural and economic life. For the Christian-Socials, antisemitism was not primarily racial (though the Christian workers' movement was more radical in this respect) but religious in content, strongly shaped by the traditional anti-Judaism of the Catholic Church. Catholic priests were in the forefront of attacks on Jewish influence in all fields of modern culture – including the press, theatre, law, and the medical sciences. Some Austrian bishops, like Alois Hudal for example, saw no inherent contradiction between Christian teachings and those of Nazi nationalism and racial ideology.[42] But under the leadership of Ignaz Seipel (himself a Catholic priest) the Christian-Socials tended to use antisemitism above all as a weapon against the social democrats, much as Lueger had done at the turn of the century. The continuing prominent role of Jews in the inter-war leadership of the Austrian Social-Democratic Party made this an effective tactic.[43]

The quasi-fascist Heimwehr movement, primarily anti-socialist in its political orientation and influenced by Italian models, also tended to focus its attacks on 'Jewish Marxists' rather than Jews as a racial group *per se*. Its antisemitism was at times moderate and at times radical, depending on the nature of the constituency to which it was trying to appeal. Thus its leader Prince Starhemberg could declare in a speech in 1930 that the Heimwehr was committed to a 'people's state' where every 'racial comrade' (*Volksgenosse*) would have the right to work and bread. 'By a *Volksgenosse* [he added] I mean only one inspired by the race instinct of the Germans in whose veins German blood flows. I do not include in "the people" those foreign flat-footed parasites from the East who exploit us'.[44] Yet four years later, the same Starhemberg was asserting that the Heimwehr totally rejected Nazi racial theories and had nothing against Jews who disapproved of internationalism and were not a threat to the State.

The Austrian Nazis, whose strength steadily increased after 1930, were more consistent, uninhibited, and uncompromising in their antisemitism than other Austrian political parties, though much of their programme on the 'Jewish Question' was essentially derivative. They were helped by the growth of unemployment in Austria in the wake of the Great Depression and Hitler's rise to power in Germany, which immediately led to the removal of Jews from the civil service and the cultural life of the Reich. During the Dollfuss/Schuschnigg years (1934–8) their influence was, however, temporarily contained by a government that rejected racial antisemitism (while allowing a relatively passive form of discrimination) and did not wish to appear to be knuckling under to German pressure to persecute the Jews.

The fragility of this interlude was revealed in the aftermath of the 1938 *Anschluss* which demonstrated the broad support that Nazi anti-Jewish policy had in Vienna and throughout Austria as a whole. Pillaging of Jewish property became a substitute for the unfulfilled 'anticapitalist' promises of the national socialist programme and a means for overcoming the acute housing shortage in Vienna.[45] 'Aryanization' of Jewish dwellings seemed an easy solution to the radical Nazis, and spontaneous raids on Jewish homes had already begun in March 1938. In this respect Austria was far ahead of Germany, though it lagged behind in matters of social policy and in the economic sphere in general. Not for nothing did Goering and Himmler praise the 'achievements' of Austrian Nazis like Hans Fischbock and Eichmann in the field of 'aryanization' and the forced 'emigration of Jews', modelling their actions on what they had done in a short space of time in Austria. The 'Ostmark', as it was now called, was also in advance of Reich law in taking legislative steps barring Jews from certain professions, removing children from schools, restricting their freedom of movement and so on.

It was also no accident that the 'Final Solution' of the Jewish question during the Second World War was linked to so many figures who were born in Austria, including Hitler himself, Eichmann, Kaltenbrunner, Globocnik, Seyss-Inquart, and many of the commanders of Nazi death-camps in Poland. Popular antisemitism had existed in Austria at a greater level of intensity for at least seventy years before the Holocaust than anywhere else in western or central Europe. Since the days of Lueger and von Schoenerer, the process of political conditioning, the socio-economic tensions, and the ideological groundwork which shaped Hitler's own outlook had also prepared his Austrian countrymen for the notion of a 'final reckoning with the Jews'. Ever since the great immigration of Jews to Vienna beginning in the 1860s and 1870s, antisemitism had been an ever-present reality in Austrian public life, with the promise of material benefits for the Gentile middle and lower middle classes accruing from a possible expulsion of the Jews.

There were, moreover, striking parallels between the conditions in Weimar Germany and the post-1918 Austrian Republic which made

Austrians particularly receptive to Hitler's national socialism and the rabid antisemitism of his movement. The trauma of the 1918 defeat and the refusal of the Allies to permit the *Anschluss* already undoubtedly embittered many Austrians (of all political persuasions) who saw no viable future for their dismembered country, bereft of its former empire.

The Austrian Nazis profited from this German national resentment in Austria and from the chronic economic situation that adversely affected broad strata of the population in the wake of the Great Depression. By early 1933 a third of the electorate was voting Nazi in elections and the much vaunted recovery in the Third Reich appeared to prove that only the *Anschluss* would bring economic salvation.[46] The Austrian Nazis had moreover accepted Hitler as their leader ever since 1926. He was not only an Austrian but the leader of a much bigger German party, who had gone to prison for his attempt to start a 'national revolution' in Munich. In the eyes of his Austrian admirers he enjoyed the halo of martyrdom and, given the internal divisions and factional rivalries within Austrian fascism, Hitler had little difficulty in imposing his leadership on the Austrian party.[47]

Hitler's success was further facilitated by the fact that before 1938 most Austrians felt that they were Germans and that there was no such thing as Austrian nationalism. The *grossdeutsch* tradition was very much alive not only among Nazis and German nationalists in Austria but even in the social democratic and Christian-Social camps. Long before the First World War it had been ideologically linked to racial antisemitism as an indispensable weapon in the struggle for the defence of 'Germandom'. Religious and anti-capitalist traditions of Jew-hatred also retained their potency and were in fact exacerbated in the troubled period after 1918. In Austria, as in Germany, the loss of the war was attributed to the machinations of 'traitors' – invariably Jews and socialists. Similarly, the adverse effects of capitalism on the 'little man' were blamed on the conspiracy of Jewish capitalists, bankers, and industrialists in league with the 'Jewish' leaders of the social democratic party. The weak democratic traditions in Austria, as in Germany, the intensity of class conflict, the 'Red Scare', the lack of political stability, and massive unemployment combined to provide the fascist and antisemitic movements with a mass following. Even the working classes in Austria did not prove immune to the appeals of national socialist and anti-Jewish propaganda in the late 1930s.[48]

Against this background, the major role played by Austrians in the persecution and annihilation of the Jews becomes more comprehensible. Austrian Jews were scarcely the victims of an antisemitic policy arising from German national socialism even if it took Hitler's 'invasion' to release all the pent-up anti-Jewish passions in the Austrian population. Viennese Jews, in particular, had long been a target of popular antisemitism in Austria, resulting from their high social and economic status and the prominent role they had played in the country's cultural life. Since the late nineteenth century this popular antisemitism had found political expression in the programmes of virtually all Austrian parties, except for the social democrats – and even their defence of Jews had been singularly lukewarm and half-hearted. We have already seen how this indigenous tradition of Austrian antisemitism shaped Hitler's own *Weltanschauung* and thereby constituted a significant element in the genesis of national socialist ideology.

The annihilation of the Viennese Jews in the Third Reich would exhibit a similar dynamic of hostility towards the Jews to that which already existed in Vienna around 1900, at the time that the young Hitler first acquired the fundamentals of his Manichean racist antisemitism. The same underlying economic and status anxiety of the threatened middle layers of Austrian society made them so receptive to Nazi anti-Jewish policy – which spoke a language long familiar to the Viennese. The *Anschluss* of 1938 was not therefore simply an invasion, occupation, or transfer of power but had elements of a popular rising discharged with special violence and brutality against the Jewish part of the population. The events of March/April 1938 demonstrated that antisemitism in Vienna in particular was more intense than that in the neighbouring German Reich. Hence one can only agree with the chilling conclusion of the Austrian historian, Gerhard Botz: 'In consequence, from 1938 on Vienna was always a few steps ahead of Germany in the process of persecution of the Jews. Not only were the comparable measures applied earlier in Vienna than in Germany, but they could also count on much broader support among the non-Jewish population. Here, the organizational instruments and procedures could be developed which would later be applied by Eichmann in the "Final Solution".'[49]

Part 2

Culture, Marginality, and Identity

6

The Jewishness of Sigmund Freud[1]

On the occasion of his 70th birthday in 1926, Sigmund Freud wrote to his friend and disciple Marie Bonaparte with a characteristic touch of irony:

> The Jewish societies in Vienna and the University of Jerusalem (of which I am a trustee), in short the Jews altogether, have celebrated me like a national hero, although my service to the Jewish cause is confined to the single point that I have never denied my Jewishness. The official world – the University of Vienna, Academy, Medical Association – completely ignored the occasion. Rightly, I think; it was only honest. I could not have looked upon their congratulations and honours as sincere.[2]

In the same letter Freud singled out the celebration of the Jewish lodge 'to which I have belonged for twenty years' and the speech in his honour made there by his private physician Professor Ludwig Braun (1867–1936), 'which cast a spell over the whole audience, including my family'. Braun, who joined the Viennese lodge of the *B'nai B'rith* in 1900 (three years after Freud) and had known the founder of psychoanalysis for nearly forty years, defined him in his celebrating speech as a *Ganzjude*.

Freud's quality of wholeness, his ability to recognize the unity of nature and mind behind discordant surface phenomena, his independence from religious dogma or conventional taboos, and especially his courage in opposing the rest of society, had stamped him as a genuine Jew. In his spiritual 'optimism', tenacious persistence, dignity, and composure in the face of social rejection he had exhibited precisely those traits which explained why Jews had always been in the forefront of the fight for freedom. These same characteristics, Professor Braun suggested, had naturally drawn Freud to the *B'nai B'rith* and its humanitarian ideals. They had also been expressed in his brainchild, the new science of psychoanalysis, which Braun described as an 'authentically Jewish conception of life' (*Lebensanschauung*), devoted to seeking the general laws of nature and fearlessly exploring the depths of the mind.[3]

Freud's own address to the *B'nai B'rith* on 6 May 1926, with its strong affirmation of his 'Jewish nature', of the humanitarian goals of the Viennese lodge, and its importance as a forum for independent-minded men of principle, amplified Braun's remarks and demonstrated his high regard for the ethical fraternity. Beyond that, it also provided an important testimony to his personal development, beliefs, and the nature of his Jewish identification. Freud recalled that this attraction to the lodge had crystallized in the years after 1895 when he had felt like a virtual pariah in Vienna.

> On the one hand I had gained the first insight into the depths of human instinct, had seen many things which were sobering, at first even frightening; on the other hand the disclosure of my unpopular discoveries led to my losing most of my personal relationships at that time. I felt as though outlawed, shunned by all. This isolation aroused in me the longing for a circle of excellent men with high ideals who would accept me in friendship despite my temerity. Your lodge was described to me as the place where I could find such men. That you are Jews could only be welcome to me, for I was myself a Jew, and it has always appeared to me not only undignified, but outright foolish to deny it. What tied me to Jewry was – I have to admit it – not the faith, not even the national pride, for I was always an unbeliever, have been brought up without religion, but not without respect for the so-called 'ethical' demand of human civilization. Whenever I have experienced feelings of national exaltation, I have tried to suppress them as disastrous and unfair, frightened by the warning example of those nations among which we Jews live. But there remained enough to make the attraction of Jews and Judaism irresistible, many dark emotional powers [*Dunkelmächte*] all the stronger the less they could be expressed in words, as well as the clear consciousness of an inner identity, the familiarity of the same psychological structure [*die Heimlichkeit der gleichen seelischen Konstruktion*].[4]

According to Freud, this 'uncanny' primordial feeling of solidarity, with its particularist ethnic nexus and common psychic structure, had nothing to do with Jewish religious identity. Though he could not define it, these 'dark emotional powers' were in fact profoundly rooted in the Galician Jewish background from which he originated and to which he was to remain attached all his life in a typically ambivalent fashion. His personality had indeed been formed in an east European Jewish home and then nurtured in the semi-proletarian Leopoldstadt district of Vienna to which Freud's parents had moved in 1859 from his birthplace in Freiberg, Moravia (now Příbor, Czechoslovakia).

Freud's father Jakob, born in 1815 in the Galician *shtetl* of Tsymenitz, was originally an observant Jew, the son of a Chassidic rabbi. Steeped in Jewish learning and rituals he had remained strictly orthodox until the age of 20 when he moved to Freiberg. Replying to a correspondent in 1930, Sigmund Freud observed in this connection:

It may interest you to hear that my father did indeed come from a Chassidic background. He was forty-one when I was born and had been estranged from his native environment for almost twenty years. My education was so un-Jewish that today I cannot even read your dedication, which is evidently written in Hebrew. In later life I have often regretted this lack in my education [*dieses Stück meiner Unbildung*].[5]

This recollection is consistent with the fact that, by the time the family had migrated to Vienna for economic reasons, Jakob Freud had already abandoned many of his earlier religious observances. But he still remained Jewish to the core – in his appearance (he had a long beard and dignified countenance), his ability to recite the Passover *Seder* service by heart, his diligent study of the Talmud, and his knowledge of Hebrew literature.

On his son's 35th birthday, Jakob Freud proudly gave him the rebound copy of the Bible which Sigmund had read as a boy, with a special Hebrew dedication written in the spirit of Jewish religious tradition:

To my Dear Son, Solomon. [Freud's Hebrew name was Shlomo, in memory of his paternal grandfather.] It was in the seventh year of your life that the spirit of G–d began to stir you and spake to you thus 'Go thou and pore over the book which I wrote, and there will burst open for thee springs of understanding, knowledge and reason. It is indeed the book of books. Sages have delved into it and legislators have derived from it knowledge and law.' Thou hast seen the vision of the Almighty. Thou hast listened and ventured and achieved, soaring on the wings of the wind.[6]

The gift, a token of his father's 'undying love', was clearly intended to impress upon Sigmund the continuing importance of the religious tradition in which he had been raised. Yet Jakob Freud must surely have been aware that, in his son's eyes, the religious rituals of Judaism had long seemed to be empty and meaningless. Indeed the vehemence of Sigmund Freud's antipathy to Judaism as a religion was almost certainly connected with his symbolic rejection of the father who could no longer properly observe or transmit to him, fully intact, the traditional Jewish way of life. Like so many other Jewish fathers of this transitional generation, the textile merchant Jakob Freud had brought to Vienna only fragments of the living tradition from his ghetto community in the countryside. But this residual loyalty to Judaism was no longer sufficient for the generation forced to live between two worlds and two cultures. The inherent duplicity of their situation produced for a whole generation of socially and spiritually uprooted young Viennese Jews a sense of inner conflict, imposture, and despair – the kind of localized neuroses out of which Sigmund Freud was eventually to construct his universalist psychoanalytic typology. In that sense, the Oedipus complex can indeed be seen – in Marthe Robert's terms – as the portrait writ large of the primordial 'murdered father', Jakob Freud.

Sigmund Freud's father-complex, of which he became fully aware only during his own self-analysis following Jakob's death on 23 October 1896, was closely linked to an early childhood experience that concerned antisemitism. During one of their strolls together in Vienna, when Sigmund was 11 or 12 years old, Jakob Freud had recounted an incident that had occurred many years earlier during his own youth in Freiberg. A local Gentile had come up to him, knocked his *Streimel* (fur hat) into the mud, and ordered him off the pavement. Instead of resisting this impudent behaviour, Jakob Freud had calmly picked up his cap in the roadway. For Jakob the point of the anecdote was to illustrate how much the condition of Jews had improved since the 1830s. However, this 'unheroic' conduct by his father deeply shocked Freud and left an indelible trauma on his mind. 'I contrasted this situation, which did not please me, with another, more in harmony with my sentiments – the scene in which Hannibal's father, Hamilcar Barca, made his son swear before the household altar to take vengeance on the Romans. Ever since then Hannibal has had a place in my fantasies.'

Freud recalled this incident in *The Interpretation of Dreams* (1900), but had not initially noticed that in the first edition he mistakenly gave the name 'Hasdrubal' (Hannibal's brother) in place of the Carthaginian general's real father Hamilcar Barca. In *The Psychopathology of Everyday Life* he subsequently explained that he had been unable to forgive the lack of courage of his own father, Jakob Freud, towards 'the enemies of our people'. It was this stinging memory of paternal cowardice that caused Sigmund's 'astonishing' error with regard to Hasdrubal.[7]

Sigmund Freud is unlikely to have felt a similar shame with regard to his mother, a prime source of his unshakeable courage and self-confidence. This youthful and dominant woman, *née* Amalia Nathanson (1835–1930), who came originally from Brody in north-east Galicia, had arrived in Vienna when she was still a child (she actually witnessed the 1848 Revolution). She was a typical Polish Jewess – 'impatient, self-willed, sharp-witted and highly intelligent'. The centre of the family, full of tender concern and devotion towards her eldest son, Amalia Freud had never been fully acculturated. According to the recollections of her grandson, Martin Freud, Amalia still retained the language, manners, and beliefs of her native environment. She belonged to a 'peculiar race' distinct not only from the Gentiles,

> but absolutely different from Jews who had lived in the West for some generations . . . . These Galician Jews had little grace and no manners; and their women were certainly not what we should call 'ladies'. They were highly emotional and easily carried away by their feelings . . . . These women were not easy to live with and grandmother Amalia, a true representative of her race, was no exception. She had great vitality and much impatience.[8]

A similar affectionate ambivalence towards the *Ostjuden* from whom he sprang was shown by Martin's father, Sigmund Freud. For years he fondly collected Galician Jewish anecdotes and jokes, some of which he used in his book *Der Witz und seine Beziehung zum Unbewussten* (1905) and regarded as being 'of deep significance'.[9] Mostly they treated the aversion of Galician Jews to baths, the wiles of Jewish marriage brokers, the impudence of *schnorrers*, and the superstitions of the *Wunderrabbiner* (miracle-rabbis). Freud himself noted the prevalence of self-criticism in these jokes which 'have grown up on the soil of Jewish popular life'. Unlike jokes told about Jews by foreigners, which rarely rose above the level of brutal derision, the anecdotes created by Jews themselves were based on a knowledge of 'their real faults as well as the connection between them and their good qualities'. Whether cynical, merely sceptical, tendentious, or absurd, this humour realistically reflected, according to Freud, the 'manifold and hopeless miseries of the Jews', the ambiguous relationship between rich and poor, the 'democratic mode of thinking of Jews', and their ability to laugh at their own characteristics.

Freud's Jewish identity during his late school years and the period of his university studies had been decidedly ambivalent under the contradictory pressures of assimilation to German culture, social radicalism, and rising antisemitism. From 1873 to 1878 Freud was an active member of the *Leseverein der deutschen Studenten Wiens*, a radical student society wholly committed to the German nationalist cause.[10] Already an enthusiastic Darwinist and materialist, he was increasingly attracted to scientific modernism and anti-clerical liberalism. The young Freud was particularly drawn to the north German physicalist school of Helmholtz whose foremost representative in Vienna was another Protestant German, his greatly admired teacher, Ernst Brücke. At this time he began to study the materialist German philosopher Ludwig Feuerbach whose anthropological psychology of religion had a considerable impact on his radical views.

Freud also reacted sharply, like other members of the *Leseverein*, to the Ritter von Ofenheim scandal which helped discredit Austro-liberalism in the eyes of a whole generation of nationalist German students.[11] But whereas the Ofenheim affair politicized many of the *Leseverein* students, Freud began at precisely this point to lose his interest in politics and devote himself increasingly to science. Philosophical and religious radicalism interested him far more after 1875 than political radicalism of the nationalist or social democratic variety. He now came under the decisive influence of the great medical teachers at the University of Vienna, such as the Berlin-born physiologist Ernst Wilhelm Brücke (1819–92) in whose laboratory he learnt the art of detailed scientific observation between 1876 and 1882; the brilliant psychiatrist from Dresden, Theodor Meynert (1833–92) who specialized in the anatomy of the brain; and yet another German, Richard Krafft-Ebing (1840–1902), author of *Psychopathia sexualis: Eine Klinisch-forensische Studie* (1886).

The inspirational example of these great scientists from Germany helped to counteract the bitter disappointment which Freud felt at encountering rampant antisemitism in the Viennese student body on entering the University in 1873.[12] In his *Autobiographical Study*, Freud openly confronted the issue:

> Above all, I found that I was expected to feel myself inferior and an alien because I was a Jew. I refused absolutely to do the first of these things. I have never been able to see why I should feel ashamed of my descent or, as people were beginning to say, of my race. I put up, without much regret, with my non-acceptance into the community; for it seemed to me that in spite of this exclusion an active worker could not fail to find some nook or cranny in the framework of humanity. These first impressions at the University, however, had one consequence which was afterwards to prove important; for at an early age I was made familiar with the fate of being in the Opposition and of being put under the ban of the 'compact majority'. The foundations were thus laid for a certain degree of independence of judgment.[13]

Having grown up in the more tolerant, optimistic atmosphere of Austrian political liberalism in the 1860s and early 1870s, when assimilation and social acceptance still seemed relatively painless, Freud's sense of shock was understandable. Nevertheless it had not been his first encounter with the new antisemitism. In the higher classes of the Sperl *Gymnasium* in the Leopoldstadt, the rapid influx of Jews had already provoked a reaction which made him 'realize the consequences of belonging to an alien race' and he was forced by the 'antisemitic feeling among my classmates to take a definite stand'.

Sigmund Freud's response to Jews and Judaism during his late adolescence was marked by considerable equivocation, as his letters to a close Rumanian friend, Eduard Silberstein (1857–1925), make plain. He was steadily moving away from the traditional customs, rituals, and pieties of his east European home environment. Not only did he proudly proclaim himself as 'godless', refusing to observe the Jewish festivals which his father still held sacred, but, in letters to friends, he indulged in open mockery of Jewish ritual observances. Reminders of his own provincial background and ties with unassimilated Jews from eastern Europe began to grate on his nerves. An encounter with just such a family on the return trip from Freiberg, Moravia, to Vienna in September 1872, prompted him to make some violently deprecatory remarks in a letter to his friend Emil Fluss.

> Now this Jew talked the same way as I had heard thousands of others talk before, even in Freiberg. His face seemed familiar – he was typical. So was the boy with whom he discussed religion. He was cut from the cloth from which fate makes swindlers when the time is ripe: cunning, mendacious, kept by his adoring relatives in the belief that he is a great talent, but unprincipled and without character. I have enough of this rabble.[14]

The transparent desire to dissociate himself from such undesirable provincial Jewish characteristics coincided with Freud's growing aspirations to identify with liberal German *Kultur*.[15] By the time he had entered medical school in Vienna, Freud clearly regarded Jewish religious traditions as thoroughly anachronistic and looked to German-Austrian democratic ideals as the basis for social integration and assimilation. At the same time he was trying to sever his connections with the *Ostjuden*, the 'alien race' who were the initial target of German national antisemitism.[16]

Freud's letters from Vienna to his future wife Martha Bernays in Hamburg reveal however a more positive side to his Jewish identity at this time. Martha was the granddaughter of the orthodox Sephardi Rabbi Isaac Bernays (1792–1848) of Hamburg and her parents were strictly observant Jews. Martha herself observed *Kashrut*, fasted on Yom Kippur (in spite of Freud's remonstrations) and at the outset of their long engagement never wrote to her fiancé on the Sabbath.

In a remarkable letter to Martha which he composed in Hamburg, the 26-year-old Freud, taking into account her sensitivities and curious about her family, recounted to her in great detail a meeting with a local Jewish stationer who had turned out to be a disciple of her grandfather, the *Chacham* Bernays. This old Jewish shopkeeper, whose name was Nathan, had proved to be a mine of information about her family background; about the *Chacham* ('a quite extraordinary person' who had 'taught religion with great imaginativeness and humaneness') and about the profound pedagogical value of the Holy Scriptures. In spite of his own intransigent atheism, Freud had been fascinated by this Jewish stationer's exposition of Isaac Bernays's teachings. The whole encounter reminded him of Lessing's famous humanist drama, *Nathan the Wise*.[17]

Religion was no longer treated as a rigid dogma, it became an object of reflection for the satisfaction of cultivated artistic taste and of intensified logical efforts, and the teacher of Hamburg, Isaac Bernays, recommended it finally not because it happened to exist and had been declared holy, but because he was pleased by the deeper meaning which he found in it or which he projected into it . . . . His teacher, he continued, had been no ascetic. The Jew, he said, is the finest flower of mankind, and is made for enjoyment. Jews despise anyone who lacks the ability to enjoy . . . . The law commands the Jew to appreciate every pleasure, however small, to say grace over every fruit which makes him aware of the beautiful world in which it is grown. The Jew is made for joy and joy for the Jew. The teacher illustrated this with the gradual importance of joy in the Holy Days [*Steigerung der Feste*].[18]

Freud declared to Martha that, on taking his leave, he 'was more deeply moved than the old Jew could possibly guess' and ended his letter on a decidedly upbeat note: 'And as for us, this is what I believe: even if the form wherein the old Jews were happy no longer offers us any shelter, something of the core, of the essence of this meaningful and life-affirming Judaism will not be absent from our home.'[19]

Freud's respect for the ethical and pedagogical values of Judaism had been strongly shaped during his adolescence by an able religious instructor, Samuel Hammerschlag, who had taught him Bible studies at the Leopoldstadt *Gymnasium*.[20] Dr Hammerschlag, like the moderate German religious reformers Ludwig Philippson and Adolf Jellinek, had aimed at a balanced synthesis of thought and feeling in Jewish religious instruction; this served him in Freud's words 'as a way of educating toward love of the humanities, and from the material of Jewish history he was able to find the means of tapping the sources of enthusiasm hidden in the hearts of young people'.[21] Freud saw in him, above all, a teacher who possessed 'the gift of leaving ineradicable impressions on the development of their pupils. A spark of the same fire which animated the spirit of the great Jewish seers and prophets burned in him'.

Freud's feelings of Jewish pride and solidarity had been particularly sparked in the 1880s by the hostile atmosphere he encountered at the Vienna Hospital, but its deeper sources lay in his own maturing personality and desire for independence. Significantly, during his stay in Paris in the winter of 1885–6, Freud further consolidated this more positive sense of Jewish identity, along with confidence in his own abilities and future path in life. His studies with the famous French neurologist Jean Martin Charcot (after whom he named one of his sons) opened up new insights into the nature of hysterical repression and its connection with sexuality. In Charcot he saw not only a great scientist but a liberator and enlightened secularizer determined, in William

McGrath's words, 'to free his patients from the oppressive weight of dogmatic misconceptions'.[27] Freud found the atmosphere in Charcot's clinic 'very informal and democratic'. The French physician had inspired in him 'an entirely new idea about perfection' and a growing dissatisfaction with the Viennese scientific milieu which he had temporarily left.[23]

The gradual shift in Freud's self-definition was reinforced by the icy reception which his new ideas on hysteria received following his return from Paris to Vienna and appearance before the *Gesellschaft der Aerzte* (Society of Medicine) in the winter of 1886. In his *Autobiographical Study* Freud cryptically recalled:

> The impression that the high authorities had rejected my innovations remained unshaken; and with my hysteria in men and my production of 'hysterical paralyses by suggestion', I found myself forced into the Opposition. As I was soon afterwards excluded from the laboratory of cerebral anatomy and for a whole session had nowhere to deliver my lectures, I withdrew from academic life and ceased to attend the learned societies. It is a whole generation since I have visited the *Gesellschaft der Aerzte.*[24]

Freud's bitterness towards the Medical Society derived not only from its authoritarian, dogmatic rejection of new scientific ideas but also from the socio-political pressures that were building up in Vienna. In a letter of February 1888 to the Berlin Jewish physiologist, Wilhelm Fliess (1858–1928), who was soon to become his main solace and ego support, Freud reported on a terrible row at the Vienna Medical Society. 'They wanted to force us to subscribe to a new weekly which is intended to represent the pure, elevated and Christian views of certain dignitaries who have long since forgotten what work is like. They will naturally carry their proposal through; I feel very inclined to resign.'[25]

Freud's Jewish identity evidently thrived on this type of adversarial relationship to the 'compact majority' in Catholic Vienna, whose outlook he openly despised. Disgusted by the whole atmosphere of *fin-de-siècle* Vienna and the antisemitic tendencies which had infiltrated the medical faculty, the academic administration, and municipal politics, he increasingly withdrew into his own therapeutic work with patients. As he informed Wilhelm Fliess in a letter on 11 March 1900: 'I hate Vienna with a positively personal hatred and, just the contrary of the giant Antaeus, I draw fresh strength whenever I remove my feet from the soil of the city which is my home.'[26]

His correspondence with Fliess during the 1890s reveals a man virtually cut off from the wider society, living in and for his intimate family circle, patients, and Jewish friends, mainly doctors like Leopold Königstein and Oscar Rie (1863–1911) with whom he played taroc once a week. His scientific work was proceeding well but very much in splendid isolation.[27] By 1894 even his close professional contact with Josef Breuer had ended and he was thrown back entirely on his own intellectual resources. Politics barely interested him, with the exception of the antisemitic successes in the Viennese municipal elections which prompted a few lapidary remarks to Fliess on 23 September 1895: 'the Liberals were beaten by forty-six seats to nil, and in the second district by thirty-two seats to fourteen. I voted after all. Our district remained liberal.'[28]

Lueger's non-confirmation in office following an imperial veto prompted Freud to light up a cigar in joy but can scarcely be taken as indicating a passionate interest in Austrian politics. Nevertheless Freud was angry at one of Fliess's friends for his tolerant evaluation of Lueger. Writing to Fliess on 25 May 1899 he reported: 'I treated him badly because of this. D. [Dernburg] wanted to persuade us that here all is very well . . . and that we are unfair in complaining so bitterly. I still think we know better.'[29]

The popular successes of Lueger's Christian-Social movement could only have confirmed Freud in his low estimate of most Viennese non-Jews and of human nature in general. But the antisemitic triumph constituted a more immediate source of anxiety and bitterness for it directly affected his promotion prospects at the university. Since his appointment in 1885 as *Privatdozent* (the lowest rung on the academic ladder), Freud's professional ambitions and hopes for a professorship had been thwarted – a source of deep frustration that constantly recurred in his recorded dreams. On 8 February 1897 he wrote to Fliess that his friend Professor Hermann Nothnagel and Krafft-Ebing were going to propose him for the coveted professorship but the former had warned him that the chances were slim. 'You know the further difficulties. It may do no more than put you on the *tapis*.'[30]

Freud believed, not without reason, that the Minister of Education was highly unlikely to accept the proposal out of 'denominational considerations'. One of his closest Jewish friends, Leopold Königstein, whose own promotion had been delayed for years, had already confirmed Freud's suspicions on this score. The existing political constellation in early 1897 following Lueger's confirmation as Mayor of Vienna and the dependence of Count Badeni's shaky government on Christian-Socialist support, made the promotion of Jews in the Austrian universities particularly difficult. It was against this depressing background that Freud's dream of the uncle with the yellow beard (February 1897) had taken place – a dream which directly related to his own professional ambitions. In the dream Freud found that he had stepped into the shoes of the minister who refused to appoint him, in order to ridicule two Jewish academics in a similar position to himself.[31] 'In mishandling my two learned and eminent colleagues because they were Jews and in treating the one as a simpleton and the other as a criminal I was behaving as though I were the Minister, I had put myself in the Minister's place.'[32]

Freud's personal crisis and his growing sense of ostracism in Viennese society were undoubtedly factors which drew him to the *B'nai B'rith* lodge which he joined on 29 September 1897. The society provided him not only with a refuge from antisemitism, a congenial Jewish atmosphere, and a sympathetic forum for expounding his psychoanalytic hypotheses but also with a framework for sharing with others the humanitarian ideals which he had held since his youth.[33] The *B'nai B'rith* brotherhood in Vienna had been created in the winter of 1894 under the pressure of antisemitic hostility. Its declared ideals were to unite 'Israelites' in prompting their own interests and those of humanity; to develop their mental and moral character; to inculcate among them the principles of philanthrophy, honour, and patriotism; to alleviate the sufferings of the poor; and to aid the victims of persecution.[34]

Freud was sympathetic to these humanitarian interests, especially approving the appeal to Enlightenment ideals of universal brotherhood and equality and their attempted synthesis with the humanistic traditions of Judaism. He was drawn to an ethical society which could provide an island of refuge within a hostile environment while not wholly severing relations with the non-Jewish world.

Freud's most active participation in the *B'nai B'rith* society during 1901–2 immediately preceded his creation of the first Viennese psychoanalytic circle which was composed, at the outset, exclusively of Jews. Not until the adhesion of the Welshman Ernest Jones and the Swiss psychiatrists Carl Gustav Jung (1875–1961) and Ludwig Binswanger (1881–1966), who in 1907 attended their first meeting in Vienna, did the psychoanalytic group include any Gentiles. This ethnic parochialism aroused deeply ambivalent feelings in Freud. On the one hand he felt at home in this intimate Jewish circle of analysts who were linked not only by their common therapeutic concerns but also by a kind of unspoken ethnic bond. At the same time, Freud strongly desired to universalize the mission and message of psychoanalysis. For this purpose the Swiss Gentile psychiatric establishment of Jung and his small group in Zurich was crucial to Freud, who made considerable efforts to ensure their allegiance. Only through their presence in the leadership of the movement could he hope to overcome the antisemitic taunt that psychoanalysis was a 'Jewish science'. Hence his well-known plea to Karl Abraham (1877–1925) on 3 May 1908: 'please be tolerant and do not forget that it is really easier for you than it is for Jung to follow my ideals, for in the first place you are completely independent, and then you are closer to my intellectual constitution because of racial kinship.'

Freud urged Abraham to show restraint in spite of what he felt to be Swiss 'deviations' in the direction of Christian spiritualism, for only through Jung's appearance on the scene had psychoanalysis 'escaped the danger of becoming a Jewish national affair'. In reply, Karl Abraham confessed eight days later:

> I find it easier to go along with you rather than with Jung. I, too, have always felt this intellectual kinship. After all, our Talmudic way of thinking cannot disappear just like that. Some days ago a small paragraph in *Jokes* strangely attracted me. When I looked at it more closely, I found that, in the technique of apposition and in its whole structure, it was completely Talmudic.[35]

Writing from Berchtesgaden on 23 July 1908, Freud did not object to Abraham's conclusions. On the contrary he frankly admitted to his Berlin disciple: 'May I say that it is consanguineous Jewish traits that attract me to you? We understand each other.' Once again Freud declared his displeasure at the quarrel between Abraham and Jung, but he did not reproach him, emphasizing instead the necessity of suffering wrongs for the greater good of the psychoanalytic cause.

> I nurse a suspicion that the suppressed antisemitism of the Swiss that spares me is deflected in reinforced form upon you. But I think that we as Jews, if we wish to join in, must develop a bit of masochism, be ready to suffer some wrong.[36]

In another letter to Abraham on 26 December 1908, Freud put the issue in slightly different but even more unequivocal terms. 'Our Aryan [*sic*] comrades are really completely indispensable to us, otherwise psychoanalysis would succumb to antisemitism.'[37]

In his correspondence with Jung, Freud expressed a similar preoccupation in more discreet and tactful language. 'For my peace of mind', he wrote to Jung on 2 September 1907,

> I tell myself that it is better for psychoanalysis . . . that you will be spared a part of the opposition that would be awaiting me, that nothing but useless repetitions would be heard if I were to say the same things all over again, and that you are more suitable as a propagandist, for I have invariably found that something in my personality, my words and ideas strike people as alien, whereas to you all hearts are open.[38]

Freud clearly regarded Jung both as his bridge to the Gentile world and as the Joshua who would carry on and eventually complete his work of conquering the Promised Land of psychiatry.[39] In a letter to Jung on 13 August 1908, Freud was quite explicit in this regard. 'With your strong and independent character; with your Germanic blood which enables you to command the sympathies of the public more readily than I, you seem better fitted than anyone else I know to carry out this mission.'[40]

Determined to establish a broader basis for the new science than that offered by his own Viennese Jewish colleagues, Freud ignored their objections and at the Nuremburg Conference of 1910 made Jung President of the International Psycho-Analytical Association.[41] He defended this step by insisting that it was essential for him 'to form ties in the world of general science'; psychoanalysis could not remain a Jewish sectarian movement if it aspired to universal significance. Therefore, according to Freud, 'Jews must be content with the modest role of preparing the ground'.[42]

Freud's confidence in Jung who had seemed ready 'to give up for my sake, certain race prejudices which he had so far permitted himself to indulge', and his belief that the Swiss psychiatrist was his obvious heir, turned out to be sadly mistaken. Freud had of course long been aware of their divergences. Jung believed, for instance, that 'the sexual terminology should be reserved only for the most extreme forms of your "libido" and that a less offensive collective term should be established';[43] he knew that Jung was struggling to free himself inwardly, as he had put it in a letter to Freud, 'from the oppressive sense of your [i.e. Freud's] paternal authority'.[44] Moreover the two men disagreed no less fundamentally on the question of myth and religion than they did over the importance of sexuality. This difference came out openly in 1910 when Freud had proposed that the psychoanalytic movement join forces with an 'International Fraternity for Ethics and Culture' to fight for common progressive ideals of world improvement and practical reform while opposing the injustice practised by reactionary states and by the Catholic church.[45] This proposal was consistent enough with the humanitarian mission that Freud had affirmed in his *B'nai B'rith* activities and subsequently transposed to psychoanalysis.

In a letter of 11 February 1910 Jung scathingly dismissed Freud's idea of an ethical fraternity as artificial, a mythical 'nothing', lacking any archaic-infantile driving force or rootedness in the deep instinct of the race.[45] Jung certainly did not think that 2,000 years of Christianity could be so easily replaced except by something equivalent in mass appeal that could reabsorb the 'ecstatic instinctual forces' inspired by its advent. The Swiss psychiatrist was not interested in practical ethics based on rationalistic presumptions but in the 'eternal truth of myth' which he believed that psychoanalysis should deliberately cultivate among intellectuals. Jung even spoke of transforming Christ back 'into the soothsaying god of the vine' (Dionysos) and rediscovering the infinite rapture and 'wantonness in our religion'.[47]

The gulf between the two men was clearly too deep to be bridged for long, especially in view of Freud's scorn for half-measures, and for circumlocutions of roundabout, non-committal phraseology on the role of sexuality in the life of the psyche. In Stefan Zweig's words, Freud was never prepared 'to hang a verbal fig-leaf in front of his convictions' so that they could be smuggled in through the back door 'without attracting disagreeable attention'.[48] He was simply not prepared to substitute polite words like 'eros' or 'love' for libido, as the Swiss would have preferred; nor could he easily swallow Jung's latent Christian mysticism and myth-centred irrationalism which would have struck a death-blow to both the scientific and the materialist foundations of psychoanalysis. Jung's defection in 1912–13 was none the less a bitter blow to Freud's hopes to make Zurich rather than Vienna the centre of psychoanalysis and, if that was possible, increased still further his distrust of 'Aryans'.[49]

Curiously enough, neither these experiences nor the refinement of his psychoanalytic insights enabled Freud to develop a convincing theory of antisemitism. Ernest Jones, one of his earliest Gentile disciples, has pointed out Freud's personal sensitivity to this issue which is certainly confirmed by our own investigations. Antisemitism of a visceral kind had been crucial in galvanizing Freud's sense of an ethnic affinity to Jews since his earliest years in Vienna. Throughout his career it had affected him and his family and in 1938 he would only narrowly escape Nazi vengeance. Yet Freud's writings and comments on this topic are minimally brief and singularly lack the kind of originality that characterized so much of his work.

Only in his last major work, *Moses and Monotheism*, can one find an implicit theory of antisemitism as deriving from the Jewish claim to be the chosen people of God. In particular, Freud mentions the 'jealousy' evoked in other peoples by this insistence that 'they were the first born, favourite child of God the Father'.[50] This 'chosenness' theme, along with the fear of castration provoked by the Hebrew custom of circumcision, seemed to Freud to be the main unconscious factors in the dynamics of antisemitism. They belonged to the secret sources, the motives buried in the unconscious and in the distant past – part of the archaic heritage of mankind. But Freud was neither inclined nor able to work out a specific psychology of antisemitism – a failing linked perhaps to his general disdain and disgust for the irrationality of the political world.

Freud's provocative last work *Moses and Monotheism* may not have illuminated the problem of antisemitism but it did highlight the ambivalences of his own Jewish identity. In place of the historical Moses of Judaism, Freud drew the highly personal portrait of a Moses who had been born an Egyptian nobleman and whose presumed murder by his 'adopted' people, the Jews, had paradoxically created Hebrew mono-theism.[51] This Moses was revered by Freud as a heroic lawmaker and creator of culture. As early as 1914, in his anonymously published essay on Michelangelo's statue of Moses in Rome, he had presented his hero as a supreme exemplar of self-control and the renunciation of powerful passions for the sake of his lawgiving mission.

In *Moses and Monotheism* he was transformed into the initiator of a repressive though ultimately beneficial revolution from above that laid the foundation of all civilized morality. In Freud's arbitrary construction, it was 'one man, the man Moses, who created the Jews'. They were his 'chosen people', and their tenacity, obstinacy, and moralism were shaped by his character and will.[52]

The 'Egyptian' Moses had given the self-esteem of the Jews a religious anchorage and therefore it was solely to him that 'this people owes its tenacity of life but also much of the hostility it has experienced and still experiences'. In Egypt the seed of monotheism had indeed failed to ripen, but among the ancient Jews it had been constantly renewed through the Hebrew prophets and gave evidence 'of a peculiar psychical aptitude in the masses who had become the Jewish people'. They alone had assumed the exacting burdens of the monotheistic religion 'in return for the reward of being the chosen people'.[53] From this exalted consciousness developed those character traits of rational intellectuality, legalism, tenacity, separateness, and moral austerity which Freud admired in the Jewish people and which were indeed reflected in his own personality.

Moses and Monotheism, written under the dark shadow of Nazism, was at once the most controversial and personal of Freud's works. It must have cost him considerable emotional pain to deprive the Jews of the man 'they take pride in as the greatest of their sons', an action which he knew would profoundly offend Jewry for national as well as religious reasons.[54] Yet this iconoclastic book, for all its obvious inadequacies, was by no means the deed of a renegade seeking to denigrate his people at its moment of supreme crisis. It should rather be seen as the paradoxical response of a consistent free-thinker and radical atheist who all his life had affirmed a stubborn identification with Jewry and with the figure of Moses, in spite of negating all forms of religious self-definition and national intoxication. It was from this ancient source of inspiration that Freud, perhaps the most un-Viennese of all Viennese Jews, had derived his indomitable power of resistance and to which he had returned at the end of his days. Through the powerful image of Moses, indelibly impressed upon the historic character of Jewry, he expressed that overcoming of magic and mysticism, that enigmatic promise of inner freedom through the exercise of reason, which gave him the courage to explore the dark side of the psyche without succumbing to despair.

7

Dilemmas of assimilation in central Europe

The exiled Czech writer Milan Kundera recently observed that central Europe in the years before Hitler owed more to the Jewish genius than perhaps any other part of the world. The Jews were the 'intellectual cement', the cosmopolitan and integrative element which added a quintessentially European colour, tone, and vitality to great cities like Berlin, Vienna, Prague, and Budapest.[1] If the collapse of the Austro-Hungarian monarchy in 1918 physically unhinged central Europe, the mass murder of its Jewish population during the Second World War can be said to have irredeemably damaged its soul. For with the disappearance of its Jewish leaven and the crushing of the smaller nations sandwiched between Russia and Germany, the brilliant melting-pot which so decisively shaped European culture in the early twentieth century has seemingly faded for ever.

The scale and magnitude of this disaster was aptly evoked for an English-speaking audience by Frederic V. Grunfeld in his *Prophets Without Honour* when he asked his readers to imagine

> that Aldous Huxley was beaten to death in a prison camp near Oxford; that T.S. Eliot had died in exile in Peru; that the aged Bernard Shaw committed suicide on a ship to South America; that Hemingway and Fitzgerald, as well as Rogers and Hammerstein, had been compelled to live out their last days in a small community in Guatemala . . . that George Gershwin had been killed trying to cross the Mexican border. That William Faulkner had learned Spanish in order to teach in a school, in Caracas; that Henry Moore had made a new career for himself in Cuba – but that W.H. Auden, Marianne Moore, Louis Armstrong, Aaron Copland and E. E. Cummings had been among those rounded up and gassed by the police . . . it sounds like a science fiction plot, absurd and wholly unbelievable. But this is what actually happened in my lifetime in the cultural life of Germany.

Nowhere is this catastrophe more palpable in its consequences than in postwar Berlin, with its physical division between east and west providing a concrete symbol of the cultural and political chasm in the heart of Europe. For Jews, too, this city has a special significance – both as beginning and end. It was here that the modern history of European Jewry started with Moses Mendelssohn (1729–86) and some 150 years later reached its macabre climax with the planning, organization, and carrying out of the Nazi 'Final Solution'. Hence, Berlin represents for Jews both a high point of achievement and creative response to Gentile surroundings (the last decades of Wilhelmine Germany and the Weimar flowering) as well as the nadir of centuries of murderous antisemitism culminating in the 'Shoah'.

The tragic end cannot be wished away but should not be used to obscure or minimize the importance of the cultural achievement and its legacy. At the same time a sober reassessment of the role of the Jews in the land of *Dichter* and *Denker* cannot but induce some melancholy reflections. From Mendelssohn to Leo Baeck, the Berlin Jews (like their co-religionists throughout central Europe) were an integral part of the great humanist civilization whose main vehicle was the German language and traditions of scholarship. But once barbarism stood at the gates, humanism proved to be a weak reed and that ponderous Christian-Germanic notion of *Kultur* (for which Biblical Hebrew has no equivalent) collapsed into servile obsequiousness before the dictates of the *Richter* and *Henker*. Against this sombre background it is all the more striking that modern Jews have for the most part retained their belief in science, rational ethics, and the autonomy of man, though the messianic faith which once inspired their humanist commitment to *Kultur* has been understandably eroded.

The key to this tenacious optimism no doubt lies deep in the foundations of the Jewish religious faith and national character as it was formed through centuries of overcoming adversity and by the experience of having outlived the mighty world-empires of the past. But the encounter with the German *Aufklärung* of the late eighteenth century was a formative experience that decisively reinforced this belief in human rationality. As George Mosse has recently pointed out, the ideal of *Bildung* (self-cultivation) which 'transcended all differences of nationality and religion through the unfolding of the individual personality' virtually became synonymous with Jewishness for many emancipated central European Jews. Having entered modernity under the sign of *Bildung* in its cosmopolitan sense – as an integral faith in education, moral perfectability, self-discipline, and aesthetic harmony – German Jews in particular would not easily renounce what had been so assiduously acquired.

There is no need to elaborate here on the significance of Lessing's *Nathan der Weise* as a symbol of the Age of Reason and Tolerance for successive generations of emancipated Jews in central Europe. Nor on the importance of Goethe's cosmopolitan serenity and classical faith in *Bildung* and humanity as a model for Jews, not only in Germany but also in eastern Europe. This was even more true of Germany's national poet, Friedrich von Schiller, whose exaltation of freedom and equality struck a particularly resonant chord in the hearts of the oppressed Polish Jews. The Austrian novelist, Joseph Roth, born in Brody (eastern Galicia) near the Russian border and educated in the local German *Gymnasium*, wrote in his poignant *Juden auf Wanderschaft* (1923):[2] 'For the East European Jews, Germany is still the land of Goethe and Schiller – the German poets whom every studious Jewish youth knows better than our Nazi grammar-school boys'. In the eastern borderlands of the former Austrian monarchy, whether in Cracow, Lemberg (Lvov), Czernowitz, or the small towns of eastern Galicia where Jews often accounted for over 50 per cent of the population, this was no exaggeration.

Ostjuden, along with more westernized Jews, had for several generations been primary bearers of German *Kultur*. As early as the 1848 Revolution this had aroused the antagonism of the Polish insurrectionists in Poznan and of the Czechs in Bohemia. In Prague, by the 1850s most Jews were not only German-speaking but effectively Germanized. In spite of the bitter reproaches of the Czech nationalists they persisted in their allegiance to a cosmopolitan *Deutschtum* even as Prague was inexorably transformed into a Czech-speaking city. (By 1900 there were 415,000 Czechs as against 25,000 Jews and only 10,000 Germans in Prague.) In 1890 74 per cent of Prague Jews still declared German to be their *Umgangssprache* though, for reasons of prudence and a desire to appease rampant Czech nationalism, the figure dropped after 1900 to under 50 per cent. But this did not undo the deep affinities which tied the Prague Jews to German language and secular culture.

Not even the rise of a fiercely antisemitic *völkisch* nationalism among German students in Prague and followers of Georg von Schoenerer in the Sudetenland, could shake the German loyalties of most Bohemian and Moravian Jews. True, some Czech Jewish intellectuals were drawn to the charismatic figure of Thomas Masaryk (who had courageously interceded against Czech popular antisemitism during the Hilsner blood libel case of 1899) and felt attracted by his call for a return to the spiritual values of Jan Hus and the Czech Reformation. But the prospects of a Czech–Jewish symbiosis would only bear fruit in the special circumstances of the first Czech Republic when the interests of both groups increasingly coincided. *Fin-de-siècle* Prague in Felix Weltsch's words remained 'a place where German literature and art were thriving-... where the most intense assimilation of the Jews to German culture was the order of the day'.

A good illustration of the prevailing attitudes in Prague is afforded by a letter written in 1914 by the liberal Czech Zionist, Hugo Bergmann, to Professor Carl Stumpf in Berlin (we shall return to this revealing document later). Bergmann is defending himself against the reproach that one cannot be both a Zionist and a 'German' philosopher.[3]

German is my mother tongue, I have attended only German schools, speak and think German. These are generally the criteria by which menbership within Germandom or the Czech nation are judged in these parts. According to these criteria I am as German as anyone and indeed more so, since I have studied at a German University and learned everything I know, *only* from Germans . . . moreover I consider German culture far superior to Czech and more deserving of promotion . . .

At the same time Bergmann emphasized that his identification with German language and *Kultur* had nothing in common with a *Germanisierungspolitik* that would deny national self-determination to 'culturally inferior' Slav peoples. Diversity was a value in itself, and the Germans who around 1700 had stood on a far lower level than the vastly superior French would have had no Goethe or Schiller had they applied contemporary criteria to themselves at that time. Bergmann quoted his Catholic philosophy teacher and mentor, Franz Brentano 'who always spoke bitterly about the Magyarisation of the smaller peoples of Hungary' to demonstrate his own disapproval of nationalistic chauvinism in east-central Europe and his sympathy for the small, oppressed peoples of the region. Indeed, precisely as a Zionist who had been nurtured on enlightened German culture, he rejected forcible assimilation, pointing out that it was by no means a tragedy 'if in Palestine today Hebrew has become the everyday language and along with the so-called 'Jargon' [Yiddish] a vehicle for literature'.[4]

Bergmann's reference to 'Magyarization' as a negative example of nationality policies (viewed from a liberal standpoint) was particularly ironic given the Magyar–Jewish alliance which had gradually emerged in greater Hungary since the 1840s. In Hungary a unique kind of political symbiosis had developed even before the 1848 Revolution between Hungarian nationalism and the Jewish reform movement. Nowhere indeed did Jews sacrifice themselves with greater fervour for the patriotic cause (in this case Magyar national liberation) than in Hungary in 1848, despite pogroms and popular resistance to their emancipation. Their identification with the Magyar struggle against Habsburg tyranny, and against brutal Russian repression (and the spectre of Pan-Slavism), was severely punished with the victory of the counter-revolution in 1849. But after 1867 the Jewish alliance with the dominant Hungarian nobility proved highly profitable to both sides. The integration and Magyarization of the Jews became an essential component in official Magyar policy, designed to neutralize the numerical weight of the Slav, German, and Rumanian minorities who constituted just over half of the population of greater Hungary.

Not surprisingly, antisemitism in pre-1914 Hungary was rather stronger among Germans, Rumanians, and Slovak villagers who resented the Jews as 'agents' of Magyarization (and of capitalist modernization) than it was among ethnic Magyars. After a brief flurry of antisemitic agitation in the early 1880s under Victor von Istoczy, the movement declined and was noticeably weaker than in the German or Slavic parts of the Habsburg monarchy. The Hungarian liberal government, for its own reasons of self-interest, repressed antisemitism more firmly than was the case elsewhere in east-central Europe. The Jews had become crucial partners in the industrialization of a predominantly agrarian society. Indeed they achieved a dramatic hegemony in the commercial and banking sectors of the economy, within the free professions and the liberal intelligentsia which was no less impressive than (though not as well-known or studied as) the German and Austrian examples.

This is less surprising when one recalls that in Budapest Jews constituted no less than 40 per cent of the pupils in the secondary schools at the turn of the century. Indeed, in some of the best Protestant and state gymnasia of Budapest before the First World War they were often the majority. They were therefore well placed to take advantage of their educational assets in the rapidly developing markets for the service professions and tended to dominate the ranks of the freelance intellectuals. As in Vienna, schooling became the key factor in social mobility and cultural assimilation. Not surprisingly, then, the percentage of Jews in the Magyarized liberal-bourgeois elite of Budapest was far above their share in the population (the same was true in Vienna, and to a lesser degree in Berlin). Nowhere else in east-central Europe, so it seemed, were social and political conditions so favourable for a swift and successful assimilation of the Jews. (This belief ignored among other factors the efficacy of the ideological and institutional barriers thrown up by Jewish orthodoxy and the Hassidic movement in the more backward parts of Hungary to the progress of Enlightenment and modernization). But appearances turned out to be deceptive. In the greatly altered circumstances of a rump Hungary after 1918, stripped off its minorities and traumatized by the short-lived communist regime of Bela Kun – followed by civil war and counter-revolutionary terror – the old 'liberal' traditions of the Magyar ruling class rapidly disappeared. Post-1918 Hungary became a pacemaker in virulent political antisemitism in contrast to the comparatively liberal, tolerant atmosphere of neighbouring Czechoslovakia, which during the Austrian period had been considerably less hospitable to Jews.

The fascinating example of partitioned Poland (1795–1918) is too complex to be dealt with here in any great detail. Moreover, apart from

Austrian Galicia, it cannot easily be defined within our chosen cultural framework. Nevertheless, a few observations on Polish–Jewish relations may help to illuminate the role of the Jews in central Europe in general. As in Hungary, the weight of Jewish orthodoxy and the strength of the Hassidic movement was a serious barrier (especially obvious in Galicia) to the acculturation and assimilation of the mass of Polish Jewry. The sheer size of the Jewish community, its spectacular rate of growth, its rapid urbanization and social differentiation, as well as its cultural distinctness meant that the problems of modernization and integration were particularly acute. Moreover, between 1815 and the First World War the majority of Polish Jews lived under Tsarist rule – a fact which tended to aggravate their relations with Gentile Poles – given the growing influence of Russian culture on the Jewish intelligentsia. The more generous attitudes fostered by Polish patriots in the first half of the nineteenth century towards Jews gave way (especially in Russian-controlled territory) to an exclusivist, organic, and antisemitic nationalism which virtually precluded any Jewish participation in Polish culture.

In Austrian Galicia, the least industralized part of partitioned Poland, antisemitism was more related to the general problems of under-development and poverty. Catholic populist movements like those of the priest Father Stojalowski took advantage of the economic tensions between Jewish middlemen and Polish peasants for political ends. The pogroms which broke out in western Galicia in 1898 drew on this primitive rural anticapitalism for which the Jew provided a ready scapegoat. Nevertheless in Austrian Poland, as in Hungary (though more equivocally), a nexus between the dominant prewar Galician nobility and the Jewish elite based on mutual economic interests (and the Polish need for Jewish allies against the Ukrainian minority) did develop and provide a modicum of security for the Jewish population. But the level of Polonization and assimilation among Galician Jews – except for a small group of 'Poles of the Mosaic faith' – remained largely insignificant before the First World War. Already by the end of the nineteenth century, the pressure of Jewish nationalism and Zionism, in addition to overriding orthodox influence, weakened the chances for assimilation on the German, Austrian, or Hungarian pattern.

The heightened nationalism of independent Poland with its many national minorities and a population of 3 million Jews (10 per cent of the total population) after 1918 further exacerbated tensions. The 'Jewish problem' as it had been inherited from the era of the three empires was resuscitated under increasingly unfavourable economic conditions. The extent of Jewish alienation from the Polish state was revealed by the startling fact that in the 1921 census only about a quarter of Polish Jews said that they were of Polish nationality. In 1931 only 381,000 Jews out of a population of over 3 million listed Polish as their native tongue.

These facts, however they are interpreted, indicate how far removed Poland had already become from the central European model of cultural, linguistic, and even political symbiosis.

The Polish example illustrates an important sociological difference between central and eastern European Jewries which greatly influenced the role which they respectively played in the general culture of the time. In Berlin and Vienna, the Jewish enlighteners could look towards and find access to the *Geisteselite* (the term is borrowed from Jacob Katz) of the Gentile middle class. Even in Prague this was the case with the educated German bourgeoisie while in Budapest the Jews, by filling the role of an absent indigenous middle class, achieved an economic and cultural nexus with the more liberal Hungarian nobility. In Poland, on the other hand, an appropriate social reference group for Jewish acculturation was missing. By the time an indigenous Polish middle class began to emerge at the end of the nineteenth century it had already been contaminated by a nationalist, antisemitic ideology. It is not surprising therefore that Jews in Galicia tended to look to the distant Emperor Franz Joseph in Vienna and the paternalistic Habsburg dynasty for their security rather than nourish dreams of an independent Polish state.

Culturally, too, for all the attraction exercised by romantic Polish nationalism on a sector of Jewish youth (not least within the Zionist movement) it was ultimately European culture as mediated through Berlin and Vienna that appealed most to the Jewish *Bildungsbürgertum* of pre-state Poland. *Deutschtum* in the universalist sense still had a great hold on the *Ostjuden* before and during the First World War. Its most sublime prophet, Hermann Cohen, the outstanding religious philosopher of the age and the renewer of Kantian philosophy in Germany, was triumphally received by the eastern Jewish masses of Russia just before the outbreak of the First World War. His notion of a unique kinship between *Deutschtum* and *Judentum* was predicated on a conception of the German 'spirit' derived from Kantian ethical idealism. When Cohen declared in 1916 that *Deutschtum* was 'the teacher of the world' and that it was the motherland of *all* Jews (the hegemony of German culture at that time extended to American as well as east European Jewry) he was still thinking in terms of the late-eighteenth-century ideals of the *Aufklärung*. It was a rational, normative construction which Cohen never confused with the actual, empirical *Deutschland*. Rather he hoped to moralize, to 'idealize' the existing Prusso-German state with its cultural and political conservatism – in which antisemitism remained a constant irritant. Cohen's 'Germanism' explicitly rejected any self-surrender of the Jewish religious inheritance, which he regarded as fully compatible with the *weltbürgerlich* humanism of 'the nation of Kant'.

Nevertheless, the discrepancy between the idealized sublimation of the German-Jewish synthesis in Cohen's work and the *empirical* reality of the German-Jewish relationship cannot be ignored. It was clearly perceived by Franz Rosenzweig, who in a letter to his parents on 20 September 1917 took issue with the self-deception involved in over-intellectualized definitions of the inner essence of *Deutschtum*:

> To be a German means to undertake fully responsibility for one's people, not just to harmonize with Goethe, Schiller, and Kant, but also with the others and above all with the inferior and average, with the assessor, the fraternity student, the petty bureaucrat, the thick skulled peasant, the pedantic school master . . . . Cohen confuses that which he as a European finds in German culture with what a German finds in it. Of course: 'German philosophy and music' are European phenomena . . . but with Cohen only the European exists, a genuine German-ism with which it could cross-fertilise is missing.

A similar criticism could have been directed at the kind of highly refined, spiritualized Europeanism exemplified by writers like Stefan Zweig and Emil Ludwig who were extremely popular during the Weimar years. Their sincere efforts to popularize the ideals of *Bildung* and classical humanism owed far more to the European Enlightenment than to an explicitly Jewish self-understanding. Nevertheless, Zweig certainly acknowledged the importance of his Jewish heritage, glorifying his Diasporic 'supra-nationality' as a source of inspiration and transcendence. For Zweig, there were no nations; only individuals and humanity as a whole. His cosmopolitan outlook led him, in common with many central European Jewish intellectuals, to stress that which united rather than divided peoples; to encourage the appreciation of alien cultures; and to act through his own writings and translations as a cultural *mediator* between the European nations.

It was a noble mission (and a characteristically 'Jewish' role) but its foundations were being sapped even as his books became bestsellers. Zweig seemed to sense as much when he wrote to Emil Ludwig in 1925: 'Sometimes I am oppressed by the feeling that we who possess an encyclopaedic knowledge, men who passionately work at extending their *Bildung*, are already a kind of fossil.'[5] Unfortunately, Jewish intellectuals like Zweig were far too unpolitical (a trait they shared with much of the German intelligentsia) to pursue more deeply the root causes of this alienation in the masses. They preferred to ignore what George Mosse has referred to as the increasing nationalization of the ideal of *Bildung* by the German middle classes since the end of the nineteenth century (soul being identified with *Volk* rather than *Geist*). They did not fully grasp how divorced they remained from popular culture and feelings. By the end of the Weimar period (as in *fin-de-siècle* Vienna thirty years earlier) German Jews often seemed to be the last upholders of the eighteenth-century faith in reason and high culture. They believed in ideals which had ceased to be held even by the *Bildungsbürgertum* with whom they identified.

This development suggests that despite their intense assimilation to German language and culture, the behaviour of Jews continued to reflect distinctive Jewish traditions; that the Jews (as Jacob Katz has suggested) never fully integrated as a *collective* into the body of German society but rather constituted a kind of separate subgroup which in some of its characteristics resembled the German bourgeoisie but in others significantly diverged from the Gentile pattern. This fact made it easier for antisemites in central Europe to claim that Jews were indeed an 'alien' element in the dominant culture whose presence could only be *zersetzend*. They could readily seize on linguistic peculiarities and a manner of speech designated by the derogatory term *mauscheln* (also used by many Jews). They could point to the lack of roots or of an organic link to the people, or else to Jewish vulgarity and tastelessness, to emphasize the foreign origin of their unwelcome competitors. All these allegations found their *locus classicus* in Richard Wagner's *Das Judentum in der Musik* (1869) which demonstrated the extent to which already in the liberal era the foundations of Jewish participation in German culture were being challenged. Even those like Gustav Freytag who favoured Jewish integration in German culture and society agreed with many of the stereotypes propagated by antisemites who opposed Jewish emancipation.

There is also a surprising degree of consensus between antisemitic perceptions of the Jewish role in German culture and that of many Jewish commentators at the time and even today. The tone and object of these respective assessments has of course been quite different, not to say diametrically opposed in most cases. What Jewish apologetics affirmed as a great contribution to human civilization and a vindication of the historic Jewish presence in the Diaspora was invariably perceived by antisemites as harmful, threatening, and destructive. In his *World of Yesterday*, Stefan Zweig describes nine-tenths of the *fin-de-siècle* Viennese culture as a creation of Jews. They were both the major producers and consumers of this culture, the 'real audience' who filled the theatres and concert halls, who bought the books and pictures, 'and with their more mobile understanding, little hampered by tradition, they were the exponents and champions of all that was new'.[6] In Zweig's glowing memorial to this lost world, the emphasis is on the intense desire of the Viennese Jews for full social integration through their cultural participation. It was part of their ambition to 'serve the glory of Vienna'; through cultural creativity they transformed their being Austrian into 'a mission to the world'.

The antisemites could only view this self-proclaimed Jewish mission with fear and alarm as a kind of swamping of indigenous tradition and talent. They, too, regarded the Jews as 'champions of all that was new', as the pioneers of modernity. Only this designation had a wholly negative connotation. It meant that Jews were destroyers of tradition, rootless subverters of hierarchy, opponents of everything that embodied classical order and form in western culture: what the Nazis in their war on modernist decadence would later label as 'Kulturbolschevismus' and the Stalinists as 'rootless cosmopolitanism'.

The association of Jews with radical politics since the 1830s, especially in Germany and Austria, reinforced these conservative stereotypes. There is a consistent thread which leads from Heinrich von Treitschke's identification of Ludwig Boerne, Heinrich Heine, and Eduard Gans as 'Oriental choir-leaders of the Revolution' to Adolf Hitler's equation of Judaism and Marxist social democracy in *fin-de-siècle* Vienna. Jews in central Europe were consistently seen by the Right after 1848 as *Ruhestörer*, as conspirators threatening the *Obrigkeitsstaat*, the fighting spirit of the nation, the integrity of the Christian faith, values, and tradition. The long line of revolutionaries and socialists of Jewish origin in German-speaking central Europe (later duplicated elsewhere with similarly unfortunate results) gave a certain credence and plausibility to the image. From Marx and Lassalle to Victor Adler and Otto Bauer, from Adolf Fischof, Moses Hess, and Johann Jacoby to the revolutionaries of 1918 who paid with their lives – Kurt Eisner, Gustav Landauer, Leviné, Rosa Luxemburg, and Leo Jogiches – Jews were in the forefront of radical social change.

Even more disconcerting for the conservative Right was the influence of the Jews on the liberal press in the two central European empires. In official circles this press was regarded as oppositional, in spite of its ostentatious patriotism and defence of German cultural interests. For the reactionary Junkers in Prussia and the clerical-conservatives in Austria it was a thorn in the flesh, while for the *petit-bourgeois* antisemitic movements of the late nineteenth century it became the symbol of capitalist corruption. Newspapers like the *Berliner Tageblatt*, the *Frankfurter Zeitung* or the *Neue Freie Presse* were indeed owned, edited, and to a certain extent written by Jews. They stood for the values of economic and political liberalism which attracted the majority of German-speaking Jews in the post-emancipation era but which never really established a decisive hegemony in central Europe. Ironically enough, some of the sharpest critics of this liberal outlook (and also of the semi-absolutist institutions in the two empires) were themselves talented and influential journalists of Jewish origin like Maximilien Harden in Berlin and Karl Kraus in Vienna.

This critique from the Right was reinforced by the offensive against bourgeois liberalism undertaken by Marxist journalists on the Left, among whom Jews also played a disproportionate role. In the Weimar period, most of the contributors and readers of the left-wing intellectual *Weltbühne* were Jews. Oblivious to the irritation and resentment they aroused in the average German *Spiessbürger*, critics like Kurt Tucholsky ridiculed not only the sins of the militarists, profiteers, and bourgeois philistines, but also seemed to be dragging everything German into the mud. Not that Tucholsky was any more sparing when it came to savage caricatures of Jewish mannerisms, modes of speech, business malpractices, or social behaviour. Like Harden and Kraus before him, he claimed to be above the parochial war of antisemites and Jews. But in December 1935, a few days before his suicide, he was obliged to recognize the grim truth in a letter to Arnold Zweig: 'Ich bin im Jahre 1911 "aus dem Judentum ausgetreten", und ich weiss, dass man das gar nicht kann.'[7]

Apostate Jews from Börne and Heine to Kraus and Tucholsky were not of course representative of Jewish communities in central Europe as a whole, even if antisemites dwelt obsessively on their alleged misdeeds. The bulk of German, Austrian, and Hungarian Jews were loyal, patriotic, and hard-working citizens who rallied to the colours in 1914 with the same intense enthusiasm as their Gentile compatriots. They felt little in common with those of their co-religionists who engaged in avant-garde cultural or political activity. Indeed, as Peter Gay has demonstrated, even among the prominent Jewish intellectuals and artists in central Europe, many were far from being cultural innovators or champions of modernism. Nevertheless it has been the minority of intellectual revolutionaries whose impact remains the deepest and has most shaped our image of the role of Jews in central European culture. As George Steiner has written: 'Without Marx or Freud, without Einstein or Kafka, without Schönberg or Wittgenstein, the spirit of modernity, the reflexes and uncertainty whereby we conduct our inner lives would not be conceivable.' It was this minority of marginal Jews who completely transformed our conventional picture of the universe, of language, society, and the human mind. Their iconoclastic shattering of time-honoured traditions, complacent certitudes, and social taboos, earned them in most cases the undying hatred of the antisemites.

The 'intellectual pre-eminence' of the Jews in the nineteenth and twentieth centuries, which attained its peak in pre-Hitler central Europe, has occasioned much speculation as to its motivations and causes. Without entering into this debate a few sociological observations may be pertinent for understanding the background. The explosion of Jewish talents took place in the context of a rapid growth of population, urbanization, and socio-economic modernization in central Europe after 1870. Capital cities like Berlin (which had only been a small town at the beginning of the century) and Vienna held over 2 million inhabitants by 1914. Budapest was probably the fastest growing city in Europe during the second half of the nineteenth century. Jewish population growth, especially in eastern Europe, was even more striking and with the ending of ghetto restrictions after 1848 led to a mass migration of Jews from the provinces to the major cities of east-central Europe. In 1871 there were already 44,000 Jews in Budapest, 40,000 in Vienna, 36,000 in Berlin, 26,000 in Lvov, and 13,000 in Prague. By 1910 the figures had risen to 203,000 in Budapest (23.1 per cent of the total population), 175,000 in Vienna (8.6 per cent), 144,000 in Berlin (nearly 4 per cent), 57,000 in Lvov (27.8 per cent), and 18,000 in Prague (8.1 per cent). In cities like Czernowitz, capital of Austrian Bukovina before 1918 (and an outpost of German culture in the east), Jews constituted more than one-third of the population and the same was true of many of the towns in Galicia.

The urbanization of the Jews took place at a faster pace than that of Gentiles in the pre-1914 era and was invariably accompanied by a higher rate of literacy and a more successful maximization of educational opportunities. We have already cited the case of Budapest. A few figures for higher education in Vienna will underline the point. After 1880, approximately one-third of all *Gymnasiasten* in Vienna were Jews (three times more than their proportion in the population) – and this was the *sine qua non* for entry into the universities. Moreover, with regard to the middle-class intake of the *Gymnasia*, the Jewish proportion was probably closer to 70 per cent. The situation was similar at the University of Vienna, where at the end of the 1880s Jews represented 48 per cent of the medical student body and 22 per cent of law students. In 1900, 23.6 per cent of all university students in Vienna, 27 per cent of students in the higher technical schools, and 43 per cent of the students in commercial colleges were Jews. Against this background it is much less surprising that Jews were so prominent in the free professions, that they played such a re- markable role in high culture, or that the German universities in central Europe became hotbeds of a racial antisemitism designed to exclude Jewish competition.

The dizzying speed of Jewish acculturation was unnerving not only to their antagonists but also to many sensitive and intelligent Jews who were themselves part of the process. Let me quote once more from Hugo Bergmann's letter of 1914 to the Berlin Professor of Philosophy, Carl Stumpf, where he touches on Jewish abilities and talent:[8] 'Unfortunately these abilities have proved only in the smallest degree to be a blessing to society. These gifted Jews are pioneers of atheism and materialism, revolutionaries and demagogues .... Jews – including even women – march at the head of the agitation against marriage and the family, participating as leaders and led in all the perversities of contemporary, urban society. What is the cause of this value reversal within three generations among members of a race whose family life was pure and chaste. It is the sad consequence of the fact that the Jews have lost their psychic balance ... they have not grown organically into European

97

culture but simply appropriated its results as they existed in 1789 or 1848. Hence they have no understanding for the history of this culture and hence they undermine its foundations.'

Hugo Bergmann's harsh verdict was echoed by another Prague-born Jewish contemporary, Franz Kafka, whose bitter reproaches to his father derived at least in part from the anguished sense of having no firm Jewish ground under his feet. It was Kafka who spoke of a whole generation of Jewish writers in central Europe drawing inspiration from the despair of having 'their hind legs bogged down in their fathers' Judaism', while their front legs could find no new ground. Yet Kafka could never rid himself of the feeling that German-Jewish literature (including his own work) was somehow conducted under false pretences; that it involved a usurpation or at best the secondhand acquisition of someone else's property ('die laute oder stillschweigende oder auch selbstquälerische Anmassung eines fremden Besitzes'). Kafka even referred to German-Jewish writing as 'gypsy literature that had stolen the German child from its cradle and trained it, in a great hurry, to perform any way because someone had to dance on the tightrope'.

As if the image of the tightrope were not disconcerting enough Kafka elsewhere refers to Jewish writing in the German language as merely a temporary expedient 'as though for someone writing his last will and testament just before he hangs himself'. Evidently, the only relief which Kafka could obtain from his tormented self-disgust was through his encounter with the Yiddish-language theatre in Prague and his dream of eventually settling in Palestine. Hugo Bergmann, who realized this dream by becoming Professor of Philosophy at the Hebrew University of Jerusalem, shared (as we have already seen) something of Kafka's aversion to the self-negating implications of the Jewish contribution to German society and letters. In harmony with his Zionist convictions he remained, however, convinced that modern Hebrew and Yiddish literature was somehow free of these defects.

Zionists had of course been consistently hostile to the intense Jewish assimilation to German culture which they saw as an undignified self-surrender and wasting of precious Jewish national assets. In 1912, in a controversial article called 'German-Jewish Parnassus', published in the fortnightly *Kunstwart*, the young German Zionist Moritz Goldstein made the case for cultural separatism. He pointed out that in Berlin Jews dominated the press, the theatres, musical life – in short they were administering 'the spiritual property of a nation which denies us our right and ability to do so'.[10] This was a dangerous and untenable situation in the long run, since literature and the arts were intimately linked to a specific homeland and to a particular people and its historic traditions.

Twenty years later another German Zionist, Theodor Lessing, came to a similar conclusion, though this did not prevent his murder by the Nazis in 1933. Looking back on the era of Jewish creativity in central Europe which was coming to an end, Lessing prophetically suggested (in 1930): 'Perhaps this brilliance was only the phosphorescent shimmer of a dying body: perhaps it was only the brief flickering of a European bonfire in which our nobility immolated itself.'

Closer to our time the late Gershom Scholem, twenty years after the *Shoah*, restated the Zionist view with particular trenchancy. In his view, there never was a German-Jewish symbiosis to begin with, but only a one-sided, unrequited love affair of the Jews for German culture. There had never been a meaningful encounter but only a tragic process of self-alienation, of self-surrender and Jewish national self-negation – a long list of 'Jewish losses to the Germans, a list of frequently astonishing Jewish talents and accomplishments that were offered up to the Germans'. Scholem believed that by rushing to disavow its own heritage the German-Jewish elite had contributed to the demoralization of Jewry and exacerbated the contempt which many Germans felt for Jews and Judaism.[11] This elite had been afflicted by an extraordinary blindness concerning the reality of the antagonism which its prominence aroused. With a few exceptions, among whom Franz Kafka occupied the first place, the literature of the period covered up the real situation.

The picture so forcefully drawn by Scholem contains a good deal of truth though it needs to be qualified in a number of respects. In the first place the sense of vulnerability and precariousness felt by Jewish intellectuals in central Europe before Hitler was rather more widespread than one might believe at first sight. Even in the 'golden age of security' before 1914, most Jews had, in Schnitzler's words, the choice 'of being counted as insensitive, obtrusive and cheeky; or of being insensitive, shy and suffering from feelings of persecution'.[12] Schnitzler's prewar novel *Der Weg ins Freie* (1907) and his drama *Professor Bernhardi* (1912) are full of Jewish characters suffering from such dilemmas. Schnitzler's own bitter frustration at antisemitism is revealed in the following succinct entry in his *Tagebuch*: 'Wie schön ist es, ein Arier zu sein – man hat sein Talent so ungestört.'[13]

In Wilhelmine Germany, even so staunch an advocate of assimilation as Walter Rathenau (the ill-fated foreign minister assassinated by *völkisch* antisemites in June 1922) had to admit in 1912 that second-class citizenship for Jews was an inescapable reality. 'In the youth of every German Jew there is a moment that he remembers his whole life: when he becomes fully conscious for the first time that he has entered the world as a second-class citizen, and that no degree of ability, or merit can ever free him from this position.'[14] Rathenau's sense of the pain of social exclusion and pariahdom was typical enough, however exceptional and un-representative his own personality may have been for German Jews as a whole. This disappointment was all the crueller to the extent that

German Jews felt that they made their contribution to German culture as Germans rather than Jews.

The element of self-deception to which Scholem referred has indeed been somewhat exaggerated. In 1926 Sigmund Freud declared to an interviewer: 'My language is German. My culture, my attainments are German. I considered myself German until I noticed the growth of anti-semitic prejudices in Germany and German Austria. Since that time, I prefer to call myself a Jew.' When did Freud in fact observe the growth of these prejudices and define himself primarily as a Jew? – at least forty years earlier, according to a letter he sent from Paris in 1886 to his future wife, Martha Bernays. Other leading Jewish artists and intellectuals came to similar conclusions at least a decade before Hitler. In 1923 the great Viennese composer Arnold Schoenberg wrote to Kandinsky:

> What I was forced to learn during the past year, I have now at last understood and shall never forget it again. Namely, that I am no German, no European, maybe not even a human being [*ein Mensch*] – at any rate the Europeans prefer the worst of their own race to me – but that I am a Jew. I am satisfied with this state of affairs. Today I do not wish to be treated as an exception.[15]

This was the beginning of Schoenberg's remarkable turning back (*tschouva*) to the Biblical sources of Judaism and Jewish identity.

This return to Judaism had always existed as an option since the beginning of the emancipation though it did not affect a significant group of acculturated Jewish intellectuals until the turn of the twentieth century. Under the influence of intellectual giants like Hermann Cohen, Leo Baeck, and Martin Buber there was a growing trend to demonstrate the contemporary and universal significance of Judaism as a counter-weight to the exclusivist claims of Protestant German theology. A younger generation of alienated Jews began to discover the truth of Leo Baeck's dictum that 'the path to our humanity leads through our Jewishness not away from it'. Through Martin Buber's *Die Geschichte des Rabbi Nachman* and *Die Legende des Baal Schem*, they rediscovered Judaism as an authentic spiritual sensibility rather than as merely a formal religion (*Konfession*) and set of ritual practices.

Through his mastery of the German language and culture, the Viennese-born Buber (who had grown up in Polish Galicia) was also able to mediate between east and west; to demonstrate that Polish Jewry might seem primitive and unsophisticated but was in reality a highly creative spiritual community. Buber helped transform the image of the *Ostjuden* from ignorant and superstitious creatures sorely in need of German *Bildung* and *Kultur* to that of a vibrant *Gemeinschaft* which heralded a new Jewish rebirth. Not only *maskilic* but even traditional German Zionist stereotypes were undermined as the *Ostjuden* became the model for authentic Jewish community, peoplehood, spirituality, and rootedness. This revolution in consciousness which Buber effected among a sector of German and east European Jewish youth before the First World War (one thinks of his influence on Polish Zionist youth in Galicia, on the *Hashomer* in Vienna, and the Bar Kochba circle in Prague) was inconceivable without the mediation of German neo-Romantic thought. Buber had after all reinterpreted Hassidism in terms of the *Erlebnismystik* of his own society and culture. Through his preoccupation with myth and *Volksgeist*, Buber was able to recover the sources of Jewish creativity and a new sense of the redemptive quality of divine revelation in the Bible.

The *démarche* pursued by Buber, Rozenzweig, and Baeck was both complementary and in some ways antithetical to that undertaken by those 'non-Jewish Jews' who became masters of modern culture. From Marx and Freud to Einstein and Schoenberg, the Jewish 'meta-rabbis' (George Steiner's catchy phrase) had a unique commitment to the life of the word, to analytic totality, to the search for laws underlying all phenomena, and to a prophetic mode of ethical activism. But they remained outsiders and exiles twice over, a kind of diaspora within the Diaspora, working outside the framework of normative Judaism. Their roots ultimately lay in the rationalist spirit of the Mendelssohnian Enlightenment and the spirit of German *Aufklärung*. They might well have agreed with the novelist Joseph Roth who wrote to Stefan Zweig on the eve of the Nazi catastrophe (22 March 1933): 'One cannot disown the 6000-year-old Jewish heritage, but equally one cannot deny the 2000-year-old non-Jewish inheritance. We stem from the "Emancipation", from Humanity, from the humane rather than from Egypt. Our ancestors are Goethe, Lessing, Herder no less than Abraham, Isaac and Jacob.'[16]

8

Walter Benjamin: a borderline tragedy

Walter Benjamin, perhaps the greatest literary critic of his age, described himself in 1931 'like one who keeps afloat on a shipwreck by climbing to the top of a mast that is already crumbling'. Nine years later, this highly idiosyncratic rebel – in the words of Hannah Arendt, perhaps the most peculiar Marxist ever produced by a movement which had more than its share of oddities – had committed suicide at the age of 48 on the Franco-Spanish border while fleeing the Nazis. Known only to a small circle of *cognoscenti* during his lifetime, the writings of the shy, introverted Benjamin, one of the last representatives of a dying species (that of the European cosmopolitan *homme de lettres*), were eventually rediscovered in the 1960s and given an honoured place in the pantheon of western Marxism. Benjamin's commitment to this ideology was however highly ambiguous (as with everything else in his secretive, enigmatic personality) and politically half-hearted, to say the least, so that his belated rehabilitation by the New Left may have obscured as much as it has revealed.

It is one of the great services of Gershom Scholem's fascinating and subtle memoir, based on a relationship extending almost twenty-five years, that it reconstitutes little-known biographical details concerning his friend's life and the intellectual comradeship between the two scholars which help to correct the rather one-sided, conventional image of Walter Benjamin. Furthermore, over and above the authentic, personal portrait of Benjamin and his intellectual milieu (names like Adorno, Horkheimer, Fritz Sternberg, Brecht, Ernst Bloch, Siegfried Kracauer, Hofmannsthal, Buber, and Magnes constantly recur in these pages) the book offers a valuable, possibly unique insight into the mind of the late Gershom Scholem himself – surely, one of the most remarkable and innovative Jewish scholars of the twentieth century.

The two young men first met in Berlin in 1915 and their experiences with the German military (they both opposed the war from a radical anarchist standpoint) intensified the friendship. In Scholem's words, what united them from the beginning was 'a resoluteness in pursuing our intellectual goals, rejection of our environment – which was basically the German-Jewish assimilated middle class – and a positive attitude toward metaphysics'. Scholem continued to see in Benjamin 'essentially a metaphysician, pure and simple, attracted by subjects which had little or no bearing on metaphysics' – such as dreams, hallucinations, clair-voyance, myths, graphology – and a scholar driven by a genuine theological search for 'absolute experience'. Benjamin's devotion to the spiritual, the central importance to him of the *religious* sphere (at least until 1927), and his belief in the transcausal connection of things and their rootedness in God, emerge clearly from Scholem's account.

Although Benjamin knew nothing of Jewish history, politics, or (except for Agnon and Bialik) of Hebrew or Yiddish literature, the theology and ethics of Judaism, along with religion, philosophy, and language, was a central theme in his conversations with Scholem and in their essay-like letters. Precisely because Benjamin's thought revolved around 'theological' categories such as truth and revelation, problems of language ('the world essence . . . from which speech arises') and transla-tion, as well as a deep-seated predisposition towards criticism and commentary, the world of Judaism retained a secret though ambivalent fascination for him. As his most important disciple, Theodor Adorno, once pointed out, Benjamin's philosophical essayism consisted 'in treating profane texts as if they were sacred'. Scholem, who to the end re-presented 'Judaism in living form' for Benjamin and served as his mentor in the area of *Kabbalah* and its teachings on language, tried to encourage these metaphysical interests in a Jewish direction.

After Scholem's own emigration to Palestine in 1923 this proved more difficult, though Benjamin continued to keep the 'Zionist' option open for himself and to promise his friend that he would shortly begin an intensive study of Hebrew. To a large extent Benjamin shared Scholem's conviction that German-Jewish involvement in politics and literature was built on a sham, and he evidently recognized in Zionism a legitimate revolt against the mendacity and self-deception of assimilated Jewish bourgeois life. His own wife Dora (the daughter of Herzl's biographer, Professor Leon Kellner) came from a Zionist milieu and it is striking that, in his correspondence with Scholem, Benjamin apparently considered emigration to Palestine even after becoming a Marxist of sorts. On the other hand, while not swayed by communist political hostility to Zionism, Benjamin was impressed by such vulgar Marxist reductionist analyses of the 'Jewish question' as Otto Heller's *Untergang des Juden-tums* (1931) and Max Horkheimer's *Die Juden und Europa* (1939) – demolished with withering scorn by Scholem in their correspondence.

Benjamin himself attributed his constant postponement of emigration plans to Palestine to the 'pathological vacillation' in his character and the pressure of other projects. In reality, this indecision may well have stemmed from a bitter realization that for him there was no personal salvation and that there were no ideological solutions for his meta-physical estrangement and radical questioning of all traditions. Once the hope of an academic career miscarried (in 1925 Professors at the University of Frankfurt had returned his *habilitation* thesis 'The origins of German tragedy' as utterly incomprehensible) Benjamin was forced to wage a seemingly endless struggle to keep himself afloat financially. On bad terms with his parents, never at home in Germany where his ideas were too unconventional to find a place in the academic hierarchy, unprepared to 'work for a living', and still vacillating between Zionism and Marxism, he could not – unlike Scholem – leap into the as yet disreputable world of *Kabbalah* and Jewish mysticism and thereby resolve his existential dilemmas.

With the breakup of his marriage and the dialectic disintegration of his metaphysical world view after 1927, the innate wanderlust, inner unrest, depressive traits, and dissatisfaction with his conditions of life caught up with Benjamin. The literary communication with Scholem which had ripened under the pressure of physical separation and political crises, though it had never been free of tensions and misunderstandings, assumed a grimmer edge in the 1930s. Between 1927 and 1938 the two friends met only twice, on both occasions in Paris, which became Benjamin's home throughout the seven years of emigration, following Hitler's rise to power. Despite Scholem's loyalty to his friend and the feel-ing of personal trust that vibrates in the letters, it was already clear that they were moving in opposed directions. Under the influence of his new friendship with Bertolt Brecht, Benjamin was drawing closer to a fitful kind of Marxism and away from Jewish concerns. Scholem, who disliked Brecht's communist politics and theoretical crudity, consistently warned his friend against the dangers to his thinking involved in trying to reconcile his mystical philosophy of language with Marxist historical materialism.

In the correspondence from the spring of 1931, enclosed in the appendix to his book, Scholem shrewdly exposes the self-deception behind much of Benjamin's Marxist theorizing, the 'astonishing incom-patibility' between his '*real* and *pretended* modes of thought'. Never one to mince words, Scholem clearly regarded Brecht's influence as disast-rous, though he continued to admire and appreciate Benjamin's un-doubted originality as a theorist and a literary critic. The latter, however, defended his use of Marxism as a heuristic-methodological stimulus while remaining largely indifferent to questions of doctrine and carefully avoiding identification with Moscow or the German Communist Party.

None the less, even Benjamin's association in the 1930s with the independent, Marxist-oriented Institute for Social Research under Max Horkheimer, on whom he depended financially for his existence in Paris, was fraught with ambiguity and tension. With the exception of Adorno, the institute had no use for Benjamin's 'undialectical' mode of thinking, his tendency to mysticism (this and his so-called 'Judaisms' also got on Brecht's nerves), and his equivocacy about progress and modern industrial civilization. Even in his 'Marxist' phase, Benjamin remained *sui generis*, an original or *inclassable*, whose essayistic work on the borderlines of philology, theology, literary criticism, history, and philosophy was too daring to be easily understood or accepted. His literary affinities remained with Goethe, Kafka, Proust, Baudelaire, and the French surrealists, his personal obsessions were with memory, the nature of allegory, and the loss of experience – themes which appeared too remote at the time from the Marxist dialectic of history. Benjamin's 'wide-eyed presentation of actuality', his literary experimentalism and concern with capturing the portrait of history through the most insignificant and fragmentary representations of reality, reflected a *poetical* mode of thought only superficially resembling the 'critical theory' of Horkheimer and the Frankfurt School.

Scholem's account documents this inner tension between metaphysics and materialism and throws a new light on the personal factors which shaped Benjamin's intellectual development. With the rise of the fascist flood in the 1930s external pressures, too, played their role in deepening the sense of isolation and despair that afflicted a whole generation of Jewish (and non-Jewish) intellectuals. Even the young Scholem, in Mandatory Palestine, was by no means immune to this mood of disillusionment, writing to Benjamin in August 1931 that 'we were victorious too early' and that this victory in the visible realm was 'the real demonism of Zionism'. In the middle of some penetrating reflections on Kafka, it is instructive to read Scholem's own agonized reappraisal of so-called 'political solutions' to the Jewish question.

> Between London and Moscow we strayed into the desert of Araby on our way to Zion, and our own hubris blocked the path that leads to our people. Thus all we have left is the productivity of one who is going down and knows it. It is this productivity in which I have buried myself for years, for, after all, where should the miracle of immortality be concealed if not here?

Following the Arab revolt of 1936 and Scholem's renewed outburst of pessimism, Benjamin – himself shocked by the growth of French antisemitism – wrote back that 'a cosmopolis like Paris has become a very fragile thing, and if what I hear about Palestine is true, a wind blows there in which even Jerusalem may start swaying like a reed'. As is clear from this letter of February 1937, Benjamin had still not completely abandoned thoughts of emigration to Palestine. Warning signs like Céline's hysterically antisemitic *Bagatelles pour un massacre* were troubling but could not shake his love of Paris. However, the shock of the Hitler-Stalin pact in 1939 struck deeper and may have contributed to reawakening Benjamin's latent suicidal inclinations. A bitter, veiled allusion (in a letter to Scholem of 11 January 1940) to the 'activities of the *Zeitgeist* that have provided the desert landscape of these days with markings unmistakable for old Bedouins like us', suggests something approaching terminal despair. Unable to swim with or against the tide in a shipwrecked Europe, and trapped by the historical-political nightmare of encroaching Nazism and his own interminable bad luck, Benjamin put an end to his own life in September 1940. As Scholem puts it in a brief but moving final chapter on Benjamin's years in emigration, his suicide 'was not a surprising irrational act but something he had prepared inwardly'.

9

The strange case of Bruno Kreisky

The role of Jewish intellectuals in the labour movements of central and eastern Europe during the past century is a well-attested fact. It led many antisemites between the wars to identify both communism and social democracy as creations of the 'subversive Jewish spirit'. Outside Tsarist Russia, the former Habsburg empire and especially German Austria provided the most striking example of a predominantly 'Jewish' leadership of a working-class movement. This is all the more remarkable since traditionalist and Catholic Austria was at the same time a classic land of antisemitism. The 'socialism of fools', as it was often derisively labelled by liberals and Marxists, could not fail to be directed against those Jews who had assumed the leadership of the Austrian labour movement since its foundation in 1889. Not surprisingly, the founder and father-figure of Austrian socialism, Victor Adler, a convert to Protestantism (at the age of 26) suffered acutely from a 'Jewish complex' and the numerous aspersions on his ancestry made by political rivals. Yet this did not prevent Adler from transmitting the typically Jewish bourgeois-humanist values of his adolescent years to the Austrian workers' movement; nor was his ethnic background an obstacle to Adler becoming as much of a revered patriarch in the eyes of the Viennese proletariat as his emperor, Franz Joseph, became for the German and Jewish bourgeoisie of the Habsburg state.

Adler's attitude to antisemitism was a mixture of cynicism, resignation, Marxist dialectic, and wry humour. Essentially he was convinced that antisemitism in Austria was endemic as long as capitalism survived and the Jews maintained their specific, particularist identity. His socialist humanism had been tempered early on by a deep psychological insight into the frailties of human nature (Adler's training had been in medicine) and mass irrationality for which there was no automatic cure. The chaos of Austro-Hungarian public life, the intensity of its nationality conflicts, the omnipresent nature of antisemitism, and the fragility of the imperial state structure no doubt explain Adler's acute sense of the psychopathology of politics. For a Jew and a Marxist, living in Habsburg Vienna was not an ideal training ground for strengthening belief in the essential goodness and innocence of mankind.

Like many educated, middle-class Jews of his generation who were deeply attached to German language and culture, Adler was however a convinced assimilationist. This led him to engage in some curious contortions in order to avoid the accusation of rival parties that the social democrats defended 'Jewish' interests. Adler took great pains to distance himself from the Jewish capitalist bourgeoisie (which was rather influential in the empire) and also from the emerging Jewish national movement. Antipathy to Rothschild and the *Geldjuden*, along with contempt for Herzl and the Zionists, had become established traditions of the Austrian social democracy in the pre-1918 era. Ironically, these attitudes were inculcated by a 'Jewish' leadership (by birth rather than conviction) determined to demonstrate how little in common it had with the *Neue Freie Presse* or with the immigrants from the Galician *shtetls*. As Adler summed it up in 1913, in reply to a query by the Belgian socialist, Camille Huysmans, as to what he felt about antisemitism: 'One must have Jews, Comrade, but not too many!'

Victor Adler's successor as leader of the Austrian socialists in the interwar period was the brilliant theoretician Otto Bauer, also a middle-class Jewish intellectual who shared his uneasiness in dealing with a seemingly intractable problem. Like his predecessor, Otto Bauer was convinced that assimilation was a historical necessity for the Jews and invented an ingenious Marxist theory to justify his conclusions. As a non-territorial minority, the Jews would be unable to survive the process of integration brought about by capitalist modernization in eastern Europe where the majority of the Jewish 'nation' was still concentrated. Like most Marxists, Bauer believed that there was no future for Jews as a corporate body within a modern, progressive society. Their traditions were outmoded, their religion obscurantist, and their social psychology corrupt and money-centred. Zionism would simply reinforce their 'ghetto' identity. As a movement against assimilation it had to be vigorously resisted in the name of the class struggle and its historic imperatives.

The future of Austrian socialism, Bauer believed, depended on its joining hands with a 'Red' Germany dominated by the powerful social-democratic labour movement. This was the socialist dream of *Anschluss* which Bauer vainly tried to apply as Foreign Minister of Austria, some seventy years after the failed bourgeois revolution of 1848 in central Europe. Throughout the interwar period Otto Bauer was haunted by the idea that the small Austrian republic (the 'dwarf' state as he called it) could not survive unless it was joined to Germany. Thus this Jewish intellectual bequeathed to the labour movement the aborted dream of a 'greater German' revolution uniting the German and Austrian working classes. The collapse of the Austrian republic in 1934, the crushing of the social democratic rising, and the Nazi *Anschluss* four years later, turned this dream into a nightmare: a terrible period of expulsion, deportation, and mass murder began for the Jews of Austria. Vienna, one of the great cultural centres of European Jewry (with over 200,000 Jews in the 1920s) had become virtually *judenrein* by 1945. On the face of it there could no longer be a 'Jewish question' in postwar Austria, nor could the socialist party again be branded as a *Judenschutztruppe*.

Against this background the career of Bruno Kreisky, Austrian Federal Chancellor between 1970 and 1983, appears all the more remarkable. Born in 1911, into the German Jewish *Grossbürgertum* of the Sudetenland, Kreisky grew up to be a militant socialist in the 1930s at a time when such activities were already illegal. Forced to flee to Sweden, where he spent the war years (most of his relatives perished in the Holocaust), he returned to Austria after the Second World War to embark on a spectacular diplomatic career. State Secretary for Foreign Affairs and then in charge of the Foreign Ministry from 1959 to 1966, Kreisky was more pragmatic and less committed to Marxism than forerunners like Otto Bauer. Like his friend and contemporary, Willy Brandt, leader of the SPD and then Federal German Chancellor, Kreisky was intent on transforming the old proletarian class-conscious party he had joined into a modernized, streamlined, progressive *Volkspartei*. This was admittedly an easier task in the neutral, postwar Austria with its consensus politics and relative stability than it had been in the harsh interwar years of class confrontation, economic depression, and the fascist menace.

A revealing symptom of how much conditions had changed was the fact that Kreisky was elected to the chairmanship of the socialist party in 1967 thanks to support from the provinces. His image was that of a pragmatic reformer who could unite radicals and moderates, a technician leading the socialists out of their ideological 'ghetto' and helping to make the party *salonfähig* even among the rural Catholic electorate. The fact that this task had devolved upon an ex-diplomat and intellectual son of a cultured Jewish bank director, in a land that traditionally identified 'Reds' with Jews and Vienna as Babylon, certainly suggested some changes had taken place. Moreover, it must be admitted that in this respect Kreisky fulfilled all expectations and indeed surpassed them to an amazing degree. Not only did the socialists become the dominant party in Austria under his leadership, representing stability as much as change, but Kreisky himself came to assume the allures of a Habsburg father-figure – a Jewish intellectual reincarnation of Kaiser Franz Joseph. Only this time he was not merely emperor of the workers (like Victor Adler before him) but king over *all* the Austrians.

This was not an easy feat in a land where registered ex-Nazis numbered more than 500,000 in a population of only 7 million, immediately after the Holocaust. The shadows of the Nazi past were longer in Austria than elsewhere – as the Waldheim affair has dramatically reminded the world in recent years. In the birthplace of such Nazi luminaries as Adolf Hitler, Eichmann, Kaltenbrunner, Seyss-Inquart, Globocnik, and many other executioners of the 'Final Solution', both racism and antisemitism had roots which were not so quickly eradicated. Nor can it be said that the Austrian socialist party did much in the way of 'overcoming the past' in the postwar years when neo-Nazism was a sensitive electoral issue, best avoided by those concerned mainly with political arithmetic.

Kreisky was by no means immune to antisemitic attacks on his leadership in the late 1960s before he had established himself fully as an Austrian statesman. Naturally he had no sympathies with Nazism or fascism, but his response to aspersions on his ancestry was in the best assimilationist traditions of a movement that had once been led by Adler and Bauer. He tended to avoid any mention of the specifically 'Jewish' victims of Nazism, to emphasize the *Deutschtum* of his family background and his remoteness from the official Jewish community.

Even more surprising for a socialist who had lost twenty-one members of his family in the Holocaust, he included in his first Cabinet a number of ex-Nazis whom he personally defended when their past was exposed. Thus in May 1970 his Minister of Agriculture, Dr Hans Öllinger, was found to have been a former SS lieutenant. Though Öllinger resigned, Kreisky's reaction was that everyone had the right to make a political mistake in his youth. He declared that he would not hesitate to reappoint Öllinger if necessary. The Minister of the Interior, Otto Rosch (who had been acquitted in 1947 on insufficient evidence for past Nazi activities), was similarly defended. Kreisky also appointed another former member of the Nazi Party as a Minister in his socialist Cabinet, which was seen in some quarters as further proof that he intended to be Chancellor of all the Austrians. A neo-Nazi paper concluded that Kreisky's principle obviously was *Wer ein Nazi ist, bestimmt die SPOE!* – an allusion to Lueger's cynical dictum – *Wer ein Jud ist, das bestimme ich.*

Kreisky's soft line on ex-Nazis was immensely popular in an Austria intent on forgetting the past. Such amnesia was also electorally profitable with large numbers of the older generation. The mild, relatively inoffensive and *gemütlich* antisemitism of pre-Waldheim Austria could not only tolerate but even welcome the fact that its Jewish-born Chancellor presided over this process of national reconciliation. Kreisky, whether he was aware of it or not, provided a perfect alibi for forgetting past unpleasantness and concentrating on the achievements of the present. Economic stability, social partnership, international prestige, and technological progress were not the least of the benefits which Austria could show during the Kreisky years.

There is no doubt that Kreisky regarded the Middle East as an area of special significance where he could display his diplomatic talents to the full and serve at the same time what he considered to be Austria's national interests. Whatever the actual merits of his Middle Eastern policy, it also unavoidably had the effect of raising a sensitive issue – his attitude to Jews and Judaism. For the state of Israel as a Jewish and a Zionist state could not be divorced from fundamental ideological issues which challenged the bases of Kreisky's own assimilationist beliefs and the nature of his Jewish identity. At the time of the Camp David talks between President Carter, Menahem Begin, and President Anwar el-Sadat, some of these assumptions came out (not for the first time) in an extraordinarily vitriolic form. During an interview at his holiday home in Majorca (published in the *Jerusalem Post*, 3 September 1978), the Austrian Chancellor referred to Israel's Prime Minister Menahem Begin as a 'political grocer', a 'little Polish lawyer from Warsaw, or whatever he was'. This rather undiplomatic language was then followed by a short tirade against the *Ostjuden* ('they are so alienated, they think in such a warped way') and against the Israelis: 'They do not grasp the subtlety in politics. They make themselves unpopular. The most hated diplomats are the Israelis . . . . They are as bad as the Africans who are also intolerable people'.

One could sympathize with Kreisky's detestation of a growing fascist mentality in Israel while at the same time being taken aback that he should himself echo some of the cruder prejudices of the Viennese back alleys. Abuse of the *Ostjuden* – a time-honoured Austrian and Viennese pastime – seemed curiously out of date in the late 1970s. Predictably it brought charges that the Austrian Chancellor must be a vintage Jewish self-hater. The Israeli satirist, Ephraim Kishon, put it rather cruelly – 'he's a got a hump and therefore proceeds to hate all hunchbacks'.

For those who disliked Kreisky it was of course tempting to dismiss his critique of Israel as a 'police state' as the neurotic fantasy of a renegade Jew striving to become the golden *goy*. Moreover, as the Chancellor of a nation which only thirty-five years earlier had been willing accomplices in implementing Hitler's murderous antisemitism, Kreisky's charges sounded a little suspect. Nevertheless, one has to recognize the complexity of Kreisky's sentiments and motives if one is to understand the nature of his attitudes towards Israel.

As a socialist, Kreisky was undoubtedly aware of the many great pioneering achievements carried out in Israel and the decisive role of the labour movement in the creation and consolidation of the Jewish state. There is no doubt that he sincerely admired this Israeli model of democratic socialism even though he reproached his colleagues in the Israeli labour party for their insensitivity to the Palestinian issue. Furthermore, there was no question of his disputing Israel's right to exist, in spite of his visceral opposition to Zionist ideology.

Kreisky did however pride himself, with some reason, on the extent of his connections with Arab leaders, including such troublemakers in the international community as Colonel Qaddafi and Yasser Arafat. The rehabilitation of Arafat was conceived by Kreisky as a central aim of his policy, and he was probably the first European statesman of stature to go down this road. Clearly the close relationship which he developed with the PLO leadership did not derive from any sympathy for terrorism. Nor could Kreisky have been unaware of the lack of *socialist* content in the PLO programme. Yet this did not deter him at every opportunity from encouraging and assisting in the international recognition of Mr Arafat.

No doubt this was a shrewd move in terms of Austrian economic and political interests in maintaining close relations with the Arab states as markets for manufactured goods and as oil suppliers. The intimacy which resulted from publicly declared identification with the Palestinian cause opened up many channels for strengthening Austria's economic position in the wake of the energy crisis of 1973. No doubt, too, it provided Kreisky with a welcome opportunity to strut on the international stage as a mediator who enjoyed the trust of both Arabs and at least some Israelis. However, Kreisky's pronouncements on the Middle East soon revealed an emotionally anti-Israeli animus that could not be explained solely by objective political judgements or Austrian *Realpolitik*. This was particularly evident in his insistence on denigrating Zionism and ignoring Jewish victims and Jewish suffering. When Kreisky did choose to recall the Holocaust, it was invariably used as a stick to beat the Israelis.

Nothing illustrated this more clearly than the Wiesenthal affair, which revealed what can only be described as the neurotic features in Kreisky's 'Jewish complex'. His clash with Simon Wiesenthal was, on the face of it, purely an internal Austrian affair and one which concerned attitudes to the Nazi past rather than the contemporary problems of the Middle East. But Kreisky's handling of the affair managed to transform it into an international scandal and demonstrates more clearly than anything else his underlying attitudes to the 'Jewish question'. It is here that one finds a classic illustration of the uncontrolled nature of his emotional animus against *Ostjuden*, the philosophy of Zionism, and the Jewish state.

Simon Wiesenthal first emerged into the public limelight as a result of the Eichmann trial in 1960 in the role which he played in tracking down the bureaucratic executor of Hitler's 'Final Solution' in Europe. The ensuing publicity gave him the impetus to establish a new documentation centre in Vienna in November 1961. (He had previously founded a smaller centre in Linz to investigate war crimes but this had to close down in 1954 because of general public apathy and lack of support from the authorities.)

From his private top-floor flat in a shabby apartment building in one of Vienna's garment districts, Wiesenthal carried on a meticulous, patient search for wanted Nazi criminals, aided only by a few volunteers, and by tip-offs from sympathizers and information in different parts of the world. He succeeded in bringing to justice such notorious mass-murderers as the Austrian Franz Stangl (Commandant of Treblinka), Erich Rajakovitch (Eichmann's aide), and the Vilna hangman, Franz Maurer. Gradually the mass media built up their own legend around this lonely figure, who was depicted as a kind of cross between an Old Testament prophet and a self-appointed avenger.

The truth was, however, simpler than the legend. Wiesenthal was a survivor of the Holocaust, a Galician Jew who had been shunted around by the Germans from one concentration camp to the next until he was eventually liberated by the Americans from Mauthausen in 1945. Like Kreisky he had lost all his relatives in the Holocaust; but his reaction to this tragedy was very different. As he told the *Sunday Times* (20 October 1974):

> I do what I do as a symbol for the future. When history looks back on this period I want people to know that the Nazis were not able to kill millions of people and get away with it. My Documentation Centre is the last organisation in the world still hunting Nazis. If I stopped now, the Nazis would say: 'The Jews are giving up . . . '

Wiesenthal's activities aroused little enthusiasm among most Austrians. Traditionally one of the most antisemitic countries in Europe, imperial Austria had cradled Karl Lueger's 'Christian-socialist' movement and Georg von Schoenerer's 'Pan-Germanism', two ideologies whose endemic Judeophobia had inspired Adolf Hitler during his early years in Vienna before 1914. During the First Republic the 'Jewish question' had been politically exploited with a cynicism that made Hitler's rapturous welcome in Vienna in 1938 only too understandable. But by the time that the Third Reich collapsed, emigration and Nazi mass-murder had liquidated most of Vienna's 200,000 Jews, who had once not only provided the leaders but also voted *en masse* for the prewar Austrian socialist party. When Kreisky returned to Austria from Sweden in 1950, it was no longer the Jews but the ex-Nazis who posed a delicate political problem.

Both the conservatives and the socialists now found themselves competing with the small Freedom Party (FPOE) for the electoral support of these ex-Nazis who virtually held the narrow balance between the leading political parties. Largely for this reason, there was a tendency, even within the SPOE (Austrian socialist party) to play down the magnitude of the crimes committed against the Jews on Austrian soil. Rather than seeking to 'master the past' (*Bewältigung der Vergangenheit*, as the Germans call it), expediency was rationalized by references to the need to heal old wounds and make a fresh start. No political party in Austria was ready to risk unpopularity by alienating former supporters of Hitler or more specifically by upholding Jewish claims to compensation.

In this climate of opinion, Simon Wiesenthal's fight to bring the mass-murderers to justice could count on little government or public support.

Yet Wiesenthal did not come into open conflict with the Austrian government until the elections of 1970 brought the socialists to power with a narrow parliamentary majority. As a result of his revelations it was discovered that a number of socialist ministers in Kreisky's Cabinet had a Nazi background. Wiesenthal's disclosures led him onto a direct collision course with Kreisky and the ruling socialist party. At its conference in June 1970 the SPOE issued a clear warning through its general secretary, Leopold Gratz (then Minister of Education). 'Es wird sich bald zeigen, ob dieser Staat die private Fehme-Organisation des Ing. Wiesenthal noch braucht [We shall soon see whether our society still needs Wiesenthal's personal "Star Chamber" courts].' Gratz, at the time widely regarded as Kreisky's protégé, had served warning that the socialist government was looking for a pretext to close down Wiesenthal's 'private police and informers' organisation'. Kreisky and his colleagues in the government clearly regarded Wiesenthal's investigation of former Nazis as a festering sore from a bygone age.

They found unexpected allies in the communist bloc, especially in Poland where a campaign was started, alleging that Wiesenthal had himself been a Nazi 'collaborator'. The Poles, incensed by his exposure of the role played by ex-fascists in the entourage of General Moczar and antisemites high up in the communist party apparatus, were out for Wiesenthal's blood. In the aftermath of the so-called 'anti-Zionist' crusade in Poland they had little compunction about fabricating evidence against Wiesenthal. In this they were joined by *Komsomolskaya Pravda*, the Soviet communist youth newspaper, which alleged that the Vienna documentation centre was backed by the Israeli secret service, the CIA, and British Intelligence. Both the Russians and Poles accused Wiesenthal of manufacturing false propaganda concerning antisemitism in communist countries.

In Austria itself, the anti-Wiesenthal campaign was openly encouraged by Chancellor Kreisky. In an interview with the Dutch socialist news-paper, *Vrij Nederland*, he described the Nazi hunter as a 'Jewish fascist' – 'happily, one finds reactionaries also amongst Jews, as well as thieves, murderers and prostitutes', the Austrian Chancellor was quoted as saying. Wiesenthal responded by calling Kreisky a 'renegade' and pointing out that Austria was the only country in Europe, twenty-five years after the war, which still had former Nazis in its government and which protected war criminals from prosecution. In the changing climate of public opinion – a decade before Waldheim – it appeared as if former Nazi party members were guiltless but those who investigated their past could be slandered with impunity!

It was, however, apparent that Wiesenthal was waging an unequal struggle in a country where war criminals were either acquitted or handed derisory sentences, where ex-Nazis still had electoral leverage but the Jewish community had no influence at all. Confronted with the massive indifference if not open hostility of the population at large, Wiesenthal's persistence appeared increasingly quixotic.

Matters finally came to a head following the spectacular socialist victory at the polls in October 1975. The election results were a personal triumph for 'Kaiser Bruno' who, after twenty-five years of active participation in Austrian public life, appeared to stand at the pinnacle of his career. He was the man who had led the SPOE out of the working-class 'ghetto' in the 1960s to the greatest electoral victory in its history. Before the elections most pundits had assumed that Kreisky would only be able to form a new government through a coalition with the small Freedom Party led by Friedrich Peter. For the latter, this would have meant the end of twenty-six years in the political wilderness. Under Peter's leadership, the FPOE (which had once been a haven for ex-Nazis) had swung away from right-wing extremism towards a more liberal posture. Kreisky had let it be known that he would have no objections to an alliance with Herr Peter, should the socialists fail to win an absolute majority.

However, just before election day, Wiesenthal revealed that Peter had been involved in war crimes against the Jews in Nazi-occupied Russian territory during the Second World War. He claimed that the First SS Infantry Brigade, in which Herr Peter had been a tank commander, was responsible for the murder of 10,513 innocent men, women, and children, most of them Jews. Peter admitted he had indeed been a member of this Waffen-SS unit but denied personal involvement in any shootings or 'illegal acts'. Once the election results became known and it was clear that Kreisky had no further need of his coalition with Herr Peter's party, the matter might have been allowed to rest. But the Federal Chancellor chose to interpret Wiesenthal's disclosures as an organized campaign 'to bring me down'. He asserted that Wiesenthal had promised a 'small circle of people' to do this, because they thought that he (Kreisky) had not fulfilled his task 'in the service of Israel'. Speaking to newspapermen, he branded this 'ideology' about his indifference to Israel as a form of 'mysterious racism' and a 'posthumous assumption of Nazi ideas in reverse'. In a slashing attack on Wiesenthal which led the latter to institute libel proceedings, Kreisky accused him of using 'political Mafia' methods. In the event of a trial, the Federal Chancellor declared himself ready to request the lifting of his parliamentary immunity, so that he could substantiate his charges in court.

Not only the Austrian press was surprised at the vehemence of this reaction. For the next two months the world was to learn that Kreisky was unexpectedly self-conscious about his Jewish origins and anxious to affirm his 'Austrianism'. He had always made it clear that he regarded harping on his background by outsiders, especially Israelis, as an impertinent, if not malicious attempt to undermine his political position. At the same time he now felt free to give vent to his antipathy towards Zionism in a manner unprecedented among postwar Austrian politicians. This hostility was not altogether new, for shortly before the October 1973 Middle East war, Kreisky had angered Israelis by closing the transit camp for Soviet Jews at Schoenau Castle and coldly ignored the appeals of an anguished Golda Meir to reconsider his decision. Nevertheless his action had widespread support among Austrians, who did not wish to see their country become an Arab-Israeli battleground. Moreover, he had not closed Austria altogether to Russian-Jewish emigrants, a fact which was not lost on the Israeli government.

But the Wiesenthal affair had clearly activated his dislike of what he took to be 'Zionist' interference in Austria's internal affairs. He now claimed that in every nationalism, but especially Zionism, there was an element of racism and intolerance. He advanced his classic assimilationist belief that 'there is no Jewish nation, only a Jewish religious community [*Religionsgemeinschaft*] or a community of faith'. Kreisky even declared that the concept of a Jewish people was 'unscientific', a standpoint which delighted the PLO and led the Israeli Foreign Ministry to ask for a clarification which he promptly characterized as 'impudent arrogance'. To those among his critics who accused him of self-hatred he responded by saying that 'the fact of being a Jew is for me without meaning' and angrily denied that he was a 'Jewish anti-Semite like Marx'. Kreisky's argument – that he did not belong to the Jewish community since he could not betray something to which he was not attached – had a certain logic. Yet in his anxiety to be more Austrian than the Austrians, 'to prove his total separation from everything Jewish', he tended to undermine his own case. Press comment in both Germany and Austria did not fail to point up the malaise concealed behind Kreisky's pronouncement on the Wiesenthal affair.

Der Spiegel (17 November 1975) quoted extracts from an interview with the Chancellor by the Israeli journalist Zeev Barth which reinforced the suspicion. Kreisky was quoted as saying that Wiesenthal came 'from a quite different milieu' (the *Ostjuden* again!) and that he had harmed the good name of Austria. 'Der Mann muss verschwinden' was his unequivocal verdict. Questioned as to what he meant by 'Mafia methods', the Chancellor thundered that he would not tolerate any cross-examination before the Israeli or Jewish public and that he had been subjected to 'unheard-of impudence'. Kreisky's parting salvo (apparently intended as a witticism) made headlines round the world: 'Wenn die Juden ein Volk sind, so ist es ein mieses Volk' (If the Jews are a people, then they are a wretched people). Significantly in a letter to *Der Spiegel* a week later Kreisky qualified this remark as follows: 'Ein Volk, das keines ist, kann also auch kein mieses sein' (A people that does not exist cannot be wretched).

At the same time he escalated his attacks on Wiesenthal, claiming that he had evidence to show that the latter had indeed collaborated with the Gestapo during the war. This wild insinuation did not prevent him from continuing to defend Herr Peter's *proven* Nazi past. The Chancellor's confrontation tactics did not escape criticism in Austria itself where the anti-fascist resistance (*Widerstandsbewegung*) protested vigorously as did the local Jewish community and also the communist organ, the *Volkstimme*. Even within the SPOE there was much uneasiness about Kreisky's insistence on a court battle and an evident desire to cool tempers. Nevertheless, public opinion was too hostile to Wiesenthal to worry unduly about the affair, and Kreisky's popularity suffered no decline.

Interestingly enough, the most vocal support for Kreisky's attitude came from the neo-Nazis in Germany and Austria who could scarcely restrain their joy at the spectacle of a Jewish-born Chancellor neutralizing their most persistent adversary. By the end of 1975 Kreisky had become a patriotic hero for the advocates of radical *völkisch* nationalism, an honorary 'Aryan' *par excellence*. The *Deutsche National-Zeitung* loudly approved the Chancellor's outbursts against 'boundless Zionist intolerance' and his rejection of any special loyalty to Jewish concerns. It enthusiastically publicized his protestations of loyalty to the Austrian *Heimat*. Here was a *deutschnational* leader after their own heart, a 'Mosaic' German whose ancestors on both sides of the family had been German-speaking teachers, doctors, Reichstag deputies, and Habsburg officials for centuries. The neo-Nazis had no doubts about the true meaning of Kreisky's attacks on Wiesenthal: 'Kreisky will die Aussöhnung mit den früheren Nationalsozialisten' (Kreisky wants a reconciliation with the ex-Nazis). Thanks to this Austro-Marxist Jewish Chancellor they had finally achieved social respectability!

Right-wing Austrians – a full decade before they elected an ex-Nazi as president – could feel justified in their belief that it was better to have been an SS man between 1938 and 1945 than to be an anti-fascist in the 1970s or 1980s. Had not Kreisky made it clear that the file was finally to be closed on the past, that the persecutors of yesterday were to be welcomed back into the national fold? In their own anti-Zionist and anti-Jewish propaganda they could now freely invoke the indubitable authority of the Austrian Chancellor. Even in his autobiography, Kreisky repeated his earlier charges that 'orthodox Zionism' is a form of 'racism'.

The Arab world was as electrified as the neo-Nazis by Kreisky's stance in the Wiesenthal affair and by his subsequent pronouncements on the Middle East conflict. In an interview in the Beirut daily, *Al Anwar* (20 November 1975), Kreisky was reported as saying: 'I am the only one who can stand up to him [Wiesenthal] because of my Jewish origin, anybody else trying to stand up to him would immediately be accused of being anti-Semitic and against the Jews.'

Such declarations were naturally grist to the mill of the pro-Arab propaganda machine. Kreisky was depicted as striking a blow against 'Zionist' political pressures, intimidation, and efforts to discredit the Palestinian cause. Anti-Nazi witchhunts, according to this version of the affair, were nothing but a diversion by Zionists against their own 'fascist' crimes in Palestine! Protests against Kreisky were dismissed as an orchestrated conspiracy to remove from office a politician who favoured a 'non-racist' solution to the Palestinian question. The London-based *Free Palestine* in its December 1975 issue approvingly quoted Kreisky as follows:

> I don't submit to Zionism. I reject it. It is true I am of Jewish origin and that my family is Jewish, but this does not mean I have a special commitment to the Zionist State and the Israelis. I reject that completely . . . . When Zionists ask those of Jewish faith outside Israel to be bound by a special commitment to the State of Israel and to work for it as though they were Israeli citizens, they are adopting a wrong political line which leads to the isolation of these Jewish citizens from their national motherland and leaves them forever isolated in their communities . . . there is nothing which binds me to Israel or to what is called the Jewish 'people' or to Zionism.

The Palestinians were particularly appreciative of Kreisky's warm sympathy for their cause. The PLO leader Yasser Arafat (in an interview broadcast on Austrian television) thanked him publicly for 'bravely resisting Zionist blackmail attempts', following the siege of OPEC headquarters in Vienna in December 1975. The six terrorists led by the Venezuelan 'Carlos' had at one point held hostage all the oil ministers of the OPEC countries, including Sheik Yamani of Saudi Arabia. Their action had been designed to strike a blow for the so-called Arab 'rejection front', yet though they had murdered three people Kreisky gave them free passage out of Austria without much hesitation. No doubt his primary objective was to 'save lives', but the speed of his capitulation suggested that, as in the Schoenau Castle affair two years earlier, he was a soft target for terrorist demands.

Hence it is not surprising to find that Kreisky consistently refused to condemn PLO terrorism even while pursuing his mediation efforts in the Middle East. After the massacre of innocent civilians on the Tel Aviv highway in March 1978, Kreisky's reaction was also breathtakingly cool. He described them as 'victims of Israel's short-sighted policy' which denied Palestinians the right to self-determination. The latter had disproved 'in the most terrible manner' Israel's contention that they did not exist. In other words, it was the Israeli government (and not the PLO which had allegedly been pursuing 'a rather moderate policy') which was ultimately responsible for the massacre. Following these tactless remarks the Austrian trade union federation felt obliged to express its regret to the *Histadrut* in Israel for 'statements belittling this act of terrorism as being the result of Israeli Government policy. Terrorism is no way to peace'.

None of this stopped Kreisky in his capacity as chairman of the Socialist International fact-finding mission on the Middle East from constantly maintaining that the PLO was ready to recognize Israel and respect its sovereignty. One of the first European leaders to regard the PLO as the sole legitimate representative of the Palestinians, he consistently insisted that only by reaching an agreement with it could peace be achieved in the area. In Kreisky's opinion the Palestinian issue is the heart of the conflict and it can only be resolved by complete Israeli withdrawal from *all* occupied territories, and the creation of an independent Palestinian state. This view might be more plausible if Kreisky had not shown such a one-sided disregard for Israel's legitimate security needs and spent so much energy in attacking Zionism while totally ignoring Arab responsibilities in perpetuating the conflict. Though he has never publicly denied Israel's right to exist as a state, his ideological view of the conflict is such as to undercut the legitimacy of the national movement that created the Jewish state. In an interview for a special supplement on the Arab world in *Die Presse* (January 1978), Kreisky spelled out his premises:

> In my opinion, the Jews are no nation. For me, the different Jewish groups are communities of fate . . . Jews live everywhere in the world. They have much more in common in both appearance and way of life with their host peoples than they have with each other . . . . There exist jet-black Jews, Indian Jews, and Mongolian Jews.

Interestingly enough this position is remarkably close to Article 20 of the Palestinian National Covenant which also insists that the Jews are not a nation and that Zionism is therefore a false, artificial, and reactionary phenomenon: 'Judaism, in its character as a religion, is not a nationality with an independent existence.' It is no accident that Yasser Arafat always refers to the Jews as a *religious* group when speaking of the future Palestinian state in which Christian, Jew, and Muslim will live in harmony. The point behind this is that only Palestinian Arabs would possess national rights in this 'secular, democratic State'. Dr Kreisky, who has been so generous in his abuse of Zionism, has never gone on record to criticize the discriminatory premises behind this concept of Palestinian Arab nationalism.

The underlying reason for the double standard lies in the Austro-Marxist tradition of which Kreisky remains perhaps the last surviving representative. Since his youth, the Austrian Chancellor had been a great admirer of Otto Bauer, whose theories provided the intellectual inspiration for the Viennese Austro-Marxist school. Like Bauer he came from a

Germanized *grossbürgerlich* background which was ultra-assimilationist. In this milieu the transition to socialist ideology did not exclude a powerful dose of *deutschnationalismus* but it very definitely ruled out any sympathy with the Jewish national renaissance. As we have seen, Otto Bauer like his fellow Austro-Marxists, Karl Kautsky, and Victor Adler, went to great lengths to deny the Jews of eastern Europe the right to their cultural-national autonomy and self-determination. Such a demand even when it was made by Jewish workers was considered neither viable nor desirable. The theories of the Austro-Marxist school insisted that the Jewish people was a *fictive* entity, doomed to extinction because it lacked a common language or territory. They were at best a 'community of fate' (one of Kreisky's favourite terms) whose cohesion was only a temporary product of socio-economic circumstances. Antisemitism alone had created the mirage of Jewish 'unity' – and once it had dissolved in the classless socialist society of the future, the 'chimerical' Jewish nation would disappear with it. When Zionism emerged, predicated on the belief that territorial concentration in Palestine would crystallize the renaissance of the Jewish nation, the Austro-Marxists decried it as a romantic utopian delusion.

The success of Zionism in achieving its aim did not lead to a thoughtful, self-critical revision of Marxist theory. On the contrary, the belief that 'complete assimilation' was the only progressive solution to the 'Jewish question' persisted, in spite of the Nazi genocide and the creation of Israel – indeed it was now transformed into a dogmatic *idée fixe*. The assertions of Kautsky, Lenin, Rosa Luxemburg, and the prewar Austro-Marxists that the Jews were not a nation had a certain appearance of validity in their time. But the repetition of these claims after 1948 involves the substitution of ideological fiction for reality. It has led many on the Left into the *cul-de-sac* of neo-antisemitism in the desperate effort to make Zionism the scapegoat for their badly mistaken prognoses. Instead of adapting theory to the facts they have sought to argue that Jewish nationalism must by its very nature be separatist, reactionary, and ultimately even racist.

It is disappointing that an experienced, pragmatic statesman like Bruno Kreisky should, when it comes to the Jewish problem, have fallen victim to this dogmatic mode of thinking. But the phenomenon is neither new nor is it especially mysterious. Long before the emergence of Israel as an independent state, assimilated Jewish Marxists expressed their ethnic death wish in the demand that the Jewish collectivity should disappear. Bruno Kreisky's outbursts against Israel and the 'warped' mentality of the *Ostjuden* may best be seen as a footnote to the central European tradition.

10

The Fassbinder controversy

Rainer Werner Fassbinder's *Der Müll, die Stadt und der Tod* (Garbage, the City and Death) is a nightmarish vision of a metropolis that devours its men and women, turning them into living corpses. It describes a world that is hard, inhuman, and glacial, in language that is at times poetic but more often unbearably coarse and obscene. The characters are mainly social outcasts – prostitutes, pimps, transvestites, sado-masochists, dwarfs – with a corrupt police president and a couple of unrepentant old Nazis thrown in for good measure. Dominating them all is the figure of a 'rich Jew' (nameless throughout the play) who in one of his early monologues declares:

> I buy old houses in this city, tear them down, build new ones which I sell at a good profit. The city protects me, it has to. For in addition, I am a Jew. The police chief is my friend, one could call it that, the mayor is happy to invite me and I can also rely on the town councillors. The city needs the unscrupulous business man who can help change its appearance. I couldn't care less if children cry, if the old and feeble suffer . . . . I disregard people's screams of fury.

This character of the 'rich Jew' was not in fact an invention of the playwright but was taken from the novel by Gerhard Zwerenz – published in 1972 – under the title *Die Erde ist unbewohnbar wie der Mond* (The Earth is as uninhabitable as the Moon). Zwerenz had depicted a rich Jewish real-estate speculator called Abraham who in the late 1960s and early 1970s along with others of his ilk had helped turn the West End of Frankfurt into a concrete wasteland of high-rise office blocks, banks, and insurance buildings. Behind this depiction was a certain social reality – namely the disproportionate role of a number of Jews from the east (virtually all survivors of the concentration camps) who settled in postwar Frankfurt and became involved in developing and reconstructing various properties on behalf of the city. It was a notorious fact that these Polish Jews owned substantial parts of the Frankfurt red-light district (*Bahnhofsviertel*) in addition to the intermediary role played by some of their co-religionists between the city and the banks.

Zwerenz's novel also reflected the conditions of economic boom in the early 1970s in Frankfurt: a time when the ruling SPD together with the bankers, city planners, and real-estate developers modernized and trans-formed the topography of the West-End – where much of Frankfurt's Jewish bourgeoisie had lived before 1933. The new edifices of glass and steel were not however erected without a fight. Many older residents were brutally evicted with the aid of the police. The 'housing struggle' was sharpened by the fact that young squatters influenced by Frankfurt's bohemian counter-culture joined hands with old established tenants to fight the 'speculators'. The fact that rich Jews like Ignaz Bubis (who was actually chairman of the local Jewish community) were so prominent in this land speculation gave a definite antisemitic slant to the spontaneous populist revolt against the property developers. The suspicion in many left-wing circles was that Jews had been deliberately selected to do the *Dreckarbeit* of an unrestrained, monopoly capitalism because of their relative immunity from criticism in a post-Holocaust Germany. This was certainly the feeling of both Zwerenz and Fassbinder who compared their 'manipulation' by the municipality with the way that rich court Jews were used by rulers and princes in eighteenth-century Europe.

By the time mercurial Fassbinder arrived in Frankfurt to become principal of the *Theater am Turm* (Theatre at the Tower) in the mid 1970s he was already a prominent and most successful film maker with a strong artistic commitment to the weak, oppressed, and under-privileged groups in modern society. At the same time, this *enfant terrible* of the German cinema who would die only seven years later (at the early age of 37) from a drug overdose, had struck a low point in his career. Constantly quarrelling with his collaborators he soon permanent-ly left Frankfurt for Berlin, but not before he had written *Garbage* – his poisoned gift to a city he had always detested. The entire play was hastily written on a transatlantic flight in 1975 and was never reworked by the author though he did write a screenplay for the film *Schatten der Engel* (Shadow of Angels) which was more closely based on Zwerenz's novel. Curiously enough, this film version made by the Swiss director Daniel Schmid never aroused much controversy.

Fassbinder's play had been published by Suhrkampf in 1976 but was soon withdrawn following attacks on its alleged antisemitism. Joachim Fest, the biographer of Hitler and an editor of the conservative *Frankfurter Allgemeine Zeitung*, even accused Fassbinder of 'left-wing fascism'. The playwright responded in the same year by claiming that he had written *Garbage* in reaction to the conditions he had encountered in Frankfurt. He had given expression to the antisemitism that already flourished there, precisely as a result of the taboo on criticizing Jews. Recalling his own youth in postwar Germany, Fassbinder told the interviewer that 'creating a sense of taboo about Jews can lead to open hostility against them. When I met a Jew as a child, I was always told behind a cupped hand: This is a Jew, be good, be friendly . . . . I have never felt that this was the right attitude'. His own position was that 'it is far better to discuss things in order to make them less dangerous rather than talk about them in a hushed way'.

The playwright declared himself frightened by the hysterical reaction which his play had aroused in some quarters and, quoting Robert Neumann's remark that 'philosemites are antisemites who love Jews', he suggested that the motives of his critics needed closer scrutiny. While not going as far as Zwerenz who declared 'left-wing antisemitism' to be a contradiction in terms. Fassbinder pointed to his own anti-fascist record as proof of the absurdity of some of the accusations made against him. Moreover he insisted on the freedom of the artist to employ methods which were perhaps debatable or even dangerous as a way of getting over his message. Literature without risk might be responsible but it would not be alive!

Fassbinder emphasized with some justice that the author could not be identified with the statements of his characters. Thus the single most blatantly antisemitic and controversial lines in *Garbage* are put into the mouth of a resentful old Nazi, Hans von Glück:

> He sucks us dry, the Jew. He drinks our blood and puts us in the wrong, because he's a Jew and we have to bear the guilt. And the Jew bears the blame, because he makes us guilty simply by his being here. If he had only remained where he came from, or if they had only gassed him, then I would be able to sleep better today. But they forgot to gas him. That is no joke, thus it thinks in me [*so denkt es in mir*]. I rub my hands when I picture how the breath goes out of him in the gas chamber.

Clearly these sentiments with their dark, brooding, murderous obsessiveness do not express Fassbinder's opinions on the 'Jewish question'. Even in the context of the play they are quite exceptional in their virulence. But they are neither introduced, artistically interpreted, motivated, or put into any sort of context by the author. Not only is there no insight into the deeper springs of this antisemitism but, as the late Jean Améry pointed out, there is no sense of history, psychology, or moral dignity displayed by the playwright concerning the probable effects of such a representation. The same might be said of Fassbinder's portrayal of the 'rich Jew'. Not only is he a ruthless speculator, swindler, bloodsucker, and friend of the establishment, he also frequents and financially supports the prostitute Roma B., whom at the end of the play he strangles with his tie. Indeed, sexual as well as financial omnipotence is attributed to the ugly, old Jew thus reinforcing some of the classic stereotypes of Christian and Nazi antisemitism. Cold, calculating, greedy, and vengeful it is difficult to find in him a single redeeming feature – though he is certainly no worse than the rest of Fassbinder's unappetizing gallery of outcasts. But while the other characters have names, only the Jew remains generic and abstract – the mythic personification of 'finance capital'. Inevitably he recalls such stage archetypes from Elizabethan drama as Marlowe's *Jew of Malta* or Shakespeare's Shylock in his Machiavellian intrigue, rapacity, and vengefulness. In a German context, the associations must of course be even more disturbing. When the 'rich Jew' seeks to humiliate her father (a Nazi and a transvestite!) by sexually violating Roma B., one thinks of Jud Süss – the ravisher of Christian-Aryan womanhood in the notorious Nazi propaganda film. While the myth of the lascivious, sexually potent Jewish speculator appears to come straight out of *Der Stürmer*.

Garbage therefore offers the strange paradox of a play that is ostensibly anticapitalist and anti-fascist while producing the classic stereotypes of antisemitic mythology. We are in effect asked to take these unpleasant images and associations as a kind of implicit satire of the *petit-bourgeois* mentality that laid the seed-bed of Nazism. 'So denkt es in mir' says the unrepentant Nazi but his feelings seem to emerge from the depths of some mysterious German essence: if only the Jew were not there, the German could sleep peacefully, at one with himself, free of guilt. While the 'rich Jew' in turn echoes some primordial Jewish seeking for revenge, for the eternal pound of flesh squeezed from the innocent Christian. Perhaps, for Fassbinder, this Jew was really intended as a victim of the system which produced and reified him but this hardly modifies his pitiless, vindictive, and amoral character. Moreover, Fassbinder and his defenders in their insistence on the autonomy of art overlook the fact that texts do not function in an empty space but in a historical context. Stereotypes like the 'rich Jew' are not simple, unmediated reflections of social reality. After all, there are far more Protestant, Catholic, or atheist speculators in Frankfurt than there are rapacious Jews. But in the context of western Christian culture (and even more that of modern German history) the Shylock myth has tremendous resonance. A character called the 'rich Christian', the 'rich Muslim', or the 'rich atheist' would fall flat precisely because he cannot evoke any mythic or archetypal associations. Thus the claim (made by many of its defenders) that *Garbage* was primarily a critique of capitalism and of the inhuman, oppressive *Baupolitik* of the municipality, seems disingenuous. For even if the Jew is presented merely as a manipulated instrument of the system – which is by no means clear in the text – the logic of the stereotypes stays in place. They preserve their original charge and echo.

These issues came to the foreground with renewed force when in October 1985, three years after Fassbinder's death and in accordance with his testament, the newly appointed principal of the Frankfurt Theatre, Gunther Rühle, finally attempted to stage the play. Rühle, previously a well-known critic of the *Frankfurter Allgemeine Zeitung* (who had opposed the play) now insisted that the time had come to lift the ban and free the city from the stigma of encouraging censorship. Echoing Fassbinder he pleaded for laying aside the outdated taboos concerning criticism of Jews in the Federal Republic ('der Jude muss wieder kritisierbar sein'). One remark of Rühle, in particular, was to shock many observers. He was quoted as saying that 'Die Schonzeit ist vorbei' – 'the no-hunting season is over' – which some commentators interpreted as meaning that a new hunting season for Jews could now begin! Rühle's unfortunate phrase (which he subsequently denied using) nevertheless expressed a real shift in German public consciousness which is essential for understanding what lay behind the new Fassbinder controversy – namely the desire for a so-called 'normalization' of the German past. Those who were calling for an abolition of taboos relating to the treatment of Jews were also implicitly seeking release from feelings of abnormality, guilt, and suffocation engendered by German responsibility for the mass murder of 6 million Jews.

This desire for 'normalization' exists both on the Left and the Right though it obviously has different motivations and goals. Fassbinder and his supporters, for example, undoubtedly saw elements of continuity between the Third Reich and the postwar Federal Republic. For the antifascist Left it was capitalism which engendered fascism and antisemitism and, from this universalistic perspective, the removing of taboos about the 'Jewish question' (*Enttabuisierung*) must be an integral part of the anticapitalist critique. Postwar Germany, they held, could only master its 'abnormal' past by a radical unmasking of those elements of dehumanization, alienation, and technocratic capitalism which persisted in the present. There is no doubt, for example, that an iconoclastic artist like Fassbinder saw clear elements of crypto-Nazism lurking behind the complacent façade of *Modell-Deutschland* and the 'economic miracle' of the postwar years. *Garbage* was one way of tearing down this façade by attacking its hypocritical 'philosemitism', seen as a mask for social injustice. The quasi-fascist system of monopoly capitalism merely used the Jewish speculators whom it 'protected' as a gesture of *Wiedergutmachung*, in order to cloak greed with the mantle of moral respectability.

Normalization on the Right meant something rather different. First and foremost it meant a reconciliation with the German past along the lines that Chancellor Kohl had indicated at Bitburg. The Second World

War was to be treated from the German side as far as possible like any other war. The Nazi regime was not fundamentally different from other 'totalitarian' terror regimes and the crimes it committed 'in the name of the German people' could not imply any collective guilt. Naturally Kohl and the conservatives paid lip-service to 'those unfortunate years' and the sufferings of their Jewish *Mitbürger* (fellow-citizens) but the emphasis in the mid-1980s had clearly shifted to creating a past more consonant with West Germany's growing national assertiveness and self-con-fidence. The memory of the Holocaust could not be allowed to infringe upon the imperatives of Allied reconciliation. This does not mean that the Kohl government encouraged antisemitism. But it did introduce into legislation a parallel between the offence of denying that Auschwitz happened and denial of the crimes committed against Germans expelled from eastern Europe after 1945. Since no Germans had ever denied that the latter took place, this levelling and rather grotesque comparison can only be seen as another step on the road to throwing off the moral burden of the past.

Another indication of the steady erosion of sensitivity on the political Right can be found in the remarks of the young Bavarian deputy Hermann Fellner (a personal favourite of Kohl) attacking Jewish survivors who had yet to be paid compensation for their slave labour by the Flick concern. The CSU deputy complained that 'Jews are quick to speak up when they hear the tinkling of money in German cash-registers.' His scarcely concealed desire to bring the *Wiedergutmachung* (repara-tions) to an end undoubtedly struck a responsive chord in many Germans. If that were not enough, the mayor of a small town in north-Rhine Westphalia, Graf von Spree, suggested that the only way to solve his budget deficit problem might be to kill 'a few rich Jews'. Fassbinder's *reiche Jude* was evidently not so mythical as some critics had assumed.

Against this background, a certain scepticism concerning conservative motivations in attacking Fassbinder's play and supporting the protests of the Jewish community is certainly called for. Those on the Right who had shown at Bitburg, during the German battle of the historians (*Historikerstreit*) and in questions relating to Israel or to *Wiedergutmachung*, a growing resentment at reminders of the Nazi past, seem poorly placed to condemn 'left-wing antisemitism'. Politically however such a tactic might seem rewarding. As a bohemian, homosexual drug addict and leftist iconoclast, Fassbinder provided an ideal target. The Right was not interested in his kind of 'normalization' with its assault on the unacceptable face of capitalism and respectable middle-class values and taboos. Here was a case where conservatives who regarded Fassbinder and his friends as little better than professional pornographers could pose as '*scheinheilige Philosemiten*' (pious philosemites), not to mention their role as defenders of bourgeois propriety and good taste!

126

For German Jews the Fassbinder controversy presented a different kind of problem. The 30,000 Jews in the postwar Federal Republic had lived in a decidedly inconspicuous manner until the time of the Frankfurt theatre scandal. Not even the public debate over Bitburg appeared to have shaken them out of their low-key, almost invisible existence. The Fassbinder controversy, especially for the younger generation who had grown up in postwar Germany, seemed like a liberation from a self-imposed ghetto in which they had previously lived. Suddenly their social integration and personal identity – whether as Jews or Germans or something undefined – could no longer be taken for granted. They were no longer willing to be objects in a monologue conducted by Germans among themselves. They firmly rejected the return to the kind of normality being advocated by supporters of the play but the very act of demonstrating against it forced them to redefine their identity as Jews in a new way.

For the older generation, residence in postwar Germany had always been considered something temporary. The Jews from the east kept largely to themselves, avoiding the public sphere and social contacts with Germans except for business purposes. Their low profile may have been connected as much with guilt feelings at living in the land of the murderers as with fear at reawakening latent feelings of antisemitism in their German neighbours. The community identified strongly with Israel but was otherwise almost wholly depoliticized. Nothing could have been further from its values of material success and bourgeois respectability than the kind of milieu of pariahs and social outcasts in which the 'rich Jew' of *Garbage* actually moves. Postwar German Jews certainly had no desire to be seen in the company of such marginalized sexual outsiders or as victims of capitalist alienation. On another level, however, in linking Jews with financial speculation, desire for revenge on the Germans for past sufferings, and a certain privileged status resulting from the Holocaust, the play did strike a raw nerve. *Garbage*, for all its failings, does hold up a kind of distorting mirror to a disturbing and unhealthy reality of postwar German-Jewish existence. The protests against 'subsidized antisemitism' of the demonstrators who occupied the stage of the Frankfurt *Schauspielhaus* at the end of October 1985 ignored this truth. Understandably, they were not ready only forty years after the end of the war to accept Fassbinder's 'rich Jew' as a collective self-image, let alone as a gesture of 'reconciliation' or as a contribution to German-Jewish dialogue! If some Jews had perhaps abused the relative immunity from criticism that they enjoyed in the wake of the Holocaust, this was no ground for generalizing about 'die Juden', 'Jewish capital', or 'Jewish power' as a whole.

The slogan of the protestors against the play was, ironically enough, the same as that of its advocates – 'Wehret den Anfängen' (Beware of the beginnings) though the reference was to two different facets of the Nazi experience. The protestors (who included, apart from the Frankfurt Jews, members of the CDU, the FDP liberals, a section of the SPD, and representatives of the churches and of the more conservative press) were warning against the danger of lending legitimacy to rising antisemitism in West Germany. They regarded the play not only as intrinsically antisemitic but also as politically imprudent and aesthetically worthless. On the other side stood the vast majority of the Frankfurt intelligentsia, of the centre-Left and radical-Left literati, the Greens, the Young Socialists, a number of key liberal newspapers, and a small group of Jewish leftists. They recalled the precedent of the Nazi book-burning, defended the absolute right to free speech, and favoured a more open discussion of antisemitism.

Though opinions crossed political and ideological boundaries, German Jews opposing the play generally found more allies on the Right than the Left and among the older rather than the younger generation. True, there were also those like Daniel Cohn-Bendit who defended Fassbinder against charges of antisemitism and favoured performing the play yet congratulated the Jewish community on its militant 'occupation' of the Frankfurt theatre! Others doubted whether the theatre was the right forum for dealing with such sensitive and complex issues in the first place. Though there was much criticism of Rühle's efforts to force a conception of 'positive normality' down the throats of Frankfurt Jewry by producing the play, there was also some unease at the fact that Jews and their supporters appeared to be favouring censorship and the restriction of free speech. Was Auschwitz again being used to silence criticism of Jewish behaviour? This was a charge all too frequently made on the German New Left since the late 1960s with regard mainly to Israel. Was the Holocaust being instrumentalized by the German conservative establishment in order to repress criticism of capitalism? Why did the same CDU mayor who condemned Fassbinder award Frankfurt's prestigious Goethe prize to such a renowned fellow-traveller of Nazism as the writer Ernst Jünger? And why did the official Jewish community not protest? Why did it remain silent as it had done even over the Bitburg affair? What, in other words, was so wicked about Fassbinder?

These and many other problems were aired though not always answered in the course of the passionate if rather chaotic public debate sparked off by the protests against staging the play. The issues clearly transcended the narrow questions of whether *Garbage* was indeed 'antisemitic', whether it was an artistically worthwhile play, whether it was tactful to produce it in West Germany, or whether the theatre could provide an appropriate catharsis for the Republic's Holocaust complex. Preserving or destroying taboos, clichés, and stereotypes about the Jews was seen to involve the larger uncertainty of the meaning of 'normalization' in the German-Jewish context. The image of robust normality which Kohl's Germany was seeking to project in other spheres began to falter when confronted with the kind of moral and historical grey zone represented by the Fassbinder affair. Coming as it did in the wake of Bitburg, the controversy demonstrated the fragility, the difficulties, and also the challenge of coexistence between Germans and Jews in the wake of the Holocaust.

Part 3

Jews, the Left, and Zionism

11

French socialism and the Dreyfus affair

The famous French writer, Charles Péguy, looking back on the Dreyfus affair in 1910, described it as *une affaire élue*. From his new-found vantage point as a French Catholic patriot, the affair appeared to be the crossroads in three eminent histories – of France, of Israel, and of Christianity.[1] But, forgetting his own past, he omitted to add that it was also a crisis in the history of French socialism.

The affair, which began in November 1894 with the announcement that a Jewish officer named Captain Dreyfus had been arrested and charged with selling military secrets to Germany, only ended in July 1906 with Dreyfus receiving the *Légion d'Honneur* and full exoneration from the French Supreme Court; yet in reality it has never ended, still remaining a source of controversy to political factions and to historians alike, long after its main protagonists have passed from the scene. At its height, between 1897 and 1900, the affair aroused such mass hysteria and extraordinary passions throughout France that no political party, no institution, no religious group, no family, no thinking individual was left unaffected. As a rising political force in the 1890s, the French socialist movement was inevitably obliged to adopt a position on an issue which had provoked an almost mortal crisis in the body politic of France. Strangely enough, French socialist attitudes to this upheaval have never been studied in depth and it is the purpose of this article to offer a starting point.[2]

One must bear in mind that at the outset of the affair, in 1894, the French socialist movement was divided into five separate organizations – the Guesdists, Blanquists, Broussists, Allemanists, and Independent socialists. Each of these groups had its own doctrine, its own tactics, its own political style – and it was the Dreyfus affair which first brought about conditions for the unification of all these factions into one socialist party. The Guesdists represented Marxism in France, in a peculiarly hard, narrow, sectarian sense; their great strength was their discipline and organization, especially in the industrial north.[3] The Blanquists had the oldest tradition among the French socialist groupings, an insurrectionary, patriotic image, strongly coloured by their prominent role in the Paris Commune. The Broussists (or Possibilists) were a Gallic version of Fabian socialism, believing in municipal democracy, gradual reform, republicanism, and the slow infiltration by socialists of government and administration. The Allemanists were a more militant splinter group, disillusioned with the parliamentary reformism of the 'Possibilists', advocates of syndicalism, the superiority of manual workers, and the General Strike. Like the Possibilists, they were influential in the Parisian region, and represented a libertarian current in socialism.[4] The Independent socialists were basically free-floating orators, parliamentarians, and journalists, attracted to socialism out of a mixture of idealistic and opportunistic motives. They were much influenced by Benoît Malon's concept of 'integral socialism', rooted in the French utopian rather than the Marxian school of socialist ideology. It was from this group that many of the leading socialist Dreyfusards, like Jaurès, Gérault-Richard, Rouanet, and Fournière, were recruited.

The Dreyfus affair in its first phase attracted little attention in the socialist camp, which had no more reason in 1894 than had the rest of the French public to doubt that he was guilty of high treason. The case had been tried in a closed court-martial and details surrounding the trial and the evidence remained obscure. The only aspect of the case which did at that time interest socialist opinion was the apparent reluctance of the military judges to apply the death penalty. Indeed, on 22 December 1894 in the Chamber of Deputies, Jean Jaurès, the leader of the Independent socialists, accused the judges of leniency towards Dreyfus because he was a wealthy officer.[5] In an article written four days later, Jaurès spoke of 'enormous Jewish pressure which has been far from ineffective' in averting the death penalty (envisaged by article 76 of the military code) for the guilty officer.[6] Other comments in the contemporary socialist press were equally unfavourable. *Le Chambard Socialiste*, edited by Gérault-Richard, sarcastically contrasted the treatment which an ordinary soldier might expect in similar circumstances, with the deportation for life of Dreyfus.[7] The headline in *Le Travailleur* was simply 'À mort le traître'. Emile Pouget in the anarchist *Le Père Peinard* reported the arrest of Dreyfus in his own inimitable slang: 'One of their rapacious officers, an Alsatian yid [*youtre*], Dreyfus, a big carrot at the War Ministry, has sold off a pile of military secrets to Germany.'[8] In other words anarchists, like socialists, did not take the affair very seriously at the outset, regarding Dreyfus as a rich officer who had betrayed his country and escaped lightly. Only Maurice Charnay, in the Allemanist paper *Le Parti Ouvrier*, suggested that Dreyfus might possibly have been the victim of a judicial error.[9]

The case began to take a new turn in August 1896 when Colonel Picquart discovered that another officer, Major Esterhazy, was spying for the Germans. By September 1896 Picquart was convinced that Dreyfus had been mistakenly condemned instead of Esterhazy, and informed his superiors of his conclusions. In December 1896 they had Picquart removed to North Africa where it was hoped that he would cause no more trouble. In September 1896, Mathieu Dreyfus, brother of the accused, had begun a press campaign, based on Picquart's discoveries, to win the support of influential people for a revision of the case. Finally, in November 1896, Bernard Lazare, a Jewish journalist whose services had been enlisted by the Dreyfus family, published a pamphlet in Brussels, entitled *Une erreur judiciale: la vérité sur l'affaire Dreyfus*, which for the first time clearly exposed the case for revision.

Lazare was a well-known revolutionary anarchist, highly respected in left-wing circles, but his pamphlet on the Dreyfus case was coldly received in the socialist press. Even such future Dreyfusard leaders as Clemenceau and Jaurès reacted with hostile indifference when Lazare sought to win their support for a revision of the case. Like the majority of radicals and socialists, they could see no evidence of any judicial error, nor did they accept that Dreyfus had been chosen as a scapegoat because of his race, as Lazare maintained. Writing in *La Petite République* in November 1896, the Guesdist propagandist, Alexandre Zévaès, cynically expressed the prevailing left-wing attitude to Lazare's pamphlet. He described the Jewish journalist as a 'high-life anarchist' and 'one of the faithful admirers of his Majesty Rothschild'.[10] The implication was that Lazare, in asserting Dreyfus's innocence, had sold out to the so-called 'Jewish syndicate' of which Rothschild was presumed to be the head. Even Lazare's anarchist colleagues dismissed his assumption of a judicial error as highly improbable. André Girard, in *Les Temps Nouveaux*, wrote at the end of November 1896: 'I believe that I can say, without being taxed with antisemitism, that this reason [that Dreyfus was a Jew] does not appear conclusive, and would rather be a reason for the opposite to have happened'.[11] Anarchists were particularly loath to believe that a rich officer, a member of the privileged military caste, could have been selected as a scapegoat by his superiors. Dreyfus's Jewish origins, moreover, made the Left even more hostile and suspicious of efforts to obtain a revision of the case. Anti-Jewish stereotypes of Jewish bankers, replete with hooked nose, fat lips, and greedy eyes exuding the 'Semitic' love of gold, were commonplace in the leftist press at that time. The 'smell of Panama', in which German-Jewish financiers had been implicated at the heart of the scandal, was still in the air – and hung like an ominous cloud over the Dreyfus case. Drumont's *Libre Parole*, Rochefort's *L'Intransigeant*, and the Assumptionist *La Croix* exploited these circumstances to inject the masses with an increasingly rabid xenophobic and antisemitic hysteria.[12] The ordinary Frenchman was daily being told that the Jews were spies, taking orders from across the Rhine, and that they were corrupt mercenaries seeking to subvert the French army and French institutions – and few men of the Left were yet ready to challenge these assumptions.

Indeed, in the provincial socialist press in 1897 there were overt examples of antisemitism. For example, the Guesdist organ in the south, *La République Sociale* (Narbonne), wrote in February 1897 that the French government was being manipulated by the 'Yids of high finance' who were trying to rehabilitate Dreyfus so that they could continue undisturbed their rapacious dealings on the stock exchange.[13] Only the Allemanists among the socialist groupings deplored the inquisitorial atmosphere which was developing around attempts to secure a revision of the trial. In an article on 5 November 1897 Maurice Charnay warned socialists that, by submitting to *raison d'état*, they were creating a precedent which might one day lead to their following Dreyfus to Devil's Island.[14] Emile Joindy, in the same paper (*Le Parti Ouvrier*) expressed his shock at the fact that a Jew could not obtain justice from a civilized nation. Jean Jaurès, however, writing in *La Petite République* at the end of November 1897, expressed the majority socialist view at that time – which saw nothing to choose between the Jewish and the Catholic bourgeoisie – 'if the smell of the ghetto is often nauseating, the aroma of suspect Catholic adventurers like the Esterhazys and co. also sickens the passer-by'.[15] For Jaurès, the affair was still merely a struggle for power and influence within the middle class, of no concern to the workers. The fact that *Le Figaro* (normally a conservative government newspaper) was campaigning against the Army chiefs was proof to Jaurès that it had been bribed by the 'Jewish' syndicate. On 11 December 1897 he argued that the rehabilitation of Dreyfus could only serve the 'opportunist' clique (by which he meant the Jewish financiers and their supporters) already discredited in the Panama scandal.[16] The Jews, he suggested, were trying to free themselves from the odium of treason which recent scandals had attached to them, so that they could continue to exploit republican institutions. Both the pro- and anti-Dreyfus factions were merely a sordid reflection of material interests, of bourgeois blindness, stupidity, and egoism, according to the pre-Dreyfusard Jaurès. Guesde, Vaillant, and Jaurès, the three leading figures in French socialism, all abstained on 4 December 1897 when a nationalist resolution in the Chamber of Deputies condemned the 'odious' campaign of the Dreyfusards, maligning the honour of the Army.

Socialists of all shades and groupings continued until January 1898 to regard Dreyfus as a traitor and those who sought his rehabilitation – whether his family entourage, Joseph Reinach, Scheurer-Kestner, or Colonel Picquart – with hostility and distaste. It was Zola's forceful intervention in *L'Aurore* on 13 January 1898 which first shook the socialists out of their complacent assumption that the rich 'Panamist' clique and the Rothschilds stood behind the pro-Dreyfus campaign. Zola's trenchant attack on the general staff for complicity in suppressing the truth, for conspiring through forgery and lies to convict an innocent man, dissolved much of the mystery and confusion surrounding the original trial. With the appearance of Zola's 'J'accuse', the affair moved from the judicial to the political plane – and Esterhazy's acquittal, two days earlier, appeared in a new light – as a 'crime against humanity'.

Zola's initiative divided the parliamentary socialist group which met to discuss it into two distinct factions. The moderates, led by Alexandre Millerand and René Viviani (who were in the majority until June 1898), argued that intervention in an unpopular cause, like that of Dreyfus, would be electorally imprudent.[17] Zola, after all, was only a bourgeois, and the socialist movement should not be towed along in the wake of a bourgeois writer. Jules Guesde, on the other hand, led the radical faction, asserting that Zola's was the most revolutionary action of the century and condemning arguments of electoral expediency.[18] This stand taken by Guesde is all the more striking, in view of his subsequent, much criticized, neutrality in the affair. Vaillant and Jaurès supported Guesde's position, but the result was a compromise – the socialist manifesto of 19 January 1898 which appeared in *La Lanterne* the next day, bearing the signature of thirty-two parliamentary socialist deputies.[19]

The socialist manifesto was the first attempt by the French Left at drawing up an official and coherent position towards the Dreyfus campaign. Composed by Jaurès, with the help of Guesde and Vaillant, it coolly viewed the whole affair as an internecine feud between the clerical and 'opportunist' factions of the bourgeoisie for the privilege of deciding who should obtain the lion's share in exploiting the working class. According to the manifesto, the Catholics hoped that France 'would be delivered to that famished, stone-broke Christian nobility, who pay court to the Jews, show off at their receptions, dance at their balls, and meditate between two waltzes and two loans how to strangle both debt and debtor.'[20]

On the other hand,

the Jewish capitalists, after all the scandals which have discredited them, needed to rehabilitate themselves somewhat, to preserve their share of the profits. If they could show that there had been a judicial error or public prejudice, then they could indirectly seek through this rehabilitation of an individual belonging to their own class – and together with their opportunist allies – to restore the good name of the whole Judaizing and Panamist clique.[21]

As for the hypocritical double-talk about the rights of man, this was merely intended, according to the manifesto, 'to wash out the stains of

Israel'. It concluded that between the Jew, Reinach, and the Catholic De Mun, the working class had nothing to choose and should preserve its complete neutrality.

In order to put this statement in its correct perspective, one has to remember that it was written against the background of a mounting and irrational campaign leading to antisemitic violence in French cities. Since 17 January 1898 there had been riots, demonstrations, and pillaging of Jewish stores in Marseilles, Paris, Bordeaux, Nantes, Rennes, Orleans, Grenoble, Toulouse, Montpellier, Lille, Le Havre, and other French towns. In Algiers, Oran, and Constantine there had been a veritable pogrom with 158 Jewish shops plundered and the murder and rape of Jewish women. In Paris, antisemitic gangs of rowdies controlled the streets: Zola's house was guarded day and night by police for fear that he might be lynched by enraged students and royalists. It was the same mob who had sung hosannas at Esterhazy's acquittal, parading along the boulevards and crying 'Death to Zola! Death to the Jews!' Yet in this atmosphere of mass hysteria all that the manifesto had to say about the activities of the antisemites was that 'they were incipient socialists [*Ceux-là sont des socialistes qui commencent*]'.

A few days later, Jaurès, writing in *La Petite République*, cynically remarked that behind Zola's 'brave and noble initiative', 'the whole suspect gang of sly, greedy Jewish scum wait for some kind of indirect rehabilitation, propitious for new crimes'.[22] In the aftermath of Zola's generous gesture 'the birds of prey swoop down, who make their profit from the seed of justice before it has sprung forth'.[23] Jaurès repeated that the working class should be seduced neither by the Dreyfusards nor by the clerical nationalists, with their war-cry 'Mort aux Juifs', which he merely described as a 'caricature of proletarian revolution'. But Jaurès was secretly far from convinced by his own rhetoric, and we know from the evidence of Charles Andler and Léon Blum that he had already been persuaded of Dreyfus's innocence by Lucien Herr, towards the end of 1897.[24] Lucien Herr, the librarian of the École Normale Supérieure, the spiritual mentor of Jaurès and of so many socialists (and Dreyfusards), had succeeded where Bernard Lazare had failed. What held Jaurès back from launching himself into the Dreyfusard campaign was the need to be sure of his ground, and above all his loyalty to the socialist movement, which was not prepared to back a pro-Dreyfus crusade. By November 1897, despite the mildly antisemitic tone of some of his articles, he had begun to criticize the irregularities in the original trial and especially the use of a secret dossier to convict Dreyfus.[25] The ultra-nationalism of the mob during the Esterhazy and Zola trials in January 1898 clearly appalled him. There can be no doubt that Jaurès's personal sympathies already lay with that 'élite de pensée et de courage' who had taken up the cause of Dreyfus at the beginning of 1898.[26] On the other hand, realizing that the organized labour movement was not ready to follow him, Jaurès hesitated to split still further the divided ranks of French socialism. A police informer reported him on 12 February 1898 as saying: 'We cannot continue with the propaganda against the *huis clos* in the provinces: it may be all right in Paris, where antimilitarism is strong. But with our friends in the provinces we have to be careful. If prolonged, the Dreyfus Affair would be a disastrous electoral program for us.'[27]

While Jaurès wrestled with his conscience, caught between the 'half-measures, reticence, equivocation, lies, cowardice', which he had so eloquently denounced in the Chamber of Deputies on 22 January 1898, and the dictates of socialist self-interest, others were less hesitant. The Allemanists and the anarchists of *Le Libertaire* began to proclaim Dreyfus's innocence in unequivocal terms in January 1898. In an open letter to Jaurès, the Allemanist Maurice Charnay asked why he had not yet drawn the obvious conclusions from his own speech in the Chamber of Deputies? How could any socialist tribune hesitate in the face of such a clear violation of the rights of man! How could the labour movement remain passive against the invocation of 'raison d'état'?[28] Another article in *Le Parti Ouvrier* blamed the pernicious influence of Henri Rochefort over the masses and thereby over the socialist leadership, for the official reticence.[29] Socialists feared to contradict the daily propaganda of Rochefort's *L'Intransigeant,* with its uninhibited defence of the Army and of Esterhazy; they were reluctant to break with Rochefort, whose support would be valuable in the coming elections, and they were well aware of the impact of his nationalist and antisemitic propaganda among the French masses. Only the Allemanists, who detested Rochefort, were as yet prepared to risk unpopularity and see in Dreyfus not the class enemy but a symbol of humanity–not the eternal 'Judas' but the victim of a conspiracy.

Similarly, Sebastian Faure and the anarchists of *Le Libertaire* were sympathetic to Dreyfus as a victim of the military, as a Jew and an outcast, who had been made the scapegoat for the sins of the fatherland.[30] On 29 January 1898 the libertarian anarchists organized the first public demonstration, held on the Left, in favour of Dreyfus and against the 'huis clos'.[31] Sebastian Faure, the anarchist leader, in a series of articles (later published as a pamphlet entitled *Les Anarchistes et L'Affaire Dreyfus*) deplored the tendency on the Left to see in Dreyfus only an officer and a class enemy. Since his degradation, Dreyfus had become a 'pariah' of the Christian bourgeois world – a victim of the inquisitorial power of the Army and Church – which anarchists were committed to destroy.[32] But Faure's comrades in the anarchist ranks strongly opposed his pro-Dreyfusard campaign, and both *Les Temps Nouveaux* of Jean Grave and *Le Père Peinard* of Emile Pouget protested against his intervention.[33] Thus, until after the elections of May 1898, Faure remained as isolated among the anarchists in their pro-Dreyfus stand as the Allemanists were among the socialist groupings. The rank and file of the organized Left were indifferent to the affair, either accepting the silence of their leaders, or veering towards the antisemitic chauvinism of Rochefort and the nationalist Blanquists.

The socialist leaders drew different conclusions from the elections in May 1898 which had taken place under the shadow of the unresolved affair. Guesde and Vaillant decided that a 'personal campaign' in favour of Dreyfus would constitute a dangerous diversion from the basic socialist struggle to enlighten the masses and increase their class consciousness.[34]

Jaurès, on the other hand, who had thrown himself into a detailed study of the case, concluded that Dreyfus was indeed a powerful symbol of social injustice, that his cause could rally the oppressed against the traditional enemies of the working class, the Army and Church. More important still, Jaurès had come to the same conclusion as his mentor, Lucien Herr, namely that truth and justice were 'integral' and not concepts which could be narrowly confined within the sphere of class expediency.

On 7 July 1898 Cavaignac, then Minister of War in Brisson's new radical ministry, reaffirmed Dreyfus's guilt in the Chamber of Deputies, quoting a letter from the Italian Military Attaché, Panizzardi, which Colonel Picquart later showed to be a forgery. Both Millerand and his faction of Independent socialists, as well as the Guesdist deputies, approved Cavaignac's speech and regarded the affair as thereby closed. Jaurès, however, stated in *La Petite République* that he would undertake a campaign on behalf of Dreyfus, 'à titre personnel'. In an article entitled 'L'Action Socialiste', he explained that he would urge the proletariat to fight for those modest guarantees of individual liberty won in the past by bourgeois revolutions.[35] He repeated that in this struggle 'je n'engage que moi-même'. But Jaurès found willing support from Jean Allemane and Maurice Charnay in *Le Parti Ouvrier* and from Gérault-Richard, editor of *La Petite République* – which now became the forum for Jaurès's Dreyfusard campaign.

The national executive of the Guesdist POF *(Parti Ouvrier Français)* reacted unfavourably to this initiative, as did the Blanquist factions. In a declaration on 24 July 1898 the POF solemnly proclaimed that 'the workers have nothing to do with this battle, which is not their own'.[36] Signed by Guesde and Lafargue, the declaration stated that the Dreyfus affair did not concern the organized and class-conscious section of the French proletariat. The workers could have nothing to do with either of the warring bourgeois factions in the case, which would only divert them from the essential tasks of class struggle and social revolution. Socialists could not dissipate their energies for the sake of one bourgeois officer when they had a whole class to emancipate! The POF did not owe any duty to Dreyfus, but only to the working-class masses who suffered daily in the capitalist prisons.[37] Both the Allemanists and Gérault-Richard in *La Petite République* attacked this pseudo-revolutionary rhetoric as an abject surrender to the Jesuit, antisemitic gang and to the militarists of the General Staff.[38]

Even within the Guesdist ranks there was some private criticism. On 1 August 1898 Paul Lafargue (son-in-law of Karl Marx and one of the POF leaders) wrote to Guesde that the party's sectarian attitude was 'inexcusable', that its duty was to lead the 'floating masses', rather than be towed along in the wake of their apathy. 'The Workers Party, which is a political party, cannot be unconcerned with political questions which agitate the country, above all in a question where militarism, court-martials, bourgeois legality, antisemitism etc. are involved.'[39] But Lafargue's private doubts (preserved in the Guesde Archives in Amsterdam) had no influence on the official Guesdist line, which he continued faithfully to follow, in his articles for *Le Socialiste*.[40] One of the main reasons for the intransigent class strategy of the Guesdists was the desire to avert the disasters of 1830, 1848, and 1871, when the French proletariat had pulled bourgeois chestnuts out of the fire only to be ignored or massacred for its pains.[41] Another reason for the Guesdist policy was the fear of the leadership that any spontaneous agitation which might develop out of the affair would endanger the tightly organized, disciplined unity carefully built up over the past twenty years. In the Dreyfus affair, the Guesdists adopted the same attitude as during the Boulangist crisis ten years earlier, when their watchword had been 'Ni Boulanger, Ni Ferry'. Abstention in conflicts involving bourgeois parties had become an article of the Guesdist faith, the hallmark of its sectarian and dogmatic interpretation of Marxism. An identical attitude was adopted by Edouard Vaillant, the leader of the Blanquist faction, whose position on the issue of class collaboration was similar to Guesde's.

However by August 1898 the Guesdist-Blanquist position of complete neutrality in the Dreyfus Affair seemed increasingly untenable. With the discovery of the Panizzardi forgery, followed by Colonel Henry's arrest, confession, and suicide (August 11) and Esterhazy's flight, the case against Dreyfus appeared to be broken. In his series of articles entitled 'Les Preuves' (written in August/September 1898) Jaurès was demonstrating with flawless logic and unmatched eloquence both the web of conspiracy and the significance of the affair. He warned the workers that if they did not disentangle the 'complicated intrigues of reaction' and relied only on general formulas, they would be 'at the mercy of every demagogic lie'.[42] He pointed out that the exiled and degraded Dreyfus was no longer an officer and a 'bourgeois', as the French Marxists proclaimed, but a *victim*. 'He is stripped in his misery of all class character, he is nothing less than mankind itself in the deepest abyss of despair. We cannot, in the name of socialism, turn our backs on despoiled mankind.'[43]

The proletarian revolution found its meaning in the defence of 'humanity', incarnated by Dreyfus – the victim of an inhuman social order, 'a living witness to the military lie, to political cowardice and to the crimes of authority'.[44] Dreyfus in his degradation had become a 'revolutionary factor', a witness to the meaning of the rights of man, the common heritage of liberty and republican legality – which the proletariat had to preserve if it were to ensure the victory of socialism.[45] Dreyfus was the illustration of Jaurès's belief in the democratic ideology, in republican institutions, and in the future collaboration of the radical bourgeoisie and proletariat in bringing about socialism. Dreyfus was also the vindication of Jaurès's theory of *integral* justice (inspired by his teachers, Malon and Lucien Herr), and his idealistic faith in socialism as the universal conscience of mankind.

Despite the dramatic turn of events, the POF continued to oppose Jaurès's campaign as a diversion of the socialist movement into the channels of compromise with the class enemy. Nevertheless, at the Montluçon Congress of 18–25 September 1898 the terms of the POF declaration in July were somewhat softened – to allow for condemnation of the abuses of militarism and a call for the abolition of court-martials.[46] The POF Congress also passed a resolution condemning nationalism and antisemitism as deviations from the class struggle. In October 1898 the Guesdists emerged from their sectarian isolation to form a 'committee of vigilance', with other socialist groupings, against the threat of a *coup d'état* from the Right. Links with other factions were gradually strengthened and a policy of 'concentration républicaine' was approved by the POF to clear the 'counter-revolutionary bands' from the streets.[47] The process of socialist unification had received its first major impulse and this was to be one of the more enduring consequences of the Dreyfus affair.

The policy of developing co-operation with other socialist groups did not prevent the POF from continuing to attack the Dreyfusard intellectuals, radical bourgeois, and followers of Jaurès for their participation in the affair. In the eyes of *Le Socialiste* (the organ of the Guesdists), the Dreyfusards were hypocrites and dilettantes, who were indifferent to the social struggles of the proletarian masses, but were ready to turn France upside down, to save an officer of their own class.[48] In January 1899, *Le Socialiste* published a long article by a veteran Guesdist, Gabriel Deville, setting out the reasons for the continuing 'neutrality' of the POF in the affair.[49] From this article it was apparent that the party leadership considered that Dreyfus's cause was unpopular with the masses: the party could not risk losing mass support at a time when France stood in danger of a *coup* from the monarchist or nationalist Right. While the Guesdists held aloof from embracing the cause of Dreyfus, they did however take an active part in the campaign against militarism and for the defence of the Republic, which culminated in the demonstration at Longchamp in June 1899.[50]

It was also in June 1899 that the Dreyfusards won their first major victory when a retrial of Captain Dreyfus was ordered. On 12 June 1899, only nine days later, the Dupuy government fell and a ministerial crisis developed, which led to the formation of the Waldeck–Rousseau Cabinet on 26 June 1899. This government of 'republican unity' contained both the socialist, Alexandre Millerand – as Minister of Commerce – and General Gallifet ('butcher of the Paris Commune') as its Minister of War. Both Guesdists and Blanquists, who had numerous ex-Communards in their ranks, were adamantly opposed to the participation of Millerand in such a bourgeois Cabinet.[51] Henceforth 'Millerandism', as the new heresy was called, became a new arm in the struggle of the orthodox Left against Jaurès's policy of class collaboration. The Dreyfus affair was seen, not without reason, as the original sin which had led Jaurès to support the entry of Millerand (regarded as his protégé) into the government. But Jaurès, unperturbed, continued his campaign, calling it 'one of the greatest battles of the century, one of the greatest in human history'.[52] On 13 August 1899 he wrote: 'The hour of liberation is coming for the martyr, also the hour of punishment for the scoundrels.'[53]

This judgement proved slightly premature. On 11 September 1899 Dreyfus was again found guilty by a vote of 5–2, this time with 'extenuating circumstances'. But eight days later he was pardoned by President Loubet – and on 18 December 1899 Parliament granted an amnesty to all those involved in the affair (except Deroulède, Guérin, and those considered a danger to state security). Jaurès, much to the chagrin of many Dreyfusards, accepted the amnesty – which protected conspirators such as General Mercier as much as Dreyfus. Jaurès's hands were tied by his political commitment to the Waldeck–Rousseau regime of 'Republican defence' and to Millerand's continuation as a minister. This was the beginning of the alienation between Jaurès and the purely Dreyfusard socialists like Péguy who did not accept a mere amnesty.

Le Socialiste, however, saw in Jaurès's tactics the logical consequence of his abandonment of the principles of the class struggle during the affair. He had led the working class into an alliance with the radical Republican bourgeoisie which in its view could only prove illusory and detrimental to socialism.[54] This was indeed a standpoint with which many European socialists, including Bebel, Kautsky, and Rosa Luxemburg who had previously supported Jaurès's campaign for Dreyfus, could sympathize.[55] They agreed with the strictures of Guesde and Vaillant against 'Millerandism', and Jaurès's tactics were now seen in a more critical light as a form of 'opportunism'. The Guesdists continued their offensive against Dreyfusardism unabated, and Lafargue even accused Jaurès of losing interest in truth and justice as soon as Dreyfus had been pardoned.[56] This kind of criticism lacked conviction however when it came from narrow-minded 'materialists' who prided themselves on their superior indifference to 'sentimental' phrases like 'the rights of man'. More convincing was the disillusion of the ex-Dreyfusards on the Left who felt that their ideals had been betrayed by the new radical/radical-socialist/socialist coalition ('Union des Gauches') of Waldeck–Rousseau and Combes. The anarcho-syndicalists, for example, drew their own conclusions from the affair, and offered an increasingly revolutionary alternative after 1900 to Jaurès's democratic parliamentary socialism. Their hostility and indifference to parliamentarianism was further reinforced by the affair, which had underlined the impotence of the legislature and the value of direct action on the streets. Syndicalist distrust of 'politicians' and of the university intellectuals who had entered the socialist movement under the impact of Jaurès's campaign, was also strengthened. Above all there was a great bitterness in the syndicalist milieu against the 'Dreyfusards' in power, radicals, and socialists like Clemenceau, Briand, and Viviani, who had changed allegiances with unseemly haste.

It was these same former champions of 'justice' who called in the army to suppress working-class strikers and reacted with extraordinary harshness against the grievances of the masses. Sometimes this bitterness among syndicalist intellectuals had an antisemitic tinge – as in the case of Sorel, Lagardelle, Edouard Berth, and Robert Louzon. Georges Sorel's *Reflections on Violence* (1906) was symptomatic of the turning away of an ex-Dreyfusard from the democratic tradition of socialism towards the anarcho-syndicalist utopia of the 'General Strike'. Sorel nourished a special resentment against the Kantian idealism which had inspired so many Dreyfusard contemporaries, against the pacifist, humanitarian ethos of the Radical Republic, against 'laic' positivism and the parliamentarianism of Jaurès.[57].In its place he glorified the heroic 'myth' of the class war and the prospect of an act of redemptive and apocalyptic violence by the syndicalists against the decadent bourgeois Republic. Robert Louzon, another contributor to *Le Mouvement Socialiste* (a review sympathetic to syndicalism) greeted the quashing of the Rennes verdict and the exoneration of Dreyfus in July 1906 as a victory of 'le parti juif' and a defeat for Dreyfusard justice. In his view, the verdict was illegal (since no new facts or evidence had been brought forward) and merely reflected a new balance of power in which the 'Jewish' bourgeoisie had triumphed over its Jesuit rivals.[58] This was an attitude not dissimilar to that of the *Action Française*, the militant right-wing organization born out of the Dreyfus affair, which always regarded Dreyfus's rehabilitation as 'illegal'. Another militant ex-Dreyfusard who had become overtly antisemitic was Urbain Gohier, who complained in his pamphlet *La Terreur Juive* that he had not helped to overthrow Rome (the Jesuits) in order to substitute Jerusalem! 'We, the internationalist revolutionary Dreyfusards had not foreseen this result. We wished to maintain civil rights for the Jewish 'métèques' and instead we have made them masters of France.'[59]

Some syndicalists like Émile Janvion were no less antisemitic than the ex-radical Urbain Gohier and sought to persuade their colleagues that the Jews, by manipulating high finance and freemasonry, were infiltrating and neutralizing the French labour movement. During the Dreyfus affair Janvion had been one of the most militant critics of Sebastian Faure's 'philosemitism', and in 1912 he was one of the leading syndicalist voices in favour of rapprochement with the *Action Française*. The virulently antisemitic *Terre Libre,* which expressed a populist variant of anarcho-syndicalism, frequently published his tirades against the Jews and freemasons. Gustav Hervé's *La Guerre Sociale* (more in the mainstream of anarcho-syndicalism) also reflected left-wing disillusion in the aftermath of what critics called 'la mort du Dreyfusisme'. Hervé's paper pointed out that the new masters of France were as little enamoured of truth and justice as their predecessors, as ready to use the military against the workers, and as indifferent to the plight of the masses.[60]

Another disillusioned Dreyfusard, but one who immortalized the idealist crusade of his youth and remained free of antisemitism (though not of French nationalism) was Charles Péguy. In 1898–9, the young Péguy had symbolized the perfect fusion of Dreyfusard ideals and socialism, perceived as an 'inner revolution', a moral transformation of man, which would enable him to construct 'la cité harmonieuse'.[61] In the Dreyfus affair the socialist Péguy had seen the crucible of a new humanity, the assertion of the universal conscience, and that solidarity which alone could bring about 'la cité socialiste'. He had left the official socialist movement at the end of 1899, appalled by the doctrinaire rigidity of Guesde, Lafargue, and Vaillant, by their 'tartufferie', moral blindness, and authoritarianism.[62] He had founded *Les Cahiers de la Quinzaine* at the end of 1899 in order to reassert the moral integrity of the Dreyfusard socialist vision. For a time, like many 'universitaires' (especially the ex-'Normaliens') Péguy still regarded Jaurès as the embodiment of a generous, humanitarian socialism with which he could identify himself. By 1903, however, Péguy was as disillusioned as Sorel, with what he regarded as a betrayal of the Dreyfusard 'mystique' by Jaurès, the parliamentarian and socialist politican.

Jaurès's Dreyfusardism became for Péguy a symbol of the incorporation of a 'mystique' into 'politique'. He concluded that whenever the demand for integral justice was manipulated for political ends, the devaluation of the original ideals became inevitable. Péguy therefore turned away from parliamentary political socialism, which had merely used the Dreyfus affair as a means to an end (to achieve socialist unity and participation in government). What probably saved Péguy, despite his Catholic nationalism, from sliding like so many contemporaries into antisemitism was his fidelity to the memory of Bernard Lazare.

We now enter a terrain which cannot be fully explored here, but only touched upon in so far as it has a bearing on the change which the Dreyfus affair brought about in the attitudes of French socialists towards the Jewish problem. This change certainly had little to do with the role played by the French Jewish community during the affair, which was almost non-existent.[63] Nor did it have much to do with the personality of Dreyfus, which did not exactly inspire even such an ardent Dreyfusard as Charles Péguy.[64] The 'hero' of the affair was really its anti-hero, the incarnation of Alsatian rigidity, of snobbish condescension, and 'noblesse oblige' *vis-à-vis* his less fortunate brethren from the east, a proud, ambitious officer, a millionaire, and a French patriot.[65] What enthusiasm could most socialists, let alone simple workers, summon up for such a 'privileged' victim, who was not only a class enemy, ready to mow them down when in uniform – but, worse, a rich Jew!? It is indeed a tribute to the moral greatness of the Dreyfusards that they saw beyond the man, his class, his race and religion, his personality, and focused on the principle. At a time when the antisemitic hysteria was raging in France, when few Jews were ready to defend Dreyfus for fear that their attitude be 'imputed to any distinction or solidarity of race',[66] it took courage to be a Dreyfusard. For socialists, who had contributed not a little to the dissemination of antisemitic stereotypes in France, it was no less difficult to interest the workers in a Jewish officer. What finally induced a part of the socialist movement to follow Jaurès and throw its weight behind the Dreyfusard campaign was the traditional hatred of nobility and Church, and the fear of a right-wing *coup* rather than concern for Dreyfus. The French workers could be mobilized to defend the Republic and obstruct the intrigues of the Army and Church, but not so readily for an individual, whose cause as Daniel Halévy noted 'was never popular'.[67]

Most socialists were unwilling to confront the issue of antisemitism head on, until it was apparent that the gangrene was threatening to infiltrate deep into the labour ranks. The prevailing antisemitic stereotypes against Jewish bankers and financiers, which had a tenacious foothold among French socialists, were only slowly supplanted by a more objective and realistic attitude to the Jews; the Dreyfus affair, by exposing the counter-revolutionary role of antisemitism as a powerful weapon in the arsenal of the clerical and nationalist Right, contributed to this process of clarification. Socialists like Gustave Rouanet, Jaurès, Gérault-Richard, and Eugene Fournière, who had all in the previous decade flirted with a mild antisemitism, began unequivocally to denounce it after 1899. The affair crystallized the break between the nationalistic, Catholic, and pseudo-socialist Right and the increasingly anti-clerical, antimilitarist, and internationalist Left. It was no longer possible for nationalist or Catholic antisemites like Barrès, Drumont, and Henri Rochefort to appear on the same platform as socialists and be labelled as such.

The break with antisemitism on the French Left, as a result of the affair, was by no means complete however. An interesting perspective on this fact is afforded by the reaction of the immigrant Jewish working class in France, who were especially affected by the antisemitic campaign. Apart from a handful of Jewish intellectuals, like Joseph Reinach, Léon Blum, Daniel Halévy and his fellow contributors to *La Revue Blanche*, and above all Bernard Lazare, they were the only section of the French Jewish community to react publicly to the affair.[68] Existing on the fringes of the Parisian Jewish community, their socio-economic position, immigrant status, and previous experience of oppression and persecution in eastern Europe made them susceptible to revolutionary ideas – but also especially sensitive to antisemitism. A glimpse into the reactions of this marginal section of the Jewish community is offered by the pamphlet entitled *Lettre des ouvriers juifs de Paris au parti socialiste français*, published in 1898. It was signed by Karpel (head of the hatmakers union) and Dinner, librarian of the Yiddish Bibliothèque des ouvriers juifs de Paris, and issued by the 'Bibliothèque d'Éducation Libertaire', typography credited to Jean Allemane.[69]

It seems highly probable that Bernard Lazare had a hand in both financing and editing the pamphlet, which was largely anarchist in its content. What is interesting in our context is the critique directed by the pamphlet against the 'attentisme' of the French socialist party, and its apparent lack of vigour in combating antisemitism. The pamphlet pointed out that anti-Dreyfusard socialists (who at that time were in the majority) persisted in identifying the Jews exclusively as members of the wealthy *haute-bourgeoisie*. The authors commented with some bitterness:

> We perceive that whenever one speaks of the Jews, whether in the medieval or the modern sense, the existence of a Jewish proletariat is forgotten; it is apparently believed that the Jews are all rich men, bankers. And yet, we are, alas!, the most proletarian people in the world. Doubly so, both as a class and as a nation; for we are at the same time, class pariahs and the pariah of the nations.[70]

The pamphlet insisted that the majority of the 8–9 million Jews in the world were oppressed, persecuted, disinherited, exiled, and living in abject poverty. Yet the French socialists had singularly ignored the existence of this worldwide Jewish proletariat, just as it had ignored the dangerous revival in France of slumbering violent instincts and Judeophobia. Socialist passivity in the face of this threat to civilization was a sad fact, according to the authors of the pamphlet: for the mass of Jewish proletarians looked to socialism as their sole defence, as the inheritor of the traditions of the French Revolution and the rights of man.[71] Jewish workers had been disillusioned by the lack of a frank, indignant, and energetic stand by the French socialists when 'there is a whole Jewish proletariat, which alone is the victim of antisemitism'.[72] The pamphlet accused the French socialists (not without cause) of believing that antisemitism was 'profitable' to the labour movement – that 'class-hatred could be superimposed onto Jew-hatred'. 'In other words, your attitude is a compromise on the political level between the old barbarian desires, the old ferocious appetites, and the new humanitarian and libertarian aspirations.'[73]

Socialist propaganda against Jewish capitalists and bankers had rebounded in the Dreyfus affair, encouraging hatred against Jews in general, including the immigrant Jewish workers of Paris. The pamphlet concluded with an appeal, not untinged with pathos, calling on the French socialists, in the name of fraternity and their best revolutionary traditions, to take the defence of the oppressed and suffering Jews. Whether this appeal had any direct impact on the attitudes of the French socialists to the Jewish problem is difficult to assess. A number of articles did appear however in *La Petite République* in 1899, dealing for the first time with the problem of the Jewish proletariat.[74] Both Jaurès and Rouanet referred to this aspect of the affair in their speeches and articles in the summer of 1899, especially in relation to Algeria.[75] In anarchist circles, some attention was also paid to Jewish rights, which had been placed in jeopardy by the antisemitic campaign during the Dreyfus affair. The Jewish anarchist, Henri Dhorr, insisted in an article for *Le Libertaire* in September 1899 on 'le droit d'être juif' as a human right, which could not be renounced in the name of a false internationalism.[76] The founder of French syndicalism and inspirer of the labour exchanges, Fernand Pelloutier, also spoke eloquently of the Jewish contribution to civilization, and especially to revolutionary thought.[77] Above all, Bernard Lazare, in an open letter in *L'Aurore,* asserted the Jewish self-consciousness and sense of mission, so lacking in the assimilated French-Jewish bourgeoisie. Explaining why he had interceded for Dreyfus, Lazare declared: 'I want it to be said that I was the first to have spoken, that it was a Jew who first stood up for the Jewish martyr . . . . a Jew who knew to what an outcast, disinherited, ill-starred people he belonged, and drew from this consciousness the will to fight for justice and truth.'[78]

For Lazare, Dreyfus was nothing less than a symbol of the martyred Jewish people, past and present – 'the tragic image of the Algerian Jews, beaten and pillaged' – of the Russian, Galician, and Rumanian Jews of the eastern ghettoes, of the suffering Jewish proletariat of London and New York.[79] Something of this passion and universal vision also communicated itself to the best of the French socialists, who fought in the name of the republican 'mystique' and the revolutionary tradition. Hence, by an extraordinary transmutation, a wealthy Jewish officer could become for Jaurès and his supporters the symbol of the martyred proletariat. For as he pointed out, if the proletariat did not intervene against the crimes of bourgeois society, it became an accomplice, itself responsible for those crimes – 'and therefore it is no longer merely a dark spot on the declining capitalist sun, but a blight on the rising socialist sun. We did not want this stigma of shame on the dawn of the proletariat.'[80]

It was a tribute to the moral and political perception of Jaurès that he was able to utilize the *élan* derived from the affair to rally the French proletariat against the threat of militarism, clericalism, and the collapse of the Republic. Despite all the hesitations, waverings, and initial reluctance, Jaurès's campaign awakened French socialism from its fratricidal struggles and lethargy, and thereby saved its honour.

12

A Parisian patricide

During the decade since *les évenéments* of May 1968 a new generation of *philosophes* began to analyse and dissect the myths and illusions of that irruption of the future into the present. Their disappointed hopes and frustrations have led the angry men of the post-1968 generation to question bitterly the naivety of the past commitments to the goddesses of revolution, progressivism, and Marxism. The new mood of the Parisian 'philosophers' is almost aggressively apolitical, or rather *anti-étatiste.* They are bored by the barricades, contemptuously dismissive of the communist classics, and intensely mistrustful of omniscient savants who claim to know the way to universal happiness.

The ideological earthquake among the youthful elite of the 'progressive' Parisian intelligentsia has temporarily, at least, brought to a halt the double-talk and facile self-deceptions that characterized the French Left since 1945. The post-1968 new-wave philosophers have belatedly discovered the problem of totalitarianism and with it the truth about Marxism as the 'opium of the intellectuals' revealed by Professor Raymond Aron more than twenty-five years ago. The writings of Solzhenitsyn and the word Gulag have entered the vocabulary of the leftist milieu with all the impact of a delayed explosion. In the words of Bernard-Henri Lévy, the prime instigator of this 'intellectual counter-revolution', it was enough, that Solzhenitsyn spoke, 'to awaken us from our dogmatic slumber'. The Russian writer and dissident, 'the Shakespeare of our times' (Lévy), almost single-handedly delivered the new philiosophers from the prison house of their own hyper-intellectual theories and conceptual systems, to the contemplation of a brute reality, freed from the compulsive lies of ideology. It is difficult to suppress a smile at the pathos and childlike innocence with which Lévy and others have piled up superlatives to describe the fearless Dante of the twentieth century who opened their eyes to the hell of Gulag and of the *univers concentrationnaire.*

Perhaps the most sophisticated of all the former *contestataires* who re-read their Marx in the cold light of Gulag is the ex-Maoist André Glucksmann. In 1968 he published *Stratégie et Révolution en France*, which was hailed by the London-based *New Left Review* as 'the fundamental theoretical document of the younger generation of students and intellectuals who launched the movement of May'. This study was an elegant critique from the Left of the tactics adopted by the French communist party to break the back of the anti-authoritarian movement which had swept France. Adroitly marshalling his quotations from Marx and Lenin, Glucksmann argued that Gaullist state power had survived in France because the Left lacked an adequate revolutionary theory and organization able to mobilize the extra-parliamentary movement.

Seven years later, Glucksmann published his iconoclastic 'Essay on the state, Marxism and the concentration camps', entitled *La cuisinière et le mangeur d'hommes,* which contained a drastic revision of his youthful anarcho-Maoist creed. In this work, infused with the spirit of the Russian dissidents, it was apparent that Stalinism was not merely an unfortunate aberration or consequence of the all-too-human mistakes of Lenin. The original sin of totalitarianism was traced back to Karl Marx himself, and beyond him to the metaphysical tradition of western philosopy beginning with Plato. *Le mangeur d'hommes* was the omnipotent, cannibalistic state that Lenin had wished to destroy and replace by the 'administration of things' which even a simple cook could run. Far from 'withering away', however, the state produced by Russian revolution had almost immedi-ately spawned the labour camps which revealed the grim truth behind the construction of socialism.

In analysing the Russian (and Nazi) concentration-camp experience, Glucksmann drew some far-reaching conclusions: Bolshevism was the embodiment of Marxism, a science of government for the twentieth century designed to keep the plebs in harness, a 'Platonism for the people' perfectly adapted to eternalize the oppression of the masses. The true role of the philosopher was to give a voice to the suffering of the plebs, *le bon peuple*, who silently resist the pretension of the state and the *appareils* which enslave them in the name of a higher truth.

The real object of Glucksmann's assault, which is even more apparent in a more recent work, *Les Maîtres penseurs*, is the language of power. It is not simply Marxism, totalitarianism, or even politics which is evil – the source of all our afflictions resides in the notion of *le Savoir total.* Glucksmann has adapted Michel Foucault's idea of history as an impersonal demonstration of absolute rationality, the myth of an omniscient and omnipotent *Maître* (the state, *le pouvoir*), and applied it with relentless logic to the writings of the great western philosophers; Gulag is not the result of a revolution betrayed, it is in our heads. Totalitarianism is not merely a product of European or Russian history, it is Plato, Fichte, Hegel, Nietzsche, and Marx, it is the *maîtrise du maître,* the myth of the Absolute Idea.

The intellectual seeds of Gulag, of all Gulags past, present, and future, rest on metaphysical foundations. In Russia, Marxism played the role of this 'science of the state', the revealed truth in whose name the *apparatchiks* can justify every oppression. They are the incarnation of the *Logos* bequeathed by the west, the realization of the totalitarian claims of Reason. Against this gigantic imposture stands the culture of dissidence (Solzhenitsyn, Pliouchtch, Bukovsky, and so on) – those who resist without imitating what they oppose. In the west, the anarchist revolt must learn from this heroic example of anti-totalitarian thought, to combat its own police states and institutionalized oppression. Against *le mangeur d'hommes*, Glucksmann celebrates the irony of Socrates, the irreverence of Rabelais, the voice of the plebs, and the carnival of the poor.

In *Les Maîtres Penseurs* he attempts to deepen this line of thought by an extended denunciation of German philosophy from Fichte to Nietzsche. The indictment against these intellectual heavyweights of the nineteenth century is so severe that it would be tempting to read it as a Freudian case study in the mechanisms of Oedipal revolt. His former teachers stand accused of preparing the intellectual tools for the great Final Solutions of the twentieth century. Glucksmann steps into the ring and runs amok as he castrates and finishes off the fathers, whose scientific prophecies he holds responsible for the Moloch–Leviathan of totalitarian state power. German philosophy, the last flower of western metaphysics, is the mirror through which Glucksmann reinterprets the evils of European colonialism, of Vietnam, the Gulag Archipelago, and the 'science of Revolution'. Order, authority, the state – the strategy of universal domination – all are ground down and passed through the great logic machine which is German philosophy. Thanks to the *maîtres penseurs,* history and the world have become German, which for Glucksmann is only a symbol of our modern, revolutionary, European-ized chamber of horrors. 'Tout le XIX siècle allemand a premédité une révolution et nationale et socialiste' – the German ideology necessarily leads to Buchenwald and Auschwitz – but it is only 'un cas particulier' il-lustrating the age-old secrets of a decadent Europe. The fascination of this demonic Germany is that of a fiendish experimental laboratory in which the logic of Europeanization reaches its final consummation. Operation Apocalypse stands revealed in the texts, for those who can decode their true meaning. 'Ils furent les pères des idéologies régnantes qui ont programmé les solutions finales.'

Yet even Glucksmann admits that the *maîtres penseurs* were not themselves Nazis. The only direct line of affiliation was through their antisemitism, passed like a relay baton from Fichte to Hegel to Marx to

Nietzsche. For Glucksmann, this sophisticated hostility to the Jews was the inevitable corollary of the unholy alliance between German philosophy and the state. Already in Fichte the theme is announced: the Jews are a state within the state, a symbol of the particularism which must be banished from the modern world. The Germans must escape from the curse of their own dispersion and disunity, they must expel the *sans-patrie* or else conquer the Promised Land (Palestine) for them, so that they will not be contaminated by 'Jewish' ideas. Only by negating the 'Jew' in themselves can the Germans affirm themselves as a nation under the authority of a powerful state.

In Hegel the theme becomes more explicit. The Jews are the anti-state: for 2,000 years their Mosaic code and Abrahamic faith has estranged them from the holy Trinity of the *maîtres penseurs* – people/nation/state. The individualism of the Jews is for Hegel something perverse, egoistic, mad, and suicidal. It is the counter-model to the aesthetic unity of the Greek polis, with which Hegel embellishes his worship of the Prussian state as the divine consummation of the Absolute Idea. What indeed can be more antithetical to the Hegelian identification of the state with philosophical Reason than the survival of the Jewish Diaspora?

Marx stands Hegel on his head, only to discover a new 'Jewish question' implicit in his master's rejection of all particularism, that of private property. The Jews represent not so much a separatist religion as the 'bourgeois spirit', as antithetical to the domination of the state as the Mosaic faith. The spirit of capitalism is the Jewish temptation of the Germans, the power of money which crosses frontiers and escapes the omnipotent state. This universal power symbolized for Marx by Judaism is later denounced as *Das Kapital*, and the hatred of the communists will be focused on its universal ramifications. Private property and not the state must be abolished if the world is to become communist. Hence Marx emancipates himself in a 'German' manner from the so-called 'Jewish' spirit of the bourgeoisie.

Glucksmann's interpretation of German antisemitism focuses exclusively on the cult of the state which rejects the right to existence of any minorities in its midst. The Jews are perceived as a subversive element because of their *extra-statist* mission. This is what supposedly links the *maîtres penseurs* to the young Hitler in Vienna, who sees in the caftaned Jew a non-German phenomenon, inassimilable to the nation-state, and therefore inhuman. The whole of European racism is thus reduced to this simplistic schema, in which the Jews along with other 'marginal' and 'deviant' groups are portrayed as inherently antagonistic to the omnipotent claims of the modern state.

The original sin of the German ideology, according to Glucksmann, is that from the outset it became the accomplice of a secret, totalistic will-to-power. Hegel's Absolute Idea, Marx's socialized Humanity,

Nietzsche's Superman, are only metaphors for a common project – the alliance of *pouvoir* and *savoir* – in the service of universal domination. Even the contemporary division of the world between the super-powers is reduced to a struggle between basic philosophical doctrines furnished by nineteenth-century German thinkers. The bombs dropped by B52 planes over Vietnam, like the bullets fired from Russian and Chinese rifles, are ultimately expressions of the impersonal universality first enunciated by the *maîtres penseurs*. As in his earlier analyses of the Nazi and Russian concentration camps, Glucksmann appears to have abandoned any attempt at the rational explanation of historical events. In his efforts to de-ideologize the twentieth-century nightmare he has fallen victim to a mode of thinking which seems no less doctrinaire than the hyper-intellectual megalomania he decries throughout his latest work. In place of a Marxism purged of its Hegelian paternity we are left with an ahistorical pessimism which endlessly turns on itself within a closed universe of philosophical discourse; a philosophy of *désillusion* which negates reason itself in the name of some vague plebeian populism. Swimming in the dizzy circle of his own abstractions, Glucksmann dissolves the actual movement of history into a series of witty but depressing encounters with the alleged bankruptcy of western philosophy.

It would not be difficult to expose the contradictions and occasional absurdities in Glucksmann's patricidal assault on the German ideology. What is more significant is that this ingenious but somewhat abstruse work should become a bestseller in France, where it has evidently filled an intellectual void. Its anti-Marxism, spiced with a touch of the old anarchist *contestation*, has ensured it an audience both with the 'lost generation' of May 1968 and those alarmed by the prospects of a left-wing government in France. Its indictment of the German philosophical school which has dominated post-war French thought fell on receptive ears in the Parisian literary world, which is far from immune to the anti-German sentiments that have swept the country in recent years. Above all, *les maîtres penseurs* captures a mood of disenchantment with ideology, of pessimistic irrationalism and malaise, which has seized the post-Marxist Parisian intelligentsia.

13

The ghost of Leon Trotsky

Despite all the attention which he has received in more recent years, Leon Trotsky remains an enigmatic figure. Few revolutionaries in modern history have been the object of such partisan commentary and aroused such strong feelings among admirers and detractors alike. In Soviet Russia and the socialist countries, Trotsky's name was until recently virtually erased from the annals of the Russian Revolution, dropped down the memory-hole and forgotten. 'Trotskyism' remains, however, as an ideological bogey to be ritually denounced, even though its organizational base in the Soviet Union was extirpated more than fifty years ago. Stalin's heirs seem unable to come to grips with the ghost of the murdered Trotsky, without whom there might have been no Bolshevik Revolution and whose heroic leadership saved the infant Soviet state from extinction in the years of the civil war.

In the west, too, 'Trotskyism' is something of a bogey, even though its endemic sectarianism, dogmatic rigidity, and in-fighting have prevented it from gaining any real foothold in the working class. In spite of media hysteria, which at one time blamed the disintegration of the Labour Party on 'Trotskyist' subversion, the movement in Britain, as elsewhere, maintains a very fragmented existence (there are currently at least four organizations which claim to be the authentic heirs of Trotsky's Fourth International). Its main inroads have been made among the so-called intellectual *avant-garde* and in the student milieu, or else by seeking to take over such current causes as feminism, Black Power, workers' control, and the defence of oppressed minority groups.

Modern Trotskyism, in its attempts to recruit a mass following, has in fact found itself obliged to move away from the legacy of its founder, whose charisma serves today as little more than a vehicle for romanticized revolutionary myths. The western working class having disappointed all Trotsky's expectations of it as the lever of world revolution, his followers began in the 1960s to appropriate the Third World as an outlet for their own political illusions.

Following this shift of perspective, it is not surprising that the Trotskyists should have become the unconditional partisans of the Palestinian cause, its most vociferous and militant spearhead on British, French, and American campuses. In their vilification of Israel as a 'racist', chauvinist, imperialist state which must be eliminated by armed struggle, the Trotskyists have outgunned all their rivals on the Left – including the Maoists, Stalinists, and anarcho-communists.

In the pathetically inflated verbal militancy and violence of their anti-Israel rhetoric, there is little to choose between such groups as the Socialist Workers' Party, the Workers' Revolutionary Party, or the International Marxist Group – to say nothing of the other tiny splinter organizations which claim to represent the true Bolshevik–Leninist heritage.

Yet for all their organizational weaknesses, there is no denying the intensity, the tenacity, and, at times, even the efficacy of the campaigns which the Trotskyists have waged against Israel and Zionism and against the National Front and racism in Britain. Undoubtedly, much of their propaganda has been essentially manipulative, seeking to extend their mass base among students and immigrant workers in Great Britain by in-filtrating such organizations as the Anti-Nazi League; and in the Near East they doubtless hope that the destruction of a Zionist Israel would facilitate the creation of a united, socialist Middle Eastern federation.

But the Vanessa Redgraves, the Tariq Alis, the Tony Cliffs, and the Paul Foots of this world have never satisfactorily explained how an Arab 'Liberation' of Palestine, with all its reactionary and potentially genoci-dal implications, can be reconciled with an *anti-racist* position. Their unconditional support for the PLO which openly sees itself as the spearhead of a militant Arabism (and, since the rise of the Ayatollah Khomeini, of a renascent Islam) and which denies all non-Arab, non-Moslem minorities the right to national self-determination, is in flat contradiction to any socialist precepts.

Indeed, in their eagerness to appropriate for their own purposes the anti-colonial and pro-Palestinian bandwagon, the Trotskyists have moved increasingly away from the teachings of their own founding father. Leon Trotsky's anti-Zionism had a quite different origin and motivation, and it was never so blindly dogmatic and totalistic as that of his followers; nor did he ever go on record as supporting the Palestinian Arab national movement, of whose anti-imperialist credentials he was justifiably sceptical. Trotsky's own position on the Jewish question was essentially dictated by his genuinely universalist perspectives and dis-regard for the reality of national and ethnic boundaries. As a young Russian revolutionary he believed that to make the Jews a special topic of discussion or to engage in a particularist struggle against antisemitism was superfluous. The advent of a classless, socialist society would automatically 'solve' the problem.

At the Second Congress of the Russian Social Democratic Party in 1903 (which witnessed the split between the Bolsheviks and Mensheviks), the 23-year-old Trotsky led the assault on the Bund, which claimed the exclusive right to organize and represent Jewish workers in the party. Trotsky, who had never worked among the Jewish proletariat and knew no Yiddish, outraged the delegates of the Bund by using his Jewish origin as a weapon against them. (Today, the many Trotskyist leaders of Jewish background do precisely the same thing when they stigmatize Zionism; they trade on their origins when it is expedient, but bend over backwards to deny their Jewishness when it no longer suits them.) It was, however, characteristic of Trotsky that he should present the demands of the Bund for Jewish cultural autonomy as a vote of mistrust in non-Jewish party members and as being opposed to socialist internationalism.

Like other equally assimilated Jews from a 'Russified' or Polonized milieu, such as Zinoviev, Kamenev, Sverdlov, Karl Radek, or Rosa Luxemburg, Trotsky could not abide any expression of Jewish ethnicity or self-conscious Jewish identification. As he once told the leader of the Bund, Vladimir Medem, Trotsky considered himself neither a Russian nor a Jew, but a social democrat. Imagine Lenin or Stalin giving such a reply! But for those non-Jewish Jews who had allegedly 'transcended' the boundaries of Judaism (Isaac Deutscher's phrase), such self-negation was the *sine qua non* of their cosmopolitan stance. It was made possible by a passionate and burning faith in the advent of a truly classless, nationless, and atheistic social order where all barriers inherited from the past would disappear. Any attempts to maintain Jewish or other forms of particularism, as in the Bund or the Zionist movement, seemed reactionary to the radicals of Trotsky's generation. But their optimism has proved to be ill-founded, a fact which the mature Trotsky himself came to recognize, albeit rather belatedly.

For a few years, following the Bolshevik *putsch* in November 1917, it did indeed seem that the world revolution might be on the agenda, and in this period Trotsky's own origins were no handicap to his playing a decisive role in events. In 1917, and again during the civil war, he was able to mobilize the energies of the Russian workers and peasants, to instil in them the belief that they were the *avant-garde* of the world proletariat, marching towards the Promised Land of socialism. But this secular messianism of which Trotsky was the most zealous Bolshevik apostle and armed prophet rebounded on him once the heroic period of struggle was over. Significantly, as Stalin's doctrine of 'Socialism in One Country' (with its appeal to Russian national messianism) gained ground after the death of Lenin in 1924, Trotsky found himself branded as an oppositionist, then as a heretic, and finally as an alien intruder and saboteur in the Bolshevik party. In the late 1920s, unmistakeably antisemitic motifs appeared in the agitation against Trotsky's Left opposition – the first indication of Stalin's personal Judeophobia and his readiness to exploit the popular prejudices of the Russian masses.

Trotsky now recognized that Soviet antisemitism was a reality that could not be ignored and one which had greatly disadvantaged his oppositional movement. On the other hand, his own feelings about Jews remained ambivalent and not untainted with prejudice. At the time of the Revolution and in the early years of the Soviet regime, he had arrogantly sent away Jewish delegations and he distrusted the motives of those Jews who joined the party or the Red Army. In his view, it was their embittered national feelings rather than their class experiences, or else it was pure opportunism, which had made them identify with the Bolsheviks.

How deep this suspicion went is shown by Trotsky's intervention in 1940 in the internal feuds which divided the SWP (an explicitly Trotskyist group in America and then the largest organization in the Fourth International) over its class composition. Trotsky favoured the mid-western non-Jewish 'workers' faction led by James Cannon against the New York Jewish 'intellectuals' led by Martin Abern and Max Schachtman. Trotsky wanted his American followers to orient them-selves towards the factories, the strikes, and the unions in order to ensure 'a more healthy atmosphere inside the party'; hence he called for the Jewish 'petty-bourgeois' and intellectual elements to be removed from 'their habitual conservative milieu' and dissolved in the real labour movement.

Trotsky was careful to state that 'the question of the Jewish intellec-tuals and semi-intellectuals of New York is a social, not a national question' but it is not surprising that Schachtman and Abern saw this stance as catering to antisemitism inside the movement! In any event, Trotsky's attitude has not prevented the movement he founded from being dominated by Jewish intellectuals like Ernest Mandel, Tony Cliff, Alain Krivine, Daniel Ben Said – all of whom, along with other Trotskyist authors, ranging from Isaac Deutscher and Abram Leon to George Novack and Nathan Weinstock, have been militantly anti-Zionist.

This neo-Trotskyist generation ignores Trotsky's own change of position on the Jewish question in the mid-1930s as a result of the ferocity of Nazi antisemitism. The fact that this had occurred in the most advanced capitalist country in Europe obliged Trotsky to revise his earlier optimistic prognosis that assimilation would automatically re-solve the Jewish predicament. Although he did not abandon his long-term belief that only the overthrow of capitalism on a global scale could provide ultimate salvation for Jews. Trotsky now saw the need for a short-term solution.

In an interview given in Mexico City in 1937, he even accepted that the Jews might require territorial concentration and an independent republic of their own in what he called the 'transitional historical period'. He did not exclude the establishment of such a territorial base for Jewry in Palestine (or elsewhere), though he was convinced that it could not succeed under the aegis of decaying capitalism and British imperialism. Thus, without abandoning his Marxist approach, Trotsky modified his position in order to 'reckon with the fact that the Jewish nation will maintain itself for an entire epoch to come'. There was no hint in this interview of any support for Arab national demands in Palestine and there is no compelling reason to think that Trotsky would have supported them today.

Trotsky's belated sensitivity to the tragic burdens facing the Jewish people at the end of the 1930s (he even foresaw the coming Holocaust) might well have been an unconscious echo of his own plight as a hunted exile seeking refuge in Turkey, France, Norway, and Mexico, yet finding no rest from the vengefulness of his implacable adversary, Joseph Stalin. Stalin had turned Trotsky into the archetypal 'wandering Jew', expelled and demonologized by the docile instruments of communist orthodoxy. Much like his co-religionists in Hitler's Germany, Trotsky found himself on a 'planet without a visa', crushed between the totalitarian juggernauts of Stalinism and fascism.

A socialist Zionist, who visited him in Mexico in 1937 and engaged him in a long conversation about Palestine, poignantly observed: 'A feeling accompanied me all the time that he was a Jew, a wandering Jew, without a fatherland.' Three years later, this last great survivor of the era of Bolshevik internationalism was cut down with an ice-pick by one of Stalin's agents as the Holocaust descended on the people he had left behind.

14

Vladimir Jabotinsky – a reassessment

Like many other ideologies, Zionism can be seen as the transmutation of a religious impulse into secular politics. In certain respects a revolt against the Jewish tradition and a radical attempt to break out of the parochial mould of Jewish history, Zionism, as an ideology, has never altogether transcended the past; rather it has aimed to politicize an age-old traditional belief in the restoration of the Jews to Zion and to substitute a secular, historical messianism, strongly marked by the nineteenth-century cult of progress, for the atrophied eschatological messianism of orthodox Judaism.

The 'revisionist' movement founded by the brilliant Russian Jewish publicist, Vladimir Jabotinsky (1880–1940), is perhaps the best example of Zionism as a purely political concept, of that *étatiste* tradition pioneered by Theodor Herzl at the turn of the century. Revisionism – the term itself derives from Jabotinsky's fight (beginning in 1923) for a revision of the political line of Zionism – was more fixated than any other trend within the movement on the goal of a Jewish state. Though this may seem surprising today, the preoccupation with a Jewish state was initially by no means as central to Zionism as it has been to other national movements – indeed not until the second half of the 1930s can it be said that the state idea emerged as a major priority for most Zionists. Although Theodor Herzl's pamphlet *Der Judenstaat*, whose very title embodied an *étatiste* programme, had appeared as early as 1896, the Basle Programme, which was hammered out a year later, contained no reference to the need for a state; instead, it said that Zionism aimed at the 'creation of a home [*Heimstätte*] for the Jewish people in Palestine to be secured by public law'. Twenty years later, the Balfour Declaration spoke of a 'national home for the Jewish people', a formula that allowed for a great deal of flexibility; it not only meant different things to the British, the Jews, and the Arabs but allowed for various interpretations within the Zionist camp.

Although no self-respecting Zionist would have disavowed the view that their ultimate aim was a Jewish state, this was not yet seen by the movement as a whole as a major nor even as a necessary condition for the realization of Zionism. The exception to the rule was provided by Vladimir Jabotinsky, one of the most flamboyant personalities in the history of Zionism, who had founded the Revisionist Party in 1925 having become disillusioned with the cautious, step-by-step policy of the Zionist executive and what he came to regard as its appeasement of the British and the Arabs in Palestine. For Jabotinsky and his followers, a Jewish state enjoying full independence and a clear Jewish majority was the only acceptable goal for Zionism. But at the beginning of the 1930s his definition of Zionist aims – which included the call for mass evacuation of Jews from eastern Europe and extensive Jewish settlement on both sides of the river Jordan – was decisively rejected. By 1935 Jabotinsky set up his independent New Zionist Organization, whose headquarters were in London. Yet, ironically enough, within four years the goal of the Jewish state, which he had consistently advocated, had become a practical necessity to which the Yishuv and the World Zionist Organization (WZO) were firmly committed. The rise of Nazism, the economic disintegration of Jewish life in Poland, and the Arab revolt and reorientation of British policy in Palestine, made the need for a Jewish state appear as a categorical imperative to most Zionists. Jabotinsky did not live to see this major shift in Zionist policy which was symbolized by the Biltmore Programme of 1942, but he can fairly be said to have been its forerunner.

No other Zionist leader had so consistently advocated the state-idea which he had linked organically to the creation of a Jewish majority in Palestine to be achieved by large-scale, rapid immigration. This mass immigration was designed not only to salvage and rescue the Jews of eastern Europe but at the same time to reinforce the Jewish claim to independent statehood. In order to absorb several million Jews in addition to the indigenous Arab population (whose future was to be that of a national minority group with equal rights and cultural autonomy but under Jewish sovereignty), the state would have to include Transjordan – that is, to be a Jewish state comprising both banks of the Jordan. Western Palestine alone would simply be too small to hold the mass exodus that Jabotinsky envisaged. It was 'rational' analysis and logical deduction rather than any sentimental nostalgic yearnings or biblical fundamentalism which drove the revisionist leader to demand the expansion of Jewish control over the whole of British Mandatory Palestine – as it had been originally designated in 1920.

Jabotinsky, it must be emphasized, was not a religiously observant Jew nor did he believe in a meta-historical bond (that is, a mystical bond directly derived from divine election) between the Jewish people and the

biblical land of Israel. His nationalism had *secular* rather than traditionalist roots. He was a child of the rationalist, positivist nineteenth century;
an agnostic who disliked obscurantism and for whom religion was
essentially a private affair. Like Herzl he could utilize a quasi-religious
pathos on occasion as an instrument of mass propaganda and in 1935 the
revisionists even included a religious clause in their platform, reflecting
the beliefs of many of their rank-and-file supporters; but this was
essentially a tactical concession. Jabotinsky never sought, for example, to
ground Israel's territorial claims in biblical promises (this appears to be a
comparatively recent development in Zionist ultra-nationalist ideology)
or to argue that settlement of the whole land of Israel was a divine
commandment. His nationalism emphasized the importance of the
secular symbols of state, territory, and political sovereignty – and to
achieve these goals he called, above all, for the inculcation of military
(rather than religious) virtues into Jewish youth.

Indeed, Jabotinsky's secularism was no less radical than that of the
labour Zionists with regard to the assault on traditional Jewish values.
Like Ben-Gurion, Jabotinsky despised the *Galut* (he had nothing in
himself of the *Galut* Jew) for its lack of inner spiritual freedom, its
submissiveness, inertia, and fatalism. Coming as he did from a Russified
assimilated home in Odessa, thoroughly impregnated with the values of
Russian and world literature, Jabotinsky never felt at ease with the
culture, the habits, the way of life of the *shtetl*. The ethos of the *cheder*, the
Yeshivah, or Jewish folklore had played no part in forming his character.
On the contrary, his vision of a reborn Jewish nation, modern, secular,
unashamedly western, aimed at abolishing forever the traits of the ghetto.
The *Galut* mentality had to be expunged; in their own homeland the Jews
would finally be able to clip off the physical and spiritual side-curls which
they had grown in the Diaspora. *Galut* represented something more than
simply political or economic oppression, social or individual discrimination; for the emancipated Russo-Jewish intelligentsia of Jabotinsky's
generation it was a *mentalité*, an amalgamation of negative characteristics
including such unattractive qualities as cowardice, self-surrender, spiritual
decadence, passivity, and social parasitism.

The ghetto Jew, the *Zhid* as Jabotinsky scathingly called him, was the
antithesis of that new Hebrew which the revisionist movement aimed to
forge in the crucible of armed struggle – a fearless, proud warrior, capable
of taking his fate in his own hands, of shedding blood for his fatherland,
endowed with the virtues of heroism, self-sacrifice, generosity, upright-
ness, idealism, and spiritual purity. The aesthetic ideals of chivalry,
honour, beauty, and gentlemanly conduct summed up in the Hebrew
word *Hadar*, expressed a world view and a doctrine that clearly
embodied the revisionist revolt against ghetto Judaism. Jabotinsky's
vision of *Malchut Yisrael* (the Kingdom of Israel), his evocation of the
Davidic kingdom, of the Maccabees, Bar Kochba, and so on – above all

his novel *Samson*, where the hero tells the people that they must do everything to get iron – 'for there is nothing more valuable in the world' – are essentially a form of radical pedagogy and therapy for a people that has lost its pride and self-confidence in exile and is close to despair; at the same time, by invoking and praising heroic virtues, the values of centralized leadership, unity, and discipline, and by stressing the importance of outward forms (all of which earned Jabotinsky the undeserved epithet of 'fascist' in his time), the revisionists aimed to mobilize the dormant mass energies necessary for any movement of national rebirth.

It is, of course, true that militaristic symbols and an undue emphasis on armed struggle were part of Jabotinskyian 'revisionism'. 'In blood and fire Judea fell and in blood and fire it will arise' – in the 1930s the labour Zionists seized on these features of 'revisionism' to brand Jabotinsky as a 'Jewish fascist' and imitator of Hitler and Mussolini. The charge was not wholly misleading when applied to some of the Palestinian neo-revisionists such as Abba Achimeir who did indeed call on Jabotinsky to become their *Duce*; but notwithstanding the militaristic cult in Betar (the revisionist youth movement), Jabotinsky himself retained an old-fashioned liberal dislike of totalitarianism, dictatorship, and police states. He sharply attacked those of his followers who, for a time, saw in Hitlerism a genuine national-liberation movement. In 1932 he wrote:

> I believe in the ideological patrimony of the nineteenth century, the century of Garibaldi and Lincoln, Gladstone and Hugo . . . . Today's ideological fashion is: a human being is in essence dishonest and stupid, and he should not, therefore, be given the right to govern himself; freedom leads to perdition, equality is a lie, society needs leaders, orders and a stick . . . . I don't want this kind of creed; better not to live at all than to live under such a system.

This is not the credo of a potential fascist dictator. If anything it testifies to the anarchist streak in Jabotinsky's makeup, and his doctrine of *Pan-Basilea* (every man is king) – the unabashed individualism which led him to proclaim that every single human being is a kingdom unto himself and to argue that the individual must be granted almost unlimited freedom and retain the final veto in respect of all measures, even those designed to improve his lot. Society in his view was made for the individual, not vice-versa. Arthur Koestler's remark that Jabotinsky was 'a National Liberal in the great nineteenth century tradition, a revolutionary of the 1848 brand, successor to Garibaldi and Mazzini' might seem closer to the mark than efforts to bracket him with D'Annunzio or Mussolini.

Yet the issue is a complex one that cannot be settled simply by quoting Jabotinsky's well-known detestation of the *Polizei-Staat* and the robot-like servitude of the masses in totalitarian societies. Undoubtedly, the

Italian connection is important here and deserves some attention since Italy (where Jabotinsky had lived as a student after leaving Russia) became a second fatherland to him. Born in the cosmopolitan Black Sea port of Odessa with its sunny carefree atmosphere, Jabotinsky was, moreover, spiritually a Hellene, a man of the Mediterranean, a great admirer of the classical Graeco-Roman tradition, and of its virtues of logic, beauty, and harmony. Jabotinsky's prose style (he signed his articles under the Italian pseudonym Altalena), with its conciseness, simplicity, and Latinate clarity, reflects this influence no less than his aesthetic politics, his nationalist romanticism and populist techniques, his emphasis on youth, and his uninhibited occidentalism. Jabotinsky not only wrote poetry in Italian, he even designed a scheme to Latinize the Hebrew alphabet. It was at the feet of Italian professors like Benedetto Croce, Enrico Ferri, and Antonio Labriola that he first absorbed the socialist ideals of his youth – which he later utterly repudiated after the Russian Revolution – and it was in Rome that he first studied history, sociology, and philology.

In his autobiography, Jabotinsky wrote:

> If I have a spiritual homeland, it is Italy much more than Russia.... From the day of my arrival here, I became fully integrated into the society of Italian youth, and its life I lived until I left Italy. All my views on problems of nationalism, the state and society were developed during those same years under Italian influence.... The legend of Garibaldi, the writings of Mazzini, the poetry of Leopardi and Giusti have enriched and deepened my superficial Zionism from an instinctive feeling, they made it into a doctrine.

But which image of Italy – liberal or fascist – was decisive in moulding Jabotinsky's social, political, and aesthetic views? According to Professor Shlomo Avineri, in a stimulating and incisive essay on Jabotinsky's political thought, it was, above all, the post-Risorgimento nationalist experience, the demise of liberalism, and the new doctrines of *sacro egoismo* whose seed-bed was *fin-de-siècle* Italy – cradle of Marinetti's futurism, revolutionary syndicalism, and the elitist themes of Mosca, Pareto, and Michels. Jabotinsky's belief that 'there is no value in the world higher than the nation and the fatherland, there is no deity in the universe to which one should sacrifice these two most precious jewels' clearly derived more from his preoccupation with the nationality problems in Europe rather than from any specific analysis of the Jewish question. Moreover, according to Avineri, Jabotinsky had to become a racial determinist in order to bolster scientifically his theory about the supremacy of the nation, even though he did not personally believe in 'pure' races.

In an article written in 1913 he affirmed his belief in a 'racial community' endowed with a 'special racial psychology' and emphasized that ethnic communities are distinguished from each other by their racial appearance. It was the 'racial psychology of the community' which in Jabotinsky's opinion determined the economy, the social organization, religion, philosophy, literature, and even the legislation of different peoples. Race was the primary, the essential component of the nation (a view incidentally shared by the pioneer Zionist socialist, Moses Hess), whereas territory, religion, and language were only its attributes. A superior race would take care not to be contaminated by alien influences; 'for such a superior race', Jabotinsky wrote in 1913, 'the authority of an alien element is organically disgusting and detestable'. In a polemic against a Russian antisemitic writer, Jabotinsky claimed that the Jews, by virtue of their self-awareness and refusal to be harnessed to the foreign yoke, constituted precisely such a superior race. Avineri also points to some other dubious aspects of Jabotinsky's nationalism which reflected his vitalistic ideology and preoccupation with the need for authenticity, uniqueness, separatism, and originality. Thus, he endorsed Ukrainian nationalism in spite of its violent antisemitism and xenophobia – because through its literature it had manifested a talent for independent cultural creativity and a healthy rejection of alien influences whether Russian, Polish, or Jewish.

Jabotinsky's flirtation in 1921 with the anticommunist Ukrainian independence movement led by Semyon Petlyura (whose name became synonymous with the most brutal massacres of Jewish history before Hitler) may not, therefore, have been purely tactical or motivated only by his hatred of Bolshevism, but the consequence of a deeper affinity. These examples are a salutary reminder of the narrow borderline that exists at the best of times, between nationalism and chauvinism, romanticism and racism, patriotism and crypto-fascism, forceful leadership and the cult of violence. Precisely because Jabotinsky was so strongly moulded by the most modern trends of European cultural life, his doctrines tend to reflect such ambivalences more clearly than those of other Zionist leaders. The lack of any specifically Jewish ingredient, if anything, heightens this impression.

There was indeed something manifestly pagan, even *goyish*, in Jabotinsky's ethnocentricity, which makes the efforts of contemporary Israel's increasingly illiberal and conservative-nationalist camp to claim him as its spiritual godfather not entirely convincing. Not for nothing did the firebrand from Odessa like to call himself a *goyishe kop* and emphasize the debt of the Jew to the Gentile. The *goy*, according to Jabotinsky, was neither brute nor angel. It was a legacy of the ghetto to view him as a foreign or hostile force; just as it was assimilationist self-hatred to bow down before him or ape his cultural superiority. Nevertheless it had to be recognized that the non-Jewish world was a great creative force, from which Jewish nationalism had much to learn, especially in the field of political thought and action. At the second

Revisionist World Congress in Paris (December 1926) Jabotinsky spoke admiringly of 'morenu ve' rabenu ha' Goy' (our teacher and mentor the Gentile).

> It is time that the Jewish people began to have confidence in the *Goyim*. The *Goyim* have not produced only Hamans; they have also produced great idealists who have given their blood for the cause of humanity. I say 'morenu ve' rabenu ha'Goy'. We must collaborate with the non-Jewish world.

It is interesting to note that this passionate Zionist awakener of Jewish youth, who came to favour the complete Hebraization of the Diaspora, proudly modelled himself on Gentile nationalism. In *Samson*, his best-known didactic novel, Jabotinsky selects the most pagan of biblical figures and appears to share his hero's admiration for the vitality of the Philistines, their cult of power, and their worship of nature. In his novel, *Samson*, there is an episode (mentioned by Shlomo Avineri) where the protagonist recalls the excitement he felt as a spectator at a religious pagan festival in Gaza where a beardless priest was leading the dancers at the temple:

> the beardless priest turned pale and seemed to submerge his eyes in those of the dancers, which were fixed responsively on his. He grew paler and paler, all the repressed fervour of the crowd seemed to concentrate within his breast till it threatened to choke him. Samson felt the blood stream to his head . . . . Suddenly, with a rapid, almost imperceptible movement, the priest raised his baton, and all the white figures in the square sank down on their left knee and threw their right arm towards heaven – a single movement, a single, abrupt, murderous harmony.

We are told that Samson leaves the scene feeling that 'here, in this spectacle of thousands obeying a single will, he had caught a glimpse of the great secrets of builders of nations'. Mass rallies, discipline, pagan rites, ceremony, hierarchy, parades – all this suggests the hysterical, overheated nationalism of central Europe between the wars, while the right-arm salute of the massed Philistines also has unmistakeable affinities with the fascist style. Similarly, the violent anti-Marxism of the revisionists in Palestine during the 1930s evoked unpleasant parallels with what was happening in Germany, Italy, and eastern Europe. Yet, in his younger days as a socialist idealist (in Russia before 1914) Jabotinsky had been the darling of the labour Zionist parties, and in wartime Palestine Poalei Zion supported his campaign for a Jewish legion and his early anti-appeasement policy. But Jabotinsky always opposed class ideology.

Subsequently he became even more convinced that proletarian class organizations, strikes, and the doctrine of class struggle were incompatible with Zionism, that they were inapplicable to a country undergoing colonization and detrimental to the integrity and unity of the Hebrew nation. In 1920, in a personal letter about the Histadrut (whose control of economic life in the Yishuv was perceived as a malignant tumour by the revisionists) and the socialist parties, Jabotinsky remarked that 'their disease is an organic one: I call it *shaatnez*' (counterfeit, a forbidden mixture, that is, cloth combining wool and linen). No movement could survive which served two such incompatible ideals. He believed it was inevitable that, sooner or later, the socialism of the left-wing parties in Palestine would lead to a renunciation of the principles of a Jewish state and a Jewish majority. Jabotinsky's bitter polemical tone in dismissing the red banner as an 'alien rag' and in calling on his followers to smash organized labour was matched on the other side by equally demagogic references by Ben-Gurion to 'Vladimir Hitler'.

The polemics did, however, reflect fundamental differences. Jabotinsky categorically opposed even the principle of giving the working class any special status, let alone the Marxist idea that it represented the vanguard of progress and the redemption of humanity. In this respect he called on his followers to conduct a remorseless struggle against all working-class parties (in his mind there was no difference between social democrats and communists) to destroy their hegemony in the Yishuv and the monopoly of the Histadrut. In place of class war, he proposed a corporatist system of mandatory arbitration, with a national arbiter supplanting strikes and trade-union activities in the national interest. The establishment of a trades' Parliament, to which each person would elect representatives according to the corporation or guild to which he belonged, was one of Jabotinsky's pet ideas for organizing social and economic life in Palestine. There would be professional corporations for those participating in industry, commerce, agriculture, banking, finance, trade, the professions, clerical jobs, and so forth; they would elect representatives to the trades' Parliament which would oversee and control economic life and represent the Yishuv in dealing with the British government as well as establishing the arbitration system from the top downwards.

This was not a form of *laissez-faire* liberalism but closer in spirit to the *étatistic*, hierarchical corporatism in vogue in the 1930s, even though Jabotinsky claimed to be defending the interests of the Jewish *Mittelstand* (artisans, shopkeepers, small settlers) and the private sector against the 'collectivist' colonies. As early as 1927, Jabotinsky had claimed in his famous 'We the bourgeois' article that the labour-dominated Yishuv discriminated against the middle class, and he deplored what he described as the 'inferiority complex' of the Jewish bourgeoisie. There was no reason to be ashamed of being bourgeois – after all, the middle classes were the standard-bearers of the great ideals of the nineteenth century, and the real enemies of the totalitarian police state. But in one-sidedly defending the historical record of capitalism and driving the revisionists into a frontal attack on the labour movement in Palestine, Jabotinsky undoubtedly made one of the most tragic mistakes of his career. It was another aspect of his refusal to compromise, his predilection for *either–or* solutions in politics. Whether it was in reaction to his own flirtation with socialist ideas in his youth, a logical product of his integral nationalism, a consequence of his bitterness at the Bolshevik revolution, or his liberal-aristocratic disdain for all collectivist ideologies, Jabotinsky expended vast amounts of energy (much of it futile) in combating socialist ideas. But the violent campaign of the revisionists against organized labour narrowed much of their potential appeal. The movement, lacking as it did settlements, economic enterprises, and institutions of its own, found it difficult to make significant headway, in spite of the desperate plight of the Jewish masses in eastern Europe in the 1930s.

The scale of their tragedy, which Jabotinsky felt deeply, gave an urgency and radicalism to his appeals which were, as always, delivered with dramatic eloquence. He had no doubt that eastern Europe was 'a zone of incurable antisemitism', that an elemental flood would soon engulf eastern European Jewry, forcing it to emigrate, and hence he proposed a mass transfer to Palestine. Between 1936 and 1939 he sought to come to an agreement on this with Polish government circles (without condoning Polish antisemitism, as has been often suggested, or depriving Jews of their rights), but by September/October 1939 he had probably realized that Polish Jewry, the mainstay of Zionism, was doomed. Jabotinsky's policy of mass evacuation, predicated as it was on his prophetic intuition that the majority of Jews in the *Galut* were doomed, depended for its implementation on the balance of power in Palestine. Ever since the 1920s he had opposed piecemeal, slow-motion colonization in Palestine and, with the impending calamity in Europe, his objections to so-called 'practical Zionism' with its apparent political submissiveness to the British Colonial Office, became sharper.

The growing clash with the British was undoubtedly a source of pain to Jabotinsky who, in his own way, believed in the Anglo-Jewish partnership as much as Chaim Weizmann. His faith in England and his pro-British sentiments had previously been buttressed by the conviction that anti-Zionism did not correspond to Britain's true interests. Nevertheless, by 1936 (and especially after Ben-Josef's hanging in 1938) the decline of British power and the shift in imperial policy towards the Arabs had become more apparent. For Jabotinsky, who had always sought to establish a Jewish state under the protection and patronage of Great

Britain, this presented a real dilemma. A substitute was needed (hence the training camps for Betar in fascist Italy and Pilsudski's Poland), and the inevitability of confrontation with Britain could no longer be avoided. For a politician who had always asserted the absolute identity of British and Zionist interests in the Middle East and looked forward to their extensive 'collaboration', and for a leader who claimed that a Jewish legion would be the best defence for British imperial interests in the region, this was a cruel setback. To be sure, he never gave way to the kind of anti-British feeling that emerged in the Irgun and even more in Lehi. He continued to believe that British public opinion could be won over by a 'political offensive', a campaign of information to demonstrate where Britain's true interest lay. But although he was officially Supreme Commander of the Irgun he had little influence on its daily activities in Palestine and his preference for global diplomatic and political methods was not shared by his more activist followers who preferred direct action and reliance on armed force. Jabotinsky toyed briefly with the idea of a Jewish coup in Palestine but in the end he remained faithful to the first article in his own credo: 'B'reshit bara Elohim et ha-politica' (In the beginning God created politics).

Yet Jabotinsky never had the patience, the sense for factional combat, the tactical finesse, or the common sense to succeed in Zionist politics. Rather like Leon Trotsky, another Russian Jewish intellectual whom he resembled in character and temperament, Jabotinsky was a brilliant orator and journalist, a mass spellbinder at his best in a crisis; distrustful of routine, compromise, half-measures; imaginative, emotional, flamboyant, artistic, but lacking the solidarity, responsibility, and sound judgement necessary for a sustained political leadership. To the end, he underestimated the slow, tedious, painful process by means of which Jewish Palestine was actually built. Perhaps nowhere was his impatience and political naivety more evident than in his attitude to the Arab question, which unfortunately appears to have left an indelible mark on the Jewish-Zionist psyche – namely in establishing the image of inevitable conflict and the impossibility of any solution except through force. For Jabotinsky, peace with the Arabs was an illusion. Since they would never agree to a *modus vivendi*, the Arabs would have to accept the inevitability of their becoming a minority in Palestine. Zionism could only be implemented against their wishes, though Jabotinsky always insisted that they would enjoy equal civil rights as individuals under Jewish rule.

Jabotinsky's uncompromising stance towards the Arabs reflected, at least in part, a Eurocentric world view which involved a disdainful attitude towards a backward, non-European culture. Whereas he was prepared to support the right to self-determination of the most obscure and relatively backward European nationalities, such as Latvians,

Estonians, Ukrainians, Albanians, Serbs, and Croats, and to emphasize their originality and distinctive culture, this generosity did not apply to the Arabs. Their claim to Palestine could not be put on the same footing as that of the Zionists. Jabotinsky always stressed that the Jews were a *European* people, an occidental nation embedded in Europe which was the focus of their cultural future. Sephardi as well as Ashkenazi Jews were part of this European world of spirituality not of the Levantine Orient. In this context, Jabotinsky even quoted Nordau to the effect that 'we come to the Land of Israel in order to push the moral frontiers of Europe up to the Euphrates'.

This insistence on the western and European character of Zionism and the implied denigration of Arab and Muslim culture was by no means confined to Jabotinsky – it was shared by Weizmann, Ben-Gurion, and most of the labour Zionist camp. The main difference was that the revisionists expressed it with greater frankness, lacking as they did the political sophistication of their rivals. It has had the fateful consequence of leading the Zionist movement to believe that minority status for the Palestine Arabs is no hardship at all, that they can be denied their national rights, since only Jewish nationalism is legitimate and authentic. This is an outlook that may have been plausible and even understandable in the heyday of European colonial domination over the Third World – today it may prove to be a misleading and even dangerous anachronism.

15

Between prophecy and politics

At a time when the Jewish world has been moving steadily towards the Right in both Israel and the Diaspora, it is perhaps salutary and instructive to look back at a period when socialist movements flourished in all the major centres of Russian Jewish life; not only in the Pale of Settlement where Jews lived in a condition of almost permanent crisis under the pogromist Tsarist regime, but also in America, England, Palestine – in fact wherever the Russian-Jewish political subculture put down roots. Indeed, one of the most remarkable features of Jewish socialism which helps to explain its universalist aspirations is precisely the similarity of the socio-economic and cultural conditions which shaped Russian-Jewish existence at the turn of the century across three continents. Underlying this geographical dispersion created by the mass migrations from Tsarist Russia was a common pattern of political culture forged by the Russian-Jewish intelligentsia and radical youth together with politically educated workers. The Yiddish language was its *lingua franca*, the clothing industry and sweatshop its economic base, trade-union politics, ideologically committed parties, and self-defence units its hallmarks – whether it was based in Vilna, Minsk, Bialystok, the East End of London, or the Lower East Side of New York. Even in the Ottoman backwater of early-twentieth-century Palestine, where Jewish socialism developed in a Hebrew-speaking, agricultural context and soon adopted a more nationalist orientation, the underlying pattern clearly derived from the Russian Pale with its impassioned, internal Jewish political debates.

In confronting these and other mutations of the Jewish revolutionary movement across the world the historian is faced with a rich and often bewildering kaleidoscope of constantly changing ideologies, programmes, and political organizations. Not only must he describe and account for the endless swings, oscillations, and ideological reversals within the Jewish socialist world but he must also analyse the dynamics of interaction between the different parts of this subculture which

171

operated in such diverse environments. This task calls for an unusual degree of knowledge in the fields of Jewish and labour history, of Russian and Russian-Jewish culture, a high level of linguistic skills, and an approach as international in scope as that of his subject. It is the great achievement of Professor Jonathan Frankel's book* that he has been able to synthesize these multiple facets in a work that displays analytical powers of a high order and manages to throw fresh light on the central role of Jewish socialism in the emergence of a modern Jewish politics.

Professor Frankel has organized his book around the clash between socialist internationalism and Jewish nationalism within the Russian-Jewish labour movement and its offshoots overseas, mainly in America and Palestine. The recurring dilemmas which confronted Jewish socialists before 1917 – socialist revolution in Russia or mass evacuation of Jews abroad, colonization in Zion or some other territory, civil or national rights in the Diaspora, class war or interclass co-operation, maximal or minimal programmes, elitist or mass strategies, Jewish national culture or a new proletarian culture essentially socialist in content – are of course no longer the stuff of mainstream Jewish politics. Nevertheless these issues are central to an understanding of the process of modernization undergone by a highly traditional minority people – the Jews – mirroring as they did many of its predicaments as it entered the twentieth century. The extraordinary energy and restlessness of that *fin-de-siècle* generation of politically involved, radical Jewish youth, its alienation and desperate search for a new identity based on a synthesis of secular nationalism and socialism, its aspiration to total change through collective action, testify to the magnitude of the crisis which they faced. Their messianic dreams, their utopianism and spirit of self-sacrifice nourished in part on the example of Russian populism, may strike the contemporary reader as anachronistic and even quaint, yet, without their legacy, the modern state of Israel and the democratization of Jewish life in the Diaspora might never have come into being.

Professor Frankel begins his book with two well-drawn portraits of Moses Hess and Aron Liberman, whose oscillations between Jewish and socialist messianism, nationalism, and internationalism anticipated many of the inner tensions of the Russian-Jewish intelligentsia in the late nineteenth century. The tragic fate of Liberman, who committed suicide in Syracuse in 1880, symbolized in certain respects the identity conflicts that continued to plague Jews who wished to work among their own people while espousing cosmopolitan socialist ideals. The doubts, uncertainties, and ambivalence of Hess and Liberman later found expression in the dualism of a worldwide Jewish labour movement

---

* *Prophecy and Politics. Socialism, Nationalism and the Russian Jews, 1862–1917* (Cambridge 1981).

constantly torn between the desire for participation in revolutionary internationalist politics and the demand for Jewish national rights.

This dualism had its roots in the traumatic upheaval of 1881 and its consequences, which Professor Frankel analyses in great detail. On the one hand the pogroms of that fateful year appeared to destroy the prospects of western-style emancipation in Russia, giving birth to the Hovevei Zion movement and the vision of exodus. At the same time it thrust the previously estranged Russian Jewish intelligentsia into a leadership role, challenging the wealthy Petersburg oligarchy and the traditional politics of *shtadlanut*. Though the emigration fever temporarily subsided, the sense of living in an intensely hostile environment remained and led to a new emphasis on auto-emancipation. The shared belief in the need for an autonomous labour movement, the casting off of the yoke of established religion and tradition, the utopian faith in a radically new society – common to both Zionist and anti-Zionist Jewish socialism – ultimately goes back to the trauma of 1881. Then, however, alternative and opposed strategies appeared on the scene as the Russian-Jewish intelligentsia, cast in the role of national saviour by the Jewish masses, sought to resolve the universalist/particularist dilemma.

The open hostility of Russian society, and the lukewarm (even approving) attitude of the socialist movement to the pogroms, cast severe doubts on Jewish efforts to assimilate, to absorb Russian culture and participate fully in the revolutionary cause, temporarily undermining the prestige of internationalism. The debate between the *Amerikantsy* (such as the Odessa *Am Olam* group) who stressed the enormous absorptive capacity of the United States and dreamed in some cases of a communal life in America, and the *Palestinsty* (Palestinophiles) with their essentially nationalist ideology, reflected what was to be a dilemma that continues to the present day. The Jewish masses voted with their feet for America (over a million Russian Jews emigrated there between 1880 and 1910) while a trickle of Zionists went to Palestine where they confronted the hostility of the Turkish government and the practical difficulties of colonization, sustained only by their fanatical determination to inaugurate a national revival. Both migrations bore the imprint of the Russian radical milieu, while adapting in different ways to their respective environments. America initially provided a fertile soil for propaganda and enlightenment in the populist tradition (and for anarchism and social democratic Marxism), for militant secularism, trade-union organization, and class conflict – however surprising this may appear today. The cultivation of Yiddish and Americanization went hand in hand for this first generation of Russian Jewish immigrants who sought to integrate fully in the new society.

The *Bilu* in Palestine, on the other hand, while quantitatively negligible, economically dependent, and administratively confined (by

Rothschild paternalism), appealed more to Jewish national consciousness and pride along with that sense of communalism and self-sacrifice
which they had imbibed from the Russian populist tradition. Neither the
emigration movement nor Palestinian settlement, however, produced
results which were initially commensurate with the proclaimed goals of
auto-emancipation and national self-liberation. They could not radically
change the pattern of life for 6 million Jews in Russia still suffering from
acute poverty, unemployment, harassment, and persecution. The official
antisemitism of the Tsarist regime exacted its own price, inevitably
encouraging the involvement of Jewish youth in Russian revolutionary
politics. It was the Bund, the force which dominated Jewish politics in
the Pale of Settlement between 1897 and 1905, that best succeeded,
initially, in channelling and organizing the revolutionary energies of the
Jewish masses, especially in the western regions of the Russian empire.

Professor Frankel deals extensively with the paradox of the Bund,
which brought the concept of a *general* Russian revolution into the
heartland of the Jewish world and yet was the first Jewish party to adopt
the idea of national autonomy. He demonstrates how both Russian
political conditions and influences from abroad (especially by the
Bundist intelligentsia in the Russian colonies of Switzerland and
Germany) created a trend towards national self-help and emphasis on
Yiddish culture. Conflicting pressures from the rival Palestinophile trend
in the Russian Pale, the nationalist wing of the Polish socialist movement, from the assimilationist tendencies of the Russian revolutionary
parties, as well as from Yiddish-speaking socialists abroad, drove the
Bund into an erratic middle course on the national question. It could
never successfully resolve the demand for full autonomy for the Jewish
proletariat with its loyalty to the Russian social democratic party that it
had done so much to found in 1898.

The nationalist wing of the Bund led by John Mill and Vladimir
Kossovsky was committed to the idea of a modern Jewish nation, as
developed by Zhitlovsky, which was worldwide in scope, socialist and
secular in content, Yiddish-speaking in form. It favoured a non-Zionist,
national solution to the Jewish question in the framework of a multi-
national, federal democratic Russia where territorial nationality would
be irrelevant. The internationalist wing was loyal above all to the idea of
a Russian-centred revolutionary party in which Jewish workers would
fight with non-Jewish workers (Russians, Poles, Latvians, and so on) for
political democracy and civil rights. The Bund, writes Frankel, reflected
'the divided soul of the modern Jewish intelligentsia' but it never
crystallized a clear ideological position, concerned as it was, primarily,
with 'practical questions'. Though a strongly centralized conspiratorial
party, it was never monolithic, seeking, according to Frankel, to avoid
schisms by common sense and compromise on ideological issues. This

interpretation may well be open to question and it is perhaps surprising that the author barely mentions the leader of the Bund, Vladimir Medem, in this context. Medem, no less important a figure than Zhitlovsky, Syrkin, or Borochov, and more significant than Liberman, surely deserved a chapter in his own right.

It was, however, the rise of the militant *Iskra* tendency led by Lenin and Martov, with its determination to restore doctrinal orthodoxy in the Russian party and to establish hegemony over the fragmented labour movement, which was to place the Bund before cruel choices that it was poorly equipped to deal with. Attacked as a 'state within a state' in the Russian party, accused of separatism and nationalist deviations despite its anti-Zionism, it was driven out in 1903 of the very movement it had helped to found and readmitted only on very harsh terms. As Professor Frankel remarks, the schism of 1903 foreshadowed in a way the subsequent fate of the Bund and indeed of Russian Jewry in the Soviet Union. By late 1905 the Bund was no longer in full control of the 'Jewish street' having been outflanked by more radical and more nationalist trends among Russian Jewry. The terrible pogroms of October 1905 with their attendant chaos, anarchy, and reaction fragmented the Jewish Left into innumerable parties, and led to a loss of faith in the victory of the Russian Revolution and a crisis of confidence in the Bund, from which, according to the author, it never fully recovered. Once again, this interpretation may be open to dispute, for the Bund still remained the leading party of the Jewish proletariat, and in interwar Poland it was hardly on the decline. What is certain is that the initial euphoria of the 1905 revolution, when Russian Jewry had felt that their fate would be decided by the all-Russian political power struggle and thrown themselves into the fight, did give way to bitter disillusion. Not only the Bund but also the Zionists and the 'assimilationists' found themselves in disarray and overshadowed by parties in the Pale variously combining revolutionary socialism, planned emigration, and Jewish nationalism.

Professor Frankel gives an excellent account of the ideological noma-dism of this period, providing insightful portraits of such figures as Chaim Zhitlovsky, Nachman Syrkin, and Ber Borochov wrestling with the dilemmas of reconciling socialism and nationalism. Zhitlovsky, revolutionary Yiddishist and Russian Narodnik, one-time ideologist of the Bund and later its opponent, pro- and anti-territorialist, SR and later pro-Bolshevik, epitomized many of the bewildering shifts of the time in his own ideological pirouettes. The eccentric Syrkin, heir of Moses Hess and messianic prophet of a Jewish socialist state, territorialist and utopian dreamer, irredeemably pessimistic about the Jewish future in *Goles* yet determined to take up arms against oppression in the Diaspora, was another who seemed to embody the frenzied tensions of his generation. 'What elsewhere is utopia, among the Jews is a necessity' was crazy Nachman's answer to those who derided his pre-Marxian visions of prophetic redemption in Palestine. Even Ber Borochov, *teoretik* and *praktik*, agitator and *referent*, the supreme exponent of monistic Marxism in the Zionist movement, emerges in Frankel's account as a far more enigmatic and contradictory figure than is generally assumed – 'a man struggling in the sea of doubt and grasping for the firm rock of faith'. The monolithic figure of legend who allegedly believed in the omnipotence of sociological processes was in fact initially a follower of Usshishkin and an advocate of the *avant-garde* elitism of the pioneer youth who spearheaded the Second *Aliyah*. His monistic, proletarian ideology forged in the crisis years (1903–6) reversed his earlier position in order to save the pro-Palestinian remnants of Poale Zion from extinction as the Russian revolutionary tide ran high. Borochovism, born out of the need to justify Zionism in strict Marxist terms and show how it could be united with revolutionary activism, was abandoned by its founder in 1917 much to the confusion of his disciples. Frankel adeptly reveals how the impressive Borochovist edifice of abstract logic resulted from practical political needs and profound inner contradictions which were common to an entire generation of Russian-Jewish intellectuals.

In Palestine, Borochov's disciples in the Poale Zion and their rivals in *Ha-Poel Ha-Tsair*, shaped by the Russian revolutionary ethos transplanted to a harsh, unfamiliar environment, faced more immediate and unprecedented problems. How could these semi-intellectuals stand on their feet as workers? How could they *democratize* the institutional life of the old Yishuv and organize the local Jewish community against its will into a power base to win concessions from the Ottoman Turks? How could they become the hub of a national renaissance without a mass influx of Jewish proletarians to follow the revolutionary vanguard? How could they keep labour in Jewish hands while professing adherence to internationalist socialist ideals? The Arab question, contrary to certain fashionable assumptions, did indeed concern them and largely explains why the Palestinian Jewish labour movement was more overt, pronounced, and militant in its nationalism than the mother parties in Russia. The land belongs to those who work it – this was the official credo of Jewish socialists in Palestine determined to create a healthy Jewish working class as the basis of national renewal.

The idea that there was *one* Arab people in Palestine with *national* rights was, however, largely repressed since it conflicted with the aim of the socialist Zionists to become a majority and their own desire for national self-assertion. Indeed the slogan 'In blood and fire Judea fell, in blood and fire Judea shall rise', often attributed to the revisionist movement, was in fact invented by the Russian Poale Zion and adopted by its offshoot, the members of Bar Giora in Palestine. Militant socialist nationalism came naturally to the graduates of the 1905 Russian

Revolution who had already been trained in self-defence and in the highly conspiratorial style of politics, continued in Palestine by the secret order of armed watchmen, *Ha-Shomer*.

Along with the desire for national self-liberation, this new generation openly sought, above all, natural simplicity, egalitarianism, and freedom from conventional restraints and tradition, by rebelling against the old Yishuv which it saw as a mirror-image of the Russian Pale and based on oligarchy, 'theocratic' rule, and economic parasitism. Imbued with the concept of an alternative society brought from Russia, the pioneer Jewish youth tried to build their new utopia outside the existing social framework once it became apparent that the old Yishuv opposed their methods. Adapting to environmental realities, the Poale Zion in Palestine gradually abandoned their Marxist dogmas, Yiddish-oriented agitation, and emphasis on the urban workers, and after 1909 the national wing of the party in Galilee turned to co-operative pioneer settlement and the project of worker *Kvutsot*. For their part, the rival organization *Ha Poel Ha-Tsair* had never believed in the 'proletarian' strategy in the first place, had always stressed Hebrew more than Yiddish, and was more consciously Zionist, rejecting the idea of participation in Russian revolutionary politics as a futile diversion of energy. By the First World War both the labour parties had opted for the third way, beyond capitalism and communism – that of co-operative farming based on self-labour, pioneered by the German Zionist thinker, Franz Oppenheimer. This constructivist socialism, strongly supported by the Berlin School of Zionism (Otto Warburg, Arthur Ruppin) and the Austrian Poale Zion, was financially backed by Zionist capital (from the World Zionist Organization and the Jewish National Fund) assisted by the Palestine Office (under Ruppin) and made possible by the egalitarian enthusiasm of the pioneer youth who above all sought freedom from the outside control of farmers, planters, employers, and managers.

By eliminating wage labour the system of *Kvutsot* and *Moshavim* had the added advantage of seeming to solve the 'Arab question' for the colonists, who had come to the conclusion that the Arab worker would always be a majority in enterprises based on private capital. As Professor Frankel shows, the Arab worker (and also the Oriental Jew) was in fact a major weapon in the hands of the Jewish employers and farmers; when faced by strikes, walkouts, and threats of violence the management could simply replace the truculent 'Russians' with a cheaper, more amenable labour force. The Yemenite workers, family men ready and able to live on subsistence wages (in contrast to the hot-headed, generally single and frequently wandering Russian Jews) could, like the Arabs, be used to break the organized labour movement. Ultra-traditionalist, settled in their way of life, and hard-working, the Yemenites had little in common with the free-thinking, radical socialists from the Pale, drunk on the phraseology of the class war, ever disputing wages, constantly ready to strike against employers and even to threaten physically those who hired Arab labour. Such psychological instability, wanderlust, and an insatiable appetite for ideological discussion belonged to an alien world – that of revolutionary Russia whose convulsions had spilled out on to the fields of Palestine a unique species of worker – *intelligent*.

In Palestine the belief in centralized party discipline, doctrinal unity, and orthodoxy which was part of the Russian inheritance was eventually modified by circumstances, but continued to shape the history of the Yishuv along with the ideology of socialist nationalism. In America, on the other hand, there was little future for orthodoxies or indeed for Jewish socialist party politics in the long run. The American Jewish labour movement was generally more successful in the socio-economic than in the political sphere – that is, in organizing a mass circulation press, trade unions, and insurance organizations to protect the interests of the new immigrants and to prepare them for full *Americanization*. As Frankel shows, it was almost impossible to maintain ideological unity in America, and the centralized structures inherited from Russia by the labour movement soon gave way to a polycentric, federalist pattern. Although the influence of socialist ideas was indeed great on the first waves of Russian Jews in the United States, the organized socialist movement remained relatively weak in terms of Jewish votes and membership and failed to break the two-party system. In New York, where over half a million Jews were crowded on the Lower East Side (and the Yiddish socialist paper *Forverts* sold 200,000 copies daily) the power of the democratic party machine remained predominant. This was not only because many immigrants initially lacked the vote or feared that to vote for the socialists was an un-American act that might affect future immigration policies. Nor was it simply because Russian Jews were good strikers but poor unionists. What mattered to the Russian Jews in America was, above all, survival in the urban jungle. They dreamed of escaping the chains of manual labour and the sweatshop, of accumulating capital through thrift and initiative, by 'making it' and becoming their own boss.

In the long run, socialism could not secure a firm political base in these conditions of rapid turnover of Jewish labour, of social mobility, restlessness, and a rampant competitive ethos. Moreover, the patterns of fragmentation, the emphasis on grassroots organization and polycentrism in American life were ultimately resistant to revolutionary change just as they militated against the centralized political unity of the Jewish labour movement or indeed of American Jewry as a whole. The socialists in the United States had to function according to the laws of the marketplace and appeal to a great mass of Jews whose interest they had to maintain in competition with many other forces – unlike in Russia where politics was of necessity essentially conspiratorial and dominated by professional party cadres, or in Palestine where it was conducted among small, cohesive pioneer-worker groups. Hence, American-Jewish socialism with its *ad hoc* populism, its politics of noise, publicity, and frenetic activity, and its reliance on the star system, inevitably reflected the environment of an open society in all of its ideological multiplicity and seasonal variations. At the same time, Jewish socialism in America was more internationalist and cosmopolitan than the Jewish labour movements in Russia or Palestine.

This was especially true of Jews active in the English-speaking sections of the American socialist party and also in many key Yiddish-speaking sections, but the melting-pot ideology was no less an article of faith for the mass-circulation Yiddish press. In the United States, the anti-religious, anti-national type of cosmopolitan, Yiddish-speaking (but not 'Jewish') socialist, who believed in the amalgamation of different nations into one mankind, found a favourable terrain – which helps explain why American-style Bundism never really flourished. Internationalist in normal times, the Jewish labour movement none the less shifted to inter-class co-operation and increasing support for Jewish nationalism in times of emergency and crisis. Abraham Cahan, the charismatic editor of *Forverts*, for example, justified his emotional reaction to the persecution of kith and kin by declaring: 'The pogroms and the Dreyfus case – they are our Holy Land.'

When it came to the Kishinev pogrom or the atrocities of October 1905, there was in truth no place for national self-abnegation, and uptown, establishment German Jews could co-operate with socialist forces in searching for a home for Russian Jewry. A united front in fund-raising and inter-class collaboration only emerged, however, in response to major crises overseas, and even then American-Jewish socialists remained divided over class strategy, failed to sustain their credibility or popular interest, and ultimately lost the struggle for hegemony over the Jewish masses.

In contrast to Russia and Palestine, Jewish politics in America remained, then, a seasonal phenomenon, the politics of philanthropy rather than national and social liberation. Professor Frankel shows that, by 1917, on the eve of the founding of the American Jewish Congress, the Jewish labour movement in the US was already on the outside, the *yidn* having been outmanoeuvred by the German-Jewish *yahudim* (who dominated the American Jewish Committee) and the rising Zionist leadership. The successes in the field of mass trade unionism were not translated into proletarian unity, which was impossible to achieve among the feuding parties transplanted from Russia, such as the Bund, Poale Zion, the socialist territorialists, and so on. It was the liberal, oligarchically organized American Jewish Committee which took the initiative in the defence of Russian Jews and in pressuring the US government to abandon the Russian-American commercial treaty (a first victory for the 'Jewish lobby'). It was the 'German' Jews led by Schiff and Marshall who organized the politics of relief and rescue as well as leading the campaign against immigration restrictions to the United States. Similarly, when it came to calls for the democratization of the Jewish community, for mass participation and a representative body expressing the political unity of American Jewry, it was the Zionists and not the Jewish labour leadership who emerged as the driving force that led to the creation of the American Jewish Congress. By 1917 the Zionist movement had already become a major force within American Jewry, whereas Jewish socialism had begun its slow decline.

Elsewhere in the Jewish world, the new era opened up by the Bolshevik Revolution and the Balfour Declaration – both occurring in the fateful month of November 1917 – created new polarities and hopes no less crucial for the future of the Jewish people. But the search for a Jewish solution to the Jewish question – one that would be universal and particular, socialist and national, scientific and messianic, continued to drive a generation of radicals committed to the myth of total change.

16

Zionism as a Jewish revolution

Alexis de Tocqueville once observed that the great French Revolution of 1789 had two very distinct phases – the first which sought the 'abolition of everything in the past', the second which tried to reconnect with that same past from which the French had cut themselves off. In the case of Zionism its basic tasks and objectives were not simply to destroy a given socio-political structure, or even to achieve national independence after an interval of 2,000 years. The Zionist revolution derived most of its peculiar features from the fact that it was a revolt against historic destiny itself or, as Ben-Gurion once put it, 'against the unique destiny of a unique people'.

Zionism sought to give the Jews that inner sense of freedom which would make them masters of their fate by ending the sense of dependence, moral, material, cultural, and political, upon others. According to the classical Zionist diagnosis the Jewish problem was rooted in the fact that Jews lacked a national and political framework in which they could determine their fate as a people. Until this fundamental anomaly of Jewish life was reversed, the Jews as a people would not really belong to any existing order. Since the creation of the state of Israel, this particular anomaly has largely disappeared without necessarily resolving other ambiguities present in the Zionist project. The very success of the Zionist revolution in changing the course of Jewish history and giving birth to a new Israeli nation may in fact have contributed to obscuring its roots and problematic character.

Before seeking however to draw any balance sheet between promise and fulfilment one must re-examine the self-understanding of the pioneers who made the Zionist revolution and dreamed of 'the complete ingathering of the exiles into a socialist Jewish State'. What was the nature of their beliefs and how did they view their role in relation to the Jewish people and humanity as a whole? In a speech in Haifa made in 1944 before a gathering of youth leaders, David Ben-Gurion asserted that

the twenty youths who founded the first *kvutzah* more than thirty
years ago on the banks of the Jordan did more for humanity and
Jewish history, for the Jewish and international workers' movement,
than all the Jewish socialists and revolutionaries who followed the
chariots of the revolution among the great nations and mocked the
insignificant and peculiar efforts of the pioneers in Israel.

Making due allowance for the Palestino-centrism and downgrading of
the Diaspora implicit in this view, what is nevertheless striking is its
assumption of a natural and spontaneous solidarity between Jewish and
international labour. The Jewish national renaissance was seen by Ben-
Gurion as

> part of a tremendous movement which involves all of humanity – the
> world revolution, whose aims are the redemption of man from every
> form of enslavement, discrimination, and exploitation, no matter
> whether the victims are nations, races, religions, or one of the sexes.
> Our revolution differs from all others because our destiny is different,
> but the difference serves to unite us with others and not to estrange us.

Ben-Gurion went on to emphasize that, while preserving its moral and
intellectual individuality, Zionism would have to cultivate its international partnership with 'the makers of the world revolution, with the
workers of all nations', a partnership based on equal rights rather than
equal strength. It is obvious that for the founding fathers of modern Israel
the Zionist revolution extended beyond the realm of politics and the
creation of a state as an end in itself. The Jewish national renaissance was
seen by its originators in Palestine not only as a vanguard movement of
the Jewish people but also as an integral, if distinctive, battalion of an international army.

The motif tends to become obscured in those accounts which depict
the Jewish national idea as the main, or even the sole, ideological driving
force of Zionism. The latter never really constituted a 'normal' national
risorgimento nor can it be viewed simply as a Jewish reaction to modern
antisemitism, however much this influenced the actual content of Zionist
ideology. Revolutions are not born simply of despair or the desire to
escape from intolerable conditions, though both these factors stimulated
the search for a radical solution to the Jewish problem. At the turn of the
century in the Russian Pale of Settlement the poverty, destitution, and
pogroms suffered by the Jewish masses favoured the growth of Bundism
and territorialism as much if not more than Zionism. Moreover one must
never forget that not one of these 'national' solutions to the Jewish
predicament enjoyed anything like the popularity of mass emigration to
the United States.

What motivated the *Bilu'im* of the 1880s and 1890s – the first
organized group of young Russian Jews who pioneered the modern

return to Eretz Israel – was their belief that this was an act of personal emancipation which, through the return to the ancestral soil, would have exemplary significance for the Jewish people. The revival of Jewish agriculture and Jewish labour in Eretz Israel implied a rejection of the isolationist immobilism of orthodox Jewry and of the passive, sacrificial role assigned to the Jews in Russia and eastern Europe. The settlers of the first *aliyah* saw themselves as an *avant-garde* of the Jewish people even if they had as yet no clear vision of national redemption. But why choose Zion? From a purely rational standpoint, none of the early Zionist theorists – not Lilienblum, Pinsker, Herzl, or Borochov – had a completely convincing answer. Their analyses, couched in the secular, scientific, or Marxist vocabulary of the nineteenth century, obscure more than they illuminate the central theme of Zionism – the return to Zion and the restoration of the link between the Jewish people and its ancestral land. As Arthur Hertzberg has pointed out, for the Jewish historian it is this *messianic* theme, rather than nationalism as such, which is central to Zionism.

The messianic link to Zion and the emotional fervour which it generated enabled the Jewish national movement to reawaken dormant energies in Jewish life which it transferred from the religious to the sociopolitical sphere. But this transference necessarily involved a revolt against Jewish tradition if only because it took many of its ideals from liberal and progressive trends in the non-Jewish world. The secular messianism of marginal, assimilated Jewish intellectuals like Moses Hess, Bernard Lazare, and Theodor Herzl reflected their subjective consciousness of a 'Jewish problem' created by European antisemitism; but the modern, secular ideology they helped to forge succeeded in undermining Jewish tradition only because of an objective need, the social decay and non-productivization of the Jewish masses in Russia and eastern Europe.

Socialist Zionism was the logical response to this need, at least under Russian conditions. It insisted more than any other version of Zionist ideology on the interdependence of social and national regeneration in a future Jewish homeland. It looked to the poorer, downtrodden classes of the Jewish people, who could not assimilate to the non-Jewish environment, to find the road to national emancipation. Nachman Syrkin, the first theorist of labour Zionism, did not overlook the messianic implications of the new ideology for the Jewish people. 'The messianic hope, which was always the greatest dream of exiled Jewry', would, he predicted, 'be transformed into political action' by fusing socialism with Zionism in a Jewish state. In this secular utopia, Israel would again become 'the chosen of the peoples!'

Ber Borochov, the leading theorist of Marxist Zionism, also saw the goal of a Jewish state essentially as a means to an end – in this case to facilitate the class struggle of the Jewish proletariat and thereby its participation in the world revolution. Zionism was conceived by Borochov and his followers primarily as an ideological weapon of the Jewish working class, which because of its landlessness and dispersion was separated from the primary processes of production. There could be no cure to its structural impotence in the Diaspora. Only in a national homeland, where it could return to productive occupations, would the Jewish people effectively contribute to the struggle against capitalistic exploitation and national oppression.

Neither Syrkin nor Borochov went to live in Palestine, unlike Aharon David Gordon, the secular mystic and patron saint of the early Palestinian Jewish labour movement. His 'religion of labour' with its revolt against the stunted, parasitic economy of the ghetto, strongly influenced the settlers of the second *aliyah*. They shared his belief that only manual labour could create a Jewish national revival in Palestine based on sacrifice, physical effort, and a life close to nature. 'This is a way of life', wrote Gordon, 'which requires a radical change, a complete change, a complete revolution in our *Galut* notions and attitudes and in our Galut way of life.'

Gordon's philosophy, with its fusion of radical populism and idealistic nationalism, perfectly expressed the ethos of that pioneering minority who came to Palestine from Tsarist Russia in the decade before 1914. Mostly young men and women of *petit-bourgeois* origins, they were rebels against the establishment of their day, nonconformists who rejected accepted values, parental authority, and the mediocrity of an un-adventurous, *shtetl* existence. They believed profoundly in the symbiotic attachment of a people to its soil and that personal labour (*avodah atzmait*) was the road to self-emancipation. They had turned their backs on the Diaspora and on bourgeois society, on Europe and on urban civilization, in order to be reborn as new men in a new land. Implicit in their creed was the conviction that only the tillers of the soil had a right to speak for the nation. For the Borochovists of Poale Zion this conviction was expressed in terms of Marxist class ideology – though there were as yet no classes in Palestine. The Gordonians of Ha-Poel Ha-Tsair on the other hand gave a national dimension to the 'religion of labour'.

The pioneers of the second *aliyah* had carried the social-revolutionary ideas nurtured in their Russian environment into what was then a decaying backwater of the Ottoman empire, where there was no industrial base, urban working class, or capitalist bourgeoisie. Everything had to be built from scratch – the land, the people, the new society. The pioneers approached the practical tasks of colonization in a spirit very different from that of white settler-colonialists in other parts of Africa and Asia. Their guiding vision – to create a Jewish peasantry and working class as the basis of a renascent nation – was truly remote from the ideals of European colonialism at the turn of the century. Nothing was further from the mental horizons of Russian and east European Jews than the *colon* sense of superiority backed by the military and police power of a mother country. They abhorred the idea of exploiting indigenous Arab labour and any manifestation of economic inequality. Their opposition to the colonial pattern of exploitation, exemplified by the philanthropic paternalism of the settlements run by agents of Baron Edmond de Rothschild, is eloquent testimony to this social-revolutionary ethos of early Zionism. They understood that the colonialist social norms which were crystallizing in the old Yishuv would undermine their national ideal of regeneration and their socialist convictions. If left unchecked this would have destroyed the core of their Zionist faith – that personal labour on the soil of Eretz Israel was the only road to freedom and personal dignity. In their own eyes daily contact with the soil gave a moral and legal foundation to their presence in Palestine. They saw themselves as colonizers of the soil not of the Palestinian Arabs.

Today it is fashionable to equate Zionism with various forms of 'white' colonialism practised in non-European parts of the world. The slogan of *Kibbush ha-avoda* (the conquest of labour), for example, which for the Zionist settlers meant settling the land in accordance with socialist principles of agricultural co-operation, might today be interpreted as a hypocritical rationalization of secret colonialist ambitions. Alternatively it might be viewed as a kind of socio-economic apartheid designed to exclude Arab labour from any participation in building the new society. Such an interpretation assumes that the Arab problem was really perceived as central by the early Zionist settlers and that 'colonial' attitudes continued to prevail beneath a veneer of socialist rhetoric. In fact the *chalutzim* of the second *aliyah* felt more antagonism towards the Jewish employers (plantation owners and operators) than towards the Arab peasant or worker. True, there was desperate competition for jobs between the Jewish settler and the Arab *fellah*, which was in a sense disguised by the Marxist-populist vocabulary of early Zionism. But the Hebrew colonists' feeling of moral superiority was grounded in precisely those factors which separated them from the colonialist prejudices of European *conquistadores* in other parts of the world; the original social practice and vision which inspired the kibbutzim was a sense of personal fulfilment in a life based on physical labour. The rejection of the use of cheap Arab labour was logically consistent with the socialism of settlers who consciously wished to avoid a colonial system in which Jews were employers and Arabs were workers.

Nevertheless it would be foolish to overlook the element of self-deception in early Zionism concerning the probable future course of Jewish–Arab relations in Palestine. Precisely because of their revolutionary convictions the pioneer settlers tended to underestimate the importance of Palestinian Arab nationalism and to assume, naively, that the Arabs would be satisfied with the material benefits they derived from the Jewish presence. Socialist Zionism encouraged the view that there was no genuine basis to the emerging Arab–Jewish conflict and that an alliance was possible between Jewish workers and the downtrodden Arab masses. In the 1920s and 1930s, for example, Zionist labour leaders conveniently blamed the hostility of the Palestinian Arabs on the divide-and-rule policy of British imperialism and the vested interests of the Arab feudal classes in preserving their privileges. The latter in turn had little difficulty in persuading the Arab masses that the Zionists were 'Bolsheviks', importers of an alien, subversive ideology as well as dangerous competitors to the Arab *fellah*. Between the socialist Zionism of Jewish settlers and the anti-Marxist ideology of rising Arab nationalism there was little common ground on which the class co-operation envisaged by some early leaders of the Histadrut could flourish.

The revolutionary spirit that pervaded early Zionism was greatly reinforced by the third *aliyah* between 1919 and 1924 which brought to Palestine some 35,000 young Jewish men and women dedicated to the ideals of socialist messianism. They were as committed to the notion of *chalutziut* as their predecessors, and endowed it with some of the collectivist *élan* inspired by the Russian Revolution. They hired themselves out as drainage or construction workers and they joined road gangs; they dreamed of building a new land free from the shackles of European capitalism, of covering Palestine with a network of independent, loosely federated collectives and co-operative bodies. These *chalutzim* were the spearhead of the drive towards a self-sufficient Jewish workers' commonwealth. In the 1920s a well-organized kibbutz-oriented sector created by the Ha-Shomer Hatzair and Left Poale Zion settlers reinforced the collectivist tendencies in the Yishuv. The kibbutzim of the Ha-Shomer Hatzair, as one observer put it, were like monastic orders without God. Their Marxist orthodoxy was probably unequalled by any other non-communist movement in the world, and although they jealously guarded their independence, they looked to the Soviet Union as their 'second fatherland'.

From its earliest beginnings, social-revolutionary Zionism in Palestine has manifested a passionate Hebraism which was an integral part of its vision of a renascent Judea. The adoption of the Hebrew language was for the Palestinian pioneer a question involving his whole outlook on life, society, and Jewish history. Hebrew was a vital symbol of this revolt against the Diaspora, an assertion of authenticity, freedom, and the destruction of a traditional identity which had become petrified in religious orthodoxy.

It was no accident, moreover, that many of the founding fathers of modern Israel were unabashed atheists, strongly opposed to 'clerical' influence even if they invoked the prophets of Israel for purely secular purposes when it suited them. Later they made their peace with the Jewish religious establishment for political reasons and some even began to espouse a sentimental religiosity with a strongly nationalist colouring. But this should not blind one to the radical critique of Judaism as such in much of early Zionist literature. Iconoclasts like Joseph Chaim Brenner and Micah Joseph Berdichevski who sought a Nietzschean transvaluation of values with regard to Judaism are perhaps extreme examples but they do underline the hostility of early Zionism to the parochialism of Jewish tradition. As Berdichevski put it: 'Our hearts, ardent for life, sense that the resurrection of Israel depends on a revolution – the Jews must come first, before Judaism – the living man, before the legacy of his ancestors.' Brenner, from a more consciously proletarian perspective, fiercely attacked the ghetto heritage, the self-glorification of the martyr-people, the illusory sense of superiority over the Gentile. His despairing hope was that Zion would forge a new, better, healthier Jew – a genuine proletarian. 'Our urge for life', wrote Brenner, 'whispers hopefully in our ear: Workers' Settlements, Workers' Settlements. Workers' Settlements – this is our revolution. The only one.'

But the ideology of early Zionism never entailed a root-and-branch sweeping away of the old world. Berl Katznelson, an outstanding trade-union organizer and one of the most representative figures of the Palestinian Jewish labour movement, recognized that Zionism was a 'revolt against servility within the revolution'. Katznelson emphasized the difference between 'primitive revolutionism', by which he meant the ruthless, irresponsible destruction of a cultural heritage – and 're-volutionary constructivism', which preserved the fruitful and creative elements of a religious tradition. In this respect, for all their anti-clerical, anti-Galut, and anti-assimilationist outlook, the Jewish labour leaders were probably less radical than Jabotinsky and his militant 'revisionist' Zionists.

One of the restraining factors on labour Zionism between the wars was its dependence on financial assistance from the World Zionist Organiza-tion. Another was the fact that, although they had been formed by the Russian political culture and favoured collectivist methods of political and economic organization, the leaders of Aḥdut Ha-avodah and the Histadrut lacked real coercive power. They were inevitably forced to compromise, to accept democratic procedures and to avoid attempting to impose their ideology on members. For all their enthusiasm for the Bolshevik Revolution, the Zionist socialist leadership remained pragmatic rather than dogmatic, 'constructivist' rather than revolution-ary, in their basic political methods. Their ideology had to remain flexible in order to attract diverse political groups to follow their leadership. For example, had they insisted on kibbutz communism as the only way to colonize the country they would not have been followed by the majority of workers. Though the kibbutz was regarded by many as a superior social structure and general obeisance was paid in the labour movement to the supremacy of collectivist ideas the leadership did not dictate this mode of life to its rank-and-file.

Another constraint was the fact that from the 1920s onwards Zionism became increasingly synonymous with the task of organizing large-scale immigration and providing employment for the newcomers. Thus economic activity and the problems of colonization determined party politics. The political style of the labour leadership had to adapt by the end of the decade to an essentially middle-class *aliyah* from Poland of people with their own financial resources and able to start their own businesses. As in the case of relations with the World Zionist Organization, which was controlled by non-socialist elements, this inevitably modified revolutionary currents in the pre-state Yishuv. Moreover the membership of the labour movement was increasingly dominated by the growth of an urban working class with its own sectional interests which pushed the leadership in a reformist direction. But it was above all through their control of the Histadrut, the centre of socio-economic organization in the Yishuv, that the labour movement and, in particular, the party apparatus of Aḥdut Ha-avodah emerged as the decisive political force in Palestine. By the mid 1930s even the middle-class parties identified labour Zionism with the national goal of building Palestine.

The bureaucratization of revolutionary impulses in early Zionism has nevertheless become more apparent with the cult of the 'state' that developed after 1948. The pioneering, frontier ethos is largely a thing of the past. Similarly there is little scope for the creative, even anarcho-syndicalist species of libertarianism or the voluntaristic social and political bodies which characterized the pre-state period. Statism, technological efficiency, and a matter-of-fact attitude to public affairs have long since supplanted the kind of idealism which marked off the Yishuv among young, developing societies in other parts of the world. The state has since 1948 been the dynamic, nation-building element. Its twin pillars, the bureaucracy and, above all, the Army, rather than the Histadrut, have become the focus of national loyalties. Are we perhaps confronted here with the typical post-revolutionary situation of a national liberation movement that comes to exercise power and manipulates ideology as a legitimating instrument of its political domination?

Familiar as this pattern may appear it overlooks the specific place of Zionism in Jewish history. For the significance of the Zionist Revolution was not so much in the birth of a new nation as a result of the Israeli war of independence but in its efforts to normalize the condition and status of the Jews as a people. In 1948 it appeared to some, like the writer Arthur Koestler, that with the establishment of Israel every Jew had to make a choice – either to become a citizen of the new state or be absorbed into the Gentile world. This either–or attitude was also reflected in a different way in the Israel-centred Zionist rejection of the Diaspora. For a time it really seemed as if the gulf between Israeli and Jew would grow wider, that there was no common identity. Had this happened, Zionism would have succeeded in its most revolutionary aim – to become part of the general history of modern man by breaking out of what it regarded in purely negative terms as the powerless predicament of the *Galut* Jew. In that case Zionism might well have produced a new nation of Hebrew-speaking Gentiles, a state in which *Israelization* (understood as a form of collective assimilation) would inevitably undermine the Jewish heritage. For the French sociologist, Georges Friedmann, writing in 1965, history appeared to be moving in this direction. To his mind there was no Jewish but only an Israeli nation, the majority of whose inhabitants were not religiously observant, and therefore not, strictly speaking, Jews.

There were Israelis, too, in the 1950s who saw in the growing separation between Israeli and Jewish consciousness a desirable conclusion to the Zionist revolution. They wanted a healthy, vigorous, non-religious culture based on 'Hebrew' identity and severed from foreign Diaspora roots. The Canaanite literary group and a few politicians like Uri Avnery denied any common ground between Israel and the Diaspora Jews. They appealed to the narcissism of the *sabra*, glorifying the fact that he was 'un-Jewish' in physique, outlook, and way of life. Already Herzl's political Zionism had been a form of Gentile nationalism – a translation into Jewish terms of a political idea, alien to Jewish tradition. The emphasis on flags, patriotic songs, uniforms, chivalry, and stirring speeches praising archaic communitarian traditions – the whole mystique of the *Volk* – belonged more to central European nationalism than to Judaism and the Jewish spiritual legacy. Even less 'Jewish' was the revisionist outlook of Vladimir Jabotinsky, who liked to refer to himself as a *goyisher kop* ('a gentile brain') and whose emphasis on militarism and national sovereignty was a logical extension of Herzlian Zionism.

Moreover, whether it came from the Right or Left, the vocabulary of abuse against Diaspora Jews in Zionist literature has only been surpassed in overtly anti-Semitic literature. The implicit assumption was that Jewish life in the *Galut* was intrinsically immoral or 'parasitic'. The panacea of the Zionist Right was for Jews to emulate the Gentiles in respect of physical strength, toughness, and military prowess. On the Left the solution was to transform the non-productive middleman, intermediary, or shopkeeper into a productive worker – in other words to make the Jew into a Hebrew-speaking *goy* through manual labour. What was *hachshara* (Zionist vocational training) asked Yehezkel Kaufman, Professor of Bible Studies at the Hebrew University, in 1934? His reply was a deliberate satire on the unconscious anti-Jewish stereotype in labour Zionism: *hachshara* was, firstly, 'preparation for Gentile jobs, the self-preparation of the Jewish worker to become a Gentile . . . to do Gentile work . . . to make profit the way Gentiles do . . . . The Jewish village lass shall live like a Gentile country girl'.

A rabbinical scholar, Yerachmiel Domb, writing in 1958, emphasized the connection between Zionism and Marxism, and the gulf which separated both from Torah Judaism. Zionism was in his view a form of Gentile nationalism strongly influenced by Gentile socialism and communism.

> When Marxism affected the world, either in its radical communist form, or in a milder socialist form, it also succeeded in impressing on the capitalist world the importance of planning, of trying to map out schemes for the future of the whole of mankind in the greatest possible detail. Zionism, with its completely worldly Gentile approach, also took to planning very eagerly and in itself constituted a plan for the political and material solution of the Jewish problem. Marxist ideas were incorporated into it in all their severity. The Zionist collective settlements have been praised by different circles as accurate expressions of the fulfilment of Marxist ideas.

For a representative of *Neturei Karta* (the ultra-orthodox 'guardians of the Holy City') like Domb, it was evident that Zionism, like Marxism, was an atheistic *Weltanschauung*, completely antithetical to Torah Judaism.

In what way has Zionism been a 'Jewish' revolution? In what sense can one speak of the Jewishness of Israel? Is classical Zionism any longer relevant to the relationship between Israel and Diaspora Jewry? Clearly since the Six Day War of 1967 one can speak of a growing 'Zionization' of the Diaspora or perhaps more accurately of an Israel-centred Diasporism. Though Zionism is clearly not able to solve many questions concerning the human condition of Jews and Judaism outside Israel, the interdependence of the Jewish state and of the Diaspora for Jewish survival is more clearly recognized. The moral and political isolation of Israel since 1973 has heightened the realization on both sides that Israel is within the Jewish people and not something separate from it.

The normalization thesis which underpinned the Zionist revolution – in the political sphere that Israel must become a nation like other nations and in the socio-economic sphere that it must have a healthy class structure – has been undermined. Equally problematic is the call of messianic Zionism to 'liquidate' the Diaspora, an eventuality that looks increasingly improbable. Not only socialist Zionism but secular Zionism as a whole is in crisis. The radical mystique of a pioneering society has exhausted its original inspiration. The early Zionist sense of a grand and unique destiny, of Israel as a light to the Gentiles, of a unique message to come forth from Zion, has for the present disappeared. Zionism has not really solved the problems of Jewry, but like all great transformations in the life of peoples, it has created new ones. The antisemitism of the Gentiles which it sought to eradicate has found a new source of encouragement in Israel itself; the process of assimilation which it sought to counter remains rampant; the exile from which it wishes to redeem Jewry remains more attractive for the majority than the Jewish state itself, no least because the latter cannot promise either peace or security to its citizens.

Nothing has illustrated more clearly the bankruptcy of the normalization thesis than the frequent attacks on Israel in the United Nations, questioning her very legitimacy. Israel has discovered that in the family of nations it has no permanent alliance on which it can rely. The only true solidarity it has known is that of the once despised Diaspora which has correctly recognized in the new anti-Zionism a threat to its own existence. For the Diaspora the sense of Jewish peoplehood is now focused on Israel, which has become the geo-political centre of a scattered, but single people – however problematic or objectionable this may appear to some. At the same time this has meant a drawing of Jews into the mainstream of world history to an unprecedented extent not only with all its risks but also its challenges.

The greatest of these challenges for the immediate future is to bring to an end the Arab–Israeli conflict. Yet paradoxically it may well be that the intractable reality of Arab enmity has done more for the *Judaization* of Israel than any other single factor, and helped to forge the interdependence between Zionism and the Diaspora which a generation ago appeared much less likely. Sadly enough, it is Arab hostility that has brought to light parallels between the Israeli and Jewish destiny never dreamed of by the theorists of early Zionism. In many respects the insistence of the Arabs on the *de-Zionization* of Israel is analogous to the demand of European Christian societies for the de-Judaization of the Jews as a price for their acceptance. The Israelis are a small, dynamic people in the Middle East perceived by the Arab majority as alien and unassimilable. This was the traditional fate of the Jew in the Gentile world. In this respect, at least, the Zionist revolt against historic destiny appears to have come full circle. The Israelis have discovered what it means to be a people alone. From this awareness may yet be born a new sense of the Jewishness of Israel.

Part 4

From Antisemitism to Anti-Zionism

17

Antisemitism and the origins of Zionism

It has long been recognized that the re-emergence of antisemitism in Russia and the west at the end of the nineteenth century was an important factor in the rise of modern Jewish nationalism. The fact that this resurgence of antisemitism was closely connected with the growth of non-Jewish nationalism, and in central Europe took the form of organized political movements seeking to reverse Jewish emancipation, inevitably left its mark on the classical theorists of Zionism. The opening sentences of Leo Pinsker's *Auto-Emancipation* betray not only the feeling of despair engendered by the Russian pogroms of 1881 but also the wider awareness that the 'Jewish question' might indeed be an organic, endemic feature of Jewish existence *throughout* the Diaspora. 'The eternal problem presented by the Jewish Question stirs men today as it did ages ago. It remains unresolved, like the squaring of the circle.' Later in his pamphlet, Pinsker went on to diagnose Judeophobia as a 'psychic aberration' of the Gentiles, 'a disease transmitted for two thousand years', which by its very nature was incurable.

Pinsker's view was reiterated by early east European Zionist thinkers like Nahum Sokolow and Ahad Ha'am who shared his belief that the people of Israel appeared to other nations as a 'disembodied spirit', a 'ghost nation', whose survival without a common territory aroused feelings of fear and hatred. Fifteen years later, the political Zionism of an unabashed westerner like Theodor Herzl, while eschewing such quasi-metaphysical speculations, recognized the chronic malaise of anti-semitism as a real danger to the physical security of Jews and therefore advocated the setting up of a Jewish state. Herzl deduced from the experience of the 1890s, which had witnessed the rapid growth of antisemitism throughout western and central Europe, that Jews would never be fully accepted in non-Jewish environments. Antisemitism implied that Jews would have to create their own politically independent territory – a Jewish national state – in self-defence against the rise of exclusive, integral nationalisms which had obstructed the process of assimilation into European society. Already Pinsker had seen that the Jews 'form a distinctive element which cannot be assimilated, which cannot be readily digested by any nation'. The legal emancipation of the Jews, 'the crowning achievement of our century', had not brought about *social* emancipation or the elimination of the national character of the Jews. A similar analysis was made by Herzl and Max Nordau who were led by the Dreyfus affair to conclude that in view of modern antisemitism the full emancipation of the Jews could not be achieved without a separate Jewish nationalism and the establishment of a national territory.

The crucial role played by the re-emergence of antisemitism in the genesis of Jewish nationalism was from the outset a source of hostile criticism from Jewish adversaries of Zionism – whether orthodox, conservative, liberal, or socialist. It was argued that both antisemites and Jewish nationalists unduly stressed the 'foreignness' of the Jews and that Zionists were in effect encouraging the removal of Jews from their native lands. By insisting on the existence of a Jewish 'nationality', Zionists were giving credence to the antisemitic claim that in each 'host country' the Jews constituted an alien element. Members of the anti-Zionist socialist Bund in eastern Europe even saw in Zionism a shameful *surrender* to antisemitism, an implicit recognition of the validity of the old cry: 'Jews, get out!' These socialist Jews like their revolutionary colleagues in Russia believed that antisemitism was an ephemeral phenomenon which would disappear with the triumph of socialist ideals and the advent of a classless society. They underestimated the strength of nationalism and religious prejudices, blinding themselves to the pervasiveness and perseverance of antisemitism because of their commitment to socialist ideology. The same blindness to the impact of antisemitism was evident in the hopes of liberal, assimilationist Jews who had opted for integration into European society and persisted in regarding both antisemitism and Zionism as reactionary phenomena engendered by panic and despair. The assimilationist critics of Zionism claimed that by directing their magnifying glass exclusively on the Jewish people, both antisemites and Jewish nationalists distorted the real trends of the time; they had misread Jew-hatred as an 'eternal force' governing the relations of Jews and Gentiles everywhere and throughout history. Some of this criticism, no doubt, appeared to be justified in the relatively stable bourgeois society of pre-1914 Europe which had not yet witnessed anything like the full destructive potential of racial antisemitism. The theory of the 'eternity of antisemitism in an eternal world of nations', the belief that every Gentile must become 'a conscious or subconscious Jew-hater' (Hannah Arendt) through living with Jews, undoubtedly appeared to many observers before 1914 as the fantasy of an overheated imagination.

The optimism of the critics of Jewish nationalism tended, however, to downplay the long history of Christian antisemitism whose tenacity and ability to adapt to new circumstances was clearly demonstrated throughout the nineteenth century. The rise of new racial doctrines in France and western Europe after 1850 and the growing conservative-reactionary character of German nationalism were further danger-signals misread by most assimilated Jews. Their importance was, however, intuitively understood by the socialist Moses Hess, the first secular Jew to adopt Jewish nationalism, who wrote his *Rome and Jerusalem* in 1862, twenty years before the Russian pogroms and the rise of political antisemitism in Germany. Hess concluded that the Jew would inevitably become the scapegoat of racial prejudice, irrespective of his efforts to cast off his Jewishness through conversion, religious reform, education, or assimilation. 'The Germans', he wrote, 'hate the religion of the Jews less than they hate their race – they hate the peculiar faith of the Jews less than their peculiar noses.' The Jews would always remain 'strangers among the nations', their noses could not be reformed and their black, wavy hair 'will not be changed into blond by conversion or straightened out by constant combing'. Although still a socialist, Hess's insistence on the *biological* impossibility of assimilation in Germany and the alien character of the Jew was arguably a kind of racism on the rebound, a response to existing social antisemitism before this had manifested itself in a political mass movement. He even glorified those traits mocked and caricatured by the antisemites as evidence to prove that the Jews are indeed a fully-fledged nation, one which had moreover a vitality and unique messianic destiny of its own. Interestingly enough, as Jacob Katz has pointed out, Hess's identification of the Jews as a *nation* was approved by Bruno Bauer, the ex-radical Hegelian turned Prussian conservative, in a review published in the *Berliner Revue* in 1863. Bauer was arguably one of the key intellectual links between the early-nineteenth-century radical critique of Judaism (in which Hess and Karl Marx had participated) and the rising racial antisemitism of the 1880s. Unlike Hess, Bruno Bauer in his *Das Judentum in der Fremde* (Jewry Abroad, 1863) denied that the Jews had the ability to create a state of their own – they were doomed by their 'parasitic' nature to live in exile. But though uninterested (like most antisemites) in a positive regeneration of Jewish existence, he shared Hess's national-racial concept of Judaism. From opposite standpoints and with different intentions Jewish nationalists and antisemites, as we shall see, could frequently find common ground in their critique of liberal emancipation and their belief that the Jews were not a confession but a *nation*.

It should be remembered that early-nineteenth-century German antisemitism constantly emphasized that the social cohesion of Jewry, its separatism and mutual solidarity, in a word its 'national' character, disqualified Jews from emancipation. This was precisely the argument of the German philosopher Arthur Schopenhauer who wrote: 'The rest of the Jews are the fatherland of the Jews . . . and no community on earth sticks so firmly together as does this.' Jacob Katz has, in a sense, vindicated Schopenhauer's point by arguing that it was *not* the emergence of antisemitism as a political movement which provoked the Jewish national movement but 'modern antisemitism was itself a reaction to Jewish proto-nationalism, to the incapacity and unwillingness of Jewry to divest itself of all the characteristics of national life except that of religion'. The eruption of organized antisemitism in central Europe in the 1880s therefore was only the second phase of a dialectical process and itself the *response* to the persistence of a Jewish proto-nation.

Katz also discusses the delicate question of an identity of objectives and even co-operation between Jewish nationalists and antisemites, pointing out that both camps responded to the ideological confusion in defining Jews in a rationalist era and a post-theological, secular society. Subsequent history, he argues, has shown the illusion behind the classical Zionist thesis that antisemitism resulted from actual strains produced by the *social* symbiosis of Jews and Gentiles living together. The assumption that Jew-hatred would disappear by removing the *external stimulus* (that is, the Jews) from entanglement in non-Jewish society has not proved itself in practice. Jewish nationalists failed to see that radical antisemitism *denies the right of Jewish existence* (including a Jewish state) *per se* and that Zionism itself would come to be perceived as part of the perennial Jewish conspiracy. This analysis, while certainly suggestive, does not satisfactorily explain the precise *historical* relationship between Jewish nationalism and antisemitism, nor the degree to which the conceptual framework of both movements was really identical. It does, however, underline that the Jews, even in western and central Europe, remained throughout the nineteenth century a conspicuous, anomalous, troubling phenomenon in the age of emancipation; that they retained the physical and mental attributes of a special collectivity, religious nonconformity and elements of a distinct culture, as well as remaining concentrated in certain economic fields. Thus, for all those opposed to the emancipation process, the Jews were easily seen as an 'unassimilable' element.

The existence of this 'proto-nationalism' did not seem to affect the self-perception of Jews themselves until the qualitative change which occurred with the rise of political antisemitism in central Europe at the end of the 1870s. Even then the politics of assimilation remained dominant in Germany, France, Britain, Austria, and Hungary until the First World War (and beyond) in spite of successive waves of antisemitism and its eventual emergence as a major political force. Thus, when pre-1914 antisemitism is described as the great external stimulus which produced Jewish nationalism, one must never forget that, at least in the west, one is talking about its effect on a relatively small minority of Jews. The overwhelming majority of western or central European Jews did not draw Zionist or nationalist conclusions from the rise of political antisemitism at least before the First World War. They believed that assimilation would dispose of the 'Jewish question'; they wanted to be Germans, Frenchmen, Poles, Hungarians, or Austrians and nothing but that; and many believed it was possible to steer a middle course between assimilation and Jewish identification. Were their aspirations a form of 'false consciousness', a dangerous delusion, a misreading of the real historical situation? Certainly the Zionist perception of antisemitism and its critique of assimilation from Moses Hess in the 1860s to Herzl and Ahad Ha'am at the turn of the century seems more realistic in the light of subsequent events. But at the time?

German Jews were undeniably perplexed when antisemitism burst on the scene at the end of the 1870s and, like their French counterparts twenty years later, they appeared initially to have lost their ability to react. Yet in the case of German Jewry, this situation had changed by the mid-1890s through the existence of such self-defence agencies as the *Centralverein*. The rejection of Jewish *national* identity did not, it should be stressed, necessarily prevent Jews from defending themselves or arriving at a positive definition of Jewishness. The struggle against antisemitism in Germany and Austria did lead, for example, to a certain revitalization of Jewish communal organizations (and greater stress on the shaped historical fate of the Jews and their common culture) without any overt assertion of Jewish national or Zionist sentiment. In France, on the other hand, the upsurge of antisemitism in the 1890s and the Dreyfus affair did *not* fundamentally alter the traditional policy of silence and reliance on republican institutions to protect Jewish lives and property. The Zionist response to antisemitism, in this context, as in Germany and Austria, was actually perceived by the majority of Jews as dangerous and calling into question Jewish loyalties to the adopted fatherland. Indeed, as we have shown, it was precisely the 'assimilationists' in the west who argued that Zionists had adopted the outlook of the enemies of the Jews. Moreover they claimed, especially after 1900, that political antisemitism was on the decline and that Jews could reasonably anticipate peaceful progress towards full integration. Interestingly enough, both the dominant big bourgeois oligarchy which still controlled Jewish communal organizations, and the most extreme Jewish radicals alienated from Jewish life, shared this diagnosis. In Germany, before 1914, one could admittedly make the case that the growth of antisemitism was not a foregone conclusion though it was a good deal more widespread than most Jews wished to believe. In France, moreover, the actual outcome of the Dreyfus affair and the secular anti-clerical thrust of the Third

Republic encouraged optimism that the growth of antisemitism could be checked and thrown back.

Hence it is not surprising that the analysis of antisemitism made by Zionists like Pinsker and Herzl which stressed its endemic features and its resistance to all reason or logic did not have an immediate appeal to most western Jews. What did it mean to them to be defined as members of a 'ghost people', as foreigners or guests in the lands of their residence? The thesis that antisemitism was a 'psychic aberration', or an unmanageable symptom of national conflict, appeared to cut the ground under their feet. The gap between east and west was evident when Pinsker explained in 1882 to the leading rabbi of Vienna, Adolf Jellinek, the implications for Russian Jewry of German antisemitism – namely, that

> if a nation as highly civilized as the Germans can tolerate antisemitic scenes in the capital of the German Reich – if a court chaplain [Stoecker] agitates and rages against those who profess Judaism and arouses the most brutal hatred against equal citizens of the same Reich, and a brilliant and all-powerful statesman [Bismarck] permits them to be reviled and stigmatized as pariahs etc . . . . why then should the Russian press not denounce Russian Jewry as aliens and intruders?

Jellinek's response, beyond advising his anguished Russian-Jewish visitor to take a cure in the south, was characteristic of most liberal western Jews: 'that would mean to accept the view of our implacable foes who deny that we have any true patriotic feelings for Europe'. It was not that most German or Austrian Jews were unconcerned or dismissive of the new antisemitism, but there was still a very significant difference in their eyes between semi-barbarous, pogromist Russia and rule of law in the west.

Russian Jews, like Pinsker, Lilienblum, or Sokolow, had before them not only the antisemitism of mob violence but also the example of actual encouragement of the mob by the Russian authorities and support from sections of the revolutionary movement. They looked at Germany through Russian eyes and concluded that emancipation western-style would not solve their problem. Only auto-emancipation, a revival of national policy and collective will, could secure the future of the Jews. Judeophobia was too deeply rooted to be fought by logic, reason, or enlightenment: whether it was interpreted as a form of social pathology, a hereditary psychosis, as a 'normal' form of national egotism, or as a product of banal socio-economic rivalries, Russian-style pogroms and the parallel emergence of antisemitism in 'civilized' Germany convinced early Jewish nationalists that social integration would not work. Nor was western civilization immune from the ancient scourge of Jew-hatred for, as Lilienblum and Pinsker argued, it was a direct result of the anomalous condition of a homeless, extra-territorial nation. Those who by the end of the century had drawn similar conclusions in the west, like Max Nordau, Theodor Herzl, or Bernard Lazare in France, were *exceptions* – marginal Jewish intellectuals who came to see in antisemitism a 'post-emancipation' phenomenon rather than a relic of medieval prejudices, a counter-movement against liberalism that had decisive implications for the future of Jewry. Herzl wrote in 1899 that he was led to Zionism

> by the new enemy which attacked us just when we were in the process of complete assimilation; by anti-Semitism. I am still aware what an impression it made upon me when I, in the year 1882, read Dühring's book on the Jewish question [*Die Judenfrage als Rassen-Sitten-und Kulturfrage*], a book which is as full of hate as it is brilliant. I think that prior to it I really no longer knew that I was a Jew. Dühring's book had an effect on me as if I had received a blow on the head. And that same thing probably happened to many a Western Jew who had already forgotten his peoplehood. The anti-Semites awakened it . . .

What disturbed the young Herzl was the thought that if a sharp intellect like Dühring insisted on the necessity for racial segregation between Jew and non-Jew, then what could be expected of the un-educated and unrestrained masses? Dühring's book alone was not, of course, enough to convert the young Herzl to Jewish nationalism. At that time he believed too strongly in the power of Germanization and the complete absorption of the Jewish race and religion in the Gentile environment. Even his exit from the German-Austrian student fratern-ity, Albia, in 1883 (after a public commemoration of Wagner's death degenerated into an antisemitic demonstration) did not bring about any fundamental change.

The antisemitic ideology of the German-Austrian *Burschenschaften*, which, in the spirit of Dühring, postulated a deep and fundamental racial antagonism between 'Aryan' and Jew, did, however, influence the foundation in 1883 of the first Jewish nationalist students' organization, Kadimah. Thirteen years before Herzl's conversion to Zionism in Paris, these Jewish students at the University of Vienna, overwhelmingly from eastern Europe and shaken by the Russian pogroms, had begun to give institutional form to Leo Pinsker's teachings. As university students they suffered directly from the actions of the Pan-German nationalist fraternities who had begun excluding Jews from membership since 1878. This exclusive policy affected school associations, gymnastic clubs (*Turnvereine*), and German cultural societies. The sharpening national conflict accompanied by humiliating reminders of Jewish 'racial' in-feriority convinced young Viennese Jewish students like Nathan Birn-baum that assimilation was not only a *cul-de-sac* but was actually exacerbating antisemitism. It was no accident that Jewish students and marginalized intellectuals, some of them born in Russia and eastern Europe, were to play such a crucial role in the crystallization of Jewish nationalist ideology in central and western Europe. No other group in Jewish society proved as sensitive to the social conflicts and discrimination generated by the emancipation of the Jews in an era of intense nationalism. Leo Pinsker's dictum that '*legal* emancipation is not *social* emancipation', later reiterated by Nordau and Lazare, spoke to their own marginal situation which had led them to experience social discrimination as a form of national oppression. Physically removed from the heartland of the Jewish masses in Russia and Galicia (though those who were born there had experienced its ethnic-traditional sense of Jewish peoplehood), they existed in a kind of spiritual and socio-economic vacuum in the universities of central Europe having broken with the communal framework of Judaism. Too poor to be philanthropists and too rich to be *schnorrers*, those who came from *petit-bourgeois* families found no place in the Jewish communities of central and western Europe organized, as they were, around charity. They had to earn their daily bread and find their self-respect outside of Jewish society. The rise of organized antisemitism after 1880 threw them back on their own resources. The ideology of Jewish nationalism provided them with a way back to Jewish life and to their own people, a new means of expressing their solidarity with the masses they had left behind and a resolution of their identity conflict.

They were strongly influenced not only by *Judennot* and the antisemitism which had dramatically exposed their marginal position in Gentile society, but also by the general ideological impact of central European culture which they absorbed at the universities in Germany and Austria-Hungary. The inculcation of values derived from German *Kultur* and *Bildung* led them to a critical perspective on assimilated Jewish society, whose materialistic outlook they openly despised. As men in transition between traditional and modern society, they found in Jewish nationalism a means of self-assertion and social integration. Whether in Berlin, Vienna, or even Paris, they were the *avant-garde* of a national movement whose real centre of gravity remained in Tsarist Russia but which was beginning slowly to spread to the western Diaspora. Central European antisemitism provided the outside stimulus for their re-evaluation of Jewish tradition in a modern, secular spirit. They applied the *Kulturkritik* of the age to their own people in the spirit of self-criticism aimed at the physical and moral regeneration of the *Galut* Jew.

At times this critique was indeed difficult to distinguish from the antisemitic argumentation and their attack on assimilated liberal Jewry was not always free from self-hatred or the imitative pattern of remoulding the Jewish people according to the standards of 'normal' nations. The Zionists and Jewish nationalists in central Europe tended to stress Gentile values such as physical fitness, outward beauty, dignified appearance, civility, and so on. They sought to integrate aspects of the antisemitic critique of Jews as an educative method for regenerating a morally 'corrupted' decadent Diaspora. Even racial premises and arguments were sometimes used in analysing the problem of Jewish physical and moral 'degeneration' with the blithe innocence that was still possible in an age where the possible operative conclusions of race-thinking were as yet unknown.

It is not surprising therefore that the leading French antisemite, Edouard Drumont, should have welcomed the Zionist solution proposed by Theodor Herzl as well as admiring the writings of the revolutionary Jewish nationalist, Bernard Lazare. In 1894, Lazare had published in Paris his *Antisémitisme: son histoire et ses causes*, a work which clearly showed the influence of Drumont. He argued that 'the general causes of anti-Semitism have always resided in Israel itself, and not in those who antagonized it', and Drumont welcomed his analysis, calling it 'the only book among the numerous and pitiful publications favourable to the Jews that the anti-Semitic movement had brought forth and which deserves to be read through to the end'. Lazare was only saying 'what we have been saying every day, only he says it differently than we do'. Drumont also praised Herzl's *Der Judenstaat* on its appearance (Herzl incidentally had noted in his diary on 12 June 1895 'I owe Drumont a great deal of the present freedom of my concepts, because he is an artist'). Like Herzl, Drumont believed that the Jews ought to leave Europe, only for different reasons. Drumont's goal was to rid France of alien intruders, that of Herzl to save Jews. Was this 'collaboration', as critics of Zionism would argue? Did it stem from a parallel world view? From a purely liberal standpoint there was indeed a similarity between Herzl and Drumont's outlook. Both agreed that modern antisemitism was an inevitable consequence of Jewish emancipation. They thought that in a society 'free of Jews', the element of friction would be removed. Antisemites and Zionists could agree that assimilation had failed, even if Drumont saw the Jewish problem as essentially *racial* (since the Jew could never assimilate for biological reasons) while Herzl argued that it was a national question. This difference was significant in so far as the racist antisemites (Drumont like Dühring before him) saw *no place at all* even for a small remnant of fully assimilated Jews in Europe, whereas Herzl believed that those who regarded themselves as Jewish Frenchmen, for example, with no attachment to their Jewish origins could be peacefully absorbed in their native country *after* the main exodus to a Jewish state.

There was, however, a convergence of views on the question of immigration, both antisemites and Zionists believing that the influx of too many Jews in a particular society automatically produced a hostile backlash. It was not only immigration itself but the concentration of Jews in certain occupations (such as in the free professions and finance) which aroused Gentile animosity. Increasingly Jewish wealth, and the over-production of 'mediocre intellects' who then staffed the revolutionary parties, exacerbated popular resentment – a diagnosis calculated to appeal to antisemites who interpreted it as proof of an organized Jewish conspiracy to undermine 'Christian' society. Herzl, like the young Bernard Lazare, who had railed in 1890 against the influx of *Ostjuden* into France as the direct cause of French antisemitism, believed that Jewish immigration would have to be channelled and controlled if the 'Jewish question' was not simply to be passed on to new lands of emigration. The Jewish state was designed, *inter alia*, to solve this problem and he, Herzl, believed with some reason that here was an area where he could make common cause with 'reasonable' antisemites.

Herzl's view of antisemitism indeed assumed that even Jew-haters are ultimately rational beings who will act in their self-interest once they have understood it. However pessimistic his assessment of the prospects of assimilation in European society, he remained an optimist in his conviction that antisemitism could be 'used' to solve the Jewish question in a mutually satisfactory manner for all parties. In Arthur Hertzberg's words, he assumed (like the Zionists who came after him) that anti-semitism could be guaranteed to remain at a certain temperature – 'hot enough to push the Jews out, but, in a basically liberal world' it would never 'break the ultimate bonds of decency'. It would be 'the visa to the Jew's passport into the world of modernity', 'the engine, driving the train towards Zion'. In that sense, Hertzberg is surely right that the Zionist analysis of antisemitism was 'one of the great acts of faith in liberalism that was produced by the nineteenth century'.

From this perspective the traditional charge made by liberals in the past and by the Left today, that classical Zionism is simply a mirror-image of antisemitism, ultimately misses the point. If Zionism can be 'accused' of anything, it is not that it took antisemitism at face-value, or too seriously, but that it failed to take it seriously enough. The classical Zionist thinkers correctly deduced, in contrast to the prevailing liberal and socialist consensus, that there was a real 'Jewish question' in Europe which would not automatically disappear with the spread of more democracy, social equality, modernization, and technological progress. What they failed to foresee was the potential genocidal logic still only latent in the antisemitism of the nineteenth century, which was however to climax in the destruction of European Jewry by the Nazis.

Zionism, itself, was ultimately too much an integral part of the tradition of European enlightenment and emancipation to envisage such a macabre consummation. It perceived lucidly enough some of the dangers confronting the Jews in European society at the turn of the century and proposed a solution that might indeed have avoided the disasters that subsequently followed. By the time the Zionist solution was finally implemented it was too late for the 6 million Jews whose fate had been sealed by the collapse of the European nation-state system and the failure of democratic forces to resist in time the Nazi onslaught.

18

The myth of the Jew in contemporary France

In 1791, revolutionary France, inspired by the ideals of the Enlightenment, the rights of man, and republican equality was the first European nation to emancipate the Jews fully. Yet, by the end of the nineteenth century, France was competing for top honours in the league table of European antisemitism. The Dreyfus affair, with its paroxysm of hatred and verbal violence directed at the small Jewish community, exposed unsuspected depths of Judeophobia which forty years later culminated in the Vichy regime. In recent years, historical research has demonstrated the degree to which France was a laboratory for ideologies of 'scientific' racism and an original, distinctive form of fascism. The extent of French collaboration with the Nazis under the Vichy regime and its responsibility for the deportation of Jews to the death camps underlines the importance of this independent tradition. The persistence and continuity of such traditions in the postwar era suggests that antisemitic myths may be more embedded in French culture and society than is commonly believed. Indeed, one might well ask which other European nation (with the exception of Germany) can offer so impressive a literary legacy of antisemitism as that which extends from Voltaire and the Encylopaedists through Drumont, Barrès, and Maurras to Bernanos, Drieu de la Rochelle, Céline, Gide, and Giraudoux? This antisemitism exploited a rich vein of right-wing Catholic tradition, modern fascist ideas, secularist anti-Judaism, the anticapitalism of the populist Left, and pseudo-scientific race theories.

Nevertheless, the impact of the Holocaust and popular sympathy in France for the newly created state of Israel, encouraged many to believe that anti-Jewish obsessions might become a thing of the past. For two decades a deceptive calm reigned on the surface until, in 1967, President Charles De Gaulle's notorious 'sermon to the Hebrews' renewed the suspended debate on the 'Jewish question'. As Henry Weinberg shows in a thought-provoking and solidly documented book,* it was as if a protective shield had suddenly been removed. De Gaulle, the most impressive figure in modern French history, the symbol of its most cherished aspirations for freedom and national independence, was accusing not only the Israeli state but the Jewish people of arrogance, elitism, and expansionist ambitions. Long-entrenched stereotypes about Jewish wealth, power, and the urge to 'dominate' resurfaced in the wake of Israel's spectacular victory and the General's unequivocal condemnation of its actions.

In retrospect, it would seem that a new era of antisemitism had been inaugurated. Jewish criticism of the French government's pro-Arab policies quickly led in some Gaullist circles to charges of dual loyalty and insinuations that Jewish solidarity was incompatible with the security of the French state and its national interests.

De Gaulle's successors, Pompidou and Giscard d'Estaing, continued this trend in their respective ways. Pompidou, in particular, displayed a growing antagonism towards Israel and its Jewish supporters in France and the United States. France increasingly voted with the Arabs at the United Nations, blamed Israel for the oil crisis, and created difficulties for it in the European Economic Community. Under Giscard, assistance was provided for Iraq's nuclear programme, close ties were established with oil-rich Arab states, and official French flirtations with Arafat paved the way for legitimizing the PLO in the eyes of western public opinion. One of the consequences of this policy was a new laxity and tolerance towards Middle Eastern terrorist organizations, marked by the French release in 1977 of Abu Daoud, who had masterminded the Olympic Games massacre of Israeli athletes five years earlier. Ironically, by the 1980s Paris had been turned into a battleground for a complex myriad of Arab terrorist groups.

Since the late 1960s a parallel development on the French Left reinforced the official pro-Arab trend. The French Communist Party (a much more powerful force twenty years ago) expressed its 'solidarity' with the Palestinians by vituperative denunciations of Israeli 'imperialism' and world Zionism. True to its Stalinist traditions it presented Israel not only as an aggressive, militarist state and agent of American interests but linked its nefarious role on the world stage to the machinations of international Jewish bankers. The antisemitic tone of some of this propaganda fused older patterns of nineteenth-century socialist Judeophobia in France with totalitarian amalgams derived from the Soviet Stalinist arsenal. Not surprisingly, it has been one of the major

* *The Myth of the Jew in France, 1967–1982* (Toronto 1987).

purveyors in France of the canard that Zionism is a form of racism and Israel a postwar reincarnation of the Third Reich.

Such rhetorical excesses were also a commonplace of the many *gauchiste* sects which flourished in France during the decade which followed the Six Day War. More extreme than the communists, their commitment to the 'liberation of Palestine' explicitly envisaged the destruction or 'dismantling' of the Jewish state. This leftist anti-Zionism (best qualified as the anti-imperialism of fools) went hand in hand with an *anti-racism* which excluded the Jews from the doubtful benefits of its compassion. The old cry of 'Mort aux Juifs!' (once the preserve of the French Right) was more than once to be heard at extreme Left demonstrations against Israel in the early 1970s. A violent offspring of this pro-Palestinian *gauchisme*, the *Action Directe* of the 1980s, even combined bomb attacks on Jewish or Zionist targets with its goal of overthrowing French democracy itself.

The visceral racism and antisemitism of the Neo-Nazi Right in France, which never altogether disappeared in the postwar years, also found encouragement in the new climate of suspicion towards Jews engendered in the 1970s. In contrast to the extreme Left, their racism has been uninhibited and able to exploit a real social problem, the growing hostility of the French population to North African Arab immigrants. The scale of this immigration and the xenophobia it engendered has provided the basis for the rise of Europe's strongest neo-fascist movement, the Front National led by Le Pen. Its rhetoric of 'La France aux Français', while officially eschewing explicit and blatant antisemitism, recalls the traditions of Drumont and Maurras as well as the fascist leagues of the 1930s. Between the lines of its assaults on prominent French politicians of Jewish origin like Simone Veil and Robert Badinter one can easily detect the time-honoured themes of the radical French Right for whom the Jews are as always a 'colonizing' power in France.

No less disturbing for French Jews is the preoccupation of the Right with the so-called Holocaust hoax (which has also found more than a few echoes on the extreme Left). In its efforts to clean up the image of Nazi crimes and thereby to rehabilitate the fascist legacy, the French Right has not hesitated to disseminate the monstrous lie that the murder of 6 million Jews was a deliberately fabricated myth serving the interests of Israel. Similar charges have been made by neo-Nazis throughout the western world and sponsored or subsidized by Arab money. But in France the new 'revisionism' found a particularly fertile terrain, encouraged by advocates like Professor Robert Faurisson and providing the subject for a university dissertation along similar lines that was initially approved by the academic authorities. In an interview published in *L'Express* (28 October–4 November 1978) the former Commissioner for

Jewish questions under Vichy, Darquier de Pellepoix, gave an even uglier twist to neo-Nazi revisionism, asserting that only vermin had been gassed during the war. This was not the only example of a new fascination with fascist antisemitism. *La mode rétro* in the French cinema during the 1970s, the revival of interest in the SS, in the Gestapo, and in the Vichy period, the publication of memoirs by former French fascists, the rediscovery of Céline, and so on all, contributed in their different ways to the erosion of post-Holocaust taboos. A former Pétain admirer, Alfred Fabre-Luce, could revive some of the oldest clichés about the Jews (claiming they had always brought persecution down on their own heads) and be granted a respectful hearing.

This intellectual climate which accompanied the closing years of Giscard D'Estaing's regime (with its suggestive echoes of the Vichy past) tended to turn antisemitism into just another political opinion. Against this background, the assassination of Henri Curiel (1978) and Pierre Goldman (1979), the flurry of antisemitic graffiti on Paris subway walls, the growing number of terror attacks against Jewish targets in France, the harassment of Jewish students, and the desecration of cemeteries appear less surprising. Thus the assault on the liberal synagogue in the Rue Copernic (1980) – seen as a turning point by many French Jews – did not come out of the blue. It was the logical climax of more than a decade of subtle incitement and official laxity which seemed to have isolated French Jews and made them stand apart from other Frenchmen.

Shmuel Trigano's controversial book, *La République et les juifs: après Copernic* (1982), clearly reflected this mood, indicting the French Republic for allegedly having failed the Jews, in effect abdicating their responsibility for protecting life and limb. Trigano put forward the somewhat bizarre thesis that the historic role of the Jews in France had always been to play 'hostage for the Republic', to abandon their own identity totally while upholding the myths of liberal republican ideology. According to Trigano, the government had *not* maintained its side of the bargain – to take a firm stand against antisemitism – thereby breaking the revolutionary contract. Copernic was thereby inscribed in a pattern of hostility of the French state, going back to the destruction of Jewish autonomous identity by centralizing Jacobinism and to the Napoleonic 'Infamous Decrees', rather than to the anti-republican forces which had traditionally been the main support of antisemitism in France. This was a provocative thesis but decidedly thin on historical evidence. What was, however, symptomatic of a wider Jewish malaise in Trigano's work was the prevailing sense of fear and insecurity among many French Jews who felt increasingly alienated from the mainstream of French society. This anxiety generated by the memories of Vichy and the continuing pattern of antisemitism in postwar France had already been revealed on the eve of Copernic by the interviews with a broad cross-section of French Jews, conducted by André Harris and Alain de Sedouy in *Juifs et Français* (1979).

The consistent antagonism to the Jewish state displayed by the 'progressive' French intelligentsia since 1967, especially in the prestigious *Le Monde*, was a further source of anxiety and concern for many French Jews, especially when it began to slide into the murky waters of anti-Jewish prejudice.

Nothing illustrates this malaise more clearly than the French media antagonism towards the Jews and Israel in the wake of the Lebanon war of 1982. For a few months at the height of the hostilities, it appeared as if a new witch-hunt was in progress. Wild accusations about the 'genocide' of the Palestinian people were rampant across the French political spectrum. Communists, Trotskyists, left-wing socialists, Gaullists, 'progressive' Catholics, pro-Palestinian and Arab intellectuals all added their voices to that of *Le Monde*, which reprovingly wrote of 'le fascisme aux couleurs d' Israel'. Israelis were branded as Nazis, and hoary Christian clichés about Old Testament fanaticism and the tribal-racist character of Judaism found a new lease of life. Where are these great humanitarians today, as Syria crushes Lebanon in its iron grip and Shi'ites remorselessly starve the Palestinian camps into submission?

There is no denying the anguish of French Jewry in the wake of this media assault and the deadly terrorist attack on Goldenberg's delicatessen in the old Jewish quarter of Paris. But one must be careful not to exaggerate the extent and intensity of postwar French antisemitism in spite of understandable fears provoked by its continued persistence and longevity. France is not, after all, an antisemitic state. Not only is there full Jewish equality but the success of French Jews in virtually all areas of French life has been impressive, even astounding in some respects. Catholic efforts to eradicate Judeophobia have been sincere and contributed much to an erosion of the old religiously-based antagonism to Jews and Judaism. François Mitterand since his accession to the presidency in 1981 has confirmed what his past record already suggested – that his empathy and understanding for the Jewish people is equal, if not superior to that of any major French political leader in the past. Public opinion polls also suggest a diminution in the intensity of popular antisemitism, though in a country as volatile and rife with political passion as France, such data are unpredictable and sudden changes may easily occur.

But if the level of contemporary antisemitism in France is open to question, its influence on current shifts in Jewish self-consciousness and identity is undeniable. The reopening of a 'Jewish question' in France has provoked a reawakening of interest in Judaism, a greater concern for Israel, and a return to Jewish sources of inspiration. There has been a reassessment of the old assimilationist ideology that survived the Dreyfus affair and even the trauma of Vichy. Unconditional loyalty to France no longer seemed in the 1980s to provide protection against physical or verbal threats. Traditional ideologies of French republican patriotism or secular Marxist universalism have become more problematic, especially if they are to be bought at the expense of Jewish identity. Nor is the traditional submissiveness of the established communal leadership to the French state appropriate to the new situation. The reign of the notables, symbolized by the Rothschild hegemony in communal affairs, is a thing of the past.

What has partly replaced it is a new style of political activism, a new Jewish militancy and assertiveness represented by organizations like Le Renouveau Juif. Many French Jews are no longer afraid of manifesting their particularism. They no longer fear the charge of dual loyalty or of acting as an organized political pressure group even if this entails a conflict with government policy. In place of the *Juif honteux* we have a greater pride in Jewishness. They no longer wish to disappear as Jews but rather to affirm their solidarity and commitment to Israel and with other Jewish communities outside France. The Frenchman 'of the Mosaic persuasion' and even the Israelite of nineteenth-century vintage is a declining species, though he may yet account for one-third of the Jewish population in France.

Henry Weinberg's explanation for this mutation involves multiple factors which he links dialectically with the antisemitic pressures of the French environment since 1967. He attributes a decisive influence to Israel (excessively in my view), seeing in its bravado and in the model of the fighting Jew standing up for his independence an inspiration for the reassertion of a positive Jewish identity. Certainly, since 1967, the traditional coolness of French Jews towards Zionism (which as far back as 1897 prompted Theodor Herzl to write them off as potential adherents to the cause) has faded and the commitment of the community to Israel runs deep. But many of the signs of revitalization in French Judaism to which Weinberg himself points suggest that Zionism may only have been a catalyst which leads off in other directions. Thus the renewal of interest in Yiddish, in the Sephardi heritage and folklore, the turn from Marx and Mao to the Talmud and *Kabbalah*, the greater observance of *kashrut*, the impact of the Lubavitcher Hassidim, and the neo-Diasporism of some French-Jewish intellectuals are scarcely marks of a Zionist renaissance in France. They testify to a significant thirst for Jewish authenticity and the rediscovery of Jewish roots which transcend a Zionist ideology that may have less appeal to French-Jewish youth than is sometimes assumed.

The return to traditional Jewish texts in the writings of intellectuals like Levinas, Trigano, or, at a more superficial level, of Bernard-Henri Lévy, represents perhaps the search for an authentic Jewish message, long distorted by western Christendom and by secular emancipationist ideologies which alienated French Jews from their own heritage. Such a search may also entail a critique of Zionism whose political philosophy is predicated on the same Jacobin nation-state model which is being reassessed in France.

In the case of Trigano, as we have seen, the critique extends beyond an attack on Jacobin centralism *per se* and its monolithic concept of culture to a wholesale rejection of French republican traditions, for having emasculated the originality and creativity of Judaism. According to Trigano the re-examination of Jewish identity and the reassessment of its cultural heritage cannot be based on traditions of the host country. Nor can it find inspiration in the concept of cultural pluralism put forward by Richard Marienstras in his *Être un peuple en diaspora* (1975) which drew parallels between the Jewish revival and that of regionalist ethnic identities (Basque, Breton, Occitans, Corsican, etc.) which have a *territorial* basis. Trigano rightly rejects this model but he is unduly harsh about the recognition by the socialists of *le droit à la différence* – that is, lending support to minority cultural groups – as constituting a danger to the integrity of French Judaism. Even more far-fetched is the attempt to see the Sephardim as the sole bearers of an *authentic* Jewish heritage in France (one that is religious in inspiration, rooted in mysticism and philosophy) as opposed to 'Ashkenazi' thinkers (Lévy, Finkielkraut, Glucksmann, and so on) whose Judaism is merely a reaction to the antisemitism of their Christian environment. However there are different modes of defining Jewish identity among Ashkenazim and Sephardim in contemporary France which have their background in distinctive cultural traditions. Nor can one ignore the crucial importance of the North African immigration in the 1960s for the demographic, socio-economic, and cultural profile of French Jewry today.

The greater assertiveness of French Jews and their emotional solidarity with Israel clearly owes much to this immigration. Its influence on communal institutions, attitudes, and intellectual trends is much less clear, as is its effect on French perceptions of Jewry. Unlike the east European Jewish immigrants between the wars, the North African Jews were already acculturated and not subjected to the xenophobic backlash of earlier generations of newcomers. Moreover their Jewish identity had a stronger basis in religious tradition, in family ties and the experience of Mediterranean societies only superficially touched by the secularizing influence of modernity. How long they are likely to resist the assimilationist pull of French society and culture, given current rates of intermarriage and the endemic weakness of Jewish communal structures in France, must however remain an open question.

But recent studies of Jewish identity in France do suggest that the older ideology of assimilation may have reached a *cul-de-sac*. As Dominique

Schnapper already pointed out in her *Juifs et Israélites* (1980), even in the most integrated milieu of French Jewry there has been a degree of return to a more Jewish identity in the past twenty years. For some, this has taken the form of a religious awakening or emphasis on a distinct cultural identity; for others it has been more immediately associated with Zionism, with solidarity towards the Jewish people as a whole, or resistance to antisemitism. The heterogeneity of these responses, especially among intellectuals and in the younger generation, is perhaps the mark of a community still in the process of becoming, though one whose creative promise gives rise to a cautious optimism concerning its future.

19

Global anti-Zionism in the 1980s*

Mr President, my purpose this evening is to trace some of the links between anti-Zionism and classical antisemitism as they have found expression in recent times. This task is all the more urgent as it has become increasingly apparent since the early 1970s that there has been an orchestrated campaign against the Jewish state, Zionism, and the Jewish people as a whole; a campaign whose impact constitutes a serious threat to our status in the world and ultimately to our very existence. This campaign has now acquired such a global dimension and resonance that I believe it can be compared to the threat posed to Jews by Nazism in the period of its upsurge – *before* it assumed governmental power; this in spite of the very considerable differences in the status of the Jews and attitudes towards them in the non-Jewish world which existed then and now. In spite of all the positive changes which occurred in the wake of the Holocaust, the last decade with its cumulative anti-Zionism has led to a dangerous regression which calls into question the over-optimistic assumptions of the 1950s and 1960s. Then it was still believed that Israel would constitute a completely new beginning and by its very existence lead to the gradual disappearance of antisemitism in the Gentile world. Indeed, the opposite has happened. Not only have anti-Zionism and antisemitism, historically distinct and even antithetical ideologies, become interrelated: Israel itself is today the prime cause and pretext of a partly novel form of antisemitism, as puzzling as it is disturbing.

Time is too short for me to analyse all the manifold paradoxical features of this phenomenon tonight. I will therefore focus my remarks on two aspects only, both of which are interconnected and which have assumed particular importance in the last four or five years, the attempt

---

*Lecture delivered in Hebrew to the Study Circle on World Jewry held in the residence of the President of Israel, Chaim Herzog, in Jerusalem at the end of 1984.

to stigmatize Israel as a 'Nazi' state and the parallel campaign by some anti-Zionist circles to rewrite the history of the Holocaust as a 'Zionist conspiracy' or as a collaboration between Nazis and Zionists to murder the Jewish masses in Europe! The very extremism of such claims makes it tempting to dismiss them as the sick product of a lunatic fringe with which no sane person could ever hope to influence public opinion. Unfortunately this is not quite the case, and bitter experience has taught us that such paranoid distortions of reality can reach a wide audience and exercise a fateful impact on the future. Moreover, it is precisely the equation of Zionism with Nazism which is in my opinion the most characteristic mode of the new antisemitic anti-Zionism in the early 1980s, one which inverts all our assumptions and therefore deserves special attention and consideration.

This is not an easy subject to discuss for emotional reasons on which I do not need to elaborate in this forum. But there are also methodological and intellectual difficulties. How can we be sure that anti-Zionism, even of the more extreme kind that I shall be discussing, is not primarily motivated by sympathy with the Palestinian cause or opposition to specific Israeli policies? In other words, is it not perhaps the case that even the most vehement anti-Zionism is not really inspired by hatred of Jews? We all know that in the nineteenth century Jews themselves were among the leading opponents of Zionism, and to this day ultra-Orthodox Judaism sharply denounces the Zionist 'heresy' and the state of Israel. Many left-wing and liberal Jews in the Diaspora who oppose Zionism would vehemently deny that they are antisemitic and yet some of these Jews openly compare Zionism with Nazism. This fact has provided an effective smokescreen for Soviet, Arab, and neo-Nazi antisemites to claim that they are 'only' against Israel even as they openly discriminate against, threaten, or attack Diaspora Jews.

Anti-Zionism has undoubtedly provided a wonderful alibi for anti-semitism *in deeds* to cover itself with a theoretical halo of virginal purity and good intentions. It has also permitted antisemitic stereotypes to enter areas of the world, particularly in Asia and Africa, where there was previously no tradition or cultural substructure of Judeophobia. At the same time in the postwar western democracies anti-Zionism has provided a vehicle for the re-emergence of anti-Jewish attitudes which were for some twenty to twenty-five years partially submerged. This does not appear to me to be an accidental connection or mere coincidence of events. On the other hand, our analytic understanding is complicated by the fact that today nobody wishes to declare himself openly as an antisemite. Even neo-Nazis in the west are careful to wrap their racial mania in the appropriate 'anti-Zionist' terminology: while on the Left those who shout loudest against 'Nazi' Israel are usually self-proclaimed militant anti-racists.

So today we are seemingly confronted by an antisemitism which springs to the defence of all victims of racial oppression *except* the Jews – the paradigmatic example of such victims – who are now transformed into perpetrators and prototypes of racism! The 'Zionism is Nazism' libel has built on this inversion of images which goes much deeper than is often realized here in Israel. Perhaps only people like myself, who have lived most of their lives in the Diaspora and witnessed the transformation that occurred in the 1970s (in my own case in England), can really grasp the full significance of this change. This does not mean that we should therefore stick the label of antisemitism on all forms of anti-Zionism, let alone on all criticisms of the state of Israel and its policies. We have enemies enough without unnecessarily extending their number by unwarranted accusations. Moreover, even if they were not anti-Jewish, contemporary forms of anti-Zionism would be dangerous enough in their own right to demand a searching analysis and effort to develop an antidote.

But it appears to me that there is a basic continuity between classical antisemitism and contemporary anti-Zionism which can and should guide us in our search. Both ideologies seek in practice to deprive the Jew of his right to an equal place in the world; to limit his activity and freedom of movement, his human, civic, and political rights, and even his very right to exist – at least in the more radical formulations. Both antisemitism and anti-Zionism imply that the Jews have no claim to be a free, independent people like other peoples, to define themselves according to universally acceptable criteria of self-determination, or to enjoy the fruits of individual or collective emancipation. Thus both ideologies are built on the negation of Jewish rights and seek to drive the Jews back into a ghetto – whether it be physical or symbolic. The Jews must be confined to the status of a pariah nation. In a word, they do not belong.

For the European antisemites of the late nineteenth century, Jews did not belong to European Christian culture. They were 'Semites' or 'Asiatics', eternally alien to Christian, 'Aryan' society. For contemporary anti-Zionists, in particular for most of our Arab neighbours, Israel is ironically enough an alien western implant in the Middle East, without roots in the region or any right to a legitimate, equal, and autonomous presence as a sovereign state. The goal of Arab anti-Zionism is ultimately to reduce Israel (or the Jews as a collectivity) to their age-old humiliated status under Islam, as *dhimmis* – 'protected' by Muslim 'tolerance' and living on grace rather than by right in their midst. This type of anti-Zionism seeks to de-emancipate the Jews as an independent nation, much as modern secular European antisemitism insistently sought to de-emancipate the Jews as free and equal individuals in civil society and as an integral part of the body politic of the nation-state. Anti-Zionism continues the discriminatory theory and practice of classical antisemitism, transferring it to an *international* plane. It wishes to re-ghettoize the Jewish nation, just as post-emancipation antisemites sought to return the Jewish community to the pre-modern ghetto.

In both cases, we witness a conscious effort to *delegitimize* Jewish self-definition and to undermine the dominant mode of Jewish group existence. In the Middle Ages the main thrust of this delegitimation was anti-Judaism – directed by the Christian church against the religion by which Jews as a whole defined themselves; in the era of emancipation, it took the secular, 'scientific' form of antisemitism – Jews are an inferior race and therefore do not deserve civil equality or else they are dangerous parasites and must be excluded from human society.

In the postwar era of the Jewish state (that is, after 1948), delegitimation is no longer primarily racial or religious but *ideological* and *political*. There are several reasons for this change. In the first place, racial delegitimation in the post-1945 world, which has been decolonized and where 'racism' is officially considered by the Third World as the original sin of humanity, is an ineffective weapon. Religious bigotry is also widely considered as a reactionary phenomenon – especially in the west – though much less so in the Islamic world where it continues to play a very significant role in Arab anti-Zionism. On the other hand ideological opposition, particularly when it employs the fashionable 'progressive' terminology of anti-imperialism, is generally acceptable.

The second major reason is that Israel has become the main embodiment in Jewish and non-Jewish eyes of the modern Jewish group identity and is therefore the obvious target for antisemitic invective. Delegitimation of Israel and its ideological basis – Zionism – is the most direct way in our time to damage Jewish interests and prepare the way for the destruction of Jewish identity. This is clear enough to the Soviet Union, the Arab and Muslim states, and the Jew-baiters all over the world. It is not apparently clear to many Jews and non-Jewish liberals who still lend their hand, often unconsciously and without always understanding the logical consequences, to the enemies of Israel.

The Soviet Union has played a special role in the worldwide campaign of delegitimation of Zionism, Judaism, and Israel since the late 1960s. It has taken over in practice the heritage of Nazi antisemitism, and already in Stalin's last years the paranoid theory of the world Jewish conspiracy, in Marxist–Leninist disguise, acquired an 'anti-Zionist' tinge. In the past fifteen years, it has also been the Soviet Union which has stood in the forefront of the global campaign to equate Zionism with Nazism, just as it orchestrated the infamous 'Zionism is Racism' resolution at the UN in November 1975 in conjunction with the Arab states. The slander that Israel is a 'Nazi' state should be seen as an escalation of the earlier campaign, one which in the early 1980s has moreover achieved some resonance in the west, especially after the violence and destruction in Lebanon. The Arab role in the propagation of the Zionist–Nazi equation is today no less significant, but in the past it was not so evident – possibly for the reason that many Arab nationalists in the early postwar period still identified with Hitler and Nazism. Their only regret was that the Germans had failed truly to complete the 'Final Solution' and as a result the state of Israel had emerged.

For the Arabs and above all the Palestinian leadership, the Holocaust was never really absorbed in its horrific dimensions of inhumanity, and the real collaboration of certain Arab leaders (beginning with the Grand Mufti of Jerusalem) with the Nazis was repressed. Instead the Nazi Holocaust was perceived mainly as a political tool in the hands of Zionism. To counteract this weapon, the Palestinian tragedy had to be inflated into a new and even more horrific Holocaust instigated by Israel itself. Zionism was allegedly responsible for this terrible and unique crime; hence Ahmed Shukeiry (the first leader of the PLO) could declare in a UN speech of 4 December 1961: 'Zionism was nastier than Fascism, uglier than Nazism, more hateful than imperialism, more dangerous than imperialism. Zionism was a combination of all of these traits.'

In the late 1960s the PLO began to grasp the utility of projecting the Nazi horror directly onto Israel and utilizing the prestige of the European anti-Nazi resistance for their own cause. For western consumption, PLO propaganda now stressed the similarities between the Palestinians' condition in the Middle East (as a result of Israeli 'oppression') and that of the Jews of Europe under Hitler's rule. Were not they (the Palestine Arabs), too, a homeless, persecuted people, evicted from their lands, defenceless, stateless, refugees deprived of independence and basic human dignity? One can recognize the factual elements in this presentation without necessarily sharing the extremely one-sided and demonological view of Zionism as the sole or even main culprit responsible for this state of affairs.

What is more important for our purpose tonight is the real impact of this inversion of traditional images of persecutors and victims on western public opinion since 1967. It was a major propaganda coup for the PLO that it partly succeeded in adapting 'Zionist' terminology for its own purposes – turning the symbolism of the 'return' of an exiled people to its homeland against Israel itself. This campaign is implicitly anti-Jewish in a subtle and insidious sense, deliberately playing on the guilt feelings and sensibilities of Europeans regarding the Holocaust. By destroying or driving the Jews out of Europe, it is argued, Zionism led to an even greater 'crime' – the expulsion of Palestinian Arabs by Israeli Jews. Therefore it is the moral responsibility of the west to support the Palestinians unconditionally. How often one has heard this Arab argument repeated by European statesmen and intellectuals in the past fifteen years to justify pro-Arab policies generally adopted for quite different and very cynical reasons of self-interest.

At the same time, Arab propaganda has deliberately sought to strip the Nazi Holocaust of its unique and Jewish content – that is, when Arab money is not actually financing the publication of so-called 'revisionist' literature, which denies that the murder of 6 million Jews ever took place! These efforts did not achieve much resonance in the west until the Lebanon war. Suddenly a significant section of the western press – by no means 'anti-Zionist' in an ideological sense – began to draw startling parallels between Lebanon and Lidice, Israelis and Nazis, the Star of David and the Swastika, the Palestinians and the embattled Jews of the Warsaw Ghetto. Was this antisemitism, latent or manifest, old or new, or simply media sensationalism and the desire to package a great human tragedy in black and white terms, with the Israelis as the natural villians?

Perhaps antisemitism is not quite the right word, though, as the former editor of the London *Observer*, Conor Cruise O'Brien, pointed out in that newspaper, in June 1982. For the people in question, to quote this astute observer, were 'even extravagantly philo-Semitic these days, in their feelings for the Arabic-speaking branch of the Semitic linguistic family'. O'Brien suggested a new term, 'anti-Jewism' – 'it's an ugly word, so it fits nicely'. He proposed 'a pragmatic test, for possible "anti-Jewism", in discussion of Israel' – namely 'if your interlocutor can't keep Hitler out of the conversation, if he is . . . feverishly turning Jews into Nazis and Arabs into Jews – why then I think you may well be talking to an anti-Jewist'.

The O'Brien litmus test is certainly a useful guide for identifying a major component of contemporary antisemitic anti-Zionism in both east and west. In the communist world, this type of 'anti-Jewism' dates back at least thirty years to the period of the Slansky trial in Czechoslovakia and the so-called 'Doctor's Plot' orchestrated by the dying Stalin. But it only attained full force after the massive Arab defeat in June 1967, when the USSR, to revive its own damaged prestige, embarked on a systematic campaign to discredit Israel, Zionism, and Judaism totally. One of its most widely used weapons was the remorseless repetition of the legend that the Zionists had already sought in the 1930s to create a 'pro-Nazi' state in the Middle East, that they had actively participated with the Germans in the mass destruction of European Jewry, that they had sabotaged Jewish resistance in the ghettos, and served as a 'fifth column' for the Wehrmacht in the conquered territories of Europe. Both Nazis and Zionists supposedly signed secret agreements which condemned the Jews of Europe to the gas chambers in return for German support for Jewish 'fascist' aims in Palestine!

The interesting fact is that in recent years these grotesque Soviet blood-libels have been taken up by a part of the radical Left – especially the Trotskyists – in western Europe and America. This trend is most striking in Great Britain, of which I have the greatest first-hand experience – a country which in the last decade has proved increasingly receptive to the most varied kinds of anti-Zionist rhetoric. The willingness of supposedly anti-Soviet radical leftists to swallow these made-in-Russia fabrications provides food for thought. Are they in fact nothing but puppets of His Master's Voice in Moscow or bought lackeys of Arab petro-dollars? Perhaps in some cases, this is indeed the reason. But the truth, I think, is more disturbing than that. Anti-Zionism has, in the past fifteen to twenty years, gradually become an integral part of the cultural code of many Leftist and liberal circles – an enemy on a par with imperialism, racism, and militarism – and invariably identified with these evils.

Precisely because it sees itself as 'anti-fascist', this western radical culture is militantly anti-Zionist and can very easily slide into the ultimate step of equating Nazism with Zionism, the Third Reich with Israel, the Wehrmacht with *Tsahal*. Unlike the radical Right, it does not desire the rehabilitation of Nazism, it does not deny the Holocaust, and at least in theory it believes that antisemitism is a reactionary, racist doctrine to be fought no less strongly than Zionism itself. Nevertheless, I would claim that the falsifiers of the anti-Israeli Left who now rewrite the history of the Holocaust as a story of Nazi–Zionist 'collaboration' are no less dangerous than the neo-Nazi 'revisionists' and possibly more effective. Unlike their Soviet models, they may actually believe the libels they propagate and this gives them a certain credibility – especially when they are Jews. Their emergence was made possible by the general climate of anti-Zionist opinion in the west, greatly stimulated by the turn to the Right in Israel after 1977 and the Lebanon war, which provided the opportunity and the opening. Recent works by Lenni Brenner, such as *Zionism in the Age of the Dictators*, or Tony Greenstein's pamphlet on *Zionism – Antisemitism's Twin in Jewish Garb* – both written by Jewish Leftists (one American, the other British) – are increasingly symptomatic of the times we live in.

Much more disturbing was the way that the Lebanon war provoked an orgy of media denunciation directed at Israel's so-called 'genocide', a fantastic legend briefly given credence even in the so-called quality press in the west. Suddenly ideological opinions on the 'fascist' or 'Nazi' nature of Zionism, which had belonged to the margins of western society, were taken seriously and acquired a new respectability. Itzhak Shamir's past as an underground terrorist was, for example, scrutinized with extraordinary intensity when he became Prime Minister in 1983, and his alleged contacts with the Nazis were inflated into wild accusations about the historically rooted 'fascist' character of Zionism. Not only the radical Trotskyist fringe of the labour and left-wing press in Britain and other western countries indulged in such analogies. They could also draw sustenance, it should be pointed out, from irresponsible voices in Israel itself who are frequently quoted in anti-Zionist literature abroad to provide cover against charges of antisemitic bias and prejudice.

The anti-Zionist mood intensified across the political spectrum in the west and thus a revision of the past and present with regard to Zionism began to take place, for the first time reflecting motifs long familiar from Soviet propaganda. For example, it was now alleged that Zionism had always allied itself with reactionary forces and rabid antisemites in order to achieve its 'criminal' goals. It was not only detrimental to Diasporic Jewish interests, but it had deliberately and callously abandoned the Jews to their fate during the Holocaust. It was, moreover, a cruel racist doctrine of chosenness, which had inevitably and logically led to the 'genocidal' policies of Israel in Lebanon. In the radical leftist and neo-Nazi press, and also in writings by ultra-Orthodox Jewish fanatics, Hitler and the Nazi mass murder seemed to pale into insignificance alongside the new Israeli 'fascism' in the Middle East – depicted as a threat to humanity as a whole.

Wild rhetoric on this scale was fairly novel in the west, but in Soviet Russia it had been official Orwellian *Newspeak* since June 1967 when Soviet Ambassador Fedorenko denounced the Israeli 'war criminals' in the UN for pursuing Hitlerite policies on the West Bank, while the war was still in progress. Brezhnev himself at that time gave the signal to the Soviet media by stating that the Israeli 'invaders' were seeking to imitate the actions of the Hitlerites. The Soviets did not wait for the advent of Mr Begin or Mr Sharon to brand Israel's leaders as fascist executioners. The late Moshe Dayan and Golda Meir, leaders of the Israeli labour government, were favourite targets in the Soviet disinformation effort of the early 1970s, accused of ruthlessly pursuing the Nazi dream of *Lebensraum*, of ruling hapless Arabs in the spirit of a master-race (*Herrenvolk*), of establishing concentration camps, and even of sterilizing the local population.

At that time, however, there were few people in the west ready to credit such obvious falsehoods. The Nazi–Zionist equation only gradually infiltrated the western world, partly through the channel of the communist parties and the growing influence of Arab money and diplomacy after the oil crisis of 1973. In addition, there were local causes, at least in western Europe, which helped prepare the ground. Rising anti-Americanism (and the perception of Israel as an American stooge) was one factor; neutralist tendencies and the growing strength of the peace movements, the policy of appeasement (towards Russia and the Arabs), and the Third Worldism of many European politicians and intellectuals, exacerbated the process.

At the same time, a subtle revision of the Hitler era took place in popular works, films, and even books by serious historians which perhaps indirectly lent itself to the irresponsible comparisons that have been drawn in the early 1980s between Nazism and more current phenomena. The result of all these trends, which were to culminate in grossly disproportionate western reactions to the Lebanon war, was the definitive end of the brief era of European 'philosemitism' and pro-Israelism, which under the impact of the Holocaust had in fact sentimentalized the Jews as model victims. In their place came new victims, above all the Palestinians – themselves sacrificed, so it was suggested, by the anti-Zionists, to make way for the creation of a Jewish state in which they were fated to be objects of racist discrimination.

These symbolic post-1967 reversals of image had their origins in the subculture of the New Left in the late 1960s, which peaked just when the Six Day War had sent shock waves through the world and transformed the European and western perception of Israel and the Jews. Though the New Left quickly faded as a political force, its influence penetrated into new and more lasting trends such as the 'green' (ecological) and peace movements, feminism, a new immigrant and ethnic militancy, the impact of Arab and Third World elements and causes at western universities. The anti-Israeli and anti-Zionist ideological bias of the radical Left was considerably strengthened by these developments and it also spread into the media – especially television – where it began to exert a mass influence. By no means all of this anti-Israelism was antisemitic in intent and much of the reporting of Israel and the Middle East was no doubt motivated by sympathy for Palestinians more than by hatred of Jews. Nevertheless, the overall, cumulative effect was to create a very negative picture of the Jewish state.

It is this background along with a significant generation change which has ultimately made possible the current fashion of drawing the Zionist–Nazi parallel even in the western democracies. The political, cultural, and moral damage to Israel and the Jewish people of this process of delegitimation has been considerable, though it is not necessarily irreversible. Images are notoriously volatile and western public reaction to the Middle East in the long term is difficult to predict. One cannot say that the Arab cause has made tremendous gains in western opinion, but the erosion in Israel's standing and good name over the past decade is certainly palpable. Many Gentiles in the west and the Third World who in former times were sympathetic to the Jewish state clearly feel let down and disappointed. Sometimes this disappointment can lead to hatred. On the other hand, there are also many influential people in western politics and cultural life who have not allowed themselves to be swept along by the anti-Israeli hysteria. Moreover, in the United States, where the situation is fundamentally different in many ways from Europe, the image of Israel and Zionism, while somewhat dented, still remains largely positive.

But if the picture is not entirely black, there are many troubling points of concern. It must be realized that there is a new generation in the west which has now entered politics and is also acquiring influence in cultural life. Many of the new generation have been nourished on extremely negative ideas concerning Israel and Zionism. The image of the ugly Israeli, which they have acquired through various channels, has un-doubtedly shaped their outlook on international politics. In place of the money-grubbing Jew or the subversive Jewish revolutionary of anti-semitic mythology, they have been exposed to new and more up-to-date stereotypes – those of the militarist, racist, and now even the 'Nazi' Jew seeking to dominate the world by force. An image of lust for power and reckless militarism can already be added to the rich armoury of antisemitic typecasting nourished over generations by Christian, Muslim, Marxist, and right-wing demonology. A reflex anti-Zionism, which may not always have been anti-Jewish in origin and intention, today all too easily falls into the established groove of an endemic antisemitism that has been a central feature of civilization for more than two millennia. This development is particularly dangerous for the future of Israel and the Jewish people because, through anti-Zionism, a revival of all the latent murderous potential of antisemitism is in fact already taking place. Those responsible for decision-making in Israel have, in my opinion, been too slow to appreciate this fact and its negative political significance.

The Jews of Israel have perhaps tended in the past to dismiss the seriousness of the ideological and political enmity that has built up in the outside world towards them. Unfortunately, as recent developments have shown, what the Gentiles think and say can be as important as what the Jews actually do – words do have political consequences! The power of propaganda, of the media and images can often be as decisive as winning wars – a fact that was once very well understood by the Zionist leadership, but has tended to be forgotten in more recent years. The negative consequences of anti-Zionism have been more palpable and obvious for Israel in the international sphere – in its standing in the United Nations and its diplomatic isolation.

But the internal dangers should also not be forgotten – for example, there is the growth of isolationist and extreme nationalist currents in Israel and even the seeds of an Arabophobic tendency which in the past was much less significant. These trends need to be uprooted while they are still only potential dangers, if the anti-Zionist propaganda offensive from without is not one day to become a self-fulfilling prophecy. Israeli society is still far from corresponding to the diabolic fantasy constructed by those who seek to destroy it. But it is also no more immunized than any other democracy from disintegrative trends, from extremism, racism, and intolerance which may tear it apart from within.

There is a no less serious danger contained in the anti-Zionist drive of recent years when we come to consider Diaspora Jews. In my opinion, one of the objectives of the anti-Israel campaign has been to drive a wedge between the Jewish state and its exposed Diasporic hinterland. The more wicked and diabolical the state of Israel seems in the eyes of Gentile public opinion, the less likely Diaspora Jews are to support such a state – this is surely the calculation of our enemies. How could world Jewry back a 'Nazi' state after what happened during the Holocaust? How can it support and subsidize racial discrimination in Israel? There has, in fact, been a growing chorus of Gentile voices even in the west in recent years suggesting that Diaspora Jewry dissociate itself from this so-called 'racist', aggressive Israel or else it can expect to pay the price in terms of a justified(?) revival of antisemitism. For, as accomplices in Israeli 'crimes' through their financial and political support, Diaspora Jews are ultimately no less guilty. Clearly this type of moral and political blackmail may have its impact on Jews outside Israel and the long-term consequences are unpredictable.

It may, of course, well be that if anti-Zionism continues to assume an extremist and antisemitic character, then Diaspora Jews will be obliged to organize and mobilize themselves, and to strengthen their ties with Israel and Zionism. To some extent, the 'Zionism is Racism' campaign did eventually have this effect. On the other hand, an opposite result is no less likely. For it is, after all, easier for the Diaspora Jew to lower his profile in Israeli-related affairs when the temperature of anti-Zionism rises, or even to join in the anti-Israel consensus than it is to swim against the current. Only time can tell whether Diaspora Jewry will continue to stand by Israel in times of crisis or whether it will wilt under the pressures of a hostile non-Jewish environment.

One thing should, however, be clear from this necessarily brief overview of the current situation. Anti-Zionism of the type I have tried to describe is a poisonous flower which has deliberately encouraged a process of alienation between Israel and the nations, and between Israel and the Diaspora as well as a sense of self-alienation within Israeli society itself. It has thereby created the danger of irrational reactions on all sides in order to overcome concrete political and moral problems by violent means. Hence the urgent need to analyse and struggle against this phenomenon.

20

The new war against the Jews

The memory of the Nazi genocide against the Jews continues to cast its long shadow over the present, affecting the way people think about the major political events of our time. This preoccupation has its dangers, encouraging overheated rhetoric and demagogery, as well as outright falsification of history; terms like 'Nazi', 'fascist', 'genocide' are emptied of meaning when every group which suffers oppression, imaginary or real, brands its oppressors with the stigma of absolute evil symbolized by the German mass murder during the Second World War.

But if in democratic societies this kind of exaggeration is frequently no more than a way of attracting attention, in the totalitarian societies of the communist world hyperbolic language is neither accidental nor spontaneous. It is part of a carefully orchestrated campaign to achieve well-defined political goals. Far from being innocent, the use of Holocaust parallels in these countries is part of a major effort not only to shift attention away from the Nazi murder of the Jews but to redirect it entirely, and turn it into a means of morally discrediting the Jewish people and delegitimizing the state of Israel.

The main vehicle of this effort in recent years has been the allegation of Nazi–Zionist 'collaboration' before and during the Holocaust, and the drawing of grotesque parallels between modern Israel and the Third Reich. Contrary to widespread belief, this attempt to link Nazism and Zionism was not a product of the Israeli invasion of Lebanon in the summer of 1982 but the result of a long-prepared Soviet ideological offensive going back more than twenty-five years.

The event which first triggered the Soviet propaganda campaign was the reparations agreement concluded between the German Federal Republic and the state of Israel in 1952. Alarmed by evidence of growing ties between the two countries, Moscow, at the end of the 1950s, was already characterizing Ben-Gurion's Israel as 'a tool of the Bonn revanchists', and claiming that the price for West German economic aid was

Israeli silence about the presence of former Nazis in Adenauer's government and civil service. The capture of Adolf Eichmann by the Israeli secret service and his subsequent trial in Jerusalem in 1961 might have seemed on the face of it to make nonsense of this charge. But the Soviets, not easily discouraged, now fabricated an elaborate theory according to which the real objective of the trial was to ensure Eichmann's silence concerning secret dealings between the Zionists and the Nazis during the Second World War.

In concocting their legend of collaboration, the Soviets seized on the figure of Rudolf Kastner, a prominent Hungarian Zionist who in 1955 had been at the centre of a bitterly contested trial in Israel. Kastner had been accused after the war – in a mimeographed leaflet published by a Hungarian Jewish survivor – of being an accessory to the murder of Hungarian Jewry. He sued for libel. Though he was found guilty of collaboration, the verdict was eventually overturned by the Israel Supreme Court in January 1958, and his name was cleared. By this time Kastner himself had been killed, but his usefulness to Arab and left-wing propaganda in the west was just beginning. Over the next two decades he was to become a symbol of a so-called Nazi–Zionist 'secret deal' by means of which a small Jewish elite was preserved during the Holocaust, while millions of rank-and-file Jews were abandoned to the gas chambers. As *Tass* put it in an English broadcast on 1 February 1978: 'In 1944 Eichmann and one of the Zionist leaders, Kastner, signed an agreement on Hungarian Jews. The agreement guaranteed the lives of 600 "prominent" Jews, while condemning to death 800,000 Jews without sufficient money to pay for their lives.'

The use of the Eichmann and Kastner trials is a good illustration of the way in which Soviet propaganda has systematically misrepresented any Jewish effort at rescue through negotiation as its opposite – Zionist connivance in the 'mass destruction of Jews'. This accusation first became part of an intensive propaganda offensive around 1970, probably in order to check the Soviet-Jewish emigration movement by demonstrating that the Zionists, far from defending the interests of the Jewish people, had always betrayed them. By the mid-1970s the charge of outright co-responsibility in the Holocaust had become the staple of virtually all 'anti-Zionist' literature. To give the claim some semblance of credibility, Soviet ideologues have invented a continuity between Zionist (and non-Zionist) efforts to achieve an orderly exodus of Jews from Germany in the 1930s – at a time when the Nazi regime was still encouraging emigration – and alleged co-operation in sending Jews to the gas chambers later on, when German policy became genocidal.

Using a crude antisemitic Marxism of a type fashionable among German communists in the early 1930s, the new Soviet literature suggests that there was a class basis to the common language of Zionism and Nazism. Lev Korneyev, a veteran antisemitic theoretician, draws a distinction between the masses of poor Jewish workers – who he claims were the only ones murdered in the gas chambers – and the Jewish millionaires and Zionists who acted as accomplices of Nazism. Already in the 1930s, according to T. Solodar in his tract, *Wild Wormwood* (1977), the Zionist leadership under Chaim Weizmann thought it inexpedient to save older Jews; what they wanted instead were 'young people filled with the poison of fanatical nationalism and fit for armed attacks on the native population of Palestine'. The same author claims that as part of the deal with the Nazis, the German Zionists repeatedly denied to the world 'the terrible news about anti-Jewish pogroms in fascist Germany'; Korneyev has a Haganah emissary (described as 'an agent of the Zionist secret service') actually co-ordinating the *Kristallnacht* pogrom with the Nazi authorities. Thus, while communists were 'heroically' battling against fascist tyranny in the underground, the Zionists were secretly pursuing their aims in agreement with the Nazis and even encouraging their excesses.

Worse, still, while other people – Russians, Poles, Ukrainians, Byelorussians – purportedly sought to rescue Jews during the Holocaust itself, their own Zionist leaders and the international Jewish bourgeoisie abandoned them. This is the theme of such anti-Zionist pamphleteers as Vladimir Begun, Yevgeny Yevseyev, and Vladimir Skurlatov, all of whom suppress the fully documented cruelty of the special detachments of Ukrainian police, of Latvians and Lithuanians, not to speak of the real collaboration of many Poles, White Russians, and other east European peoples in the 'Final Solution'.

Other propagandists like D. I. Soyfer go even further, asserting that the Zionists actually 'took part in the mass extermination of Jews', that they 'doomed the Jews, including children, to death in the gas chambers, whereas Soviet soldiers rescued the children who were threatened with death'. Soyfer identifies the *Judenräte*, the Nazi-appointed Jewish councils in eastern Europe, with the 'Zionists' who 'sent the poor to their deaths' but 'did not touch the rich'. He also represents the Zionists as the Wehrmacht's fifth column, writing that the 'Gestapo's Zionist agents infiltrated the ranks of the resistance fighters and helped the fascists to finish them off'. Another work similarly stresses the class dimension of the Holocaust; according to the author, V. A. Semenyuk, those 'chosen' to be taken off transports to the death camps (via the secret Zionist–Nazi accords) were never representatives of the working class, but always businessmen, rabbis, bourgeois intellectuals, and above all militant Zionists.

A particularly sinister twist is given by the assertion that the Zionists were covert allies of the Nazis in the war on the Soviet Union. Thus Korneyev, writing in the popular periodical, *Ogonyok*, in August 1977, singles out the 'Zionist' fund behind many banks and monopolies in the capitalist states (especially the US), which supposedly 'extended assistance to the Nazis and collaborated with them both before the latter came to power in Germany and in the period when the Hitlerites were making preparations for world war'. Not only did the Zionists bankroll the Nazis, according to Korneyev, they also 'actively collaborated with the fascist invaders' in occupied Soviet territory during the period of the Holocaust itself.

More, even, than elsewhere, the myth of Nazi–Zionist collaboration has been pushed with special intensity in the Ukraine, probably to serve the dual purpose of sowing hatred and distrust between Ukrainians and Jews and simultaneously blackening both Zionist and Ukrainian 'bourgeois-nationalist' tendencies. R. M. Brodsky, for example, in a widely distributed Ukrainian-language pamphlet, *Zionism and Its Class Essence* (1973), asserts that Zionists were never squeamish about co-operating with slaughterers of the Jewish people, beginning with the Ukrainian Petlyurites during the Russian civil war, continuing with the White Guards, and concluding with fascist dictators like Antonescu, Mussolini, and finally Hitler. So close was this co-operation that – in Brodsky's words – 'many fascist criminals avoided the punishment they deserved only thanks to their Zionist protectors'.

It is remarkable that this scurrilous literature manufactured in the Soviet Union should find resonance in the west; but it has. Whereas some of the extreme Right have derided the Holocaust as the 'hoax of the century', others on the far Left – on the far British Left, in particular – have transformed its meaning in a no less repellent way by focusing on the theme of collaboration. To take a random sampling of comments by Trotskyist papers over the past several years: the *Socialist Worker* twisted a letter of Ben-Gurion's arguing, in December 1938, for a speedy territorial solution to the Jewish refugee problem, into a statement of cold indifference to the plight of European Jewry; the Trotskyist *News Line* volunteered the information that 'Ben-Gurion, the founding figurehead of the Israeli state, welcomed the killing of Europe's Jews because it got rid of the old and sick which the new state would not be able to absorb'; the feminist paper *Outwrite* repeated the canard that Kastner's committee in Budapest 'had helped the Nazis exterminate the bulk of Hungary's Jews in exchange for the lives of 600 prominent Zionists'; and the *Socialist Organizer*, going one step further, actually charged that Hannah Senesh – the heroic Palestinian girl who parachuted behind German lines in an attempt to save the Jews of Hungary – was betrayed to the Nazis by the Hungarian Zionists themselves.

The slander of Zionism does not stop with rewriting the past. It also seeks to imprison the present in that past, to burden the Jewish state with the ultimate stigma of reproducing the Nazi horror in its daily policies –

of being, in short, a Nazi state itself. This libel has now become an integral facet of the strategy of all those forces pursuing the political aim of dismantling Israel.

Its advantages for this purpose are obvious; the inversion of values whereby Nazi crimes are attributed to the Jewish state (and the PLO is cloaked in the mantle of anti-fascist resistance) totally undercuts the moral legitimacy of the Zionist project. At the same time, it procures for its propagators a clear conscience with regard to the past. For if the alleged victims of the Holocaust have themselves become perpetrators of 'genocide', then there is nothing for the rest of the world to feel guilty about – the slate has been wiped clean. Even antisemitism becomes legitimate, provided it is cloaked in the appropriate *anti-racist* terminology!

The Soviet offensive, carrying the myth of Nazi–Zionist collaboration full circle to describe Israel itself as a Nazi state, goes back to 1961, to the time of the Eichmann trial in Jerusalem. The analogy was still somewhat tentative then, and lacked the demonic features with which the Soviet media were later to invest it. By 1964, however, a cartoon appeared in *Izvestia* depicting West German arms sales to Israel in which the Star of David had metamorphosed into a symbol of death and destruction. Two Nazi officers are shown selling arms to an Israeli, and the caption reads: 'I recommend these first-class weapons. They have been tried and tested and used in Auchwitz and the Warsaw Ghetto.' These were still the early, relatively benign years of the Brezhnev–Kosygin regime – preceding the Six Day War – but a growing number of Soviet papers began repeating the charges that Israeli leaders had been accomplices of the Nazis, that they were now cynical allies of the 'neo-Nazi' government in Bonn, and that they themselves practised a repugnant racism at the expense of Israel's Arabs.

Such charges were disturbing enough, but it was a key meeting of the Third Committee of the United Nations on 14 October 1965 that may more properly be regarded as the opening gambit of what was to become a sustained and successful campaign. The purpose of the meeting was to debate a motion, put forward jointly by the US and Brazil, that the UN charter on human rights should contain a clause banning antisemitism. The Soviets offered an amendment to the motion, proposing that Zionism too be included in the condemnation so that antisemitism, Zionism, and Nazism – in that order – would all be classified as 'racial crimes'. The motion never came to a vote, but the episode foreshadowed the infamous Zionism-racism resolution that was passed a decade later.

The event which decisively brought the Israel–Nazi comparison onto the world stage was the Six Day War of June 1967. Israel's lightning defeat of Moscow's Arab allies unleashed an unprecedented vilification of Zionism and the Jewish state that has not let up to this day. In the

United Nations the chief Soviet representative, Nikolai Fedorenko, accused the Israelis of 'behaving like Nazis' and demanded that the country's leaders be tried as war criminals before an international tribunal. On 2 June Moscow radio repeated the charges and four days later *Izvestia* told its readers that 'even the western correspondents compare these crimes with those the Nazis perpetrated in the occupied countries during World War II'. On 5 July Leonid Brezhnev, speaking to graduates of Soviet military academies gathered at the Kremlin, stated that 'in their atrocities against the Arab population it seems that the Israeli invaders want to copy the crimes of the Hitler invaders'.

As early as 17 June – when the war was not yet two weeks old – a leader article in the official party newspaper had headlined Israel's victory with the words 'This is genocide', and genocide remained the slogan under which the Soviet press and radio called for Israel's punishment. Communist media compared Israel's war of survival with the 'Nazi theory of the preventive blow' and portrayed Moshe Dayan as a pupil of General Rommel and an advocate of Nazi doctrines of *Lebensraum*. On 29 July 1967 *Moscow News* blamed what it termed the Zionist ideology of racial self-segregation, chosenness, purity, and exclusiveness for the 'monstrous crimes' that had been committed against the Palestinian Arab population in the occupied territories. In the journal *International Affairs*, L. Sedin argued that Tel Aviv's policy was based on German practices during the Second World War:

> There is the same immediate appointment of Gauleiters for the newly-occupied areas; the ruthless treatment of POW's and the native population; the terrorism and eviction of the population from their old homeland; the plunder and 'development' of occupied territories ... all ... sickeningly reminiscent of Hitler's 'new order in Europe'.

Komsomolskaya Pravda, not to be outdone, published an article by Yevgeny Yevesyev on 4 October 1967 drawing the standard analogies between Hitlerite Germany and Israel, but also pointing out that whereas in the fascist heyday the Zionists had been mere junior partners, now the roles were reversed: 'It is the German revanchists and militarists who are now performing services for Zionism in practical affairs.'

The reversal motif found vivid expression in many Soviet cartoons of this period. Thus in *Kazakhstanskaya Pravda* (21 June 1967) a subdued Adolf Hitler cringes before an arrogant Moshe Dayan who orders him to 'Move on!'; and in *Sovetskaya Rossiya* (2 August 1967), three hapless Arabs await their fate at the hands of an Israeli soldier, while a uniformed Nazi offers a blueprint for a gas chamber. Variations on this same theme have been endlessly repeated by Soviet cartoonists over the past seventeen years, and recently – during the Lebanese war – have also found their way into mainstream as well as left-wing newspapers in the west.

As far back as 1967, then, at the time of a war which was almost universally recognized in the west as a just war of self-defence against a mortal threat to Israel's very existence, the Soviets were already branding the Israelis as imitators of the Nazis, and filling the air with such trigger-words as *Blitzkrieg, Herrenvolk, Gauleiter*, both for the benefit of western audiences and to serve the needs of Soviet domestic policy. By the end of 1969, the Nazi analogy had been further elaborated to include the accusation of 'Zionist racism', and the concept of the 'chosen people' was increasingly being twisted into a synonym for the Nazi doctrine of the 'master race'.

If the Six Day War sparked the invention of the Soviet myth of 'Jewish Nazism', the campaign reached its first peak around 1970 in reaction to the unprecedented challenge of a Jewish national revival within the USSR and the consequent movement for Jewish emigration. Meetings were held up and down the Soviet Union denouncing 'the Zionist fascist monsters' and their alleged atrocities against Arabs. *Komsomolskaya Pravda* and other Soviet newspapers invented imaginary pogroms and massacres of Arab villagers. Defence Minister Moshe Dayan was accused of following in the footsteps of the SS and the 'mad Fuehrer', sowing death and destruction in the Middle East. But it was above all Prime Minister Golda Meir who bore the brunt. The 'fascist-imitating protectress of the Jews' was denounced by *Sovetskaya Moldavia* (10 March 1970) for having 'proclaimed the nightmare idea of "Greater Israel"' and for bringing back 'the rotten theory of racial superiority'.

Again and again, the labour leaders Golda Meir, Moshe Dayan, and even Abba Eban were equated with Hitler, and fascism and Zionism were declared identical in form and content. (Eban was described in *Radianska Ukraina* on 3 March 1970 as 'meeting near the walls of Dachau with the ideological heirs of Eichmann'.) Countless letter writers, many of Jewish origin, were mobilized to avow their Soviet patriotism, their abhorrence of Israeli actions, and their denial of any anti-Jewish discrimination in the USSR. The spectre of a 'Greater Israel' – presumably a carbon copy of the fascist 'Greater Germany' – was evoked time and again with particular relish. An article in *Sovetskaya Byelorussia* (2 April 1970) added a new wrinkle, claiming that Hitler, in his doctrines of *Lebensraum* and Aryan superiority, was himself simply repeating the ideas of Theodor Herzl, the founder of Zionism.

Long before the advent of Begin and the Likud to power, moreover, Israelis were being accused of bombing and wiping out Arab villages just as the Nazis had flattened Lidice and Oradour during the Second World War. In 1970, Yevgeny Yevseyev in a series of articles, later published as a little book called *Fascism Under the Blue Star*, suggested that the

Zionists put up a monument to Hitler, since his *Mein Kampf* had provided them with their basic dogmas. Time and again, the visual media over the next few years were to merge images of the bloodstained Star of David with the paraphernalia of Nazism, while ideologues continued to stress that Zionism was based on the same biological and racist principles as Hitlerian fascism and employed methods it had refined from the Gestapo arsenal – including torture, terror, demolition of houses, and atrocities against old men, women, and children.

The United Nations resolution of November 1975 equating Zionism with racism, masterminded by the Soviet Union with the help of the Arab states, brought to fruition the first stage of the international campaign against Israel. The emphasis had deliberately been placed on racism rather than on Nazism to win the support of the Afro-Asian bloc, for whom racial discrimination was the original sin of western colonialism in the twentieth century. For most of the Third World, indeed, the Holocaust remained a side issue, but this presented no problem to the Soviets or the Arabs since, according to the new dogma, racism and genocide were precisely what Zionism and Nazism had in common. Just as the theory of the 'racial superiority of the Aryans' had led to the gas chambers, so the alleged Zionist doctrine of racism was resulting 'in a policy of genuine genocide' (G. Kuznetsov, 'Zionism in the pillory', *Za Rubenzhom*, 21 November 1975). S. Astakhov, writing in the Moscow daily *Selskaya Zhizn* (16 November 1975), went even further and declared that genocide had been practised in Israel 'from the first days of the establishment of the state'.

The 1982 war in Lebanon thus added little that was new to Soviet rhetoric. There were the same atrocity stories, Hitlerian parallels, and distorted quotations as in the past. Indeed, *Pravda*, during the war, took pains to deny that Begin and Sharon were departing from standard Zionist theory or practice: 'The policy of genocide being carried out at this time by the Zionists in Lebanon is inseparable from Zionism as an ideology and the criminal practices of the Jewish bourgeoisie' (1 August 1982). Inseparable, that is, according to *Pravda*.

But if Moscow has been the prime source of the Nazi-Zionist comparison – propagated through its internal media and foreign broadcasts, its embassies, the international communist movement, the press of the non-aligned countries, the United Nations, the peace movement, and even a number of bourgeois newspapers and sympathetic media in western Europe – it has also had help from other sources. Arab influence, particularly, has been very important in encouraging the identification of Zionism with Nazism, though this did not become a central theme in the Arab war on Israel until fairly recently.

There are a number of possible explanations for earlier Arab reticence on the subject. The simplest might be the very well documented collaboration of Arab leaders with Nazism in the pre-1945 period. Haj Amin el-Husseini, the leader of the Palestine Arabs (known as the Grand Mufti of Jerusalem) expressed his admiration for Hitler and Nazi Germany throughout the fascist era, and sought with extraordinary persistence to win German backing for his goal of wiping out the 'Jewish national home' in Palestine. On 28 November 1941, in Berlin, the Mufti formally declared his readiness to co-operate with the Third Reich, to form a Muslim SS legion, to encourage uprisings in the Arab world, and to instigate sabotage against Great Britain. Hitler in turn promised the Mufti that the moment the German armies reached the southern exit of the Caucasus, he would give the signal for Arab liberation.

In their determination to liquidate the Jewish nucleus in Palestine, Hitler and the Mufti found a common language. Not only did the Mufti aid and abet Hitler's 'Final Solution' of the Jewish question in Europe, he even pressurized the SS leadership and allied satellite regimes in the Balkans into preventing the escape of any Jews from the inferno of the death camps. Indeed, Haj Amin el-Husseini's record of collaboration from 1933 to 1945 was so clear-cut that the Allies were obliged to classify him as a war criminal, though the British, in their anxiety to prevent more Arabs from going over the Axis, censored news of his wartime activities in Berlin.

Nor was Haj Amin el-Husseini an exceptional case. The Nazi regime aroused a high degree of enthusiasm throughout the Arab world – in Egypt, Iraq, Syria, and Lebanon as well as Palestine. Its nationalist fervour, militarism, fanatical antisemitism, and opposition to Anglo-French hegemony inspired many Arab nationalist leaders, intellectuals, and youth between the wars. Both Nasser and Sadat, among the Free Officers in Egypt, were admirers of Hitler and looked to Nazi Germany to free them from British rule. It is no accident, therefore, that in the 1950s a number of Arab countries, and especially Egypt and Syria, were to serve as havens for Nazi war criminals in hiding. Some of the most notorious of these, like Johann von Leers and Leopold Gleim, converted to Islam and continued to act as political advisers and experts on 'Jewish affairs' to the Arab regimes at war with Israel.

Given the immense sympathy for Hitler and Nazism in the Arab world in the 1950s and early 1960s, it was unlikely that a theory of Zionist Nazism could take firm root. When a leading Arab intellectual like Sadat's intimate friend, Anis Mansour, could write that 'The world is now aware of the fact that Hitler was right', or when a paper like the Jordanian English-language daily, the *Jerusalem Times*, could console Eichmann that his trial would 'one day culminate in the liquidation of the remaining six million to avenge your blood', there was little sense in accusing Israel of pursuing Hitlerian policies. On the contrary, the trend was to identify with neo-Nazi forces all over the world; this was Nasser's policy as it is today the policy of Qaddafi, of the Ayatollah Khomeini, and of the Saudis who have continued to finance 'revisionist' literature which denies the Holocaust and which propagates older antisemitic theories based on the Protocols of the Elders of Zion.

Nevertheless, there were a few ideologues in the Arab world in the 1950s and 1960s who did argue that Zionism was the heir of Nazism, and that both grew out of the same intellectual soil. Parallels were sometimes drawn between the alleged Zionist aim of a Palestine without Arabs and the national socialist goal of a *Judenrein* Germany. The leftist Baha al-Din described Zionism in 1965 as 'a school for racist fanaticism which is not inferior to Hitlerism'. Other Arab writers followed the British historian Arnold Toynbee in his contention that the Zionists were morally even worse than the Nazis for they had murdered or expelled peace-loving Arabs who had done them no injury. Ahmed Shukeiry, the first leader of the PLO, declared at the UN on 4 December 1961 that 'Zionism is nastier than fascism, uglier than Nazism, more hateful than imperialism, more dangerous than colonialism. Zionism is a combination of all these evils.' The PLO was later to adopt a variation on this theme as Article 19 of its first Palestine National Covenant.

Over the past two decades PLO strategists have increasingly seen the utility of using the Nazi label to blacken Zionism, especially when appealing to a western or 'progressive' audience. In particular PLO emissaries have sought to play up the theme of the Palestinians as the new Jews of the Middle East – exiled, landless pariahs driven from their homeland and subjected to genocidal persecution.

In this disinformation effort the PLO has been greatly helped in the west by the left-wing press and a section of the media which regarded the government of Israel as an object of loathing long before the Lebanon war. In Britain, however, such anti-Israel attitudes have moved from the radical fringe closer to the mainstream and have even begun significantly to infiltrate the Labour Party. Tony Greenstein, chairman of the Labour Committee on Palestine, has for instance been one of the more persistent advocates of the 'Zionism is Facism' myth as well as the thesis of Nazi–Zionist collaboration. Interestingly enough, one of Greenstein's discussion documents on Zionism (entitled 'Antisemitism's twin in Jewish garb') was hailed by an organ of the neo-Nazi National Front as 'excellent'. Such strange convergences between the Left and the Right are by no means new in modern history, though there is something peculiarly grotesque in the spectacle of self-confessed Nazis expressing their approval of Jewish left-wingers who equate Zionism with fascism!

Nor is it only in Britain that one sees this convergence of Left and Right on the issue of Zionism. One need only recall the statements made during the 1984 US presidential campaign by the Black Muslim leader, Louis Farrakhan. In addition to expressing the usual attitudes of Islamic fundamentalism towards the Jews and Israel, Farrakhan also made a point of asserting that the 'Zionists made a deal with Adolf Hitler', thus bringing the collaboration myth to an audience that might otherwise have not had access to it. Such is the long, insidious reach of Soviet and Arab propaganda.

But its insidious reach is longer still. In the summer of 1982, without a shred of supporting testimony and with massive evidence to the contrary, even some of the more respectable western media found it possible to liken the siege of Beirut to the Nazi siege of the Warsaw ghetto, Menachem Begin to Adolf Hitler, the Israeli defence forces to the Wehrmacht, the Ansar prison camp in South Lebanon to Dachau, and Sabra and Shatilla to Nazi 'genocide'. Those who stigmatize Israel with the obscenity of Nazism and the odium of collaboration – tragically, the one option that was never open to the murdered Jews of Europe – may or may not be aware of the peculiar etiology of the charges they mouth. Aware or not, however, in so doing they are helping to further one of the great lies of our age, and in their own way contributing to the success of one of the most sustained propaganda campaigns in modern history.

21

Under the sign of *glasnost*

During the past three years under Mikhail Gorbachev's dynamic leadership the Soviet Union has been steadily breaking way from the Stalinist legacy. The old command structure bequeathed by crash industrialization, the ossified bureaucratic apparatus, over-centralized planning and the primacy of heavy industry at the expense of consumer interests have been increasingly challenged from within the party leadership itself. Military expansionism abroad as well as cultural and political repression at home are no longer taboo subjects for criticism. The Brezhnev years are now seen as a period of stagnation and regression in the economy and of exaggerated commitments in foreign policy which led to such mistakes as the invasion of Afghanistan and a massive build-up in American military power to counter the Soviet threat. Like the de-Maoized China of Deng Xiaoping, Gorbachev's Russia sings the praises of modernization, economic efficiency, greater private initiative, and rational cost-accounting. It looks for western technology and credits, for co-operation with capitalist firms, and emphasizes the need to free the Soviet economy and society from the stranglehold of bureaucratic mismanagement and red tape. Corruption, embezzlement, bribes, and black marketeering – for decades endemic vices in the everyday life of Soviet citizens – are now regularly exposed in the media. No more are rampant alcoholism, crime, drugs, and prostitution presented as the exclusive prerogative of the decadent capitalist west. Soviet society, too, is having to come to grips with the darker corners of life in the 'socialist paradise': phony production statistics, shoddy goods, food shortages, chronically inadequate distribution, fraudulent money, mass pilfering, and a demoralized workforce.

Mr Gorbachev inherited from his predecessors a military superpower and an industrial giant with feet of clay. Its technological lag compared with its major western competitors forced his hand. To permit a continuation of the privilege, conservatism, and sloth which characterized management, or the low productivity, absenteeism, and lack of discipline in the workforce, would mean condemning the USSR to permanent economic backwardness. If the Soviet Union were successfully to compete in the age of the microprocessor it would have to change its economic structure, its work habits, its way of thinking. Scientists have to enjoy freer access to discoveries, inventions, and knowledge developed in the west; the intelligentsia have to be permitted more scope for free discussion, debate, and criticism. Huge military outlays need to be cut back to allow the civilian economy to breathe; workers must be encouraged to participate more in the life of enterprises; peasants have to be given material incentives to produce more food. The inhibitions and shackles produced by decades of secret police supervision, by an obsolescent legal system which provided little recourse for the ordinary citizen against official arbitrariness, have to be eased. Above all the Soviet Union has needed to show the rest of the world as well as its own citizens that change is possible as well as desirable, that the sclerotic monster-state forged by Stalin was not permanently frozen in the mould of mindless semi-totalitarian uniformity and repression.

Mr Gorbachev's personality has been ideally suited to this imperative of the hour. His urbane, sophisticated, self-confident, and businesslike manner contrasts all too strikingly with that of his immediate predecessors in the job: the overbearing, vain, and essentially mediocre Brezhnev, the austere, grey, and somewhat sinister Andropov and the senile, tottering party hack, Chernenko. Here at last is a Soviet leader who is relatively open, quick at repartee, smooth, and well-educated. The first genuinely post-Stalin leader of the USSR – he had no hand in Stalin's terror and therefore no need to justify or cover up his crimes.

Gorbachev's first priority has clearly been to get Russia moving again by coming to grips with its endemic failings in the economic sphere. But the practical tasks of increasing the output and quality of goods in the home and export markets, of stimulating innovation and streamlining marketing and distribution, demand an opening up of Soviet society to new technologies, new ideas, and a new ethos of competition. *Glasnost* – variously translated as 'openness', 'transparence', or 'publicity' – has been the key weapon in this campaign and sits well with Gorbachev's own mastery of public relations. The modern information revolution, intelligently applied from the top in a way consonant with the traditions of Soviet political culture, is being used to stimulate at least the appearance of change, movement, and the encouragement of innovation. *Glasnost* is the indispensable tool for the process of 'democratization' slowly being carried out in the USSR – not of course in the sense of western liberalism, pluralism, and human rights, but rather in accordance with Leninist norms. Thus Gorbachev-style socialism wants to strike a balance between central planning and local initiative, to re-establish the primacy of the economic enterprise and to breathe new life into the largely defunct 'soviets' without abandoning the monopolistic control of the Communist Party. Gorbachev has not abandoned Marxism–Leninism (there are precedents for his policy in Lenin's NEP and Khruschev's de-Stalinization during the late 1950s) nor is he selling out Russia to the west. But his *perestroika* ('restructuring') depends on a more hospitable international climate in which the spiralling costs of the arms race can be controlled. Hence his tireless efforts to prevent Reagan's star wars project from launching a new arms race in outer space and his emphasis on the responsibilities of 'global partnership' with the United States. The commonality of interests with the United States clearly ranks far higher in the current Soviet scale of priorities than support for further adventures in the Third World or backing for its myriad national liberation movements.

Against this background Soviet overtures towards Israel are both logical and consistent with Gorbachev's more pragmatic western-oriented policy. The existence of Israel is not only a fact that the Soviet Union recognizes (Gromyko's famous 'Zionist' speech of 1947 in support of a Jewish state in Palestine is more frequently cited today than it has been for many years) but she also acknowledges that it is the strongest power in the region. The USSR has always respected military power and is certainly aware of the strategic and other advantages that the United States has derived from its alliance with Israel. On the other hand the intransigent anti-Israeli and pro-Arab policy pursued for more than twenty years by the Kremlin has yielded diminishing returns in recent times. Gorbachev is evidently less keen to put all his eggs in the Arab basket or to underwrite an extremist Arab policy which has proved costly in arms, money, and prestige to the USSR. Thus Soviet backing for Palestinian self-determination is now being balanced by a new readiness to acknowledge Israel's legitimate security concerns. Indeed, the Kremlin has recently been pressurizing Yasser Arafat to recognize the existence of Israel if he wants the PLO to participate as an equal partner at an international Peace Conference. The holding of such a Conference would provide the USSR with the opportunity to restore diplomatic relations with Israel which were broken off in 1967 – an act widely recognized today in the Soviet bloc to have been a serious tactical mistake. Indeed as Mr Gorbachev recently told his most important Middle East ally, President Assad of Syria, 'the absence of relations with Israel cannot be considered normal'.

The more balanced, constructive, and rational attitude towards Israel which characterizes the current Soviet leadership has also been evident in its handling of the vexed issue of Soviet Jewish emigration. After several years of precipitous decline in Jewish emigration during the early 1980s the figures have begun to rise and nearly all the major Soviet Jewish *refusniks* have been released and permitted to go to Israel. This has been very much in the spirit of *glasnost* – understood as public relations – and reflects the evident concern of the USSR to polish its dented human rights image in the west. For the sake of better relations with the west – so vital to the future of the Soviet economy – it was obviously in the present leadership's interest to lower tensions over the Jewish issue.

Nevertheless it should not be supposed that the USSR can simply open the gates wide for a Soviet Jewish exodus. Apart from ideological arguments (why should Jews wish to leave the 'socialist paradise'?, there is no 'Jewish question' in the USSR, and so on) Gorbachev needs Jewish brains for his scientific-technological revolution. The Soviet Jews constitute a highly literate, educated group who despite some official discrimination still form a disproportionate percentage of the Soviet academic, scientific, and technical elite. Moreover the majority of Soviet Jews are highly acculturated and physically concentrated in the Russian, Ukrainian, and White Russian republics – the Slavic heartland of the USSR. They are not serious candidates for emigration to Israel (unlike the less acculturated Jews from the Soviet periphery) and Gorbachev is unlikely to give them as a present to capitalist America.

There is another factor complicating Soviet Jewish emigration policy – namely the danger that it may spark off similar demands for an exodus from Soviet Germans, Armenians, and other national minority groups. As it is, the Kremlin has some reason to fear the reawakening of the nationalities and latent national conflicts in the USSR. The violence in Soviet Armenia and neighbouring Azerbaijan between different national and religious groups has been perhaps the most spectacular recent example. But from the Baltic states to the Caucasus, from the Ukraine to Kazakhstan, the signs of centrifugal nationalism are beginning to threaten the cohesion of the world's last surviving great colonial empire and multi-national state. Ukrainian nationalism and the desire of the Baltic states to recover their national independence are by no means dead; the Kazakhs, Uzbeks, and other central Asian Muslims, doubtless encouraged by the Iranian revolution and the successful resistance of the Afghan *mujaheddin* to Soviet military might, are increasingly restless. Tensions between the European and Asian elements in the population can only be expected to grow given the declining fertility of the Slavs and the rising numbers of Soviet Muslims who today already number 65–70 million – a quarter of the entire population in the USSR. Wedged between these nationalities are the 2–3 million Jews – disliked as a 'Russifying' element by the discontented non-Russians (already over half the population – and distrusted by Russian nationalists as an unreliable, alien, and potentially disloyal national minority.

Antisemitism in the Soviet Union feeds on such partly hidden social and national antagonisms. It is exacerbated by the feeling that Jews, in spite of persecution and discrimination, are somehow a privileged sector in the population who enjoy a higher standard of education, social status, and special connections. Though their role in the state and the *apparat* since the 1940s has been very small, they remain prominent in the managerial, technical, scientific, and creative fields and therefore a target of social and economic envy. For the underprivileged, less educated strata in Soviet society antisemitism (surreptitiously encouraged by the bureaucracy and by the intense 'anti-Zionist' campaigns of the past two decades) provides a compensation for their own frustrations and the promise of increased social mobility at the expense of the Jews. Economic stagnation, food shortages, and other daily miseries of Soviet life taken in conjunction with tenacious popular prejudice makes Soviet Jewry particularly vulnerable in spite of the official ban on antisemitic propaganda and agitation. Indeed *glasnost* may well work to the disadvantage of Jews in the USSR in so far as it inevitably leads to a loosening of social controls, dislocation, and upheaval as well as to a much greater freedom to openly express ethnic, religious, and other forms of prejudice.

The most serious immediate threat to the future of Soviet Jewry remains however that of Great Russian chauvinism which has historically always been linked with antisemitism. In the Soviet period this was first encouraged by Stalin during the war years and led directly after 1945 to the notorious 'anti-cosmopolitan' campaign against the Jews. It experienced a definite revival under Brezhnev and during the 1970s a neo-Stalinist racist campaign under the thin veneer of 'anti-Zionism' was rampant in sections of the Soviet media. Publicists like Yevseyev, Skurlatov, Begun, Zhukov, Lev Korneyev, Emelianov, and Romanenko – some of whom are still active purveyors of antisemitic literature – became prominent and officially respectable. By the late 1970s a kind of neo-Nazi Right had surfaced in the USSR, semi-official and semi-underground, which enjoyed some protection at the top of the Soviet hierarchy and found a wide outlet in works of popular fiction. The belief in a 'Jewish–Masonic conspiracy' to undermine the Soviet Union, in a Jewish–Zionist plot to seize control of the world, and the depiction of Jews as eternal enemies of the Russian people and its culture became commonplaces even in official writings. This racist trend co-existed along with the more conventional Leninist mode of anti-Zionism and a virulent anti-Israeli propaganda that sought to delegitimize the Jewish state. Thus the Soviet Union officially encouraged both at home and abroad the view that Zionism was a form of racism, a species of fascism, and even an accomplice and heir of Nazism! It denounced the Zionist 'corporation' as an international Mafia of exploiters seeking to gain a hegemonistic position within monopoly capitalism and as a militant instrument of anti-Soviet and anti-communist intrigues. Within this framework an irrational antisemitism which uneasily fused Marxist, racist, Slavophile, and Black Hundred propaganda motifs could develop and expand. In the 1980s under *glasnost* it has come into the open in the guise of *Pamyat* ('Memory'), a Russian nationalist organization ostensibly devoted to the preservation of the Russian cultural heritage. In reality, *Pamyat*, while claiming to be *for* Mr Gorbachev, represents all those elements in Soviet society which hate western technological civilization, modernization, and greater liberalization. It fastens on the Jews as the symbol of these undesirable phenomena and blames them for all the disasters that have befallen the Soviet people in the twentieth century. *Pamyat* has unexpectedly demonstrated that neo-Nazism is indeed alive and well in the USSR – the land which suffered more than any other from Hitler's barbarism.

Mr Gorbachev is not a Russian nationalist of this ilk but he is no doubt well aware of the strength of such feelings among conservatives, in opposition circles, and also among the ignorant masses and sections of the Russian intelligentsia. Thus far he has avoided a head-on confrontation with the nationalists though there has been some criticism of *Pamyat* in the Soviet media. Officially he has declared that there is no place for antisemitism in a civilized society but then he has said something similar about Zionism – which can be cold comfort for most Soviet Jews. Indeed one wonders from these and other pronouncements how much Mr Gorbachev and his friends really understand about the nature of the 'Jewish problem' in the USSR. Having said that and taking into account the delicate situation in which the current 'restructuring' is taking place there may still be grounds for some guarded optimism. The logic of *perestroika* entails a radical questioning of many of the taboos which have hitherto governed Soviet society. In the long term it must be incompatible with the kind of unrestrained slander of Zionism and the Jewish people which prevailed in the Soviet media until fairly recently. Equally, the new *glasnost* should eventually entail a greater freedom for Jewish culture and religion in the USSR, perhaps even a gradual restoration of the ties that once linked Russian Jewry with the rest of the Jewish world. There is no reason why democratization should not proceed along this path, which would certainly be in the best interests of the present Soviet regime as well as of the Jewish people in the USSR. If, however, *perestroika* should fail to move Soviet society forward on the path to greater prosperity, then the Jews – not for the first time in Russian history – may have to pay a heavy price.

22

The politics of perdition

In an author's note to his by now notorious 'banned' play, *Perdition*, Jim Allen openly states that this is a work 'which shows how some Zionist leaders collaborated with the Nazis during and before the Second World War'. Loosely based on the Kastner trial of the 1950s but transplanted to the High Court of Justice in London just a month after the Six Day War of 1967, the play hammers away at the theme of complicity and betrayal of the nearly 1 million-strong Hungarian Jewish community by Zionist leaders in Jerusalem and Budapest. The villain of the piece, Dr Miklos Yaron (based on Kastner), is accused of having lulled the Budapest Jews into a false sense of security in 1944; and of having made a deal with Adolf Eichmann whereby a tiny number of rich Jews, Zionist function-aries, and relatives would be saved while the great mass of Hungarian Jewry were deported and perished in the gas chambers of Auschwitz. Of course, this accusation is not new. It was the basis of the charges made against Kastner in Israel in 1953 which were initially upheld but then overruled four years later by the Israeli Supreme Court. This proved to be too late for the main protagonist, who was assassinated by right-wing extremists convinced that he had indeed 'sold his soul to the devil'.

Nor is the use of the Kastner affair for political ends in any sense novel. In 1953 the motives of Shmuel Tamir, the right-wing lawyer who broke Kastner on the witness stand, were clearly to discredit the Mapai establishment with which the Hungarian Zionist leader was identified. This, too, was a major aim of the American Jewish playwright, Ben Hecht, whose play *Perfidy* caused a similar scandal in the United States twenty-five years ago. In many ways it anticipated Jim Allen's conspiracy theories while utilizing them for quite different purposes. Even Jim Allen's manipulation of the Kastner trial to 'prove' the identity of interests between Nazism and Zionism (before, during, and, by implica-tion, after the Holocaust) is not in the least original. As I had occasion to demonstrate in *Hitler's Apocalypse*: *Jews and the Nazi Legacy* (London,

1985) this canard has been a standard propaganda item in the Soviet Union, assiduously promoted by its multiple channels of disinformation for the past thirty years.

But Jim Allen did not need to drink at this 'poisoned well' (to pick up a metaphor from his play), since the theme of Nazi–Zionist collaboration has been widely disseminated in Britain by the Trotskyist fringe over the past seven years. Allen's fictional 'j'accuse' can draw on a fairly extensive literature in which pride of place must go to the American Jewish anti-Zionist, Lenni Brenner, whose *Zionism in the Age of the Dictators* is revealingly described by Allen as a 'goldmine source'. Not surprisingly, in that volume, published by the Ithaca Press (a leading purveyor of anti-Zionist literature in Great Britain), one can find notes by Lenni Brenner and Akiva Orr (an Israeli anti-Zionist who no longer lives in Israel) intended to buttress Allen's theses. There are also three letters of support by prominent (if ageing) veterans of the international Jewish anti-Zionist brigade: Erich Fried, Noam Chomsky, and Maxime Rodinson. All three predictably give the play a clean bill of health as far as charges of antisemitism are concerned – Chomsky without even having read it! Indeed, he goes so far as to accuse 'British establishment circles' of manifesting a 'totalitarian streak' in trying to suppress the play. For a Jewish intellectual who was ready to defend Faurisson's right to deny that the Holocaust took place, this is probably par for the course.

Rodinson is another matter. He agrees with most of Allen's points against Zionism, having for many years written along similar lines with far greater authority and talent. He rejects in some detail the equation of anti-Zionism and antisemitism. But he does point out that some of the statements in the play are schematic, that there were Jewish resistance groups, including Zionist ones, and that very few Zionists went as far as Abraham Stern in advocating a common struggle of Nazi Germans and Zionist Jews. Though Rodinson sees the core of the play as an exposure of real facts largely ignored by the general public, he allows that there probably are examples of 'minor mistakes', some overdrawing of the arguments, and arbitrary selection in Allen's work.

This is a more skilful defence than that put up by most of Allen's supporters in Britain. Indeed, reading the leading articles and letters in the national press, and the essays and comments by those for and against the play, one is forcefully struck by the level of ignorance, bias, and lack of minimal intellectual sophistication displayed by so many who took part in this debate. Perhaps only in a country like Britain, which never experienced at first hand Nazi occupation, with the resulting moral, political, and existential dilemmas for Jews and non-Jews alike, and which has so little understanding of the murderous character of ideological antisemitism, was it possible to conduct the discussion with such naivety. This applies to some of the well-intentioned Jewish apologies no less than to the predominantly left-wing anti-Zionist supporters of Jim Allen, or to the liberal defenders of unqualified free speech.

The blanket condemnation by many Jews of all Allen's arguments about Kastner or Zionist behaviour during the Nazi period was, for example, as unwise as the decision to label his play 'antisemitic' in its underlying thrust, motivation, and intent. In my view the entire Jewish leadership of that generation – including the Zionists – failed the test of the times and no useful purpose is served by covering this up. Nor can it be denied, given that the major priority of the Zionist movement at the time was indeed building Palestine, that the tragedy of Diaspora Jewry was inevitably given less attention than it deserved. Equally, one can make a reasonable case that Zionists did not fight antisemitism before 1939 with the appropriate vigour, that some Zionists favoured the principle of racial separateness, and that others wanted to develop a 'special relationship' with the Nazis for opportunistic or other reasons. To deny these points apologetically is not only stupid but unnecessary. Similar criticisms (and many far worse than these) can and have been made of the behaviour of the western democracies, German public opinion, the liberals, communists and social democrats, the USSR and others, during this same period. One wonders against whom the charge of collaboration or complicity or simply co-operation with the Nazis has not at some point been made?

Allen of course went far beyond this and was justifiably attacked by more knowledgeable critics on these grounds. It is, for example, quite untrue that the Zionist leadership in Palestine thought that European Jewry was expendable during the Holocaust. (Dinah Porat's recent book, *Manhigut be-Milkoud*, published thus far only in Hebrew, exhaustively documents the real dilemmas facing this leadership.) It is an outright libel to suggest, as Allen does, that Zionist leaders thought 'the spilling of Jewish blood would strengthen their demand for a Jewish State after the War'. The smears against Ben-Gurion, Weizmann, Gruenbaum, Sharett, and others, based on misleading quotations torn out of context and endlessly regurgitated in the anti-Zionist literature, are also quite inaccurate. So too is Allen's insistence that the Zionists were Hitler's favourite Jews. In my previously cited book I demonstrate that Hitler consistently regarded Zionism as part of the Jewish world conspiracy, even if he temporarily supported dumping unwanted German Jews in Palestine during the 1930s.

What is particularly nasty, repellent, and objectionable in Allen's work is not so much the repetition of these well-worn clichés and distortions as the transparent intent to use the terrible tragedy of Hungarian Jewry to put the present state of Israel in the dock. Again and again in the text we are told that Israel is a ghetto state, that it is racialist, expansionist, and militarist; that it 'commits outrageous crimes, then silences its critics by invoking the Holocaust'. Against this monstrosity of a state we are presented with an array of anti-Zionist Jewish witnesses (assimilationist, Bundist, and so forth) who believe in the author's anachronistic solution to antisemitism – namely the overthrow of the capitalist system and total assimilation. To cover himself even more against any insinuation of anti-Jewish prejudice (and one must admit that this is cunningly done) Allen dedicates the play 'to the Jews of Hungary who were murdered by the Nazis at Auschwitz'.

Perdition thereby presents itself both as a universalist warning against the dangers of neo-Nazism and antisemitism, while at the same time rewriting history to show that Israel and the Zionists are continuing this criminal legacy. Even the chief protagonist in the play, the Zionist Dr Yaron, is made to concede the supposedly self-evident truth that Israel is 'a nation built on the pillar of Western guilt', that it is 'the most dangerous place on earth for a Jew', and above all that it is a racist state that has expropriated the land of the Palestinians. From this one can readily understand Allen's boast that *Perdition* is a 'lethal' attack against Zionism because it touches the heart of 'the most abiding myth of modern history, the Holocaust'.

In the new left-wing 'revisionism', the Holocaust has indeed become a myth, highly serviceable for the purpose of dehumanizing the Zionist 'enemy of humanity'. The dead Jews of Hungary can be mobilized to point an accusing finger not at the British, American, or Soviet governments who refused to bomb the railway lines to Auschwitz (or the death camp itself) but at the relatively powerless Zionist movement during the Second World War. All the complexities, ambiguities, and qualifications fall away. Questions of morality and human behaviour in extreme situations, of crime and punishment, means and ends, are reduced to a new demagogic rallying cry, 'The Zionists are guilty!'

It is a sad comment on declining standards in public life and the poverty of contemporary British drama that the Royal Court Theatre should have ever considered staging this tawdry political pamphlet dressed up as a play and sought to defend its authenticity and historical accuracy. Whether 'banning' or withdrawing it was a wise decision once the mistaken commitment had been made is another matter. For the notion that Jews are somehow immune to criticism or that there was a conspiracy against the play by a wealthy, powerful Jewish clique behind the scenes is the very stuff of which antisemitism is made.

23

Soundings in the Gulf

In June 1919 David Ben-Gurion told the Provisional Council of the Jews of Palestine: 'There is no solution to this question. No solution! There is a gulf, and nothing can fill this gulf. . . . We, as a nation, want this country to be ours; the Arabs, as a nation, want this country to be theirs.' Six decades later, though the Arab–Israeli conflict no longer seems as hopelessly intractable as it once did, the question of Palestine continues to arouse intense passions on both sides. Four Arab–Israeli wars have failed to resolve the issue and bring about peace. Nevertheless, since President Sadat's historic visit to Jerusalem there has been a qualitative change in Egyptian–Israeli relations, the first beginnings of a dialogue that may yet transcend the endless cycle of bloodshed and violence. This may therefore be a propitious moment to reassess the roots of the Jewish–Arab confrontation in Palestine, which entered its modern phase with the Balfour Declaration of November 1917.

The turbulent history of the British Mandate has already produced a voluminous literature, yet many old myths and conspiracy theories still persist. Nicholas Bethell's admirably balanced narrative *The Palestine Triangle* picks up the story in 1935, a watershed in Anglo–Zionist relations, which saw the highest immigration in any year of the British Mandate. The simultaneous rise of Arab nationalism and the tidal wave of antisemitism in central and eastern Europe, which drove Jewish immigrants in ever larger numbers to Palestine, created contradictory pressures which the mandatory authorities were unable to resolve. The Arab rebellion which began in 1936 as a result of this immigration was crushed with the utmost severity by the British but ultimately led to a radical change of policy towards the Zionist enterprise. The 1939 White Paper strictly limiting Jewish immigration and settlement in Palestine, and the clashes between the mandatory power and the Zionists which began in this period and continued until 1948, were largely a consequence of the Arab revolt. The revolt also sounded the death-knell for hopes of any *modus vivendi* between Arab and Jew in Palestine, widening the gulf between the two peoples to the point where armed conflict became the dominant mode of encounter. Moreover, the revolt prompted the British to take the fateful step of granting a *locus standi* to the surrounding Arab states to intervene in the affairs of Palestine, in the illusory hope that they would moderate the demands of the Palestine Arabs.

By 1939 it was evident that Britain, conscious of its declining international position, had decided to sacrifice the Balfour Declaration for the sake of its strategic and political needs in the Middle East. This, in turn, drove Palestinian Jewry to embark on a policy of active resistance to the new White Paper policy – to the stepping up of illegal immigration, the creation of more settlements, and the development of an independent fighting force. Lord Bethell threads his way skilfully through the complex maze of the Jewish resistance movements and the British counter-measures which they provoked. Having interviewed many of the participants – politicians, soldiers, policemen, and underground fighters – he is able to provide new evidence about the activities of the Irgun, the assassination of Lord Moyne, and the King David Hotel affair. He possibly overestimates the impact of Jewish terrorism in the struggle against the mandatory regime, though there is no denying that the hanging of the two British sergeants by the Irgun was seen by many as the last straw which made the British finally decide to leave Palestine.

By 1947 Britain's Palestine policy had virtually disintegrated. Bevin, Attlee, the Foreign Office, and the Chiefs of Staff were categorically opposed to partition, believing it incompatible with British strategic needs and fearing as they did an Arab revolt in Palestine and the neighbouring countries.

The British government was convinced that the Arabs had the power to ruin Britain's Middle Eastern position; and they profoundly mis-understood the traumatic impact of the Nazi Holocaust on the Palestine Yishuv and American Jewry. British policy-makers also deluded them-selves into thinking that after the war Jewish refugees would return to or be content to remain on the Continent. At the same time they were unable to control the flood of Jewish immigration to Palestine and, in trying to enforce a rigid, unworkable policy, were led into disastrous political mistakes. The expulsion of the illegal ship *Exodus* to Germany in the summer of 1947 and the international condemnation it aroused symbolized the final bankruptcy of British rule.

A main factor in Britain's decision to leave Palestine was American pressure and intervention. Although Bevin vainly sought to co-ordinate Anglo-American policy on Palestine, neither he nor his Foreign Office and military advisers took sufficient account of President Truman's concern about the fate of the Jewish refugees in Europe. Truman's demand for the immediate immigration to Palestine of 100,000 Jewish displaced persons was seen in London as an intolerable interference with British efforts to reach a compromise settlement and an undermining of the alliance on which Britain was increasingly dependent in the postwar world. Truman's Palestine policy was not only a source of embarrassment and constant irritation to the British Labour government but also to his own state department officials. They were no more inclined than the Foreign Office to sympathize with the humanitarian imperatives and domestic political considerations which impelled the American President to support partition and the creation of an independent Jewish state.

Reading Evan Wilson's *Decision on Palestine* on how the United States came to recognize Israel one understands better the saying that foreign policy is too serious a matter to leave to the diplomats. A retired foreign service officer who worked in the Near East division of the state department during the 1940s, Mr Wilson has written a well-researched book on America's Palestine policy under Roosevelt and Truman. *Decision on Palestine* is remarkably detached, sober, and scholarly in tone. We are transposed far from the turmoil and bloodshed of the Palestine imbroglio into the orderly world of the desk men with their 'expert' opinions, memoranda, policy papers, and endless attempts to square or triangulate the circle. This is an insider's book, demonstrating an intimate knowledge of the decision-making process in the United States and giving a reasonably clear picture of the conflicting pressures which determined American policy on Palestine. Essentially Mr Wilson believes that the pro-Zionist approach was victorious because all major American opinion-makers from the Congress to the state and local governments, from the trade unions to the universities, had rallied to the Jewish cause. Officials in the state department and the defence establishment might oppose Zionism as being detrimental to America's overall interest in the Middle East, but in a democratic system the influence of domestic politics and the pivotal importance of the large Jewish vote proved more important. He stresses too that from mid-1945 onwards the control over Palestine policy had passed from the 'professionals' in the state department to the White House.

This is a source of some regret to Mr Wilson who apparently believes that American relations with the entire Arab world 'have never recovered from the events of 1947–48, when we sided with the Jews against the Arabs and advocated a solution in Palestine which went contrary to self-determination as far as the majority population of the country was concerned'. Be that as it may, the author still views the coming of the

Jewish state as inevitable and concedes that, on a number of key questions, the career men in the Near East division got their sums badly wrong. They did not foresee the Israeli victory in 1948, tending as they did 'to downgrade the Jews and upgrade the Arabs as fighting men'; they were stunned by Soviet support for Zionism in 1947–8; they did not anticipate the mass exodus of Palestine Arabs nor the mass immigration to Israel of Jews from Oriental (Arab) countries; and they continued to think in terms of a bi-national state, even when it was apparent that this was out of the question for both sides. As reasonable men they looked for a compromise, but the hard fact was that neither of the two parties wanted it.

Policy-makers in Washington and London consistently under-estimated the power of the two national ideologies, one Arab, the other Jewish, locked in territorial conflict over the destiny of Palestine. Of the two movements, it was Zionism which was until recently much the more successful in capturing the imagination of enlightened liberals, demo-crats, and socialists in the west. For a variety of complex cultural, religious, and political reasons the return of the Jews to their biblical homeland has been perceived by many Gentiles as an epochal event which deserves their understanding, sympathy, and support. The Pales-tinian Arabs, on the other hand, were rarely seen before the 1970s as a people with national rights of their own but more often as backward Orientals with an inferior culture, as non-European 'natives' whose wishes could be ignored when it came to the division of spoils in the Middle East. Such 'Orientalist' stereotypes might perhaps have in-fluenced the readiness of British statesmen to ignore the wishes of the Palestinian Arabs when they issued the Balfour Declaration at the zenith of Great Britain's imperial self-confidence. No doubt, too, Zionism may have benefited from the common tendency in the west to regard the Arab Orient as a blank space to be filled, a wilderness to be redeemed by the colonizing energy and intellect of European-educated settlers. This indeed is the central thesis of Edward Said's book, *The Question of Palestine*, and he uses it as a platform from which to indict the west (and by extension Zionism) for what he regards as its callous indifference to the Palestinian Arab tragedy. The theme of western prejudice towards Islam and the Arabs is not new (the author has expounded it at greater length in his previous work on Orientalism) but it is given a sharper polemical edge by Said's stance in this book as advocate and propagan-dist of the Palestinian cause.

Himself a man of two cultures, Palestinian-born and American-educated, a New York literary intellectual and a member of the Palestine National Council, Said has evidently experienced the tensions and ambiguities of exile in an intensely personal way. He feels himself embattled, in political terms 'an outlaw of sorts, or at any rate very much an outsider', engaged in a semi-apocalyptic confrontation with the racist metaphors fabricated by the western literary imagination. At the same time he has a compulsive need to vindicate the uniqueness of Palestinian identity, to stress the singularity of that experience in terms of the traumatic encounter with Zionism. As a result, not only is Palestinian nationalism somewhat arbitrarily detached from the context of Arab/Islamic history and politics but a distorted focus emerges whereby all significant movements in the Arab world are seen as being dominated by the Palestine question. Similarly, the Zionist project itself, viewed solely from the angle of its 'victims', is never really analysed in its own terms, but reduced to the negative function of systematically repressing the Arab reality in Palestine.

However much one may sympathize with the author's revulsion against the racist stereotypes from which the Arabs (and Palestinians) have suffered in the west, it is regrettable that he should expend so much effort in seeking to tar Zionism with the same brush. The fact that Tyrwhitt Drake, Lord Kitchener, Sir Flinders Petrie, Charles Clermont-Ganneau, Stanley Cook, and many other Victorians had a low opinion of Arab civilization does not prove that Zionism is racist, imperialist, or colonialist. None of these men were Jews, let alone Zionists. Indeed the whole pseudo-Marxist framework through which Said seeks to brand Zionism as an extension of nineteenth-century imperialist attitudes to 'subject races' seems stale and unconvincing. Nothing could have been further removed from the typical colonial prejudices manifested by white settlers towards the 'natives' in Asia and Africa than the mental horizon of the Russian and east European Jews arriving in Palestine from the turn of the century onwards. It was partly in order to avoid a colonial situation and the capitalist exploitation of indigenous labour that the early Zionists insisted so much on creating a Jewish working class and peasantry which would at the same time serve to transform their own national, social, and human existence as Jews.

Moreover, precisely because Israel is a Jewish-Zionist state it cannot meaningfully be described either as 'white' or 'western' and even Said acknowledges the spuriousness of the parallel with the Afrikaners. The fact is that Jews have never identified themselves in terms of skin colour, and in a religious-cultural sense they have always been outsiders in European Christendom. Had the author pursued this theme he would have found that Jews even more than the Arabs (and Palestinians) have been victims of the 'Orientalist' mythology of the west and that Zionism has been the only effective answer that they have found to its murderous logic. Equally, he might have been led to a deeper understanding of the necessity of Zionism had he considered the flight of Jews in the Muslim world to the new state of Israel after 1948. For these large, 2000-year-old communities, as indigenous to the Middle East as the Palestine Arabs and reduced to second-class citizenship by the quasi-theological brand of Arabism which Said himself claims to reject, a sovereign Jewish state was their only security against ever-recurring Muslim violence and fanaticism. Like the Palestinians, they, too, had to abandon homes, property, inheritances, and personal possessions. Through their successful absorption into Israel they were, however, able to overcome the fragmentation and dispersal which has continued to plague Palestinian society and politics.

The book of essays edited by Joel Migdal, *Palestinian Society and Politics* (Princeton 1980), makes an important contribution to an understanding of this last phenomenon. It examines the changing patterns of Palestinian population movement, social stratification, and communal cohesion under the impact of four different regimes – those of the Ottoman Turks, the British, the Jordanians, and the Israelis. The emergence of a distinctive Palestinian identity is analysed here in terms of the development of Palestinian village society, its urban elites, and their modes of interaction with the masses. Particular attention is paid to the decline of the old notable families who had controlled Palestinian politics under the Ottomans and British. The defeat of 1948 with its attendant traumas of flight and national dismemberment left the Palestinians disorganized and leaderless. Under Jordanian rule, only a fragmented, local leadership highly dependent on the resources and roles allocated by the regime in Amman was permitted to function. The West Bank was downgraded economically and the political centrality of Jerusalem purposely diminished. As Shaul Mishal points out in an interesting essay, the West Bank Palestinian elite was co-opted into the existing political machinery but never allowed to occupy key positions in the Hashemite hierarchy. These were reserved for East Bankers, who dominated the army, administration, and Parliament. The solution to the Palestine question was deferred to the distant future while the Jordanian regime sought to stabilize the status quo through political accommodation with Israel. The question of Palestinian self-determination was never raised since this clearly constituted a threat to Hashemite ambitions.

It was the outcome of the Six Day War which dramatically transformed the situation by bringing the whole of what had once been Mandatory Palestine west of the Jordan river under the control of the Israeli army. The humiliation of the Arab regimes re-opened the question of Palestine, aggravating the problem of Palestinian physical dispersal and displacement, intensifying animosity to the Jordanian regime, and stiffening resistance to Israeli military rule.

The Israeli occupation continued the stern security policies of the Jordanians, seeking to prevent the crystallization of new urban elites and a unified West Bank leadership. Nevertheless the massive exposure of West Bank society to the Israeli economy and culture has led to an inadvertent modernization, undermining the patriarchal norms, values and social relations on which the pre-eminence of the traditional Arab elite was based. Access to new sources of wealth and status provided by higher Israeli wages and contact with a highly technological, secular society have weakened the traditional village social networks and the old bonds of dependency in West Bank Palestinian society. New counter-elites have emerged and with them a resurgent sense of Palestinian identity.

The most important vehicle for this shift in consciousness has been the rise of the PLO, which since 1967 has been the major organizational base and institutional expression of Palestinian nationalism. Its main weakness is that it is based outside the West Bank and the major Palestinian population concentrations, and lacks control of the social resources critical to the needs of large elements of Palestinian society. On the other hand it has succeeded in mobilizing the material and moral resources of the Palestinian diaspora and in reconstituting a new national elite which has focused international attention on the Palestinian struggle for self-determination. The identification with the PLO is especially strong in the refugee camps where it embodies the apocalyptic hope of 'awda – the Palestinians' dream of returning to their places of origin. But on the West Bank, too, especially since 1973, it appears to many as the wave of the future, if only as a means to end the Israeli occupation.

The problem with the PLO is that it has never abandoned its original demands for the dismantlement of Israel and that it continues to adhere to a national covenant which not only refuses to recognize the territorial integrity of the Jewish state inside the pre-1967 borders but denies any historical connection between the Jews and Palestine. Its total ideological negation of Zionism is expressed in its claim on the whole of the former mandated territory (including Israel) to be reconstituted as a so-called 'democratic secular state' for Palestinians.

Significantly, Edward Said never discusses the covenant in any detail and evades the issue of Palestinian terrorism when arguing that an independent West Bank–Gaza state would be an important step towards peace between Israeli Jews and Palestinian Arabs. But how could such a state avoid being irredentist, seeing its future in the repossession of Israeli territory? How could it solve the refugee problem within the confines of its tiny territory? And what confidence could the Israelis have that such a state would not become a cat's paw for Soviet expansion or a launching-pad for a fifth Arab war to eliminate the Jewish state? These hard questions are ignored and we are treated instead to a vituperative assault on the great American–Egyptian–Israeli conspiracy to liquidate the question of Palestine.

The gulf then remains, and no amount of wishful thinking is likely to bridge it. Perhaps the beginning of wisdom would be to recognize that there is no absolute justice in the world, least of all in a conflict between two rights, and that there are some problems to which there are no solutions. On one point, however, Professor Said is surely right. The Israelis and Palestinians are two peoples whose past and future 'ties them inexorably together'; one can only hope with him that their encounter will yet prove to be to their mutual benefit.

24

The fundamentalist challenge

In his timely and important study *Semites and Anti-Semites*,[1] the historian Bernard Lewis reasserts the conventional wisdom which regards the Arab–Israeli conflict as being essentially *political* – 'a clash between states and peoples over real issues, not a matter of prejudice and persecution'. On the other hand he concludes that if the conflict is not quickly resolved there may be no escape 'from the unending downward spiral of mutual hate that will embitter the lives of Arabs and Jews alike'. The conflict, he observes, has engendered a growing corpus of myths, prejudices, and hatreds to the point that extremism on both sides is rampant. Classical antisemitism (which Lewis regards as distinctively Christian and European in provenance) has unmistakably infected Arab political and intellectual elites. Indeed contemporary Arab antisemitism in its vehemence, ubiquity, and obsessiveness is, he argues, becoming increasingly reminiscent of the Nazi model. This is no longer simply a matter of government initiative. In Mubarak's Egypt since the peace treaty, as a recent monograph by Rivka Yadlin has demonstrated, opposition groups ranging from the Muslim Brotherhood to the Socialist Action Party have consistently used antisemitic expressions, motifs, and slogans as part of their political activity.[2] Theological, racial, and cultural antisemitism have flourished in the 1980s. In Cairo books with titles like *The War of Survival between the Koran and the Talmud* are in demand. Christian and Islamic motifs intertwine and Muslim writers do not hesitate to spread the medieval Christian blood libel. Indeed, the current Defence Minister of Syria, Mustafa Tlas, even published a book (*The Matzah of Zion*) purporting to vindicate the notorious Damascus blood libel of 1840, when native Christians accused the local Jews of murdering a friar and his assistant, to obtain blood for the coming Passover.

The new Arab antisemitism cannot of course be divorced from the Arab–Israeli conflict. In Egypt, Syria, and other Arab lands, anti-Jewish attitudes are an integral part of the effort to *delegitimize* Israel – not on

254

the basis of its policies but rather because it embodies an intrinsically evil or *demonic essence*. In that sense there is no real distinction between Israel and the Jews, between theology and politics, for the archetype of the Jews is in fact eternally fixed by Koranic scriptures and Muslim tradition. Israel simply embodies all those nefarious Jewish characteristics – egoism, envy, perfidy, fanaticism, racism, and malevolence, and so on – which supposedly manifested themselves in their first encounter with Islam and have remained unchanged over the centuries. There is plenty of material in classical Muslim sources that can be used to vindicate the current image of the Jew as an enemy of Islam and an agent of the darkest forces of evil. No doubt the trauma of Western colonialism (which also led to the import of European antisemitic stereotypes) and the even greater shock of Israel's emergence was necessary in order to galvanize this indigenous tradition. But its roots lie in much older Muslim archetypes of the Jews as persecutors of the prophets and perverters of Allah's truth, deniers of the Islamic revelation and conspirators against its holy mission.

This dimension is explored in Ronald Nettler's *Past Trials and Present Tribulations*, a valuable essay on modern Islamic fundamentalist doctrine dealing with the Jews.[3] Nettler translates and annotates the text of the leading ideologue of Muslim fundamentalism, Sayyid Qutb, entitled *Our Struggle with the Jews*, which presents them as the most dangerous conspirators against the heritage of the Muslim community. Sowing doubt, confusion, deception, and apostasy, the Jews, according to Qutb, sought to shatter the unity of the creed and the integrity of the believers. From the time that the first Islamic community was established in seventh-century Medina, the Jews – again according to Sayyid Qutb – had plotted to undermine and destroy it with 'every weapon and all means which the scheming Jewish genius could devise'. First they had gathered together the polytheistic tribes of Arabia; then they incited civil disturbances and encouraged the Sunni–Shi'a split within Islam; they were constantly using Christianity and idolatry in their war against the Muslims which in modern times has culminated in the 'Crusader–Zionist' assault on Palestine. It was the Jews who also fomented communism, atheistic materialism, and revolution as part of their campaign against the true faith; all forms of secularism – including secular Arab nationalism – were ultimately an instrument in the hands of 'world Zionism' against the Muslim community and its creed.

Qutb's views, which undoubtedly reflect prevailing fundamentalist doctrine, express more than simply an emotionalized Islamic variant of the Protocols of Zion. Hatred of Zionism and the Jews is closely linked in this ideology with the sense of a *civilizational* crisis, a deep suspicion of modernity and desire for revenge on the west.[4] The return to early Islam and the ethos of *jihad* is part of the fundamentalist attempt to revitalize what they perceive as a Muslim culture and way of life threatened by decline and even collapse. A combination of socio-political activism, militant faith, and struggle against both internal and external enemies may yet restore past glories. Thus the *jihad* must be waged not only against Zionism and the west but also against their own secular westernizing rulers who have betrayed Islam.

For the fundamentalists, the establishment of a Jewish state on Muslim land is of course the ultimate heresy, and its victory over Muslims on the field of battle remains the ultimate disgrace. By satanizing the enemy antisemitism may well provide an essential compensatory function for Muslims who are unable to deal with Allah's abandonment of the faithful. The Zionist and the Jew, it must never be forgotten, are not only a concrete foe but no less importantly a metaphor for the general threat to Islam's destiny. Hence the struggle with Israel tends in much Islamic and Arab writing to take on the character of an *apocalyptic* conflict involving past, present, and future with no room for concession or compromise. The redemption of Islam and the Arabs (beginning with Palestine) necessarily comes to involve the destruction and downfall of Zionism and the Jews. This is not simply a local but, on the contrary, a *universal* conflict since the Muslim/Arab camp is confronted by an international conspiracy of vast dimensions. Islamic fundamentalism remains confident, however, that it will be able to mobilize the spiritual strength to overcome this conspiring Jewish power. No doubt the Islamic Revolution of 1979 which successfully overthrew the reactionary 'pro-American' and 'Zionist agent', the Shah of Iran, provided a source of hope for many Muslim radicals. However, since then Khomeini's war against the secular, Pan-Arab, and heretical regime of Saddam Hussein completely collapsed in the marshlands of the Shatt-el-Arab and the Pan-Islamic dream of unity seems as far off as ever. Far from liberating Jerusalem, Khomeini was reduced to dealing with the American and Israeli 'Satan' in order to ensure the continuation of his fanatical *jihad*!

The liberation of Jerusalem, to be sure, depends for the fundamentalists on the overcoming of apostasy, and the return to the Koran and to the principles of Islam. There can be no salvation for the Arabs until the source of their decline – the impact of secularism, modernism, and westernization – is uprooted from their midst. Precisely for this reason, however, there can be no peace agreement, no compromise, and no normalization with Zionism. Such a normalization, in the fundamentalist view, would simply facilitate the further spread of the poisons of 'racist-imperialist culture' into the heart of the Arab world. The hardcore Muslim radicals regard the fight against this danger as lying at the centre of their struggle.

Fundamentalist views of Zionism and the Jews have increasingly taken root in the Middle East in recent years. Their practical implications for Israel were already felt in the aftermath of the Lebanon war in 1982. The Shi'ite Hizbullah of Lebanon, which sprang up at that time as a militant arm of Iranian revolutionary strategy to re-establish Islamic rule in Iraq, then in Lebanon, and finally in Palestine, have demonstrated an implacable opposition to Israel. There is no doubt that they have seen themselves as the vanguard of a great Iranian-led *jihad* which could liberate Jerusalem if victory were ever achieved in the Gulf war. This war of redemption in the name of Allah, it was hoped, would provide the climactic chapter to Lebanon's long-drawn-out agony. The Hizbullah officially reject both Iranian and Arab nationalism, clinging instead to the myth of a single Muslim community. In reality their ties are much closer to Iran and their attitudes to the Arabs bear more than a trace of patronizing contempt. Only the war against Israel provides a vague common ground between them, the Sunni Muslim clergy, the Druze, and the Palestinians.

However, Islamic fundamentalism has begun in more recent months to impinge more directly on the Arab–Israeli conflict from inside the borders of Israel itself. The anger, bitterness, and disappointment of the Palestinians under Israeli occupation which erupted at the end of 1987 in the *intifada* has shown certain marks of fundamentalist influence. The growing contempt of the new generation, the *shabab* – which has known nothing but Israeli rule – not only for their occupiers but also for the Arab states and even the PLO leadership outside the territories is one indicator. This has been particularly evident in the Gaza strip whose teeming refugee camps are a fertile breeding ground for fundamentalist sentiment. The pressure of socio-economic hardship, the traditionally religious and conservative character of the local population, the proximity to Egypt (and Egyptian fundamentalism), and the impact of the Iranian revolution all played their part. So, too, did the shortsighted-ness of Israeli policy which encouraged fundamentalists to bring in money from abroad to establish kindergartens, youth clubs, sports organ-izations, mosques, and Islamic colleges in Gaza and parts of the West Bank. The Israeli military evidently hoped that fundamentalism might wean the youth of the territories away from the PLO. True, the Islamic sheikhs reject the nationalist ideology of the PLO and insist that Palestinian aspirations can only be realized by creating an Islamic state. But both ideologically and in practice, their opposition to Israel is even more intransigent than that of the Palestinian nationalists. For the ideologues of Islamic Jihad, Israel is the spearhead of 'satanic' forces aiming to create a Zionist empire from the Nile to the Euphrates. One of their main spiritual leaders in Gaza, Sheikh Rajab al-Tamimi, declared early on in the Palestinian rising that Israel, which sprang up 'on the dead bodies of the Moslem Palestinian people', was 'doomed to destruction', 'born to die'.

More recently, the leading fundamentalist organization in the occupied territories, Hamas, declared in one of the opening sentences of its official covenant that 'Israel will exist and continue to exist until Islam will obliterate it, just as it obliterated others before it.' Moreover, its chilling call for Israel's extinction is anchored in some of the hoariest myths of European racist antisemitism. Thus we read in Article 22 of the Islamic Resistance Movement's covenant:

> They [the Jews] were behind the French Revolution, the Communist Revolution and most of the revolutions we heard and hear about, here and there. With their money they formed secret societies, such as Freemasons, Rotary Clubs, the Lions and others in different parts of the world for the purpose of sabotaging societies and achieving Zionist interests.[5]

Indeed, 'world Zionism' and 'the warmongering Jews' are accused in the classic traditions of *The Protocols of the Elders of Zion* of having caused both world wars, 'through which they made huge financial gains by trading in armaments, and paved the way for the establishment of their state'.[6] The 'Capitalist West' and the 'Communist East' are both equally guilty in the eyes of the Islamic resistance for having permitted the 'illegal usurpation' of Palestine. The only answer to this perfidious conspiracy remains unswerving loyalty to the commandment of holy war (*jihad*) which, needless to say, rejects all peaceful solutions and the very notion of an international conference as anathema. Thus, although Hamas regards the PLO as an ally in its fight for one homeland against 'an enemy common to all of us' (Article 27), it sharply condemns Arafat's current so-called 'peace offensive'. Even acceptance of such anachronisms as the 1947 UN Partition Resolution on Palestine (something that Arafat favours and Al-Fatah now publicly supports) is seen as betrayal of 'an Islamic Waqf land consecrated for Moslem generations until Judgement Day'.[7]

During the rising Israel has reaped the harvest of fundamentalist hatred. Islamic teachers have been among the main choirleaders of the rioting, calling for resistance from loudspeakers attached to mosques in Gaza, the West Bank, and east Jerusalem. Islamic calls to martyrdom – cries of 'Palestine is our Holy Land' and 'Allah helps those who help themselves' – have vied with the more familiar slogans of the PLO throughout the rising. There can be little doubt that a renewed belief in God and Islam has provided a powerful emotional framework for the rebels and motivated younger Palestinians to die for their cause. Hence it is not surprising that defiance of the Israeli occupation should have taken on a more openly Islamic colouring and, in some cases, an explicit rejection of the 'corrupt' westernized lifestyle blamed by fundamentalists on daily contact with Israeli society.

The appeal of fundamentalism among the Palestinians thrives on the despair engendered by an occupation which seems endless and increasingly permanent. It gains strength from its roots in Islamic history and popular culture; from the impotence and indifference of surrounding Arab regimes who have been singularly unable to affect the fate of the Palestinians; from the failures of the PLO and of secular Arab nationalism to address convincingly the traumas of modernization. Above all it offers a seductively simple solution to the personal and collective sufferings of the Palestinians over the past four decades. Islam has always been a most effective symbolic system of the Arab world, a central inspiration for its ideals, social norms, laws, and future aspirations: a source both of legitimate authority and now for the revolt of the oppressed. Much more than Judaism, Christianity, or other world religions it has been supremely *political* in character. Indeed, as the Ayatollah Khomeini once stated: 'Islam is politics or it is nothing'. What contemporary Islam has yet to demonstrate is whether it can rise above the politics of hatred and fanaticism to regain that authentic universality and tolerance which characterized medieval Islamic civilization at its height. In concrete terms, that means accepting that Palestinian national self-determination can only come through recognition of the rights to independence and sovereignty of an Israeli Jewish state within mutually agreed and secure boundaries. The alternative is that downward spiral towards Armageddon which will reduce to ashes not only all prospects for human and social liberation in the region but turn the redemptive visions of both Islam and Judaism into a hollow mockery.

But the rise of fundamentalism, as recent events have shown, has not been confined only to Israel's Muslim population. In some respects, Israeli Jews have also been swept along by the variant of Middle Eastern fundamentalism, though the socio-political context is singularly different. For example, no religious groupings in Israel explicitly call for a holy war against the Palestinians or any of the Arab states. Indeed, Rabbi Meir Kahane's Kach movement, the closest parallel in Israel to Islamic fundamentalist antisemitism, was banned because of its racist incitement against Arabs from running for the Knesset. (Moledet, a secular right-wing nationalist party that favours the 'repatriation' of Palestinians to neighbouring Arab lands, did however obtain two seats.) Another significant difference which reflects the depth and strength of Israel's democratic ethos is the absence of any significant Jewish fundamentalist group advocating a *revolutionary* transformation of society by violent methods. True, in certain circumstances – such as a total Israeli withdrawal from all the occupied territories – one can conceive of a messianically motivated Jewish underground taking up arms even against its own legally elected government. But none of the religious parties in the Israeli parliament – who currently hold 18 of the 120 seats – believes in violence as a legitimate method of obtaining its goals.

Nevertheless there are some disturbing similarities between Muslim and Jewish fundamentalism (the Christian evangelical variety deserves a separate treatment and cannot be dealt with here) which merit more attention than they often receive.[8] Both share, for example, a commitment to expanding the scope of the religious law (Jewish *Halakhah* or Islamic *Shari'ah*) so that it govern the life of society and the state. Both advocate the rigorous enforcement of puritan standards in the field of entertainment, the media, the printed word, and education in general. They share the same long-term vision of a religiously controlled, exclusivist, and godly state – one that is inspired by zealous observance of the divine law. In such a society classic Enlightenment values of reason, tolerance, and pluralism will be seriously endangered, if not eliminated altogether. Non-Jews in the Jewish state like non-Muslims in the Muslim state risk being branded as 'infidels'; the secularists and non-believers in general might be seen as 'heretics', 'pagans', or even corrupters of youth; women will be returned to their pre-emancipatory condition; above all everything associated with the 'tainted' secular values of modern western society can expect short shrift.[8]

The Israeli election results, while scarcely providing a mandate either for religious fundamentalism or for an integral nationalist vision of Greater Israel, did reveal a striking increase in *ḥaredi* (ultra-orthodox) influence and for a time even raised the spectre of a slow drift towards this kind of theocracy. Fortunately, the formation of a broad if rather elephantine Likud–Labour coalition after weeks of agonizing negotiations seems to have closed off this particular possibility for the next few years. Apocalyptic fears of an imminent 'haredization' of Israeli society have thus far proven to be without foundation. But the underlying trends – demographic, cultural, social, and political – as well as certain features of the electoral campaign and its aftermath do provide warning signs.

One dramatic example in the elections was the intervention of the 87-year-old Lubavitcher Rebbe, Menachem Mendel Schneerson, regarded as *moshiach* (the Messiah) by many of his more fanatical adherents. The Brooklyn-based rabbi has never set foot in the Holy Land but his 'super-patriotic' Habad Hassidic movement insists that every inch of Israel belongs to the Jewish people and can never be given away! Breathing new life into the nearly defunct Agudath Israel movement (most observers believe that the missionary zeal of the Habadniks accounted for three of the five Agudah seats), they won significant support among the traditionalist (mainly Sephardi) voters of the development towns. Thus the non-Zionist Agudah was able to break out for the first time from its Yiddish-speaking medieval enclaves like Mea Shearim or Bnei Brak and draw recruits from among the children of immigrants from the North African *mellahs*.

Even more successful in this respect was another *haredi* group, Shas (the Sephardi Torah Guardians Party), which obtained six seats in the Knesset and has two ministers in the present broad coalition government. Shas's position on the territories has been hardline, and during its electoral campaign it called for tougher measures to curb the *intifada*. But the key to its popularity was its shrewd appeal to the rich spiritual heritage of Moroccan Jewry, combined with a willingness to address real social problems among contemporary Israeli youth such as drug-taking, criminality, or sexual permissiveness. It also exploited the services of a former chief rabbi, Ovadia Yosef (a much revered figure among most Sephardi Jews), who criss-crossed the country by helicopter, liberally dispersing blessings and curses to anyone who would listen.

Shas's synthesis of ethnic particularism and Torah values undoubtedly has an appeal to underprivileged Sephardim who in the past registered their resentment of the Ashkenazi labour establishment by voting Likud. By now disillusioned with both the major parties, and fed up with interminable and mostly sterile debates about peace and the territories, they have turned back to their religious roots in growing numbers. The cult of Moroccan Jewish holy men like the Baba Sali was a pointer to what might happen, though few observers expected this traditional religiosity mixed with superstition to find effective political expression. Yet the 'miracle workers' have proven to be potent vote-catchers as might have been predicted by anyone familiar with modern Jewish history since the late eighteenth century in eastern Europe or the Middle East. As the recent elections demonstrated, many Moroccan Jewish voters, in particular, have never really embraced modern secular, rational, or western values. Like their Ashkenazi *haredi* counterparts (and like many Muslim fundamentalists) they feel themselves to be at war with modern society, alienated by its pressures, dismayed by its corrosion of religious tradition and family cohesion, and deeply offended by its pluralism and permissiveness. Jewish fundamentalism, whether Zionist (in the shape of the National Religious Party under its Sephardi-oriented hawkish new leadership) or non-Zionist, has been able to fill this ideological vacuum. Like its Muslim counterparts, it has flourished against a background of collapsing secular ideologies, growing trends of irrationalism and superstition throughout the Middle East, unresolved social problems, and distrust of the critical, scientific spirit. Among Jews, as among Muslims (and Christians too), it appeals to those troubled by a loss of identity, distinctiveness, or sense of meaning to their lives – proposing in its place a new framework of belonging – which fuses ethnicity with religion.

Yet, spiritually speaking, this new fundamentalist religiosity is utterly barren. What really preoccupies the religious parties in Israel is to ensure the flow of funds to their *Yeshivot* and other institutions; to strengthen the rabbinate and the status of rabbinical courts; and to maintain formal Sabbath observance in public. Ideally, they would not permit a single bus, taxi, or tram to run on the Sabbath throughout the country. They would close down every business, restaurant, theatre, and cinema, and ban the Saturday football games – something guaranteed to outrage the Sephardi ballot-box *haredim* who, like many other Israelis, have no difficulty in combining synagogue and sport on the Sabbath. Most worrying of all to patriotic Israelis is the growing number of draft-deferments to *Yeshivah* students (presently estimated at 18,000 able-bodied young men) which, if 'haredization' really took hold, raises a very crucial question: who, in the future, will be manning the tanks and flying the planes while *am yisroel* is studying in *Yeshivot*? And who will guarantee the continuation of Israel's qualitative superiority over its enemies in the fields of science and technology, if desperately needed funds for secular education are diverted to *haredi* institutions?

Most Israelis remain secular-minded, of course, and are not likely to put up tamely with the prospect of religious coercion at any time in the near future. Indeed, public pressure in favour of a Labour–Likud coalition was no doubt motivated, at least in part, by this concern. But the observant minority who already constitute between 20 and 25 per cent of the population have larger families and their numbers are growing more rapidly. In Jerusalem during the recent elections their strength was particularly palpable and it is bound to increase in the future. Thus, demographic trends suggest a continuation of the current drift towards a more Oriental, a more *haredi* and moderately right-wing Israel – one that may be increasingly at odds with the traditionally liberal and pluralist western Jewish Diaspora. The bitterness of the 'who is a Jew?' controversy and the narrowly averted split (for the present) between Israel and its American Jewish constituency is eloquent testimony to that danger. Almost certainly Mr Shamir's readiness to make substantial concessions to Labour was due to his unwillingness to be made a prisoner of Israeli orthodox intransigence in rejecting the validity of conservative and reform conversions to Judaism. If the 'law of return' were to be amended as proposed by the religious parties in Israel there is no doubt that this would substantially reduce the enthusiasm, the readiness, and the ability of American Jewry to intervene on Israel's behalf with the American administration, the Congress, and public opinion. This is not something that Mr Shamir could afford with the *intifada* still raging and the PLO scoring diplomatic points in Algiers, Stockholm, and Geneva. The Likud leadership remains convinced, of course, that PLO moderation is purely cosmetic and that despite appearances its basic philosophy and aims remain unchanged – namely, the destruction of Israel in stages. The official Israeli position (shared also by most of the Labour leaders) is that Arafat can never be a partner for peace since the *raison d'être* of the PLO is the total 'liberation of Palestine'. The radical factions within the PLO will never renounce this objective and indeed they have not even indirectly declared their willingness to recognize Israel or to abandon armed struggle.

Even many dovish Israelis, it must be said, were also disappointed by the tortured ambiguities of the PNC (Palestine National Council) resolutions at Algiers at the end of November 1988. These statements condemned terrorism while supporting the struggle for independence by means which include violence against Israeli civilians. They supported the 1947 partition resolution calling for an Arab Palestine while ignoring the part that laid the legal foundation for Israel as a Jewish state. The resolutions did not explicitly limit the future Palestine state to the West Bank and Gaza; they simply called for these areas to be handed on a platter to the PLO by the UN following an Israeli withdrawal, without any process of direct negotiation. This is all the more disturbing for Israelis since in PLO literature the West Bank–Gaza state is only an 'interim' solution and pre-1967 Israel is still considered 'occupied Palestine'. Above all, the PNC seemed willing only to imply recognition of Israel's existence without actually doing so.

Admittedly, in Geneva Arafat did finally utter the magic words that the United States had insisted upon in order to open a dialogue with the PLO. He condemned terrorism, declared his willingness to embark on a process of negotiation, and appeared to accept the right of Israel to exist – though this was by no means the full, unequivocal acknowledgement that the majority of Israelis would find acceptable. Moreover a statement for a foreign audience, aimed primarily at the Americans, can hardly cancel out decades of terror, hijackings, and murder with which Arafat's PLO is indelibly linked. Nothing in the PLO statement can bind Palestinian fanatics like the Abu Nidal group, Abu Moussa's rebel Fatah faction, or Jibril's Syrian-controlled Popular Democratic Front for the Liberation of Palestine from pursuing their bloodstained path to total redemption. Indeed, for them, as for the Syrians and Libyans, Arafat is already beyond the pale.

Nor is there any sign in Israel of a creative response to Arafat's moves – with foreign policy now controlled by the Likud in what promises to be a sclerotic government that seems incapable of taking any bold step to solve the Palestinian problem. The 'iron fist' policy will undoubtedly continue while the uprising, despite all the international sympathy it may have generated, is unlikely to bring about any real improvement in the position of the Palestinians. In this situation, the Islamic fundamentalists, the pro-Syrian groups, and the radical PLO factions may well increase their base of support, especially if Arafat's strategy produces no tangible fruits. All these groups of 'true believers' – whether secular or religious – despise the PLO public relations offensive to win over western countries and continue to proclaim openly their desire to destroy Israel. Their capacity to sabotage any compromise settlement cannot be doubted. Thus, despite the PLO's change of course, the prospects of peace in this troubled region still remain bleak.

Notes

2 The internationalism of Rosa Luxemburg

1 Among the most important studies in the past decade are J. P. Nettl, *Rosa Luxemburg* (London/New York/Toronto 1966), 2 vols; Helmut Hirsch, *Rosa Luxemburg in Selbstzeugnissen und Bilddokumenten* (Hamburg 1969); Feliks Tych (ed.), *Rosa Luxemburg, Briefe an Leon Jogiches* (Frankfurt a.M. 1971), translation from the 1968 Polish edition published in Warsaw; Dick Howard (ed.), *Rosa Luxemburg. Selected Political Writings* (London/New York 1971); Rosa Luxemburg, *Internationalismus and Klassenkampf* (Neuwied/Berlin 1971); Rosa Luxemburg, *Le Socialisme en France 1898–1912* (Paris 1971), introduced by Daniel Guérin; Narihiko Ite (ed.), *Rosa Luxemburg u.a.: Briefe an Mathilde Jacob 1913–1918* (Tokyo 1972); Lelio Basso, *Rosa Luxemburg: A Reappraisal* (London 1975); Norman Geras, *The Legacy of Rosa Luxemburg* (1976); and more recently E. Ettinger (ed.), *Comrade and Lover. Rosa Luxemburg's Letters to Leo Jogiches* (Cambridge, Mass. 1979). Concerning the influence of her Jewishness on Rosa Luxemburg's political thought and career, both Isaac Deutscher, *The Non-Jewish Jew and Other Essays* (Oxford 1968) and J. L. Talmon, *Israel among the Nations* (London 1970) touch on this theme. For a more detailed treatment see Chapter 4 of my book, *Revolutionary Jews from Marx to Trotsky* (London/New York 1976).
2 See Rudi Dutschke's comments in 'Noch einmal: Rosa Luxemburg in der DDR', *Vorwärts* (31 July 1975). Also the thought-provoking article by Gunter Barsch, 'Die Aktualität Rosa Luxemburgs in Osteuropa', *Osteuropa* (October 1975), 848–54.
3 See Nettl, op.cit., vol.2, 787–827 on 'Luxemburgism – weapon and myth'. Also Gerhard Beier, 'Rosa Luxemburg. Zur Aktualität und Historizität einer umstrittenen Grösse', *Internationale Wissenschaftliche Korrespondenz*, Heft 2 (June 1974).
4 Rosa Luxemburg, 'Organisationsfragen der russischen Sozialdemokratie', *Die Neue Zeit*, vol. 2 (1903/4), 484–92 529–35.
5 ibid. 'The ultra-centralism advocated by Lenin seems to us in its whole character to be sustained not by a positive creative spirit but by a sterile night-watchman spirit.'
6 Rosa Luxemburg, *Leninism or Marxism? The Russian Revolution* (Ann Arbor, Mich. 1961), edited by Bertram D. Wolfe, 76–7.

7 ibid., 69.

8 ibid., 71.

9 Rosa Luxemburg, 'Kwestia narodowosciowa i autonomia', *Przegląd Socjaldemokratyczny*, no. 6 (August 1908), reprinted in *Wybór Pism*, vol. 2 (Warsaw 1959), 147–8.

10 Nettl, op. cit., Appendix 2: The National Question, 842–62 for a useful summary. Also Michael Lowy, 'Rosa Luxemburg et la question nationale', *Partisans*, no. 59–60 (May–August 1971); Arieh Yaari, 'Rosa Luxemburg ou le nihilisme nationale', *les Nouveaux Cahiers*, no. 39 (Winter 1974–5), 27–31.

11 For further details see the general introduction in Robert S. Wistrich, *Revolutionary Jews from Marx to Trotsky* (London/New York 1976).

12 Rosa Luxemburg, *Briefe an Freunde* (Hamburg 1950), edited by Benedikt Kautsky, 48–9, letter dated 16 February 1917.

13 Nettl, op.cit., 672.

14 Paul Fröhlich, *Rosa Luxemburg. Ideas in Action* (London 1972), translated from the 3rd German edition *Rosa Luxemburg, Gedanke und Tat* (Frankfurt a.M. 1967).

15 ibid.

16 See Avraham Bick (Shauli) *Merosh Tsurim* (From the Lofty Heights), subtitled *Metaknei Chevra Al Taharat Hakodesh Shalshelet Hayichusin Shel Avot Hasozialism* (Social Reformers in the Spirit of Sanctity – the Family Trees of the Fathers of Socialism) (Jerusalem 1972). Bick's essay on Rosa Luxemburg entitled 'Nesher Ha-Mekhapcha' (The Eagle of Revolution), 76–90, seeks to establish parallels between the teachings of her rabbinical ancestors and her ethical beliefs.

17 ibid.

18 ibid.

19 See the thoughtful essay by the late Hannah Arendt, 'Rosa Luxemburg', in *Men in Dark Times* (London 1973), 47.

20 Parvus, Kark Radek (whom Rosa Luxemburg detested), Jogiches, and Trotsky all compare unfavourably to her in this respect. See Joel Carmichael, *Trotsky. An Appreciation of His Life* (London 1975) for an illustration of this point.

21 Andrej Neimojewski, *Myśl Niepodłegla*, no. 153 (November 1910), 1599.

22 Rosa Luxemburg, 'Ein literarisches Bravo', *Vorwärts* (23 November 1910), 2.

23 ibid. 'Freidenkertum und Sozialdemokratie', *Vorwärts* (27 September 1910), 1–2. The authorship of both these articles, which were unsigned, was first established in *Z Pola Walki*, no. 3 (19) (1962) by Feliks Tych and Jadwiga Kaczanowska.

24 Rosa Luxemburg, 'Po Pogromie', *Młot* (The Hammer), no. 10 (8 October 1910), 1 ff.

25 ibid. Also 'Odwrót na calej linji', *Młot*, no. 2, 9 ff.

26 R. L. 'Dyskusja', *Młot* no. 14 (5 November 1910), 5–7.

27 ibid.

28 ibid. Some of these articles have now been translated by Valentina-Maria Stefanski into German for Irving Fetscher's anthology, *Marxisten gegen Antisemitismus* (Hamburg 1974); see especially 130–4, 144–5, 147–8. For a critical review of this work see Robert S. Wistrich, 'The Marxist concern with Judaism', *Patterns of Prejudice* (July/August 1975), 1–6.

29 *Protokoll über die Verhandlungen des Parteitages der Sozialdemokratischen Partei Deutschlands*, Lübeck (22–8 September 1901) (Berlin 1901), 195.

Heine, who had once been chairman of the antisemitic German Students' Association, declared: 'Unser Internationalismus bedeutet, dass jede Nation die andere achtet, und ich habe keine Missachtung gegen die russischen und polnischen Juden aber wenn Jemand als Gast zu uns kommt und uns in die Stube spuckt, so werden wir uns das nicht gefallen lassen'. See also the *Rheinische Zeitung*, 12 October 1901, 'Sozialdemokratie und Antisemitismus'.

30 ibid., 202. See also the protest by Franz Mehring, 'Einige Ketzerei', *Die Neue Zeit*, vol. 1 (1901/2), 1–4, against the attacks on Luxemburg and Parvus.

31 See Robert C. Williams, 'Russians in Germany: 1900–1914', *The Journal of Contemporary History*, vol. 1, no. 4 (October 1966), 121–50, for a general account of German attitudes to Russian *émigrés* in this period. Also Nettl, op.cit., 512–13.

32 Gustav Noske, *Erlebtes aus Aufstieg und Niedergang einer Demokratie* (Offenbac:h a.M. 1947), 27.

33 ibid.

34 On Grillenberger's reaction to Parvus, whom he described in a letter to Carl Oertel in 1895 as a 'dirty Polish Jew', see Paul Meyer, *Bruno Schoenlank. (1859–1901). Reformer der Sozialdemokratischen Tagespresse* (Hanover 1971), 76. On Eduard David's anti-Jewish feelings during the First World War, see *Das Kriegestagebuch des Reichstagsabgeordneten Eduard David 1914 bis 1918* (Dusseldorf 1966) ed. Erich Mattias and Susanne Miller. August Winnig subsequently went over from revisionism to national socialism. On antisemitic tendencies in the SPD see Edmund Silberner, *Sozialisten zur Judenfrage* (Berlin 1962) and Robert S. Wistrich, *Socialism and the Jews. The Dilemmas of Assimilation in Germany and Austria-Hungary* (London/Toronto 1982).

35 Rosa Luxemburg, *Briefe an Leon Jogiches*, 145–6.

36 See Walter Z. Laqueur, 'Zionism, the Marxist critique and the Left', *Dissent* (December 1971), 566–74; Robert S. Wistrich, 'Karl Marx, German socialists and the Jewish question 1880–1914', *Soviet Jewish Affairs*, vol. 3, no. 1 (Spring 1973). My article for the *Leo Baeck Yearbook* vol. 21 (1976), 'German social democracy and the problem of Jewish nationalism 1897–1917' deals with this aspect in greater detail.

37 Ezra Mendelsohn, *Class Struggles in the Pale* (Cambridge 1970), 35, 40.

38 See the introduction by M. Mishkinsky to the parallel Russian-Hebrew edition of the text of these speeches first made in Vilna on May Day 1892, *Four Speeches of Jewish Workers* (Jerusalem 1967).

39 L. Jogichesa-Tsyszki, 'Nowi towarzysze', in *Socjaldemokracja Królestwa Polskeigo i Litwy. Materialy i Dolumenty t. I 1893–1903*, vol. 1 (Warsaw 1957), ed. H. Buczek and F. Tych, 146–52. For a similar reaction see I. Ignatieff (pseudonym of Helphand-Parvus), 'Russian-jüdische Arbeiter über die Judenfrage', *Die Neue Zeit*, vol. 1, (1892–3) 176 ff.

40 Jogichesa-Tsyzki, op.cit.

41 See M. Mishkinsky, 'Yesodot leumiim be-Hitpatkhutah shel Tnu'at ha-poalim ha-yehudim be-Rusia' (National elements in the development of the Jewish labour movement in Russia), unpublished PhD thesis, Jerusalem 1965, 188–227; John Mill, *Pionirn un boier* (Pioneers and Builders) in Yiddish, vol. 1 (New York 1946), 133–43 150ff., 251.

42 *Internationaler Sozialistischer Arbeiter-und-Gewerkschaftskongress zu London* (London 1896), 18.

43 *Naprzód*, 14 May 1896. See Rosa Luxemburg, *Briefe an Karl und Luise*

Kautsky (Berlin 1923), 34–5, letter dated 24 May 1896, in which she enclosed her German translation of the PPS attack on her as 'a quarrelsome, hysterical female'. According to *Naprzód*, 'Der polnische Sozialismus ist nicht so tief gesunken, dass Fräulein Rosa mit der stillen Compagnie der Berdycower "Russen" das recht hatte, in seinem Namen zu sprechen.'

44 Julien Unszlicht (Sedecki), *Social-litwactwo w Polsce*: *z teorii i praktyki SDKPiL* (Cracow n.d.) For the reaction of the SDKPiL to attacks from Sedecki and Emil Haecker, editor of *Naprzód*, see for example 'Dwa Obozy', *Młot*, no. 6 (8 October 1910), 8–9.

45 Rosa Luxemburg, 'Krytyka i bibliografja', *Przegląd Socjaldemokratyczny*, IV, no. 4 (1903), 159–63, review of the Bund pamphlet, *Polska Partja Socjalistyczna żydowskim ruchu robotniczym* (London 1903).

46 Adolf Wars(zaw)ki to Kautsky, in Kautsky Archive D XXIIII 20 May 1903 (International Institute of Social History, Amsterdam).

47 Karl Kautsky 'Das Massaker von Kischineff und die Judenfrage', *Die Neue Zeit*, vol. 2, (1902–3), 303–9. Rosa Luxemburg, *Briefe an Karl und Luise Kautsky*, 59, reported in a letter on 6 June 1903 to Kautsky that her associate, Warski, was 'highly delighted' with his Kishinev article.

48 Rosa Luxemburg, 'Krytyka i bibliografja'.

49 ibid. 'Odwrot na calej linji', *Młot* (15 October 1910), 9ff.

50 ibid.

51 ibid.

51 See my *Revolutionary Jews from Marx to Trotsky*, especially the General Introduction where I take issue with Isaac Deutscher's thesis that the great 'non-Jewish Jews' (like Marx, Trotsky, and Rosa Luxemburg) 'transcended' their Judaism.

4 Karl Lueger in historical perspective

1 Friedrich Austerlitz, 'Karl Lueger', *Die Neue Zeit*, vol 2 (1900–1), 38.

2 Austerlitz, 'Die Wahlen in Wien', *Die Neue Zeit*, vol 29, no. 1 (1911), 510.

3 See Carl E. Schorske, *Fin-De-Siècle Vienna*: *Politics and Culture* (London 1980), 118–20, 132–3 on postrational politics.

4 John Weiss, *Conservatism in Europe 1770–1945. Traditionalism, Reaction and Counter-Revolution* (London 1977), 119.

5 ibid., 120.

6 ibid., 118. In point of fact, Lueger's career, far from 'emerging' in 1907, was virtually finished. The classification of his movement as belonging to the 'Radical Right' is of course problematic.

7 Adolf Hitler, *Mein Kampf* (London 1939), 95.

8 ibid.

9 See Karl R. Stadler, 'Austria', in S. J. Woolf (ed.), *European Fascism* (London 1968), 88–110. See also A. Wandruszka, 'Österreichs politische Struktur', in H. Benedikt (ed.), *Geschichte der Republik Österreich* (Vienna 1954).

10 *Stenographische Protokolle über die Sitzungen des Hauses der Abgeordneten des Reichsrates*, 17th Session (22 October 1901), vols VII–VIII, p. 7,044.

11 For a shrewd assessment of Lueger in this social context, see Ilsa Barea, *Vienna* (London 1966).

12 Sigmund Mayer, *Die Wiener Juden*: *Kommerz, Kultur, Politik 1700–1900* (Vienna/Berlin 1917), 475.

13 Wilhelm Ellenbogen, 'Der Wiener Antisemitismus', *Sozialistische Monatshefte*, vol. 1 (September 1899), 418–19.
14 ibid., 419.
15 ibid., 421.
16 ibid., 422.
17 Austerlitz, 'Karl Lueger', 40–1.
18 ibid., 43.
19 For the first systematic analysis of Austrian social democratic attitudes to Lueger and Christian socialism in general, see Robert S. Wistrich, *Socialism and the Jews. The Dilemmas of Assimilation in Germany and Austria-Hungary* (London/Toronto 1982), 250–98.
20 Kurt Skalnik, *Dr Karl Lueger: Der Mann zwischen den Zeiten* (Munich 1954), 82.
21 For examples, see my *Socialism and the Jews*, 281–2.
22 These tendencies are well reflected in Arthur Schnitzler's *Zeitroman*, which deals extensively with the Jewish question; see his *Der Weg ins Freie* (Vienna 1907).
23 A point well made by John Boyer, 'Karl Lueger and the Viennese Jews', *Leo Baeck Yearbook* vol. 26 (1981), 139–40.
24 See John Boyer, *Political Radicalism in Later Imperial Vienna. The Origins of the Christian Social Movement, 1848–1897* (Chicago 1980), for an indispensable contribution.
25 ibid. Compare Boyer's treatment with the very different perspective of Reinhold Knoll, *Zur Tradition der Christlichsozialen Partei* (Vienna/Cologne/Graz 1973).
26 Schorske, *Fin-De-Siècle Vienna*, 120. In fact, Schorske underestimates (rather than ignores) the traditionalism behind Lueger's appeal, mainly out of a desire to emphasize the novelty of his politics. Neither the category of 'postrational' nor the assumption that Christian socialism represented a genuinely new mass politics should be, however, uncritically accepted, as Boyer has convincingly shown.
27 ibid., 133.
28 ibid., 143–4.
29 Wistrich, *Socialism and the Jews*, 250–98. See also my earlier article, 'Austrian social democracy and antisemitism, 1890–1914', *Jewish Social Studies*, vol. 38 (Summer-Fall 1975), 323–33.
30 See Boyer, 'Karl Lueger and the Viennese Jews', 137, where he slightly overstates the point. Also see Earl Edmonson, *The Heimwehr and Austrian Politics 1918–1936* (Athens, Ga. 1978), on the primacy of anti-Marxism rather than antisemitism in post-1918 Austro-fascism.

5 Hitler and national socialism: the Austrian connection

1 Adolf Hitler, *Mein Kampf* (Boston 1942), 125.
2 See Robert Wistrich, *Hitler's Apocalypse* (London 1985), chapter 1.
3 *Mein Kampf*, 11,16,95,141,148.
4 See Geoffrey G. Field, *Evangelist of Race: The Germanic Vision of Houston S. Chamberlain* (New York 1981) 111.
5 Andrew G. Whiteside, *The Socialism of Fools: George Ritter von Schoenerer and Austrian Pan-Germanism* (Berkeley, Los Angeles 1975). Also Robert S. Wistrich, 'Georg von Schoenerer and the genesis of

Austrian antisemitism', *The Wiener Library Bulletin* 29, nos 39/40 (1976) 20–9.

6 For the demography of Viennese Jewry, see Robert S. Wistrich, *The Jews of Vienna in the Age of Franz Joseph* (Oxford 1989).

7 Edouard Calic (ed.), *Secret Conversations with Hitler* (New York 1971), 66–7.

8 ibid., 67.

9 Hermann Rauschning, *The Voice of Destruction* (New York 1940), 87–8.

10 *Mein Kampf* op. cit., 123.

11 ibid.

12 Karl R. Stadler, 'Provinzstadt im Dritten Reich', introduction to Gerhard Botz, *Wien vom 'Anschluss' zum Krieg. Nationalsozialistische Machtübernahme und politisch-soziale Umgestaltung am Beispiel der Stadt Wien 1938/9* (Vienna, Munich 1978) 13–27.

13 F. L. Carsten, *Fascist Movements in Austria: From Schönerer to Hitler* (London 1977), 334. 'After March 1938 the very name of Austria disappeared; even Lower Austria and Upper Austria were renamed "Lower Danube" and "Upper Danube" to eradicate any memory of Austria as a separate entity.'

14 Norman H. Baynes, *The Speeches of Adolf Hitler* (London 1942), II, 1456–7.

15 For a useful, though impressionistic account, see J. Sydney Jones, *Hitler in Vienna 1907–1913: Clues to the Future* (New York 1982).

16 See Ernst Nolte, *Three Faces of Fascism: Action Française, Italian Fascism, National Socialism* (London 1965) for further parallels.

17 Letter dated 29 November 1921, quoted in Werner Maser, *Hitler's Letters and Notes* (New York 1974), 107.

18 For a psychoanalytic interpretation of the possible connection between his mother's death from cancer of the breast, her ministration by a Jewish doctor in Vienna, Hitler's gas poisoning during the First World War, and the genesis of his Jew-hatred, see Rudolf Binion, *Hitler among the Germans* (New York 1976), 35. This theory seems highly improbable to me.

19 On Wagner, see Zvi Bacharach, 'Omanut Ve'antishemiut be'hashkafat Ha-Olam Shel Richard Wagner', *Yalkut Moreshet* 29 (1980), Hebrew.

20 *Mein Kampf*, op. cit., 55.

21 On the antipathy to *Ostjuden* at this time, see Steven E. Aschheim, *Brothers and Strangers: The East European Jew in German and German-Jewish Consciousness 1800–1923* (Wisconsin 1982), 58–79.

22 Albert Speer, *Inside the Third Reich* (London 1971), 79.

23 See Edward Bristow, *Prostitution and Prejudice: The Jewish Fight Against White Slavery* (Oxford 1982) for the historical background.

24 *Mein Kampf* op. cit., 338, 512.

25 ibid., 59. Also Aschheim, *Brothers and Strangers*, op. cit., 38,146.

26 *Mein Kampf* op. cit., 59. Also the comments by Friedrich Heer, 'Explosionen: Wien und sein Untergrund', *Emuna* 8, no. 2 (March-April 1973), 83–93.

27 John Boyer, *Political Radicalism in Late Imperial Vienna: The Origins of the Christian Social Movement 1848–1897* (Chicago 1981).

28 J. Boyer, 'Karl Lueger and the Viennese Jews', *Leo Baeck Yearbook* vol. 26 (1981), 139–40. Robert S. Wistrich, 'Karl Lueger and the ambiguities of Viennese antisemitism', *Jewish Social Studies* 45, nos 3–4 (Summer-Fall 1983), 251–62.

29 *Mein Kampf* op. cit., 100.
30 ibid, 120.
31 Stadler, 'Provinzstadt', op. cit., 19–20; August Kubizek, *The Young Hitler I Knew* (Boston 1955), 161.
32 See Jeffrey A. Goldstein, 'On racism and antisemitism in occultism and Nazism', *Yad Vashem Studies* 13 (Jerusalem 1979), 53–72.
33 On Lanz von Liebenfels, see Wilfried Daim, *Der Mann, der Hitler die Ideen gab: Von den religiösen Verirrungen einer Sektierers zum Rassenwahn des Diktators* (Munich 1958).
34 Jones, *Hitler in Vienna*, op. cit., 116–17, 123–5, Daim, *Der Mann*, op. cit., and also Wistrich, *Hitler's Apocalypse*, op. cit.
35 *Mein Kampf*, op. cit., 51, 320.
36 See Helmut Konrad, *Nationalismus und Internationalismus. Die österreichische Arbeiterbewegung vor dem Ersten Weltkrieg* (Vienna 1976), 153ff.
37 Baynes, op. cit., vol II, 1456–7. *Mein Kampf*, op. cit., 124.
38 *Mein Kampf*, op. cit., 125.
39 John Haag, 'Blood on the Ringstrasse: Vienna's students 1918–33', *The Wiener Library Bulletin* vol XXIX, new series nos. 39/40, (1976) 29–33.
40 F. L. Carsten, *Fascist Movements in Austria. From Schönerer to Hitler* (London 1977), 75–6.
41 ibid., 90.
42 J. Moser, 'Von der antisemitischen Bewegung zum Holocaust', in Klaus Lohrmann (ed.) *1,000 Jahre österreichisches Judentum* (Eisenstadt 1982), 265.
43 Bruce F. Pauley, 'Political antisemitism in interwar Vienna', in I. Oxaal *et al* (eds) *Jews, Antisemitism and Culture in Vienna* (London/New York 1987), 159–60.
44 ibid., 162.
45 Gerhard Botz, *Wien vom 'Anschluss' zum Krieg* (Vienna/Munich 1978), 406–8, 463.
46 Bruce F. Pauley, *Hitler and the Forgotten Nazis: A History of Austrian National Socialism* (Chapel Hill, NC 1987).
47 Carsten, op. cit., 334.
48 Robert Schwarz, *'Sozialismus' der Propaganda. Das Werben des 'Völkischen Beobachters' um die österreichische Arbeiterschaft 1938/9* (Vienna 1975).
49 Gerhard Botz, 'From the *Anschluss* to the Holocaust', in I. Oxaal *et al* (eds) *Jews, Antisemitism and Culture*, op. cit., 202–3.

6 The Jewishness of Sigmund Freud

1 This chapter constitutes the text of the Kaufmann Memorial Lecture delivered at the Leo Baeck College in London on 6 May 1987.
2 See *Letters of Sigmund Freud*, selected and ed. Ernest L. Freud (New York 1961), 221.
3 Dennis B. Klein, *Jewish Origins of the Psychoanalytic Movement* (Chicago/London 1985), 84–6.
4 *Letters*, op. cit., 366–7. See also Martin Freud, 'Who was Freud?' in Josef Fraenkel, *The Jews of Austria* (London 1967), 197–9.
5 *Letters*, op. cit., 395.
6 A. A. Roback, *Freudiana* (Cambridge, Mass. 1957), 92.

7 Sigmund Freud, *Zur Psychopathologie des Alltagslebens* (Frankfurt a.M. 1976), 174.
8 Martin Freud, op. cit., 202.
9 Sigmund Freud, *Jokes and Their Relation to the Unconscious* (London 1978).
10 See William J. McGrath, *Freud's Discovery of Psychoanalysis. The Politics of Hysteria* (Cornell 1986), 97ff.
11 ibid., 107–8.
12 Sigmund Freud, *An Autobiographical Study* (London 1936), 15.
13 ibid., 14–15.
14 S. Freud, 'Some early unpublished letters,' trans. Ilse Scheier, *International Journal of Psychoanalysis*, vol. 50, no. 4 (1969), 420; Klein, op. cit., 45.
15 See *Letters*, op. cit., 3–6.
16 Klein, op. cit., 46ff.
17 Freud to Martha Bernays, 23 July 1982, in *Letters*, op. cit., 20.
18 ibid., 21.
19 ibid., 22.
20 Klein, op. cit., 43–4.
21 See Freud's obituary for Hammerschlag in vol. 9 of *The Standard Edition of the Complete Psychological Works of Sigmund Freud*, ed. James Strachey, 24 vols (London 1953–75).
22 McGrath, op. cit., 152ff. for Charcot's influence on Freud.
23 *Letters*, op. cit., 185.
24 Freud, *Autobiographical Study*, 26.
25 Sigmund Freud, *The Origins of Psychoanalysis. Letters to Wilhelm Fliess* (New York 1977), 55.
26 ibid., 311.
27 ibid., 83.
28 ibid., 124.
29 Quoted in McGrath, op.cit., 184.
30 Freud, *Origins of Psychoanalysis*, 191.
31 See Marthe Robert, *D'Oedipe à Moise. Freud et la conscience juive* (Paris 1974), 159, 165–6.
32 Sigmund Freud, *The Interpretation of Dreams*, in *Standard Edition*, vol. 4, 193.
33 See Freud, *Origins of Psychoanalysis*, 238.
34 Klein, op. cit., 24ff.
35 See *A Psycho-Analytic Dialogue: The Letters of Sigmund Freud and Karl Abraham 1907–1926* (London/New York 1965), trans. Bernard Marsh and Hilda C. Abraham: Freud to Abraham, 3 May 1908, 34, and Abraham to Freud, 11 May 1908, 36.
36 ibid., 45.
37 ibid., 63.
38 Freud to Jung, 2 September 1907, in *Letters*, op. cit., 256.
39 Ernest Jones, *Sigmund Freud, Life and Work*, vol. 2 (London 1955), 37.
40 *The Freud-Jung Letters*, ed. William McGuire (Princeton 1974), 168.
41 Jones, op. cit., vol. 2, 48–9, 77.
42 Fritz Wittels, *Sigmund Freud. His Personality, His Teachings and His School* (New York 1924).
43 Jung to Freud, 31 March 1907, in *The Freud-Jung Letters*, 25.
44 ibid., letter of 2 April 1909, 275.
45 ibid., Freud to Jung, 13 January 1910, 288.
46 ibid., Jung to Freud, 11 February 1910, 293–4.
47 ibid., 294.

48 Stefan Zweig, *Freud, La Guérison par l'esprit* (Paris 1932), 134.
49 Jones, op. cit., vol. 2, 184.
50 *Moses and Monotheism*, in *Standard Edition*, vol. 23, 91.
51 See David Aberbach, 'Freud's Jewish problem', *Commentary* (June 1980), 35–9.
52 *Moses and Monotheism*, op. cit., 46.
53 ibid., 111.
54 Freud to Charles Singer, 31 October 1938, in *Letters*, op. cit., 453.

7   Dilemmas of assimilation in central Europe

1 Milan Kundera, 'The tragedy of central Europe', *New York Review of Books* (26 April 1984).
2 Joseph Roth, 'Ostjuden im Westen', *Juden auf Wanderschaft* (Kohn 1985), 11.
3 See the letters in Miriam Sambursky, 'Zionist und Philosph. Das Habilitierungsproblem des jungen Hugo Bergmann', *Bulletin des Leo Baeck Instituts*, no. 58 (1981) Brief 8, 36. My own translation.
4 ibid., 37.
5 Stefan Zweig, *Briefe an Freunde*, ed. Richard Friedenthal (Frankfurt a.M. 1978), 153.
6 Stefan Zweig, *The World of Yesterday* (New York 1943), 22.
7 Marcel Reich-Ranicki, 'Juden in der deutschen Literatur', *Die Zeit* (2 May 1969), 18.
8 Sambursky, op. cit., 37. My own translation.
9 Letter of June 1921 in Max Brod, *Franz Kafka, Briefe, 1902–1924* (Frankfurt a.M. 1955), 336ff.
10 Moritz Goldstein, 'German Jewry's dilemma. The story of a provocative essay', *Leo Baeck Yearbook*, vol. 2 (1957), 237ff.
11 Gershom Scholem, 'Wider den Mythos vom deutsch-jüdischen "Gespräch"', *Judaica 2* (Frankfurt a.M. 1986), 7ff.
12 Arthur Schnitzler, *My Youth in Vienna* (New York 1970), 6–7.
13 *Tagebuch* (4 November 1904) quoted by Egon Schwarz in *Frankfurter Allgemeine Zeitung*, no. 112 (14 May 1977).
14 Walther Rathenau, 'Staat und Judentum' (1911), *Gesammelte Schriften* (Berlin 1918), vol. I, 188–9.
15 Arnold Schoenberg, *Briefe*, ed. Edwin Stein (Mainz 1958). Letter to Wassily Kandinsky of 20 April 1923.
16 Joseph Roth, *Briefe 1911–1939*, ed. Hermann Kesten (Cologne/Berlin 1970).

11   French socialism and the Dreyfus affair

1 Charles Péguy, *Notre Jeunesse* (Paris 1969), 62.
2 The whole complex of French socialist attitudes to nationalism, militarism, and especially antisemitism, as it crystallized during the Dreyfus affair, will be treated by me in greater detail in a book to be published next year.
3 See Claude Willard, *Le Mouvement Socialiste en France (1893–1905): Les Guesdistes* (Paris 1965).
4 See Maurice Charnay, *Les Allemanistes, histoire des partis socialistes en France*, vol. 5 (Paris 1912).

5 *Journal Officiel* (24 December 1894), 2320.
6 *La Dépêche de Toulouse* (26 December 1894).
7 *Le Chambard Socialiste* (29 December 1894).
8 *Le Père Peinard*, série londonienne, no. 4, 2 Quinzaine (November 1894), 24.
9 *Le Parti Ouvrier* (7–8 January 1895); also Maurice Charnay, op. cit., 93–4.
10 *La Petite République* (10 November 1896).
11 *Les Temps Nouveaux* (21–9 November 1896), 3.
12 See Pierre Sorlin, *La Croix et les Juifs* (Paris 1967).
13 'Dreyfus et les traîtres', *La République Sociale* (8 February 1897).
14 'Il ne reviendra plus', *Le Parti Ouvrier* (5 November 1897).
15 'Idole Tarée', *La Petite République* (27 November 1897).
16 ibid., 11 December 1897.
17 Alexandre Zévaès, *Jules Guesde* (Paris 1928), 138–9.
18 ibid., 140. Also A. Zévaès, *Histoire du Socialisme et du Communisme en France* (Paris 1947), 261–3.
19 'Le Manifeste' (Réunion du Groupe Socialiste – Appel aux Prolétaires', *La Lanterne*, vol. 1 (21 January 1898). Also in Zévaès, op. cit.
20 ibid.
21 ibid.
22 'La Révolution', *La Petite République* (22 January 1898).
23 ibid.
24 See Charles Andler, *La Vie de Lucien Herr* (Paris 1932), 95, 116.
25 *La Petite République* (26 November 1897); *La Lanterne* (28 November 1897).
26 'Toute la clarté', *La Lanterne* (16 January 1898).
27 *Préfecture de Police* (Paris), Dossier no. BA 345 'L' affaire Dreyfus' (12 February 1898).
28 'Au citoyen Jaurès – lettre ouverte', *Le Parti Ouvrier* (29 January 1898).
29 ibid. (12 March 1898).
30 *Le Libertaire* (29 January – 5 February 1898).
31 ibid.
32 'Les Anarchistes et l'Affaire Dreyfus', ibid.
33 *Les Temps Nouveaux* (22–8 January 1898).
34 Zévaès, op. cit., 266.
35 *La Petite République* (19 July 1898).
36 'Declaration', *Le Socialiste* (24 July 1898).
37 See *Les Deux Méthodes*, Conférence par Jean Jaurès et Jules Guesde, Lille 1900 (Paris 1945), 31–2.
38 *Le Parti Ouvrier* (30 July 1898).
39 *Guesde Archives*, International Institute of Social History (Amsterdam August 1898).
40 'L'affaire Dreyfus et la justice militaire', *Le Socialiste* (9 October 1898).
41 'L'Esprit de classe', ibid. (28 August 1898).
42 Jean Jaurès, *Les Preuves* (Paris 1898), 11–14.
43 Quoted in Charles Rappoport, *Jean Jaurès, l'homme, le penseur, le socialiste* (Paris 1915), 43.
44 ibid.
45 ibid., 55–6.
46 *Le Socialiste* (18–25 September 1898). Report on the Sixteenth National Congress of the POF.
47 Willard, op. cit., 415.
48 'Tactique de classe', *Le Socialiste* (4 September 1898).
49 'L'Affaire Dreyfus et le Parti Socialiste', ibid. (15 January 1899).

50 ibid. (11 June 1899).
51 'Les Socialistes et le Ministère Gallifet', ibid. (2 July 1899).
52 *La Petite République* (12 August 1899).
52 ibid. (13 August 1899).
54 *Les Deux Méthodes*, 30–1.
55 See, for example, Rosa Luxemburg, Consultation Internationale, *Cahiers de la Quinzaine*, XIᵉ Cahier, Iᵉʳᵉ série (1899), 76–82.
56 'L 'affaire Dreyfus: le nouveau spectre rouge', *Le Socialiste* (3 June 1900).
57 See Georges Sorel, *Reflections on Violence*, trans. T. E. Hulme and J. Roth (New York 1961), 84–7. Also G. Sorel, *La Révolution Dreyfusienne* (Paris 1911).
58 'La faillite du Dreyfusisme', *Le Mouvement Socialiste*, no. 176 (July 1906), VI, 193–9.
59 Urbain Gohier, *La Terreur Juive* (Paris 1905).
60 *La Guerre Sociale* (24–30 June 1908).
61 See introduction to Charles Péguy, *Notes Politiques et Sociales* (Paris 1957), 23.
62 ibid., 56.
63 See Michael A. Marrus, *The Politics of Assimilation: A Study of the French Jewish Community at the Time of the Dreyfus Affair* (Oxford 1971), 176.
64 Péguy, op. cit., 73.
65 André Foucault, *Un nouvel aspect de l'Affaire Dreyfus* (Paris 1938), 310.
66 Léon Blum, *Souvenirs sur l'Affaire* (Paris 1935), 25–6.
67 Daniel Halévy, 'Apologie pour notre passé', *Cahiers de la Quinzaine*, 10ᵉᵐᵉ Cahier, II série, (1910), 71.
68 Marrus, op. cit., 176.
69 See, E. Tcherski, 'Die Dreyfus-Affare, die Arbeiter-Immigranten, un die franzosische-yiddische Firers' (Yiddish), in E. Tcherikower (ed.), *Yidn in Frankraich*, 2 vols. (New York 1942), 165–8; also H. Bulawko, 'Les Socialistes et l'Affaire', *Les Nouveaux Cahiers*, no. 27, (1971–2), 26–30.
70 *Le Prolétariat Juif* (Paris 1898), 9 (Groupe des Ouvriers Juifs Socialistes Français).
71 ibid., 19.
72 ibid., 18.
73 ibid., 17–18.
74 For example, Gaston Cogniard, 'Le Prolétariat Juif', *La Petite République*, (3 March 1899).
75 See, *Journal Officiel* (19 May 1899), 1438–1446, speech of Gustave Rouanet, the socialist deputy, on the conditions of the Jewish proletariat in Algeria.
76 'Le droit d'être juif', *Le Libertaire* (24 September 1899).
77 Pelloutier was one of the few syndicalists who was unequivocally Dreyfusard and outspokenly hostile to antisemitism. See *L'Ouvrier des deux mondes*, no. 14 (1 April 1898), 209–12.
78 *L'Aurore*, 7 June 1899, 'Lettre ouverte à M. Trarieux'.
79 ibid.
80 *Les Deux méthodes*, 12.

24 The fundamentalist challenge

1 Bernard Lewis, *Semites and Anti-Semites* (New York/London 1986).
2 Rivka Yadlin. *Anti-Zionism as Anti-Judaism in Egypt* (Hebrew edn, Jerusalem 1988).

3 Ronald E. Nettler. *Past Trials and Present Tribulations : A Muslim Fundamentalist View of the Jews* (Oxford 1987).
4 See Emmanuel Silvan, *Radical Islam* (Princeton, NJ, 1985).
5 Translated from the *Covenant of the Islamic Resistance Movement* [Hamas] (in Arabic), 18 August 1988.
6 ibid., Article 22.
7 ibid., Article 11.
8 An exception is Hava Lazarus-Yafeh, 'Contemporary fundamentalism – Judaism, Christianity, Islam', *Jerusalem Quarterly*, no. 47 (Summer 1988), 27–40.

Index of names